CHEMICAL WEAPONS

ENCYCLOPAEDIA OF BIOTERRORISM - IV

CHEMICAL WEAPONS

By

Dr. S.K. Prasad

School of Studies of Zoology & Biotechnology

Vikram University

Ujjain

First Published - 2009

Reprinted - 2026

ISBN: 978-81-8356-387-1

Chemical Weapons

Published by:

DISCOVERY PUBLISHING HOUSE
4383/4B, Ansari Road, Darya Ganj
New Delhi-110 002 (India)
Phone: +91-11-23279245, 23253475, 43596065
E-mail: discoverybooksindia@gmail.com
discoverypublishinghouse@gmail.com
web: www.discoverypublishinggroup.com

Printed at:
Infinity Imaging Systems
Delhi

Preface

The present title *"Encyclopaedia of Bioterrorism"* aims to bring historical context to present concerns about biological weapons, biological agents, chemical weapons and the potential for bioterrorism. The lack of use of biological weapons in war advocates for using biology to create a new class of weapons initially envisioned delivery systems for pathogenic aerosols that mimicked those for chemical weapons, which were mainly bombs that generated aerosols intended to kill or disable troops in a local area. This vision was quickly replaced by the concept of creating huge clouds of germs that would drift with the wind and infect people over areas of thousands of square miles. The scientists and civil and military leaders who believed in the future of biological weapons saw their potential for fulfilling the goals of total war, for the mass killing or debilitation of enemy civilians. It is often asked why biological weapons are different from any other means of destruction. The answer is that they are the only ones devised expressly to kill defenseless humans and animal and plant life, with little real battlefield potential in modern war.

When biological weapons were developed for possible retaliation against an enemy thought to be similarly armed, they fit this model of restraint. Nevertheless, germ weapons were developed and laws and political circumstances offered no guarantees against their use. Historians may seek neat explanations, but the element of uncertainty was always there. Political and military authorities differed unpredictably when it came to calculating the consequences of using biological weapons. This book also describes the new subject of bioterrorism and traces at least the beginnings of the present era, in which domestic preparedness and homeland security are major policy issue. One of the major homeland security directives is to use technology derived from medical research to protect civilians against bioterrorism. The use of biology to defined civilians against any and all biological agents is a daunting project that imposes new security restrictions more familiar to physicists in the defense establishment than to biologists.

The study of biological weapons combines knowledge from disparate fields: biology, medicine, military history, politics, law, and ethics. This book intends to give the reader a basic literacy in this complex area. The entire subject of biological weapons is characterized by an unusual degree of misinformation and even disinformation. Almost every fact in this book has several page backstory, with greater nuance and depth than a brief overview can provide. As scholars continue their work, more information and analysis will likely turn today's accepted wisdom on its head. This progress will be a healthy sign for the field, whose subject matter has often been exploited for the frightening and sometimes entertaining effect it has on the imagination.

There can be no claim to originality except in the manner of treatment and much of the information has been obtained from the books and scientific journals available in the different libraries.

The author expresses his thanks to his friends and colleagues whose continue inspirations have initiated him to bring out this book.

The author expresses his gratitude to Mr. Wasan and staff of M/s Discovery Publishing House for their whole hearted co-operation in the publication of this book.

Author

CONTENTS

1

INTRODUCTION

Although *biological* and *chemical weapons* are two separate and distinct categories, many in the public understandably lump them together. And the fact that hostile nations as well as known terrorist groups have sought to develop both underscores the need to offer at least a quick overview of the most important sues we face with chemical weapons.

In assessing the relative threat posed by biological and chemical weapons, it appears there is a trade-off. Chemical weapons, in general, are not as likely to cause mass casualties or death as biological weapons. But chemical weapons, again speaking generally, tend to be easier to make and use.

The Aum Shinrikyo case in Japan is instructive here. The Japanese doomsday cult had money—they spent an estimated $30 million on their chemical and biological terror program—and recruited scientists and graduate students with considerable technical expertise.

In the early 1990s, they tried on several occasions to release biological agents—anthrax and botulism—in Tokyo and near U.S. military installations in Japan. Each attempt failed.

Finally, in 1995, cult members filled plastic bags with the chemical agent Sarin, brought them to five different locations in the Tokyo subway system, and poked holes in the bags with umbrellas. As a result of these attacks, twelve people died, a thousand were hospitalized, and their hundred were injured. In no way to minimize the horrible pain and suffering those victimized by this cowardly attack endured. But for all of the cult's money technical skill, and persistence, its members fell far short of their goal of causing widespread death.

This gives us some perspective on the potential threat. Not that we should grow complacent, but we should recognize how difficult it is for even a well-organized, well-funded organization to plan and carry out a successful attack.

Sarin is one of a class of chemical weapons known as nerve agents. These, along with the group known as blister agents, are the two categories most often viewed as potential terrorist threats.

Difference between Chemical and Biological Attack

Both can be dispersed in the air we breathe, the water we drink, and on surfaces we routinely touch.

Signs that a *chemical attack* has occurred would be expected to appear within minutes to hours. The first indications frequently are things we can see or smell, such as dead insects and animals, coloured residues, or distinctive odors.

A *biological attack* may not make itself known for days to weeks, and there typically are no obvious environmental signatures, such as dead birds falling out of the sky. This delay allows people who have been infected to travel great distances before any medical symptoms appear. That could make it difficult to pinpoint where and when the attack took place.

Possibility of a Chemical Attack

Observe the surroundings. The signs around you will likely tell much of the story. Look out for large numbers of dead animals, birds, or fish in the same area. Note if there is a lack of insect life that you might normally expect.

What about others around you? In a chemical attack, there could be numerous people breaking out in unexplained watery blisters, choking, exhibiting dilating pupils, or experiencing breathing problems. There could be a lot of people with unexplained rashes, nausea, or disorientation. And more than one person suddenly going into convulsions is a ciear giveaway.

Be suspicious if you notice numerous surfaces with oily droplets a film, or if you see numerous surfaces of water with an oily film. With odors, the key is to notice if the odor you smell is simply out of character for the environment you are in. For example, mustard gas smells like rotten onions.

Nerve Agents

As the name implies, these chemicals work on the nervous system. Colourless and odorless in their pure state, nerve agents are extremely toxic. And they can work with frightening speed, especially if they are inhaled, as was the case in the Tokyo attack.

Nerve agents are liquid at room temperature, but also can be produced as gases or aerosols. They enter the body either through inhalation or through the skin. It is also possible to contaminate food or liquids with nerve agents.

They work by disrupting the transmission of nerve impulses within the nervous system. The nerve agent destroys an essential enzyme that acts as a messenger to let your glands and voluntary muscles know when they have been stimulated enough. When this messenger enzyme is killed, the glands and muscles continue to he stimulated uncontrollably.

The two nerve agents considered most likely to be used by terrorists are Sarin and Tabun. Tabun, originally developed as an insecticide by German chemists in the 1930s, was the very first nerve agent.

Symptoms of a Nerve Agent

It depends on how the chemical enters the body. It works very rapidly when inhaled, because the nerve agent immediately gets into the bloodstream through the blood vessels in the lungs and heads straight for the target organs.

Depending on the dose a person has been exposed to, symptoms can show up anywhere from a few minutes to one hour after the attack. The symptoms include watery eyes, runny nose, chest tightness, nausea, and vomiting. Persons exposed to a relatively high dose may experience coughing, difficulty breathing, drooling and excessive sweating, blurred vision, stomach cramps, loss of bladder and bowel control, arid twitching, jerking, staggering, or convulsions.

If exposed to a high dose, the victim may quickly go into convulsions, lose consciousness, and die of suffocation because the muscles tire and can no longer sustain breathing functions. This can happen within a matter of minutes. Exposure to nerve agents is diagnosed from the symptoms. There is no specific diagnostic test.

Treatment for Nerve Agents

There is no *antidote* or *vaccine*. As a general rule, if you see one person on the ground choking or in convulsions it likely is just a heart attack or seizure. But if you see several people fall to the ground choking and convulsing assume their has been a chemical attack and immediately leave the area and dial 911. Tell the dispatcher that a hazardous gas may have been released.

As quickly as possible, take off your clothes, place them in a plastic bag, and seal it. If your clothes are contaminated, they can spread the substance to others. Wash your skin thoroughly and aggressively with soap and water. If only water is available, wash off with water. Try to remain calm. Even if you show no signs of illness, you should be checked by a paramedic or physician responding to the scene.

If you are ill, you'll likely receive an injection of atropine, pralidoxime chloride, or diazepam to ease symptoms.

Blister Agents

Again, the name is fairly descriptive. These *chemical weapons* cause wounds that resemble *burns* or *blisters*. What the name does not tell us is that these chemicals damage the respiratory tract when inhaled. The two blister agents most widely viewed as potential terrorist threats are mustard and Lewisite.

You may have heard mustard agent referred to as mustard gas. Actually, it is liquid at room temperature, but it can also be released in the form of a gas.

Mustard agent has a long history of use as a *chemical weapon*. The German military used it extensively in World War I leaving many soldiers with permanent eye injuries and chronic respiratory illnesses. But fewer than 3 percent of U.S. mustard casualties died. It was used again in World War II, and it reportedly was used by Iraq in its war against Iran in the 1980s. Up to a thousand Iranian deaths have been attributed to mustard agent.

There are several varieties of mustard agent, including *sulfur mustard*. It's relatively simple to manufacture, but any large purchase of the precursor chemicals needed to make it would likely be detected.

As a weapon of mass destruction, mustard agent has a limited usefulness. It is more effective at incapacitating people than killing them on a large scale.

The same is true of Lewisite, which can be produced in liquid or vapour form.

Symptoms of Blister Agents

It depends on the agent. Mustard often has a delayed reaction, and it may be hours before you realize you were exposed. Lewisite, on the other hand, causes an immediate, painful reaction.

Mustard agents are colourless and almost odorless, although it's said that mustard can give off a smell similar to rotten onions.

However, the chemicals can damage the respiratory system in concentrations so low that they could not even be detected by the sense of smell.

Mustard agents typically attack the skin, eyes, lungs, and gastrointestinal tract. They may also eventually damage blood-generating organs as the agent is circulated through the body.

Reaction to a mustard attack is usually delayed, unless a high dose is involved. Once someone is exposed to mustard agent, it can take from two to twenty-four hours before symptoms appear. A mild case may cause aching, tearing eyes, red, irritated skin, hoarseness, coughing, and sneezing.

More severe exposure may cause small blisters that, over several hours, gradually combine to form large blisters. Nausea, vomiting, diarrhea, fever, loss of eyesight, and severe respiratory problems also can occur in serious cases of mustard exposure.

Exposure to Lewisite causes an immediate burning or pain in the eyes, nose, and skin. To make matters worse, fresh air increases the pain. Within minutes, skin can turn grayish owing to tissue damage. Later, severe damage to the eyes, skin, and airways may occur.

Treatment for Blister Agents

There is no vaccine for mustard or Lewisite, and there is no antidote for mustard agents. However, there is an *antidote* for *Lewisite*, known as *British anti-Lewisite*.

For any attack involving a blister agent, immediately remove all clothing, place it in a plastic bag, and seal it. Mustard and Lewisite are considered "*persistent*" in the environment, which means they won't evaporate within twenty-four hours under normal conditions. That greatly increases the chances of harming others by exposure to contaminated clothing.

If you have been exposed to mustard, flush your skin with water, then wash thoroughly with soap and water. There is a urine test to conform if you have been exposed to mustard.

If you were exposed to Lewisite, flush your skin with a very amount of household bleach, then wash thoroughly with and water. There is no specific diagnostic test for Lewisite.

Recovery from blister agents is slow, but even extensive skin damage can be cured. The key is to keep the patient free of infection. Constant medical care and plastic surgery may be necessary over several months.

OTHER CHEMICAL WEAPONS

Hydrogen cyanide is of great concern because it is so easy to make. All it takes is mixing a cyanide salt, such as *potassium cyanide*, with a strong acid. These materials are readily available and can be purchased in quantity. In fact, these chemicals and a device to mix them were found in Tokyo subway restrooms a few weeks after the Sarin nerve agent attack.

Hydrogen cyanide is a liquid that evaporates very quick lying vapors or gas to rise. Because these vapors are lighter than air, hydrogen cyanide is unlikely to be used outdoors. But it could be very effective indoors.

In small amounts, *hydrogen cyanide* would have no effect. In medium doses, it would cause dizziness, nausea, and weakness. In large amounts, it is extremely toxic, potentially causing loss of consciousness, convulsions, stopped breathing, and death within minutes.

In a famous case, hydrogen cyanide was spiked into Tylenol in the United States in 1982 and caused considerable panic. It also resulted in the development of tamper-resistant packaging to help prevent other such incidents.

2

DEFENSIVE APPROACH

As September began, Pentagon military planners were increasingly concerned about the fact that no one knew the exact numbers of protective clothing, masks, medical autoinjectors, and agent detectors; where all this equipment was located; and how quickly it would be consumed. Since the Army had been appointed the lead DoD executive agency for NBC defense in 1976, DoD expected the Army to assist the Air Force, Navy and Marine Corps to prepare for chemical warfare. The other services were also in the dark due in large part to their traditional reluctance to spend funds on NBC defense, and they had difficulty determining their INBC defense logistics status. While the Army could use its Chemical Corps officers to track units' readiness and logistics, the other services did not have a similar resource. They saw this as the combat unit commander's, rather than one central agency's, responsibility; these unit commanders, for their part, had never seriously considered preparing for the immense logistics burden that came with a chemical battlefield.

To provide ODCSLOG with an immediate action officer, the Joint Chiefs of Staff J-4 (Director for Logistics) appointed a Joint Service Coordination Committee for Chemical Defense Equipment (JSCC-CDE). Its mission was to assist in NBC defense equipment logistics prioritization and allocation of resources, maintain all DoD CDE inventory, and coordinate CDE transactions relating to the industrial base. While two other joint NBC defense panels existed, this organization was formed strictly for the management of fielded CDE during the Persian Gulf conflict. This committee reported to the Assistant DCSLOG, who in turn reported on CDE readiness through the DCSLOG to the Joint Staff. Colonel Harold Mashburn became the deputy chair for this panel, which was officially established in the first week of September.

One of the JSCC's first actions was to identify the current stock levels of CDE and the potential consumption rates of that equipment in a modern conflict. While the logistics agencies within the four services scrambled to inventory their CDE, the Institute for Defense Analysis developed a computer model to determine the consumption rates in a conflict in Southwest Asia. Gradually, a picture formed. The JSCC discovered that there were inadequate stocks of protective clothing, large vehicle protective filters and mask filters, and NAAK autoinjectors to sustain a conflict in a CB agent-contaminated environment over thirty days. The JSCC began coordinating transfers of Army protective clothing and decontaminants to the other services and tracked CDE shipments from warehouses throughout the world of the Gulf. It became a daily exercise to deal with specific logistics issues.

Some were fairly easy to resolve: for instance, the Navy wanted more of the old "*fishtail*" chemical protective boots and butyl rubber gloves from the Army; the Air Force and Navy requested bulk decontaminants such as DS-2 and STB from Army stocks. Also, marketers began calling ODCSLOG, sometimes hundreds of them each day. They had everything to offer, from lightweight microclimate cooling vests to mini-chemical detectors. Many were just get rich-quick schemes although all had to reviewed in the event that one good product was available. There were a number of tougher policy issues to face, such as who should provide for civilian protection in Saudi Arabia, when there were not enough suits for the soldiers The Israeli and Saudi Arabia, when there were not enough suits for the soldiers. The Israeli and Saudi governments were requesting protective clothing, specially US military protective clothing, and had the money to buy it. Because US military needs took priority, Colonel Mashburn had to turn their requests over to the British and German governments to be filled with their Mark IV and Saratoga suits, respectively. Although not referred by ODCSLOG, the Russians sold several million sets of their chemical protective clothing to Middle Eastern nations. Other nations, some as far away as South Korea, offered their chemical defense equipment to the Middle Eastern nations. It was seller's market, and no requests were being turned away.

Saudi government procurement of other than Army protective suits (and later the Marine Corps' similar actions) were interpreted by reporters (and other so-called military experts) to mean that the US protective clothing was inferior to the British and German brands, which was not the case. The British Mark IV, as Army validation reviews showed, was lighter in weight but less durable (making it better for heat stress but not as resistant or long-lasting to heavy concentrations of agent). The German Saratoga suit, on the other hand, might have been equal to or superior to the American clothing in many respects, but it cost nearly twice as much per suit, and there were only two producers that could manufacture the suits. The US production problem continued to be a nagging issue for the logistics planners, but shortage of chemical protective suits was a concern throughout the war, even with the promise of suit deliveries by January 1991.

Prior to their development to the Gulf, soldiers suddenly began carefully inspecting their masks. Many soldiers, for instance, had preferred large protective masks that gave easier and more comfortable fits during peacetime training exercises. Now everyone wanted smaller, tight-fitting masks. Those who found their masks inoperative had difficulties replacing them. On top of the natural wear and tear, more masks were breaking down in Saudi Arabia due to soldiers tightening their mask straps beyond the failing point; everyone wanted to cinch their masks as close to their faces as possible to minimize the chance of leaks. Pine Bluff Arsenal stepped up its mask repair and began a massive refurbishment line. Before the conflict, Pine Bluff Arsenal repaired 1,100 protective masks per week. During the conflict, Pine Bluff Arsenal repaired 1,100 protective masks per weak. During the conflict, ODCSLOG asked Pine Bluff to increase that to 5,000 masks per week.

With the deployment of several thousand government civilians, defense contractors and media crews to the Gulf, the question of protecting American citizens in theater arose. Prior to Operation Desert Shield, the Pentagon had no policy about equipping civilians or contractors with CB defense equipment. This was new concern, arising form the increased sophistication of military equipment and the American public's desire for instantaneous news reporting. The difficulty was where the Pentagon's obligation ended. Did the government bear a responsibility to protect all the Americans in Southwest Asia, including those working for the Saudi government prior to hostilities? If so, why not all civilians who resided near military areas? The shortages of protective suits and masks forced DoD to draw the line, supplying protective clothing and masks only to American military and authorized civilians in theater. This increased the pressure on Pine Bluff Arsenal to repair as many masks as it could, twenty-four hours a day, seven days a week.

Aviator protective masks across all services were at a critical juncture. The Army had just re-awarded a production contract for its MN43 protective mask in 1990, but not were being produced yet. As noted, Mr. Rick Decker and Captain Ernie Nagy at CRDEC would produce and deliver 264 M43 masks for Apache crews in the Gulf before November 1990, largely out of developmental masks and spare parts at Edgewood. Mine Safety Applications would add another 658 M43s to the total, which would cover the Apache pilots in the Gulf. The Air Force issued urgent contracts for the immediate procurement of the MBU-19/P aircrew masks. By releasing funds to be directly channeled to air logistics centers, the Air Force was able to begin production of pilot masks quickly. The Navy had developed a separate program to modify the British AR-5 aircrew mask, but it (NAVAIR) borrowed 250 AR-5 masks from the Canadian military and modified them for Marine fixed-wing and Navy helicopter aircrews the two most likely aviation candidates for chemical agent protection over land.

Collective protection equipment filters became a critical issue. Army units did not often use the *collective protection systems (CPS)* in the M1A1 tanks, or the M20 and M51 *collective protection equipment* (CPE) shelters, during field training exercises. This had led to a pattern of very low peacetime requirements and consequently, a shortage of wartime filters. This was a concern more for the many MIA1 tanks collective protection system, than the fewer mobile collective protection shelters available for command and control units. Most XVIII ABN Corps units had left their M51 shelters in the United States. These aging systems (first issued in the early 1970s) had not help up well. The generators which kept air circulating in the semi-rigid walls broke down often, and many units could not afford to dedicate a five-ton truck to move each M51 shelter. Between September and October, forty-nine older M51 CPS shelters were refurbished from depots, shipped to the Gulf and set up for medical units throughout the corps. CENTCOM forces sent more than eighty backorders for the M51s, but it would be six months to a year before the manufacturer could deliver them.

The newer M20 Simplified Collective Protection Equipment (SCPE) was not working out much better. Designed for the interiors of European buildings, they were not suitable for the military or Saudi-furnished tents in the desert. Mounting tent poles within the plastic liner without rupturing it was difficult; trying to inflate an M20 SCPE in the open left it vulnerable to the elements (and hostile fire). While some of the over 300 M20s remained in Dhahran, al-Dammam, and Riyadh, combat units in the field abandoned them. Warehouses and US civilians in the cities (and their families in the theater) could and did use the M20 systems to protect against chemical attacks. Over a thousand would be shipped to Saudi Arabia, with 128 going to the Navy for its personnel in the ports. A small number of the experimental XM28 Tent Extendable, Medical Personnel (TEMPER) SCPEs were rushed through production. Four XM28s eventually were produced, of which one made it to the Gulf during the crisis.

The few Navy ships equipped with shipboard CPE filters did not practice their collective protection any better than the Army. Far worse off were the Air Force bases; while this service had made fixed site collective protection a priority in Korea and Germany, transportable CPS was still in the laboratories. While the Marine Corps had invested in portable CPS, there were few available for MEF. As a result of low annual peacetime consumption, large filters had been ordered only to stockpile them in depots as war reserves, which led to a very small manufacturing base. While small stocks existed, it was clear that industry could not "*ramp up*" quickly enough to produce the large filters. Only one company had produced this type of carbon for the military filters, used for both individual protective mask filters and the larger filters for vehicles and shelters. Calgon Corporation was stretched to its limits over the next six months to produce the special activated limited number of large CPE filters made it to Southwest Asia prior to 1991. This made the hundreds of Abrams tank crews vulnerable to nerve agents if the filters inventory ran out, and the rear areas very vulnerable to Scud attacks due to the lack of shelters.

Defensive Battle Plans

On September 3, CENTCOM practiced its mobile defense-in-sector under a plan known as "*Desert Dragon III*," which would later be modified as the Desert Shied defense. The plan called for the 101st ABN DIV and 3d ACR to fight the initial covering-force action and soften the initial edge of an invasion. The 24th IN DIV would fight and halt the Iraqi army in the main battle area, and the 1st CAV DIV would counterattack form Assembly Area Horse to destroy the enemy.

The 82d ABN DIV would protect the ARCENT rear area and the oil fields at Abaquaiq against terrorist actions, while the Marines held the coastal regions. The operations plan assessed enemy use of chemical weapons as "likely." Since this was defensive operation, all of Iraq's air force, ballistic missiles, and its South African artillery systems (which could outrange their US counterparts) were assumed to carry both chemical and conventional munitions. Intelligence reports had noted possible chemical munitions being loaded near Iraqui artillery batteries in Kuwait. For war-gaming purposes, the military's prime targets for persistent chemical agent included the condition ports at al-Jubayl and al-Dammam, the airfields at Dhahran and Riyadh, and military logistics depots.

The chemical recon/decon plan to support this defense-in-sector counted on a number of reserve and active duty units that would not arrive until October (or later). XVIII ABN Corps NBCC identified hundreds of potential decon sites for the defending units. The 3rd ACR covering force would rely on its 89th Chemical Company. The 101st ABN DIV would receive the 761st Chemical Company and the 7/92 Recon Platoon in support as well as its organic 63rd Chemical Company. The 24th IN DIV had its 91st Chemical Company and the 5/69th Recon Platoon prepared for the main defensive effort. If the Iraqi army meant to use chemical munitions to soften up the US forces, the 24th's mechanized units were the best able, within the XVIII ABN Corps, to absorb it. The crop's 101st Chemical Company provided general decon support for the artillery batteries. The 1st CAV DIV with the Tiger Brigade had the 68th Chemical Company (and elements of the 44th), plus the 5/22 Recon Platoon, waiting in Assembly Area Horse as the counterattack force. The 82d ABN DIV had its own 21st Chemical Company, and, being in the rear area, could call on the 101st Chemical Company. The 2d Chemical Battalion was in general support to XVIII ABN Corps, covering the main logistics areas and ports with the 59th and 181st Chemical companies, the 5/25th Recon Platoon (when it arrived), and the first reserve decon unit due-in-theater, the 327th Chemical Company.

"*Desert Dragon III*" offered the planners the option of relating against Iraqi chemical use with US chemical weapons. Although the option of deploying *chemical weapons* to the Gulf had been war gamed in Internal Look-1990, there had been no further guidance for the real event. Official US policy was to reduce the likelihood of enemy chemical weapons use by threatening retaliation with similar munitions, but no one had made that policy call for CENTCOM's battle plan. Colonel Rick Read suggested two courses of action for DCSOPS to recommend to the Joint Chiefs. First the Army was preparing to remove the US chemical weapons from Germany to Johnston Island (Operation "Steel Box") is November 1990. Instead of shipping them to Jonston Island as planned, they could reroute the chemical munitions to Saudi Arabia. If the Saudi government protested the presence of nerve agents on their soil, there was a second course of action. Binary production had ceased, but the binary projectile shells themselves (minus the second component) could be shipped to the Gulf to fool the Iraqis into thinking there were US chemical munitions available for retention. Both of these options were ultimately rejected as politically too controversial. While the munitions would have offered a substantial counter to the Iraqi threat (as US military policy intended), President Bush had committed himself to the bilateral chemical weapons disarmament treaty between the Untied States and Soviet Union. Deploying chemical weapons to this conflict would seem contrary to that policy on the global political stage. Later in the month, ODCSOPS officially confirmed to CENTCOM that there would be no chemical munitions deployment to Saudi Arabia. No plans were developed for US retaliation using chemical munitions.

On September 14, the German government surprised the PM NBC Defense office by revising the terms of the Fuchs loan to make it a gift, which included the tools, parts, transportation assistance and follow-on training. In the last days of September, the German government increased the gift to a total of sixty Fuchs vehicles. This was especially magnanimous due to the fact that many of these came out of the German military's own 140 Fuchs (to be replaced later by the German government). The German military had one request: that the frantic pace of training and production be slowed down to accommodate the British and Israeli against Iraq, the training would have to expand to a six-day, ten-hour, four-week course, which would allow the trainers a less grueling schedule. Also, Thyssen Henschel would not work through Christmas holiday unless war was declared. Since the Army had its initial recon capability en route, the US government agreed to relaxing the training demands. As for the second thirty-Fox offer, HQ DA initially refused it, despite clamoring from the PM NBC Defense office. With one corps's worth of Foxes inbound, some within the department felt that there was no need to incur additional training, supply and maintenance costs. There was a concern that additional

Foxes would overload the training and employment program, and that thirty were enough for one corps. Based on that decision, Thyssen-Henschel stopped any plans to modify a second batch of thirty Fuchs vehicles. This decision would have a profound implications when it came time to develop a second corps's reconnaissance capability.

Two fox platoons from Europe arrived in Saudi Arabia on September 20, just as the Fort Hood units began to "close" in the theater. The 5/69th Recon Platoon took four foxes to the 24th IN DIV, marrying-up with the two "Nunn" vehicles for full platoon strength. The 7/92nd Recon Platoon took the remaining six Foxes to the 101st ABN DOV, with its covering force mission out front. The 5/22 Recon Platon would join the 2d Chemical Battalion in late October, with eight Foxes (six of their own and two to replace 5/69th's "Nunn" vehicles, which would become the ARCENT operational readiness floats [ORFs]). These three platoons would spend the next three months training with their division's units to familiarize them with the Foxes' capabilities. The 5/25th Recon Platoon was to arrive in Dhahran in mid-November, allowing the 1st CAV DIV to receive the 5/22d. Five of the last six Foxes were designated for 3rd ACR, with the last one joining the two "Nunn" vehicles as maintenance floats.

Because the Foxes had been fielded two years ahead of schedule, there was no military capability to maintain them within CENTCOM. Thyssen-Henchel was unable to send German civilians into a war-crisis zone, so General Dynamics Services Company (DGSC, a GDLS subsidiary) provided support contractors to maintain the systems. The PM NBC Defense office established a Fixed Fox Facility in Dhahran, to begin operations in October; it would grow to accommodate maintenance support for two other PM NBC projects, the M1 CAM and XM21 RSCAAL. However, if either a CAM or RSCAAL required major repairs, it had to be evacuate to England (for the CAMs) or to CRDEC (For the RSCAAL), for lack of spare parts. In addition, the 2d Chemical Battalion would stay at the site, once it arrived in late October. When the 490th Chemical Battalion arrived in theater, it would take over the rear area chemical defense mission, allowing the 2d Chemical Battalion to move to support SVIII ABN Corps directly.

On September 26, the 2d Chemical Battalion's advance party deployed to Saudi Arabia to prepare for the main body's arrival. Back in Houston, the 2d Chemical Battalion's main body, the 181st Chemical Company and the reserve 327th Chemical Company began their move to the ports to stage their equipment and load onto the ships. At Fort

McClellan, the 490th Chemical Battalion and three reserve chemical companies were training and readying their units for deployment. The first non-divisional decontamination unit, the 59th Chemical Company, would arrive ten weeks after the initial XVIII ABN Corps deployment. Its sister unit, the 761st Chemical Company, would be right behind, arriving at the end of October.

Protecting the Force

CENTCOM began to have particular concerns over rumors of an Iraqi threat called "*dustry mustard*" agent. This was not a new agent or a novel weapon, nor was it certain that Iraq even stockpiled the agent. The Germans in World War II had experimented with the concept. "*Dustry mustard*" is created by coating dust-sized particles with mustard agent, increasing its persistency and ability to float into cracks, gaps and crevices. The concern was that this "*dusty mustard*" would float between the gaps of the two-piece BDO and the protective mask's hood rather than being soaked into the fabric. To address this concern and prevent a panic message to the field commanders, a Pentagon team under Dr. Bob Boyle addressed the validity of the threat and how to detect "*dusty mustard.*" Edgewood, Dugway and Natick labs cooperated in determining whether the detectors would sense dusty agent and whether the suits would protect against it. Tests showed that if the suits were worn correctly, troops had little to fear and that the CAM and M256A1 kit would detect the agent. By November, ODCSOPS messages forwarded instructions on how to detect the "new" agent with existing detectors, should Iraqi forces employ "*dustry mustard.*"

In light of continuing protective suit production issues (and former dissatisfaction with the BDO's weight and heat stress) the Marine Corps announced the purchase of seventy-three thousand British Mark-IV protective suits. The Marines determined these "*lightweight*" suits to be more suitable for the desert. An overzealous Marine public affairs officer stated that the purchase was made because the suits were "better than the Army BDOs." In reality, the Mark-IV was less than fur pounds lighter than the BDO and cost nearly twice as much (a major decision point for the Army, which would have to buy millions of suits, not thousands). As the troops thought lighter meant less heat stress (which, as Natick lab tests would later show, was not the case), they perceived the Mark-IV to be the better suit. CRDEC and NRDEC were flooded with press inquiries about the quality of the Army's BDOs, requiring more lab analyses and frequent demonstrations to the press. The Air Force still sought a less bulky, nonflammable suit for its pilots, and ordered a small quantity of the experimental CWU- 66/ P one-piece protective suit through a single source without requesting bids, at a unit cost of nearly five times that of the BDOs. The Navy relied on its dwindling stocks of CPOG suits and purchased on additional 150 Mark-Ivs for Navy SEALS in-theater. All three services would use the Army BDOs once their own initial suit stockpiles were consumed.

Until the later protective suit manufacturers began their shipments, the Army dug deeper into its warehouses of older CPOGs. The CPOGs constituted up to 20 percent of the protective clothing used in the Gulf; despite their shorter exposure life (fourteen days in comparison with BDO's thirty days), they met the same challenge level of ten grams of liquid agent per square centimeter. The Natick labs worked to toughen up the BDO design around the elbows and knees, as well as to incorporate a desert-tan camouflage pattern. They also inspected the stockpiles of protective gloves to extend their shelf life past the expected expiration date. Many of the glove lots were found adequate, and the current stockpile of over four million butyl rubber gloves was prepared for shipment to the Gulf.

The Chemical School concurred in CRDEC's proposal to push the development of ten XM21 RSCAAL prototypes into the field. Despite concerns with fielding chemical defense equipment before it was ready, Lieutenant Colonel Silvernail and Colonel Barbeau requested every available chemical defense program be accelerated and fielded type-classified limited procurement (asking industry to produce a limited number of devices without full formal test and evaluation). The XM21 program was close enough to completion to permit an initial production contract through Brunswick Corporation for ten systems. These systems would permit the Army and Marine Corps commanders a limited capability for early-warning, long-range chemical agent detection. The Chemical School, in mid-October, sent a Mobile Training Team to Camp Lejeune to begin training Marines on the XM21 operation and maintenance.

The M1 CAMs had not been fully fielded, due to production problems. The final delivery of CAMs from ETG, Inc., was due in March 1990 (thirty-one months after contract award), but ETG had difficulties getting its CAMs past governmental testing and approval, projecting a two-year delay in production of the final lot. The Army had a total of 1,029 CAMs in the field from previous production runs, with another 200 as maintenance floats. Only 150 of these CAMs were in the hands of XVIII ABN Corps soldiers, leading the Army to request 500 from the Canadian Mobile Command (army) and to order an additional 495 from Graesby Ionics in Britain. The Canadian government promised to deliver the CAMs by the end of December, with Graseby's CAMs following in January.

Preparations to deal with the biological warfare threat continued as the Army's MRIID worked with NAVCENT to establish an initial biological screening capability, using the medical expertise available on the hospital ships and at the Navy Medial Research Unit at Cairo, Egypt. A team of nine Navy medical specialists occupied an abandoned Saudi hospital in Al Jubayl with lab equipment designed to deal with biohazards. Working through October, they established and tested a courier specimen transport system between Saudi Arabia and CONUS. This capability would at least allow early confirmation of any Iraqi BW attacks, rather than waiting for MRIID's test results conducted at Fort Detrick.

Major General Watson's DNA team continued its tests of the prototype biological agent detector mounted on the airplane through September and into October. The biodetection program's goals and progress were relayed through the Vice Chief of Staff, Lieutenant General Gordon Sulivan, to General Powell in early October. In mid-October test results continued to be satisfying, and it seemed that the prototype might be ready for deployment by the end of the year. The program was promising—the team could not identify a biological agent, because of the cytometer technology, but it could tell there was an increase in background readings of biological material. This would be the first indication of a potential biological agent attack. On the final day of testing, the DNA team needed some final results as to how well the detector could do. Then, tragedy struck. The pilot flew the plane into the ground; the airplane, the pilots, crew and equipment were lost. It was a real setback; it wiped out almost any hope, given the time it had taken to pull this effort together. This completely stopped DNA's biodetection project Major General Watson called CRDEC and asked them to take over the program.

Brigadier General Dave Nydam, commander of CRDEC, had appointed Colonel Gene Fuzy in September as the point of contact for CRDEC's technical support to CENTCOM, for both offensive chemical munitions and defensive NBC defense programs. Colonel Fuzy had been the last Program Manage for Binary Munitions and had begun closing out the program in July 1990. He now became responsible for the Army biological defense program, since, as mentioned earlier, the retaliatory chemical weapons option had been dropped. The new office, titled the Projection Office for Biodefense, began with the data accumulated under the DNA program. It reviewed the past history of the center's biodefense program and began identifying commercial programs that might be used. The best approach to CRDEC seemed to be to use the old XM19/XM2 Biological Detection and Warning System to provide CENTCOM and early post-attack indication of the use of biological agents. The drawbacks of using the 1970s-era detector were obvious given its large size, weight, and potential unreliability. Commercial industries might be able to field a similar system, although more fit for a laboratory than the field. CRDEC immediately began plans to update the XM2 samplers, modifying them to use commercial agent tickets that would indicate positive biological agent detections.

CRDEC proposed mounting the XM2 air samplers on vehicles, but the detectors could be operated only while stationary. If the biodetectors identified a possible positive biological warfare agent sample, the operators would have to transport the sample to a forward laboratory at KKMC or al-Jubayl for further culture testing, which could take several hours. This system had to support the entire CENTCOM theater defense, since the other services had no biodetectors ready. The Navy and Marine Corps had no biological detectors ready for the field. Under their own independent effort, the Air Force had been working on a prototype model it called "*Morning Song*," which detected only anthrax spores after a two hour sampling period. Ten devices would eventually be manufactured and shipped to air bases in the Gulf region prior to the start of the ground war.

Higher level unit training picked up after CENTCOM had developed its defensive plants in mild-October. The decon platoons of the chemical defense companies began working with the combat units on their thorough decontamination drills. Nearly every unit supported by a chemical decon platoon or company began practicing personnel and equipment decontamination. For those in the rear areas, such as in the COSCOMs, the chemical officers helped identify and train personnel to assist the medics in chemical casualty triage and decontamination prior to treatment. For instance, in 1st COSCOM, the division field bakery unit augmented the forward medical units as litter bearers and decontamination assistants. In the 24th IN DIV, Major General McCaffrey ordered continuous chemical defense training. At the individual level, all soldiers would mask every day in response to M8A1 test alarms all battalions would train in full protective clothing once a week once a month, every battalion would conduct a decontamination exercise for persistent chemical agent decon operations. Training grew to include command post exercises testing the NBC Warning and Reporting System, from corps level down to the battalions.

XVIII Airborne Corps conducted two major command post exercises to test the NBC warning and reporting system among the corps chemical staff units. The corps rear area was especially vulnerable, for three reasons first, all the logistics and support functions traditionally in the rear areas were textbook targets for any chemical weapons analyst. These troops held the majority of the reservists, most of whom had little familiarity with NBC defense operations. If the gasoline tankers, ammunitions vehicles, maintenance trucks, and medical units could not support the fighters because of chemical contamination, the corps's offensive power would drop tremendously. Second, because of the immense distance between units in the rear area (often over fifty kilometers), communication was difficult and often spotty. Because of the large numbers of support units at the base clusters (over one hundred at each cluster), sending NBC message to each was time-consuming and laborious. Not all these units had M8A1 alarms of CAMs, and they would receive little or no warning of chemical agent attacks. Last, because of the large distances, the dedicated decon units would be stretched to their limits to support all of these units. The lack of collective protection shelters increased the demands on the decon units. The exercises identified these shortfalls, and enabled the NBC elements to develop expedient solutions to keep their soldiers aware of any threats. The other divisions held their own command post exercises to test and develop familiarity with the NBC Warning and Reporting System.

The many doctors and medics deploying to the Gulf had little practical knowledge on the diagnosis and treatment of NBC-related casualties. Even the most recent references relied on data documented in the 1970s certainly these doctors had more experience with gunshot wounds than, say, chemical agent burns. While the active duty medical units required some refresher training the reserve medical units were initially even less prepared to deal with CB agent casualties. The wasn't exactly what doctors saw in their civilian practices. The Army's Medical Research Institute for Chemical Defense (MRICD) responded by sending its military doctors to the deploying active and reserve medical units to provide training in a five-day Medical Management of Chemical Casualties Course (M2C3). From October through November the M2C3 instructors traveled through Southwest Asia, providing a three-day version of the course to Army, Air Force, Navy and Marine Corps medical units, in addition to training doctors from Saudi Arabia, the United Kingdom, France, Canada and the United Arab Emirates. In all, they trained over 1,400 health care providers in theater. In November, when it was announced that VII Corps was deploying, they traveled to the US Army hospital IN Neubreucke to train those medical units deploying from Germany to the Gulf.

Continuing Concerns about Readiness

Colonel Barbeau had received a status report on XVIII ABN Corps defensive equipment preparedness in late September, and the picture was not pleasant one. The entire corps was still short just about everything- common items such as BDOs, masks, and BA3517 batteries, in addition to such more specialized needs, as additional M8A1 alarms, CAMs, and M17 SANATORs. He headed off the initial requirement for water haulers by leasing water trucks from the local community and had initiated purchases of HTH bleach to augment the DS-2 and STB supply. However, AMCCOM's National Inventory Control Point at rock Island had rejected most of the requisitions for additional chemical defense equipment. AMCCOM had not been prepared for the magnitude of the requirements, could not meet them immediately, and cancelled the requests it could not fill. Worse AMCCOM was not providing any information on what items were in short supply and which ones were just not available, and when these shortages might be resolved, AMCCOM's focus was on multi-branch commodities such as ammunition, weapon systems, and maintenance and repair equipment. There was no priority on chemical defense equipment at AMCCOM, despite CENTCOM's voiced concerns.

The M8A1 battery shortage was particularly vexing since the batteries were essentially military-version D-cells in a large plastic container, not hard to manufacture. There had been insufficient quantities prior to hostilities, and now the Army could not make up the shortages. Using the batteries too long led to false alarms, which on one appreciated. These false alarms made troops increasingly reluctant to stop operations and jump into MOPP, but if they didn't respond to the real attacks. This became areal stress-builder. Communications and Electronics Command (CECOM) responded to the battery shortage by designing and manufacturing a 450-foot cable to power the M8A1 detectors from engine batteries.

Their requests for the urgent procurement NBC protective covers and Suit, Contamination Avoidance, Liquid Protection (SCALP) suits had been heated, but none were due in any time soon. The corps NBCC requested eight million dollars buildings or even trees to cover the supplies against CB agent contamination, the rear area logistics bases remained very vulnerable. CENTCOM J-4 (logistics staff) denied the request, stating that there was no requirement set by AMCCOM. These flip-flops, combined with other unresolved logistics issues and concerns over the biological agent problem hurt the credibility of all chemical personnel throughout XVIII ABN Corps.

On October 1, Lieutenant Colonel Vicki Merryman arrived in-theater to replace the ARCENT chemical officer, who had unexpectedly left in late September. She listened to ARCENT commander Lieutenant General John Yeosock's philosophy of providing the corps with the capability to fight and acknowledged the difficulties chemical soldiers were having getting requisitions filled by the wholesale logistic system. She approached the ARCENT G-4 with the NBC defense logistic problems; he responded by identifying a Quartermaster officer on his staff as the NBC logistics specialist. This arrangement ensured that division logistics cells submitted requisitions correctly, and responsiveness to their inquiries was improved. The ARCENT NBC Cell and the G-4 NBC logistics specialist began identifying theater shortages and submitting requisitions. Supplies were transferred form Europe until the Seventh Army began having reservations about the rapid depletion of its theater reserves; overgarment requisitions shifted from the stripped-down European theater reserves to the Pacific theater was reserves.

Medical officers in the United States had a busy few months as well. Existing topical skin protectants against blister agents were old and not stocked in sufficient numbers to support the forces in the Gulf in September, MRDC accelerated its research to find an effective skin protectant, narrowing in on two promising treatments that were under development and also a commercially available protectant. After testing the three candidates, MRDC shifted the two government treatments to full development and recommended production of all three. DLA issued an order in the fall for about one million tubes of the commercial protectant, with the majority of the shipment due to arrive in early February 1991. MRDC also accelerated the development of its diazepam autoinjectors. A nerve agent attack, even if the soldier used atropine could be vulnerable to convulsions that could cause brain damage. The diazepam autoinjectors would reduce the incidents of those convulsions. Since this drug was already available to Army medics as valium, the FDA had fewer reservations about authorizing the use of this drug, even though its efficacy had not been absolutely proven (that is to say, it had not been tested on soldiers suffering from nerve agent exposure).

In early September, General Powell and the Joint Chiefs of Staff had listened to the Surgeon General's medical recommendations and forwarded the recommendations to Defense Secretary Dick Cheney. The decision was to surge vaccine production, delay the start of immunizations, and review the status of the vaccine program every two weeks. The tri-service task force began investigating both domestic and foreign production sources. Because US firms still did want to produce the medical products, even with offers of indemnity, the group began to look at European firms (as Europe's military forces had similar concerns). A Danish Company, Solvay-Duphar, was approved to produce diazepam autoinjectors, based on its past autoinjector production for European nations and an inspection of its plant.

On October 3, Secretary Cheney directed the Army to increase its vaccine production capability. By October 11 MRDC had identified the need to obtain FDA efficacy waives for the topical skin protectant, the diazepam auto injectors hepatitis A, the botulinum toxoid, J-5 monoclonal antibody and Ribavirin. DoD was not about to suggest human-volunteer agent tests to prove the efficacy of CB agent pretreatments, treatments and vaccines. By mid-October, the Joint Chiefs had agreed to request a waiver of informed consent and had began to express concerns about the stockpile size and the time needed to immunize and develop immunity. MRDC submitted to the FDA an Investigational New Drug application for the botulinum toxoid and a New Developmental Drug application for the CANA. By the end of the month the CINCCENT Surgeon had outlined an immunization plan for the delivery and use of vaccines in the theater.

The Office of the Assistant to the Secretary of Defense for Health Affairs (OASD/HA) sought a waiver of the FDA requirements for informed consent of both the botulinum vaccine and *pyridostigmine bromide* (PB) tablets, on the basis that initial testing had been good that there was established prior human use in other medical cases (although not specifically for CB agent treatment); that there were no medical alternatives; and that the need to protect the troops was a national security issue. The FDA was still concerned about soldier safety, product liability and the need to follow well-thought out and practiced regulations. However, congressional regulations would not permit testing the vaccines and antidotes on human volunteers afflicted with CB agents. DoD did not want to go ahead with unapproved products, but given the nature of the threat, was prepared to do so.

The FDA agreed to test the botulinum vaccine for safety prior to the end of the year. DoD requested and received approval to conduct an immediate study of four men to evaluate the effects of PB tablets. These tests would provide at least some indication of any health issues prior to their use by soldiers in the Gulf. But the bottom line was plain for the political and military leadership—it could not afford to ignore any possible medical solutions to the CBW threat. The leadership was aware of the intense scrutiny of the media and the American public and their concern to minimize American casualties over all else. If DoD held back on developmental vaccines and pretreatments to troops in the Gulf, and Saddam initiated CB warfare, the outcry would have been deafening. DoD had to take the risk that these drugs would save lives if CB agents were employed.

Battle Plans for Desert Storm

CENTAF's air power concept, "*instant Thunder*," had made Iraqui NBC production and storage facilities one of its highest priority targets. The designers of this plan likened the strategic campaign to a dartboard. In the bulls-eye were the command, control and communications targets, the decision-making capability of the military. In the first ring around the bulls-eye the targets involved military production and storage capability, to include factories, electric power grids, power plants and oil refineries—and NBC munitions factories. The next ring held transportation infrastructure targets: the railroads, bridges, main highways, airfields and ports. The third ring held the population centers and food sources. The outmost ring contained the least important targets—the enemy's military forces.

Through September and into October, CENTCOM began planning for a possible one-corps offensive into Kuwait. General Vuono had sent four graduates of the School of Advanced Miliary Studies, the "Jedi Knights," as they became known, to Saudi Arabia in mid-September to assist the CENTCOM headquarters with possible war game scenarios. After two weeks of planning and discussing options, the group settled on an up-the-middle attack that began just east of the Wadi al-Batin and two left-hook options that began just west of the wadi. The left-hook options left the outnumbered corps vulnerable to counterattacks by the more numerous Iraqi mechanized divisions, which could sweep around the US Army and cut off its supplies. Potential US casualties for the favored option, the up-the-middle approach, ran to two thousand dead and eight thousand wounded troops. Schwarzkopf was also concerned about the impact of chemical weapons use and the mass casualties that might result, but were impossible to estimate. Their recommendation was that another corps was necessary to defeat the Iraqi force.

On October, 11, a CENTCOM team flew to Washington to brief President Bush, Secretary Cheney, General Powell and other advisors at the White House. Brigadier General Buster Glossen briefed the Air Force strategic plan first, including its targeting of CB weapon sites at Karbala, Samarra, and Salman Pak. The plan listed eight chemical and biological main targets. Major General Robert Johnson, Schwarzkopf's chief of staff, briefed the one-corps ground offensive concept. The plan stressed the risks of significant casualties: the danger of extending the offensive from the logistics rear area, the lack of a theater reserve, and the threat that Iraqi chemical attacks would slow the tempo of combat operations. The plan called for an effective air campaign against the Iraqi ground forces, and for quick execution, before counterattacks would threaten the rear area. General Schwarzkopf's personal assessment pointed out that the one corps, as heavy corps was needed to guarantee the success of an operation to liberate Kuwait.

After he received feedback on the cone-corps offensive plan, Schwarzkopf told his Jedi Knights to plan a two-corps operation. They began on the assumptions that strategic and tactical air campaigns would wear down the air defense, ground and command-control communications units in the Kuwaiti Theater of Operations (KTO) and the Iraqi forces would use chemical weapons during the ground attack. On October 22, General powell flew to Riyadh to discuss the cone-corps versus the two-corps concept. Based on discussions with the CENTCOM staff, he brought the two-corps concept. Based on discussions with the CENTCOM staff, he brought the two-corps concept to a National Security Council meeting; the concept included activating VII Corps in Europe, bringing additional Army and Marine combat units from forces in the United States adding three more carrier groups, doubling the Air Force units, and calling up additional reserve forces. A second corps was on the way, with large implications for the logistically-sensitive NBC defense community.

With the arrival of the 59th Chemical Company on October 15 and 2d Chemicals Battalion advance party on October 19, the VIII ABN Corps could finally institute detailed and realistic plans for decontamination support throughout the theater. On October 21, the Corps NBCC conducted a corps-wide decontamination assessment. This meeting highlighted a defense strategy of contamination avoidance, reconnaissance, decon sites, and the use of weathering to defeat contamination. The chemical officers discussed the strategies available, given the massive shortage of M17 SANATORs (less than 500 in-theater), the water-hauling issue, and the critical shortage of water points. Originally, the corps NBCC had planned hundreds of decontamination sites throughout the theater. Because of the limited resources available, the 2d Chemical Battalion operations officer, Major Mike Brown, suggested that the corps change this plan to allow the battalion to mass its assets at designated priority sites.

The anticipated arrival of the 2nd Chemical Battalion and the active and reserve chemical decontamination companies allowed the CENTCOM, ARCENT and XVII ABN Corps NBCCs to breath easier. On October 26, Colonel Barbeau held a conference of all chemical staffs and units to discuss the more critical NBC defense issues. This conference allowed the chemical officers throughout the corps to meet one another and share training ideas and lessons learned on CDE problem areas. One of the prime issues was an update on the Fox platoon's training and deployment. For perhaps the first time since the deployment, the division chemical staffs were briefed in full on the NBCRS Fox fielding plan and the emerging reconnaissance strategy for the corps. Three chemical reconnaissance platoons were in theater, but there were no spare parts or maintenance facilities. General were in theater, but there were no spare parts or maintenance facilities. General Dynamics Land Systems contractors were arriving to help support the Fox (as well as other GDLS equipment, such as the M1A1 tanks).

The officers also discussed the lack of a standard NBC threat warning system throughout the theater. With assets from three Army corps present (XVIII, III and VII), no one had designated which field procedure would be used. Colonel Barbeau suggested that they build from the III Corps threat warning system. This system had been developed to guide the necessary leadership actions to prepare for a potential NBC attack but not replace the commander's delegation of MOPP levels. The NBC threat condition had Red, Amber, Green, and

While levels to define imminent, probable, possible and nil enemy attack probabilities respectively, and indicated what protective actions, other than changing MOPP levels, should be taken. This system was easily adaptable to all unit's standard operating procedures, and eliminated confusion over what states of readiness should be maintained and minimum actions required.

The main party of the 2d Chemical Battalion and the 181st and 327th Chemical companies arrived in al-Dammam on October 28 and began precombat operations in a nearby marshaling area. The 490th Chemical Battalion and 318th Chemical Company arrived in Saudi Arabia on the same day. The 761st Chemical Company joined the 101st ABN DIV on November 2. On November 5, the 2d Chemical Battalion received orders to move forward to support the XVIII ABN Corps with the 181st, the 327th and the 59th Chemical Companies, allowing the 101st chemical company to move from supporting the corps rear area to supporting the XVIII ABN Corps artillery. The 490th Chemical Battalion would provide general support to the Army's echelons above corps units in the Support Command area of responsibility. It took the 318th Chemical Company under its control, with other reserve chemical units due to join in November. Rear area support mission included decon for troops, equipment, logistical stockpiles, facilities, ports, airfields, terrain and main supply routes, on a priority basis.

Initially, there was a debate over how the rear areas would receive decontamination support. Major General Gus Pagonis, as the theater army support commander, and the XVIII ABN Corps support commander had mixed combat support units in and around the Saudi airfields and ports. Both commander expected the two chemical battalions to offer support to their respective units, the two initial non-divisional chemical companies, the 5th and 761st, only had three of their four authorized decon platoons. The continued lack of M17 SANATORs meant that XVIII ABN Corps also needed general support above and beyond its capabilities in the forward areas. Supporting the CENTCOM and ARCENT rear areas, in addition to the XVIII ABN Corps main area, would disperse the few decontamination assets available over a large area, straining their operational capabilities.

On November 9, the two chemical battalion commanders and Colonel Barbeau conferred and agreed to a division of labor. The 490th Chemical Battalion would have the responsibility for all soldiers at the King Abdul Aziz Port and Dhahran's airport. The 2nd Chemical Battalion would support the XVIII ABN Corps Rear Command Post area of responsibility in the Dhahran/Dammam complex in addition to ARCENT's rear area. The rest of the decon capability for XVIII ABN Corps would have to come from the divisional companies and the promised SANATORs, which had still not arrived.

Two more, decon companies the 371st and 413th Chemical Companies, were due on November 18; they would join the 490th Chemical Battalion for rear area support. While the CONUS chemical units were arriving, the 11th and 51st Chemical companies had been held back in Europe. With the recognition of VII Corps deployed into theater, it had emphasized "teeth" over "tail" (or combat power over logistic sustainability). As a result, the combat units would have been vulnerable if they had had to sustain combat operations immediately. Cognizant of the need to avoid that vulnerability, VII Corps would deploy the two chemical companies with their COSCOM in early December, just after the 2d ACR (the first VII Corps unit in theater). Appendix A details the task organization for the chemical units within Saudi Arabia as the beginning of November.

Approval of the two-corps offensive meant another call to the PM NBC Defense office. Just when the PM shop was about to congratulate itself for a strong (and very busy) supporting effort, it got the news that it had to equip another corps with Foxes. CENTCOM NBCC informed Colonel Evans and Lieutenant Colonel D'Andries that the new goal was to provide two corps with NBCRS Foxes by mid-January. By the end of October, less than twenty had arrived- about enough for two-thirds of one corps. And to make it more interesting, VII Corps chemical recon units were already in the theater, supporting XVIII ABN Corps! Now one month after the German government had offered a second gift of thirty Foxes, the Army accepted the vehicles. Initially, the Army was reluctant to accept more than 50 systems, as the original initial procurement was planned at 48. ASARDA had told ODCSOPS chemical division that a Marine commander in the Gulf had heard of this capability and wanted some as well. Lieutenant Colonel Willhoite and Major Newing quickly contacted the Marine Corps offices in Quantico, Virginia, and Saudi Arabia and got the commitment for ten more systems, matching the German offer of 60 systems. The delay would cost a month, since Thyssen Henchel had not committed resources to the program until the US government agreed to the gift. The first thirty vehicles would be "Americanized" by the end of November as planned; the second thirty would be fielded as four batches-five systems in December, ten each in January and February and five more in

March. This would permit an additional five platoons of Foxes to be deployed to the theater.

Lieutenant General Franks wanted a ready reconnaissance capability prior to sending his forces into the overcrowded Gulf ports and airfields. The 2d ACR's chemical recon platoon form the 87th Chemical Company bumped 3rd ACR's 89th Chemical Company on the training list, and would enter training after the 5/25th Recon Platoon in November, receiving its six NBCRS Foxes (the last of the initial thirty) in early December. While this represented an initial NBC reconnaissance capability for the deploying VII Corps recon platoons back to their own divisions in a way that let the XVIII ABN Corps divisions retain their NBC reconnaissance capability.

A second corps also meant new headaches for the medial NBC defense community. Supporting one corps with biological vaccines and atropine injectors seemed within the realm of feasibility; vaccinating two corps would mean hundreds of thousands of additional dosages, which were not available. With FDA companies, the medical community had no idea how it would meet the new requirement. There was no rest for the weary.

3

Threat to Food and Water Supply

Almost a thousand people are hospitalized each and every day in our country due to food-borne diseases. More than five thousand people die each year from such illnesses. This high fatality rate coupled with the ease with which a terrorist could obtain a harmful organism (such as the ever present *Salmonella* or *E. coli*) leads many to believe that as we consider *bioterrorism*, we are most vulnerable in our food supply. Indeed, the most notable bioterrorist attack prior to the *anthrax* events of last year was the intentional food poisoning of 751 people in 1984.

Our water supply is generally considered safe, but there still is some anxiety over the threat of bioterrorism. That threat even reaches to our farms and has given rise to another term *agroterrorism*.

Quality of Food

Generally, our food supply is among the safest on Earth. High standards are consistently maintained. But we recognize that our food is particularly vulnerable to a potential biological attack, primarily because of inadequate governmental oversight.

The Food and Drug Administration (FDA) presently has fewer than 800 food inspectors to oversee food imports at more than 300 ports of entry and to inspect 57,000 sites across the country. It is an impossible task for so few inspectors. Furthermore, the FDA inspects many food manufacturers only once every eight to ten years, and only 1 percent of all food imports are properly inspected. This leaves our food supply highly vulnerable to the deter mined terrorist.

Three of the "*major*" biochemical agents that are on the list of most likely offenders in the hands of a terrorist—*anthrax*, *tularemia*, and *botulinum toxin*—may be transmitted through the food supply. And other agents, such as *Salmonella* and *E. coli*, are also easily transmitted in that manner. So we should be doing more to inspect and protect our imported and domestic food supply. In this new age of *bioterrorism*, we can no longer take for granted the safety of our food supply.

Food Safety

It can get confusing. The Department of Agriculture (DA) and the FDA have different, but sometimes overlapping, areas of responsibility. The FDA is responsible for overseeing any food that is already on the market that may be *adulterated* or *misbranded*. The DA is responsible for inspecting all meat, poultry, and egg products before they reach the market.

The DA, through the Food Safety Inspection Service (FSIS), has more than 7,500 inspectors who are required by law to be continuously present when processing is going on at any of the nation's 6,000 meat and poultry plants.

The FDA, with between 700 and 800 inspectors, conducts about 13,000 inspections per year. Owing to inadequate resources, inspectors can only get to about 7,000 of the more than 57,000 warehouses, wholesalers, and processors under the agency's jurisdiction. The FDA also inspects about 1,700 juice processors annually.

That means the agency is only inspecting roughly 12 percent of its areas of responsibility each year. Furthermore, the FDA is supposed to inspect high-rick foods (seafood, canned foods and prepared foods) twice a year, medium-risk foods every two years, and low-risk foods every three years. You should know that these goals are not being met. And this is the food you and your family eat every day.

The FDA's inspection team includes only 175 food importation inspectors for the more than 300 ports of entry nationwide. The FDA views and inspects all food importation paperwork. However, inspectors actually sample and test only 1 percent of all food imports—a figure the FDA would like to increase to 5 percent. There are more than 4 million shipments of food imports per year.

Foodborne Disease are Potential Bioterror Threats

More than two hundred known diseases are spread through food. Each year, food-borne diseases cause 5,000 deaths, hospitalize 325,000 people, and cause 76 million illnesses.

Terrorists would be expected to choose diseases with the highest fatality rates. These include botulism, brucellosis, listeriosis, and *Vibrio vulnificus*. Here's a quick overview of the other diseases.

Brucellosis

This infectious disease is caused by the bacterium *Brucella*. The most common way people get the disease is by eating or drinking contaminated milk products. It also çan he contracted by direct contact with infected animals or animal products.

Symptoms of *brucellosis* include fever sweats, headache, hack pain, and weakness. In some cases, severe infections of the central nervous system or lining of the heart may occur. *Brucellosis* also can cause long-lasting or chronic symptoms that include recurring fevers, joint pain, and fatigue.

More than half—55 percent—of those with *brucellosis* require hospitalization, but the fatality rate is relatively low, at 5 percent. A combination of the antibiotics *doxycycline* and *rifampin* is usually prescribed for six weeks to prevent recurring illness. Depending on when treatment starts and the severity of the illness, recovery may take a few weeks to several months.

Listeriosis

Eating food contaminated with the bacterium *Listeria monocytogenes* causes this very serious disease. Symptoms include fever, muscle aches, and gastrointestinal problems such as nausea and diarrhea. If the infection spreads to the nervous system, symptoms such as headache, stiff neck, confusion, loss of balance, or convulsions may occur.

Pregnant women who contract *listeriosis* may only experience a mild, finlike illness. But the disease during pregnancy can lead to premature delivery, infection of the newborn, or even stillbirth. Infection of the fetus or newborn, however, can be prevented if antibiotics are given promptly to a pregnant woman.

Nine in ten people with listeriosis will require hospitalization, and one in five will die. Antibiotics are generally effective, but even with prompt treatment, some people with the infection will die. Those at highest risk are the elderly and persons with other serious medical problems.

Bioterrorism at the Salad Bar

A bioterrorist attack on our food supply is not merely hypothetical. It has already happened here. In September1984 an outbreak of food poisoning caused by the bacterium *Salmonella typhimurium* swept through the community of The Dalles, the quiet county seat of Wasco County, Oregon. A total of 751 people became ill, though none died. It was the largest outbreak of food-borne disease in the United States that year.

Public health and low enforcement officials were baffled. Their investigation found links to at least ten of the town's thirty-eight restaurants. Most of the restaurants where people had eaten before coming down with food poisoning had salad bars, but there was no common supplier. There did not appear to be any pattern that connected all the cases—until the criminal investigation turned up the truth o year later.

Followers of Indian guru Bhagwan Shree Rajneesh had built a huge international headquarters and commune in Wosco County and were locked in a zoning dispute with the local government. So commune members came up with a plan: If they could make enough voters sick on election day, they could influence the outcome in their favour.

In September, two months before the election, they had a test run of their plan. They prepared cultures of *Salmonella typhimurium* bacteria in their secret lab on the commune, and then commune members poured the bacteria on food items in salad bars and, in some restaurants, into coffee creamers.

Two commune members eventually pleaded guilty and went to prison for the attack.

The *Oregon* attack taught us several hard lessons. It exposed our vulnerability to the deliberate contamination of food in public places. The *Salmonella* culture used in the attack is easily obtained from raw foods bought in a grocery store, and it can be produced in large quantities with simple equipment and little expertise. Residents of The Dalles were fortunate that the cult didn't use a more lethal agent, such as *botulinum* toxin or even anthrax or tularemia.

The attack also underscored the need for health care providers and laboratories to closely cooperate and coordinate with local and state public health departments so that any future outbreaks can be detected more quickly.

And the Dalles case changed the way we look at public health emergencies. At the time, back in 1984, it never occurred to investigators that a group would deliberately contaminate food in several restaurants in on attempt to advance some twisted political or religious agenda. Now we know that if a mysterious outbreak of infectious disease occurs that fits no known pattern and doesn't seem to have any common link, the possibility of intentional contamination must be considered, and law enforcement should be called in immediately to investigate.

Vibrio vulnificus

This bacterium normally survives in warm seawater. People usually contract the disease by eating contaminated seafood or having an open wound exposed to seawater.

The bacterium causes vomiting, diarrhea, and abdominal pain. Nine in ten people with the disease require hospitalization, and 39 percent die. The disease is treated with antibiotics. Top choices are doxycycline or ceftazidime.

Quality of Water Supply

Many people initially think water, since it comes so freely to each of our homes from a common community source, would be the ideal vehicle for the bioterrorist. Thankfully, it is not. In fact, although there has been some concern about our drinking water, as evidenced recently by increased security at our reservoirs, aqueducts, and dams, it is unlikely that a future bioterrorist attack would concentrate on our water supply for a variety of reasons.

First, most experts have concluded that it would be virtually impossible to cause widespread health problems by contaminating a major public water supply. Poisoning public drinking water would require truckloads of biochemical agents that would be difficult to produce and relatively easy to spot.

Every day, massive amounts of water are pumped from our reservoirs. Most of it goes for industrial and other purposes. Relatively little is actually consumed. So any biological agent put in the water at its source would be so diluted that it would have no effect by the time it came out of your faucet.

Second, drinking water from public sources in the United States is monitored constantly by sophisticated technology, and the presence of any contaminants would likely be detected. And if that's not enough, drinking water is typically aerated and heavily chlorinated. Chlorine protects drinking water from waterborne bacteria and neutralizes many biological agents.

And if water contamination were suspected, alternative water sources almost always could be tapped. For example, New York City has twenty reservoirs from which to choose. It's possible, though still highly unlikely, that a contaminant could be placed in the system through a pipe downstream from the treatment plant. However, the water pressure is so great that even that would be extremely difficult, And the chlorine in the water would still probably offer protection.

So it is unlikely that the water supply is in danger. It certainly could not be the vehicle to deliver a weapon of mass destruction. However, the Environmental Protection Agency (EPA) is continually monitoring our risk to such an invasion.

Drinking Water Safety

Under a 1998 presidential directive, the EPA gained responsibility for protecting the nation's water supply from the threat of terrorism including bioterrorism. Since then, the EPA has been working with utilities to assess vulnerabilities, guard against attack, and respond to an emergency. In the wake of the September 11 attacks, the EPA formed the, Water Protection Task Force to develop comprehensive plans to protect our nation's water supply infrastructure, such as dams, treatment plants, and reservoirs.

The EPA also sent utilities information on steps they could take to protect their facilities and worked with the FBI to ask local law enforcement agencies to work closely with local water companies to beef up security.

Bottled Water is Safer than Tap Water

Not necessarily. Keeping bottled water on hand as part of your disaster supply kit is probably a good idea. But in most cases, to the surprise of many except those marketing it, bottled water comes from a water source no different from the water, that comes out of your tap.

The fact is, public water is more closely regulated than bottled water. So the safety of bottled water depends on the safety and security precautions taken at the bottling plant. Tap water under goes rigorous scrutiny and is protected by security measures approved by the EPA, state and local governments, and other organizations.

Water Supply Security

One of the lessons we learned from September 11 is that we must prepare as best we can for the unthinkable. The threat, though, is not that someone will dump tons and tons of a biological agent into a reservoir when nobody's looking. It's that a sewage plant could be blown up along a river, contaminating the drinking water of millions of people downstream, or that a major dam could be brought down, unleashing floodwaters on cities in the way.

In these perilous times, heightened surveillance, security, and water-quality monitoring are clearly needed. And although the likelihood of poisoning a city's water supply is considered very small, the odds increase when you start talking about smaller targets—for example, a holding tank of treated water, a water system that serves a resort or an office building, or a bottling plant for water.

WHAT IS AGROTERRORISM?

This is a word we all need to know and understand. *Agroterrorism* is the use of biological weapons against animals or crops. To date, there have been no reported cases of agroterrorism in the United States. But there is a growing consensus that we could be particularly vulnerable.

Why ? Because the technology required to stage a successful attack is relatively accessible. The resulting disruption to our economy could be significant. And we know that the Soviet Union during the Cold War and, more recently, Iraq developed anti-animal and anti-crop weapons as part of their bioweapons programs.

Unlike *bioterrorism*, the goal of *agroterrorism* would not be to cause widespread human death or illness. In fact, most of the biological agents likely to be used against animals or plants do not usually affect humans. The intent would be to radically disrupt another part of our infrastructure that we take for granted: our food supply. It would be to inspire terror by destroying something we depend on.

The economic impact of *agroterrorism* could be staggering. All we need to do is look at the costs of natural outbreaks. A 1996 outbreak of foot-and-mouth disease among swine in Taiwan resulted in almost 4 million hogs destroyed and losses to swine-related industries of $7 billion.

Britain's ongoing battle against mad cow disease has resulted in the destruction of more than 1.35 million head of cattle, at a cost of about $4.2 billion. On the basis of Britain's experience, it is estimated that the economic toll in the United States would be more than $15 billion if mad cow disease showed up on our shores.

U.S. animals and plants would be particularly susceptible to foreign diseases because they have not built up a natural resistance to them. And as agriculture has increasingly consolidated into large agribusinesses—some feedlots have as many as a hundred thousand animals—introducing a biological agent could quickly cause widespread infection.

Agroterrorism Attack against Animals

As we have seen, with bioterrorism and chemical weapons, launching a large-scale attack would require a fairly high degree of technical sophistication. An agroterrorism attack would not.

In fact, someone with just a basic understanding of micro-biology could cultivate the virus that causes foot-and-mouth disease from an infected animal in another country, bring it into America, and spread it to a herd here by swabbing the virus into an animal's nose. It is no more complicated than that.

Even a small outbreak would have significant consequences, since any outbreak of foot-and-mouth disease could trigger other countries to close their ports to animals and animal products—all from a single act of agricultural sabotage.

Agroterrorist Attack against Plants

Most crop diseases don't kill plants. They dramatically decrease their yield or diminish the quality of the plant. Just as viruses are the greatest threats to animals, fungi are plants' most dangerous enemy.

Deliberately spreading crop diseases is considerably more difficult than spreading a virus through a herd, though. For one thing, most of the biological agents likely to be used against crops are sensitive to environmental factors such as temperature, humidity, and sunlight. Plus, they don't travel airborne as fast or far as animal diseases.

One major obstacle terrorists would have to overcome is weather variables. To illustrate the difficulty consider that in 1999, top university plant pathologists, armed with a particularly virulent strain of late blight disease and test potatoes that were susceptible to the disease, were unable to create an epidemic for research purposes. The reason: drought.

However, the mere fact that a crop is exposed to a known biological agent may be enough to cause other countries to cut off imports, causing a huge ripple effect through the economy.

Mad Cow Disease

It actually bovine spongiform encephalopathy or BSE, a brain-wasting disease that has been found in cattle in eighteen countries. There has never been a case of mad cow disease in the United States, and a government-funded study recently concluded that there is little risk of American cattle contracting the incurable disease.

Still, it is a major concern because humans can contract a form of the disease by eating tainted meat, and it is always fatal. Variant

Creutzfeldt-Jakob disease (vCJD), the form that strikes humans, has killed more than a hundred Europeans, mostly in Britain.

The disease was first diagnosed in British cattle fifteen years ago. Since then, there have been more than 180,000 cases of BSE reported, all but about 1,500 of those in Britain. And the actual number of infected animals is estimated at about 1 million, although the number of cases has been steadily declining since 1993.

When the government in Britain announced in 1996 that eating contaminated meat was linked to the human form of mad cow disease, the $880-million-a-year British beef industry became worth less almost overnight. It took two years and an extensive, government-funded public relations campaign for the industry to begin to recover, the disease is believed to spread among cattle by infected feed containing meat-and-bonemeal a protein supplement made from ground-up parts of cows. The U.S. banned meat-and-bonemeal and other mammal-based animal protein in cattle feed in 1997. And European beef is banned in the United States because of concerns over mad cow disease.

Scientists believe that an aberrant protein, known as a *prion*, causes mad cow disease. *Prion* diseases are not unheard of in the United States. Although no cases of mad cow have ever been reported here, about three hundred cases of prion diseases occur in the United States each year.

About one in every million people is struck with classical *Creutzfeldt-Jakob disease*, which also can be spread by surgical instruments used in brain operations. Experts are concerned that the deadly vCJD may be more infectious than the classical form we have seen here, and that it may spread though blood or other ways. That why many U.S. blood banks won't accept blood from people who have stayed in Britain for more than three months or other parts of Europe for more than six months since 1980.

Food and Mouth Disease

Because they both broke out in Britain, many people in the United States confuse foot-and-mouth disease with mad cow disease. But they are two very different and unrelated diseases. The only thing they have in common is a devastating impact on the British economy.

Unlike mad cow disease, foot-and-mouth or hoof-and as it sometimes known—poses little danger to people, even if they eat the 'neat of infected animals. It only strikes cloven-hoofed animals like sheep, cows, goats, and pigs. And foot-and-mouth is rarely fatal.

But it is highly contagious and debilitates infected animals, leaving them unable to grow or produce milk. Last years outbreak in Britain led the United States to ban imports of animals and animal products from the European Union. Imagine if this were to hap pen to the United States!

The ban is expected to cost European exporters $400 million a year. But the economic toll on Britain is already far higher. It is estimated that the cost to British farming, tourism, and other industries will exceed $3 billion. And the effects on British agriculture will be felt for years. More than 3.5 million animals have been slaughtered in an effort to stop the spread of the virus.

The problem is that the virus is extremely resourceful. It can spread from pigs to sheep to other animals. It can spread through farm machinery. And it can spread through airborne particles. In 1981, foot-and-mouth cases showed up on the Isle of Wight just three days after an outbreak in Brittany, France. The most likely explanation is that the virus traveled 175 miles across the English Channel through the air.

Other Diseases Pose the Greatest Agroterror Threat against Animals

The International Office of Epizootics represents 155 member nations and is responsible for setting animal health standards on which international trade restrictions are based. The organization has compiled a list of the diseases that could spread rapidly and cause serious economic and public health problems. An outbreak of any one of these diseases would likely result in an international export embargo.

In addition to foot-and-mouth disease, others on the list include:

1. *Vesicular stomatitis*. Spread by insects and direct contact, such as shared feed and water troughs; affects cattle, swine, and horses; found in the United States, Mexico, Canada, the Caribbean, and Central and South America; humans can get a version resembling the flu.
2. *Swine vesicular disease*. Spread by eating infected meat; affects swine; found in Hong Kong, Japan, and Europe; can cause flu-like symptoms in humans.
3. *Rinderpest*. Also known as cattle plague. Spread by airborne droplets and direct contact with animal fluids; affects cattle, sheep, and goats; found in Africa, the Middle East, and Asia; no effect on humans.

4. *Contagious bovine pleuropneurnonia.* Spread by inhaling droplets of animal fluids; affects cattle; found in Asia, central Africa, Spain, and Portugal; no effect on humans.
5. *Lumpy skin disease.* Spread by insects; affects cattle; found in Africa; no effect on humans.
6. *Rift Valley fever.* Spread by insects, especially mosquitoes, and direct contact with blood or tissue; affects sheep and cattle; found in Africa; humans are very susceptible can be fatal, though a vaccine is available.
7. *Bluetongue.* Spread by insects; affects sheep and cattle; found in U.S., Africa, and Europe; no effect on humans,
8. *African swine fever.* Spread by ticks, eating infected meat, direct contact, and airborne aerosols within buildings; affects swine; found in Africa, the Iberian Peninsula, and Sardinia; no effect on humans.
9. *Classical swine fever.* Also known as *hog cholera.* Spread by direct contact with animal fluids and indirect contact on shoes, clothing, and equipment; affects swine; found in Africa, Asia, South and Central America, and parts of Europe; no effect on humans.
10. *Highly pathogenic avian influenza.* Also known as *fowl plague.* Spread by direct contact and through the air; affects chickens and turkeys; found worldwide; rarely affects humans, but 1997 Hong Kong epidemic killed six.
11. *Newcastle disease.* Spread by direct contact with animal feces and other secretions and contaminated feed, water, equipment human clothing; affects poultry and wild birds; found worldwide; sometimes causes brief conjunctivitis in humans after extensive exposure.

Greatest Agroterror Threat against Plants

When the Soviet Union and Iraq developed biological agents to use against crops, they targeted primarily those that would harm cereals: wheat, barley, and rye. The most likely fungi to be used against the cereal crops are stem rust of wheat, stripe rust of cereals, and powdery mildew of cereals. All are spread by airborne spores. Against corn, the bacteria that cause corn blight are at the top of the list. They would be spread by spraying. The fungi that cause rice blast and rice brown-spot disease are likely to be used against rice. Both would be spread by airborne spores. The bacteria that cause rice blight, spread by spraying, also could be used against rice. Late blight, the disease that caused the potato famine in Ireland in 1845, would be of chief concern for potato crops. It is a fungus, spread by airborne spores.

4

TERRORISTIC MOVEMENT

The Pentagon officially mobilized VII Corps on November 9, 1990; certainly, however, VII Corps had begun planing its deployment much earlier. Plans had been kicked around for the past month as to which corps within the Army should deploy to augment CENTCOM. General Vuono was emphatic that the III Corps, although partially mobilized, should not be fully deployed, leaving the United States without a major Army Corps. VII Corps in Europe had been planning a drawdown since the fall of the Berlin Wall in 1989, and so it seemed the logical choice. The Seventh Army commander, General Crosbie Saint, choice VII Corps headquarters, with its 1st AR DIV and 2d ACR, and V Corps's 3rd AR DIV and the US-based 1st DIV to deploy. On November 13, Lieutenant General Franks, as VII Corps commander, brought his commanders and primary staff to Saudi Arabia for a leader's reconnaissance. General Schwarzkopf emphasized his desire to see VII Corps in place by mid-January. VII Corps began deploying on November 21; and it would take the rest of the year and part of January to move into the theater. There were a number of immediate issues for the Corps NBC Center to work on.

One of the first issues was to collect all available CAMs in Europe for the deploying units. As mentioned, there were not many CAMs fielded, and every one was critical to preparedness. VII corps made a considered decision not to deploy any of the M20 SCPEs that the units already had, based on the trials conducted by SVIII ABN Corps. It seemed unlikely that VII Corps would have any more luck erecting these shelters in the desert. A team of technical experts from Pine Bluff Arsenal deployed to Germany, where they spent two weeks checking hundreds of protective masks for soldiers with abnormal face requirements. During the two-week period, only a half dozen solders could not be properly fitted; they were left behind in Germany.

Perhaps the greatest concern was the VII Corps's requirement that each deploying soldier have at least two unopened sets of chemical protective clothing and three NAAK with his or her mask. While a USAREUR regulation stated that every soldier have two complete sets of clothing, there was no requirement to report their on-hand status; therefore, no one has checked. As the Cold War ended troops. No one knew exactly where the suits were or how many there were, but everyone knew that there were not enough. Most suits in storage were primarily the older CPOGs. Despite the known threat in the Gulf and their potential deployment in that theater, many units had neglected to identify their shortages and request replacements. Several units had packed their extra protective suits in military containers for shipment, which took several weeks to move from Europe to Saudi Arabia, while the troops arrived in days. Last, several military units that would augment VII Corps came from CONUS; unfortunately, many were told that they would receive protective suits once in Saudi Arabia. Of course, there were no extra suits, increasing the overall shortage. As a result, the majority of VII Corps units deployed with only one set of overgarments, as had the XVIII ABN Corps.

This is not to suggest that VII Corps had been as unprepared in November as XVIII ABN Corps had been in August. The level of chemical training of forces in threat and constant REFORGER exercises. VII Corps medical personnel had the opportunity to undergo refresher training in chemical agent casualty operations. Their familiarity with French and British forces in NATO would allow them to integrate these division's NBC defense operations smoothly. Because SVIII ABN Corps had established a theater warning system, VII Corps and its attached units would adopt it as their standard while in the Gulf. Overall they would deploy in a somewhat better posture, which was good for one main reason—they would not have six months, or even much more than three months, to equip and train their forces.

Very much on the minds of Lieutenant General Franks and his division commanders was that three of their chemical recon platoons were already in Saudi Arabia, with a fourth on the way in mid-November. Two of those belonged to units remaining in Europe (3rd and 8th IN DIV), but the other two, attached to the 24th IN DIV and 2d Chemical Battalion, belonged to the deploying 1st and 3d AR DIV, respectively. As the Foxes had been one of the earliest VII Corps contributions to CENTCOM, Franks has visited the Sonthofen training and seen his NBC recon platoons off. The XVIII ABN Corps's divisions had become very comfortable with the Foxes, had made extensive plans on the assumption of retaining these vehicles, and now had to find out how to replace them.

Complicating Fox distribution were demands from the Marine Corps for a similar capability for its two divisions. On October, General Schwarzkopf had made the concession that the first ten NBCRS vehicles in-theater in January 1991 would go to the Marines (as per the earlier ODCSOPS negotiation with the marines.). No arguments from the Army commanders to redirect the vehicles could sway him. The two platoons gave the two Marine divisions a specialized NBC reconnaissance capability equal to the Army division. Although the Marines had never developed specialized chemical units and had turned down initial procurements of Foxes, they were not about to turn down this capability in the hour of their need.

Part of the solution would come from the Chemical School. The remaining three "Nunn" Fox vehicles that had been shipped to the GDLS facility in Michigan for refit were ready in September and were shipped to Fort Hood for deployment with the III Corps units. Since the German government had made its initial thirty Foxes a gift, the Chemical School requested the three "Nunn" Foxes be sent to Fort McClellan to support training of chemical reconnaissance troops. The chemical School did not have an NBCRS simulator like the one in Sonthofen and had submitted a critical-needs statement to HQ DA to acquire two Fox simulators (with laboratory), at a cost of $6.1 million. However, these would not arrive until November 1991. In the meantime they could make to do with classroom training and the three Fox vehicles on hand.

On November 3, the 1st IN DIV's chemical recon platoon from the 12th Chemical Company attended the first three-week NBCRS training course. Another chemical company would send its recon platoon to Fort McClellan in December (Training as potential replacements). One USMC platoon would arrive just before Christmas, returning prior to the beginning of the air offensive, followed by a third Army recon platoon. The 1st IN DIV's recon platoon returned to Fort Riley to deploy with its division in early January, while the two Marine recon platoons would return to Southwest Asia. All three platoons would wait for orders to pick up their Foxes from the factory at Kassel,

Germany, where they were being "Americanized." The XVIII ABN Corps's release of two recon platoons back to VII Corps would balance both corps at three recon platoons each in January, with two platoons going to the Marines.

The recon training program in Germany continued on track. Major Polley had left the German school to join the 1st IN DIV as its division chemical officer and had had an opportunity to stop by Fort McClellan to see his division's chemical soldiers' training on the Chemical School Foxes. Major Jeff Adams replaced Polley as the liaison officer at Sonthofen to continue the training. The recon platoon from 87th Chemical Company (2d ACR) arrived at Sonthofen for its training in early November. 3rd ACR's reconnaissance platoon from the 89th Chemical Company would train with it, but would deploy with its own Foxes form the second batch of thirty vehicles after the 2d ACR received its Foxes. As these troops arrived, the 5/25 Recon Platoon from 8th IN DIV was preparing to deploy to Saudi Arabia with its six Foxes.

Major General Watson had an opportunity to talk to General Schwarkopf again in November; Schwarzkopf referred him to Major General Burt Moore, US Air Force, the J-3 (operations) on the CENTCOM staff. Watson suggested to Moore that CENTCOM needed a one-star general officer to help coordinate the NBC defense requirements for the four services, especially in light of a second corps coming into the theater. The original CENTCOM deployment plan had a chemical brigade (which would have been commanded by a brigadier general or promotable colonel) that would plan, coordinate and support the non-divisional chemical defense units' actions as they moved to support one division or another or across the two corps. That had not materialized. In the minds of many senior chemical officers, the situation to date had not been fruitful, since the two corps had colonels as their chemical officers as compared to the lieutenant colonels at the higher ARCENT headquarters (Vicki Merryman) and CENTCOM headquarter (Ken Silvernail).

The two lieutenant colonels had done their best to stay abreast of growing chemical defense requirements, requisitions, and related issued of a huge force. But in a climate of general officers running the ARCENT/CENTCOM policy in the various staff offices, a lieutenant colonel did not have the horsepower to recommend and execute timely decisions. This issue had been a significant source of friction between XVIII ABN Corps's, ARCENT's and CENTCOM's NBCCs and NBC defense organizations in the United States, with respect to obtaining the timely support that XVIII ABN Corps thought it needed. A chemical general officer would have sat in on the two corps commander's war councils, enabling closer operational and logistical support and presenting a single, authoritative voice to the United States. Regardless, Major General Moore was not convinced; he told Watson that he did not see that much work for a chemical general officer in CENTCOM. This decision would affect the Army chemical defense staff and units throughout the war, denying General Schwarzkopf valuable advice and contributing to delays in assigning chemical defense units to and from the divisions.

Major General Watson did convince ODCSOPS to allow DNA to develop an Automated Nuclear, Biological and Chemical Information System, or ANBACIS. This was a computer software packaged that could take data concerning an enemy CB munitions strike, such as munition type, agent used, number of munitions, and combine it with local weather information to create a "footprint" of the downwind program for the 9th Infantry Division in Fort Lewis, Washington—a simple computer exercise to practice crude NBC agent contamination plots. It had never become more than a training tool until 1989, when the right amount of synergy between software development, program funds, and modern Army communications came about to develop it into a planning tool for military units in combat.

Major General Watson was able to authorize several million dollars to refine the ANBACIS model at DNA. IN early November, he gathered his modeling team; its members included a Navy officer (with a biological warfare agent model), Dr. Clyde Replogle from Wright-Patterson AFB (supplying a weather information model), and a small group of scientists from CRDEC (in the chemical warfare agent modeling and simulation area). Members from Los Alamos National Laboratory, contractors from the SAIC, Mitre, an JAYCOR firms, and a representative from the Air Force Global Weather Center joined the team. Over a period of about forty days they were able to develop a model that, using the Cray supercomputers at DNA, could use real-time Middle East weather information and enemy munitions data to develop footprints of the predicted contamination area quickly. The model integrated three chemical agent models (NUSSE4, PARACOMPT, and Plume) into one model (ANBACIS-II), which provided an improved depiction of CB agent collateral effects. This was light-years ahead of the current NATO ATP-45 method, which an individual manually consulted wind speed charts and a simple hand calculator to develop an (overly conservative) contamination prediction within a half hour, if the analyst was well trained.

CONTINUING CB DEFENSE PREPARATIONS

Logistics units under Major General Gus Pagonis used the time given to them to bring in every material advantage they could to improve the combat units' odds in the upcoming desert battle. One possible improvement was to upgrade the many M1 Abrams tanks in Southwest Asia to the M1A1 standard. The majority of tanks in CONUS divisions were M1s, armed with a 105 mm main gun and using the same ventilated facepiece protective system ad the M60A3 tanks used. US Army divisions in Europe were equipped with M1A2 tanks, armed with a 120 mm main gun, advanced targeting electronics, and hybrid collective protection that included an overpressure system with the ventilated facepiece. This meant that the later model tanks could keep chemical agent vapors out of their interior. They also featured micro-climate cooling vests, which were worn under the crew's protective clothing; the hybrid system would pump cool liquid through the vest, keeping the crew comfortable despite the protective clothing and fierce desert heat. Overall this enabled the crews in M1A2 tanks to fight with a lower physiological and psychological burden than those in M1s or M60A3s. The combined bonus of increased lethality and better protection was a strong incentive to upgrade the M1 systems before the ground war began. HQ AMC began the upgrade of 1032 M1 tanks in early November, with the final tanks receiving their modifications only days prior to the start of the ground war. As these tanks were upgraded and repainted to desert schemes, the 490th Chemical Battalion was tasked to support AMC by providing decon systems to wash the tanks prior to painting them.

Fox vehicles continued to roll into Southwest Asia. By establishing liaison offices at the Thyssen-Henschel site at Kassel, the Sonthofen NBC defense school, and Dhahran's King Fahd International Airfield, the PM for NBC defense school, and Dhahran's King Fahd International Airfield, the PM for NBC Defense office was able to monitor and troubleshoot the production and deployment process continuously. Thyssen-Henschel produced ten additional systems in October and November, and five of the second thirty in late December, raising the projected total end-year figure to thirty-seven modified NBCRs vehicles. There was concern that the Fox's profile resembled the Soviet-built BTR-60 (used by the Iraqi Army). To avoid fratricide, the Fox crews raised "*Jolly Roger*" flags or American flags on their radio antennas and taped large inverted Vs with florescent infrared reflecting tape on the vehicles' sides. The PM NBC Defense Office issued thousands of vehicle identification cards, meant to familiarize CENTCOM soldiers, marines and aviators with the new vehicle's silhouette.

Thirty-five General Dynamics Services Company contractors joined the AMC maintenance facility at Dhahran, where the Army had established a limited repair depot in October. The Fox facility in Dhahran grew to include a small fleet of vehicles (for the mobile organizational maintenance support of forward combat units), a second facility site at KKMC, and seven organizational maintenance teams for around-the-clock operations by February 11, 1991. The seven teams included two with the USMC, one with the British forces, two corps-level direct-support sites, and two fixed facilities.

To have another corps in-theater called for another chemical battalion to support its CB defense operations. Under the November reserve call-up ODCSOPS tapped the 457th Chemical Battalion and 413th Chemical Company from South Carolina, the 323rd chemical Company from South Dakota, the 340th Chemical Company from Texas, and the 496th Chemical Detachment (JB) from Alabama. The 496th would arrive in Saudi Arabia the day after Christmas; the rest would follow in the first week of January. All the companies were decontamination units. Although concern over insufficient decontamination assets was now not as great as it had been in August, there still was a large corps rear area that would require these additional units if chemical strikes occurred.

In early November, an advance military group from the Czechoslovakian Ministry of National Defense visited Saudi Arabia to offer assistance in the form of a Czech "*anti-chemical*" team. The unit would be stationed in the rear support area about 160 kilometers from the Iraqi border. Its main function was to detect and identify chemical agents delivered against the Saudi military's area and the Saudi population. This support was accepted by the Saudi Government, with the deployment of the Czech troops scheduled to begin in December. Officially, these units would not report to CENTCOM but were directly contracted to the Saudi government, to support Saudi forces only.

The 5/25th Recon Platoon joined the 2d Chemical Battalion on November 16 to begin a rear area support mission, allowing the 1st CAV DIV to receive the 22d Chemical Company's platoon. The 87th Chemical Company's platoon (from 2d ACR) would take the last six vehicles of the initial thirty back to Saudi Arabia in mid-December. Having accomplished the mission of reorganizing, training and equipping the four initial NBC reconnaissance platoons, Task Force Fox stood down. After all, its soldiers had to deploy with 3rd AR DIV to get into the war. The training at Sonthofen went on, however, as it did at For McClellan. Since two "float" vehicles remained available, the 490th Chemical Battalion which had ARCENT rear area. Eight chemical soldiers (five from the battalion headquarters and three from the 318th Chemical Company) traveled to Sonthofen on November 17 for the three-week course; they would arrive back in Saudi Arabia after Christmas. A Marine platoon would follow in early January, about two weeks after their colleagues began Fort McClellan's NBCRS training course. Platoons from 13th Chemical Company and 95th Chemical Company (both from 3rd COSCOM) were scheduled to enter Sonthofen training on February 8 (to be ready by mid March) as replacements prepared to replace casualties once the ground offensive began.

President Bush and a party, including Barbara Bush, Secretary of State George Baker, Chief of Staff John Sununu, National Security Advisor Brent Scowcraft, Senators George Mitchel and Bob Dole, and Representatives Tom Foley and Bob Mitchell, arrived in Saudi Arabia on November 22 for thanksgiving. The Secret Service, understandably worried about protecting the president against Scuds and CB agent attacks, ensured that the president and his party all carried MCU-2/P protective masks. Abroad Air Force 1 during the overseas flight, chemical officers had shown President Bush how to don a mask. His entourage traveled to within seventy miles of the Kuwaiti border to eat Thanksgiving dinner with the 2-18th Infantry Battalion. Three Fox NBCRS vehicles from the 5/69th Recon Platoon joined the protective phalanx of gunships, fighter planes and bodyguards. In the event of a chemical attack, the president and his group would have been whisked away in the NBCRS back to Riyadh.

On November 26, one Fox vehicle from the 92d Chemical Company hit a washout in the road during high-speed training operations, rolling several times before breaking its left front wheel and damaging the front axle. It could not be repaired in-theater and was shipped back to the depot in Kassel in December. This would leave a total of thirty-one Foxes in theater by the end of December—four recon platoons with XVIII ABN Corps (one with five vehicles and one with a "*Nunn*" vehicle), one platoon with 2d ACR, and one "*Nunn*" vehicle as the ARCENT ORF.

No Time for Cautious Decisions

Many normally accepted day-to-day operations were complicated by the CB agent threat, raising special concerns at CENTCOM that had to be answered quickly. At Dugway Proving Ground, scientists had increased their test activities to accommodate them. CENTCOM was concerned about a report that the Iraqi government had purchased forty Mistral-2 aerosol generators, which could be mounted on flatbed trucks, aircraft or boats. This agricultural sprayer consisted of a motor, a pump, a cannon-type blower assembly and storage areas for liquid and solid materials. These sprayers were designed to disperse either liquids or powders (i.e., insecticide), or both liquids and solids simultaneously. They had a military potential to disperse CB agent against the coalition if driven along the Iraq-Kuwait border, or against Navy ships and Marine forces in the Gulf if employed by small boats along the shore. DoD purchased two of these sprayers, transported them to Dugway, and used biological simulants to study their effectiveness. Other studies examined various terrorist chemical attack scenarios against command, control, communications and intelligence operations within CENTCOM. These studies remain classified to this day because of the implications of their potential applications.

One of the more sensitive issues was the disposal of contaminated bodies or US troops. The Quartermaster Corps, which has responsibility for the graves registration units, realized that mere body bags might be insufficient to seal in CB agents that might emanate from a contaminated corpse. Possibilities were to leave the corpses in Saudi Arabia or cremate the bodies prior to shipping the remains home. These were not seen as politically viable solutions. The Army Medical and Quartermaster Schools worked with Dugway Proving Ground scientists to find ways to decontaminate the bodies, check for excessive contamination, seal the remains in double body bags, and ship them back in sealed coffins to the United States. Prior to releasing the remains, the coffins would be checked again with sensitive laboratory chemical agent detectors for any leaking contamination. The details of this macabre procedure had to be tested and validated prior to its use, which meant months of careful evaluation.

A similar situation arose in shipping back formerly contaminated equipment. There was no question but that soldiers would continue to fight in their aircraft and vehicles, contaminated or not; that was a staple of chemical doctrine, to "*fight dirty*." However, when it was time to return the equipment back to CONUS, there was the possibility that contaminated tanks, helicopters and other major systems would require refit and repair by civilian and government depots. Before unprotected maintenance workers could safely handle equipment that had once been contaminated, the equipment had to be proven clean to a degree that military field detectors could not register. To achieve this very low agent level, soldiers would have to expose the equipment to intense heat for a period of time that would effectively destroy it—those $3 million tanks and $35 million helicopters—as well as the suspected contamination. Dugway Proving Ground scientists worked on procedures and laboratory equipment to screen the suspected contaminated equipment in Southwest Asia before it was loaded onto ships for the ride back, and again once the equipment arrived in the United States.

At the end of November, the UN Security Council adopted Resolution 678 by a 12-2 vote, calling for the United Nations to act against Iraq unless its forces withdrew from Kuwait by January 15. The British, French, US and Russian representatives took the opportunity to warm Iraq against "initiating the use of chemical or biological weapons." This resolution initiated increasing diplomatic pressure to warn Iraq about the consequences of using these weapons against the coalition. For the military members of the coalition, however, the fact that there was a resolution against CB warfare meant about as much as the Geneva Protocol of 1925 had meant to the Iraqis in the 1980s.

In the early morning hours of December 2, Iraq launched three Scud missiles on a test flight within its own boundaries, causing XVIII ABN Corps to institute MOPP-0 levels (Chemical protective suits within reach). This sent a clear signal to the coalition that its readiness would be tested. Colonel Barbeau sent messages throughout the corps to re-examine operating procedures and defensive equipment status in preparation for any Scud attacks that might initiate CB warfare.

CENTAF targeting lists swelled with the additional fighter and bomber wings brought in by the November call-up. Targeted NBC sites grew in number from eight to twenty in the fall, and finally to thirty-four. Target and weapons analysts worked with DNA to predict the possible collateral hazards of destroying facilities that housed radiological, bacteriological and hazardous chemical solvents. The nuclear targets were the least worry; the idea was to bury the enriched uranium under debris rather than completely destroy the reactors. IN addition to weapons production and storage sites, planners targeted the specific airfields where Iraqi forces had built chemical weapons bunkers. These included airfields at H3 (an oil-pumping site in the west), Mosul, Qayarrah West, Kirkuk, al-Taqqadum, Ubaydah bin Al Jarrah, and Shuaybah (a helicopter base). The two airfields at Tallil and an-Nasiriyah were targeted because of their proximity to the front and ability to launch air attacks into Kuwait.

DNA computer modeling showed a very small chance of any chemical agent traces traveling downwind far enough to threaten any allied troops. Basic physics explained that high concentrations of chemical agents eighty kilometers away would dissipate to sub-lethal levels long before reaching CENTCOM forces. Biological agents, however, scared the target analysts. Because any small sample of biological agent can, under optimal conditions, quickly cover a large area, there were serious and long debates over the possibility of causing an anthrax epidemic by bombing a biological weapons site. British and American troops had not begun their inoculation programs, and there was not enough vaccine for all the troops, let alone the civilian population. Biological warfare experts suggested that the risks of causing an epidemic were grossly overstated, given the extreme desert environment and distance the agent would have no travel.

Politicians and military leader in London, Washington and Moscow were still wary. The analysts offered up three options. First, they could mine the area around the bunkers with cluster bombs, denying access to the weapons. Second, they could guarantee that all the spores would die, by raising the temperature of the immediate area up to 20,000°F in three seconds–through tactical nuclear weapon employment. Some suggested that it might be morally correct to use one weapon of mass destruction to destroy another. Scientists at Yuma Proving Ground examined the effects of fuel-air explosives against bunkers holding simulated biological weapons. Last, F-117s could drop two thousand pound GBU-27 bombs on the bunkers right after dawn, followed by cluster bomb runs. This option would deny access to the sites while the sun's ultraviolet rays killed the spores that had escaped the bunker. CENTCOM's final position was to attack the biological weapons storage sites using the third option, hitting the sites with GBU-27 bombs followed by cluster bombs.

As more government civilians and defense contractors deployed to Saudi Arabia to help maintain military equipment, all had to be prepared for working within range of CB agent delivery systems. The majority of government civilians traveled to Aberdeen Proving Ground, Maryland, or Fort Jackson, South Carolina, to undergo a two-week predeployment staging. All deploying civilians had to take their immunization record, list of current medications, and their most recent eyeglass prescription (for the optical lens insert of the protective mask) to their medial screening appointment. The physicians assessed their ability to wear full protective equipment in the heat. This included identifying any history of heat stress, medical conditions that would limit the use of a mask, hearing problems that would prevent their reacting to a chemical agent alarm, and evidence of physical stress form other medical tests. Government civilians drew protective masks and protective clothing. In addition to some basic training, they attended a one day course on proper wear and maintenance of the protective mask, how to wear protective clothing, and how to administer medical antidotes. This predeployment training was vital if they were to respond properly to the expected gas alerts, especially for individuals who had never been exposed to such exercise in the military. One AMCCOM civilian commented later, "where you first hear over the radio the words 'GAS, GAS, MOPP-4' that is so frightening. And you're struggling, and all of a sudden you feel yourself breathing and you have to count one thousand one, one thousand two, so you don't lose it."

Biodefense Team Preparation

The CRDEC biodetection development team had received $20 million directly from Congress to develop and test a biological agent detector, with a deadline of January 15. The existing biodetection programs there were too immature to rush into development. CRDEC had identified two possible approaches—to see what industry could provide, or rely on the XM19 biological agent detector of the 1970s era. It narrowed down the choices to four systems. Two relied on point aerosol sampling-the previously abandoned XM2 biological agent air sampler and a commercial aerosol sampler, the PM10 Biological Aerosol Sampler/Cyclone. These systems would concentrate air particles into a saline solution. Another commercial item, Sensitive Membrane Antigen, Rapid Test (or SMART) tickets, would selectively identify biological materials in the concentrated medium through antibody reactions, indicated by a bright red spot for "*positive*." Both the commercial and military detectors required manual operation and fifteen minutes per test after forty-five minutes of aerosol collection.

The other two biodetector concepts were stand-off systems developed by Los Alamos National Laboratory (LANL) and SRI, which had begun their development under the DNA effort. LANL had developed an aircraft-mounted laser system to test alongside SRI's ground-mounted passive infrared system. A stand-off capability was desirable, since commanders wanted early warning of biological agent clouds rather than an indication that he ground that they were standing on had already been hit by BW agents. The Project Office for Biodefense transported the four systems (the two stand-off systems and the two point detectors) for testing at Yuma and Dugway, and arranged for a special environmental permission to use biological simulants and an active laser system (which involved eye-screening concerns). Ms. Donna Shandle, then the Assistant Technical Director for Testing at CRDEC, became the PO Biodefense coordinator for the testing at the proving grounds, given her past experience with the Dugway Proving Ground Test program.

While the theater biodetection concept was still forming, CENTCOM had designated the Navy Forward Laboratory as the theater medial lab for biological agent testing. Based on their collaborative work, the Army and Navy would share all incoming samples, with the NAVCENT Surgeon offering initial results to CENTCOM, and USAMRIID confirming the results at Fort Detrick. The Army planned to deploy its own forward lab from the 996th Medical Laboratory in December, equipped with advanced diagnostics equipment.

ASARDA ordered the low-rate initial production of the XM2 and commercial PM10 biological aerosols samplers on December 3, 1990. There had been no final word from CENTCOM about when or even if the systems would make it to the Gulf. Because of the pressure to get VII Corps to the Gulf and the looming deadline of the air war, CENTCOM had in January instituted strict guidelines on who was permitted to enter the theater. Even the Fox maintenance support teams had run into difficulties expanding the number of personnel at the Dhahran facility to support two corps' worth of NBCRS systems.

Initially, in late November ARCENT's G-3 had refused the biodetectors. Lieutenant Colonel Merryman distrusted the biodetectors; they were untested, previously rejected programs with no tested doctrine to back up their employment, no tried procedures on the collection, transportation, and identification of biological agents, and required 45 minutes to sample the air for one test. The point detection would not provide early warning for treatment; it would be hours after the fact before the operators knew that they had indeed been hit with biological warfare to the NBCCs. Lieutenant General Dennis Reimer, DCSOPS, pressured Brigadier General S.L. Arnold, the ARCENT G-3, to give his immediate support to the concept; there had to be a biodetection capability to give the military and political leadership some indication of the threat employment, if Iraq choose to use BW agents against CENTCOM.

In the bowels of the Pentagon, Colonel Read virtually locked Major Newing and a small group of Army, Navy and Air Force CBW specialists in a room to develop the doctrine to provide that capability. The group brainstormed to develop a doctrine using airborne stand-off biological agent detectors, the XM2 point samplers and the forward laboratories to alert CENTCOM to a biological agent attack. With the limited detectors being built (roughly a dozen), should they deploy in front of the division to allow an early warning capability? Or what would they confirm the biological agent attack? And upon confirmation of a biological warfare agent, how should they alert CENTCOM, and what then? How would they determine when it was safe to unmask after a biological agent attack? There were many thorny issues, and little time.

After three days, the groups emerged with what is still today the most accurate prediction and threat analysis on employment of anthrax and botulinum toxin. They had analyzed weather windows of opportunity, possible weapon delivery systems, triggers for employment, and war-gamed several scenarios. The result was a one-inch thick operational concept that laid the threat, provided point detection sampling and detection operations, and described the splitting of samples to theater medical labs (for immediate analysis) and CONUS labs (for international evidence if needed). If included an airborne stand-off option using a dedicated C130 to employ the detector and an AWACS for command, control and communications. As Major Newing briefed this concept in the Pentagon's briefing rooms, he sensed the Air Force's reluctance to commit these planes to a fly-by-night, ad hoc effort. Passive defense (detection) was still not favored over active defense (attacking the CW/BW sites), no matter the low battle-damage assessments.

ODCSOPS had selected the 9th Chemical Company form Fort Lewis, Washington, to take the biological agent detectors and XM21 RSCAALs into the Gulf (At the time, the 9th IN DIV was being deactivated). Two chemical officers and forty-three soldiers from the 9th Chemical Company at Fort Lewis would travel to Edgewood in mid-January to begin training and receive vaccinations. Two CRDEC officers, Captain General Minor and Captain Lloyd Plume, would join them as technical representatives and advance party for the 9th Chem's biodetection teams. The deployment concept was to sent an initial liaison team after the New Year, followed by area CB sampling teams using XM2s and XM21 RSCAALs and fixed-site teams using PM10 commercial detectors. CRDEC began to train their Biological Detachment Teams, in the hopes that ARCENT would accept them prior to the ground offensive.

ARCENT agreed on December 19 to request formally deployment of the biodetection teams. They would host the teams under the *Foreign Material Intelligence Battalion* (FMIB), attached to the 513th Military Intelligence Brigade, rather than with one of the chemical battalions (or the missing chemical brigade). The FMIB had the mission of collecting foreign military equipment, providing some on-site analysis, and shipping the equipment back to the United States for further intelligence analysis. As such, it was ideal to support the biodetection teams, although it had never worked with chemical soldiers before. One of its technical intelligence teams and the S-3 cell was already in the theater. The FMIB planned to deploy and establish a *Joint Captured Material Exploitation Center* (JCMEC) in theater by mid-January. Its operations and logistics cells had already left on December 10 to lay the foundations for the JCMEC.

The JCMEC had a technical intelligence mission. It would conduct battlefield exploitation of captured enemy equipment to determine its capabilities, limitations and vulnerabilities. Its new mission was to oversee CB agent and medical sampling to verify first use of CB agent weapons, in order to support national-level introduction of countermeasures. The 9th Chemical Company would conduct biological air sampling and provide a chemical stand-off detection capability at strategic locations across the theater front in two and three-man teams. The Army's *Technical Escort Unit* (TEU) would conduct the battlefield processing and packaging of suspected CB agent samples, and escort the suspected CB agent samples back to CONUS. If a biodetection team "hit" on a possible positive chemical or biological agent sample, it would send it to one of the labs—the Naval at KKMC—to produce an initial analysis for CENTCOM.

While the in-theater labs began their analysis, the TEU team would seal the sample in commercially-available medical hazard handling containers and send it from Dhahran to the United States on the next available flight. If the sample was suspected to be a chemical agent, it went to the CRDEC labs at Edgewood; if a suspected biological agent, it went to the USAMRIID labs at Fort Detrick. Once the sample was positively identified as either a false alarm or a real agent, the results would be forwarded to the Pentagon and CENTCOM. This was the same procedure that the Fox teams, medical preventive medicine units and special operations teams would follow if they had CB agent samples.

At least, this was the theory. In practice, a number of challenges by ahead. No one was exactly sure how this would work, since this was the first time this was the first time this sort of military sampling analysis had actually been put into operation. The equipment had been slapped together from commercial and antiquated military designs, and the operators were unfamiliar with them. There were not enough organic radio or vehicle assets to maintain twelve mobile teams across two corps and the corps support area. The forward labs required a minimum of six hours to analyze the samples after however long it took to get the samples back to the labs. To transport the samples back to CONUS, the TEU teams had to throw peacetime Army and Air Force transportation regulations about hazardous materials out the window. Last, even if CENTCOM was aware of a large-area biological attack, it had no way of knowing if a contaminated area could be cleared and rendered safe for troops after the attack. There was no way to declare "all clear" to the soldiers, as was done with the M256A1 kits for chemical agents. The whole concept had no precedent, making it difficult to estimate how quickly and how accurately it could provide answers on suspected CB samples. Yet they would be the basis for any presidential decision and CENTCOM's reaction to Iraqi CBW attacks.

5

FORENSIC SCIENCE CENTER

While Lawrence Livermore's national security accomplishments have received much publicity over the years, one Laboratory organization has gained such a stellar reputation among law enforcement, intelligence, and emergency response agencies that it is cited by Tom Clancy in his novel Shadow Watch: "I've requested assistance from the Forensic Science Center in San Francisco. It's at the Lawrence Livermore National Laboratory. I don't know if you're familiar with them."

"They did evidence analysis on the Unabomber case, the Times Square and WTC bombings in New York, probably hundreds of other investigations," Nimec said. "Uplink's had a relationship with them for years, and I've worked with them personally. The LLNL's the best group of crime detection and national security experts in the business."

Founded in 1991, the Laboratory's Forensic Science Center (FSC) offers a comprehensive range of analytical expertise to counter terrorism, aid domestic law enforcement, and verify compliance with international treaties and agreements. The center's combination of human and technological resources has made it among the best of its kind for collecting and analyzing virtually any kind of evidence, some of it no longer than a few billionths of a gram. Its resources, expertise, tools, and techniques are applied to all kinds of cases, from the September 11 World Trade Center attack to the spread of anthrax spores, from multiple homicides to nuclear materials smuggling.

FSC has a staff of 15 personnel, mostly chemists, with expertise in analytical chemistry organic chemistry, inorganic chemistry, nuclear chemistry, toxicology, pharmacology, special coatings, and forensic instrument design and fabrication. The center also drawn upon the resources of experts in Livermore's Chemistry and Materials Science and Nonproliferation. Arms Control, and International Security directorates.

The center's approach to forensic analysis maximizes the information that can be obtained from sometimes extremely small samples of explosives residue, dust particles, hair strands, blood strains, radioactive isotopes, drugs, chemicals, and clothing fibers. As Brain Andresen, until recently FSC director, says, "We're probing the lower limits of detection for many types of compounds isolated during an investigation." Even the tiniest quantities, says Andresen, are usually enough to provide compelling evidence that holds up in court. The minuscule amounts of oils remaining on fingerprints, for example, can tell the general age of suspects, their diet, and whether they smoke. In that respect, says Andresen, "Everything someone does leaves a chemical or biological signature that we can investigate."

Many forensic research projects have required FSC personnel to develop new analytical tools, forensic techniques for analyzing trace amounts of evidence, and unique sampling procedures. Several new, portable instruments have been developed that are capable of detailed analysis in the field. These tools provide important advantages when dealing with substances that may be unstable, perishable, or too toxic to bring back to the Laboratory.

Supporting International Security

Andresen notes that the term "*forensic science*" used to apply only to the scientific analysis of evidence for civil or criminal law. Increasingly, however, forensic analyses done at FSC are broadening that definition to include support for monitoring or verifying compliance with international treaties and agreements, particularly those involving weapons of mass destruction, and for countering threats of terrorism. For example, the center is contributing to the National Nuclear Security Administration's (NNSA's) Chemical and Biological National Security Program to develop and field advanced technologies to better prepare for, detect, and respond to chemical or biological incidents in the U.S.

In light of its demonstrated capabilities to analyze minute specimens, FSC was selected by the U.S. State Department in 2000 to support the Organization for the Prohibition of Chemical Weapons (OPCW) as the second U.S. certification laboratory.

OPCW, based in the Netherlands, is responsible for implementing the Chemical Weapons Convention, which bans the production, stockpiling, or use of such weapons as nerve agents and blister agents. OPCW-designated laboratories test samples collected by OPCW inspectors from sources around the world to determine whether the samples contain chemical weapon agents, their precursor chemicals, or decomposition products. The convention stipulates that all samples must be analyzed at the two OPCW-designated laboratories. Federal legislation requires that all samples taken from a U.S. facility be tested in a U.S. laboratory that is OPCW-certified.

FSC has established a separate chemical weapons analysis laboratory that is certified by the American Association for Laboratory Accreditation. To date, no actual samples have been officially collected from any site or analyzed at any laboratory. FSC, however, has been required to analyze and identify constituents of mock samples supplied by the OPCW as part of a series of proficiency tests.

According to FSC's Armando Alcaraz, "Passing the tests is a very challenging task because the samples might contain literally thousands of chemicals that are linked to chemical weapons manufacturing." He notes that the samples are sometimes spiked with certain materials to deliberately try to throw the analysis teams off track. Like the test samples, the real samples will be extremely dilute (that is, parts-per-million level) so that they can be shipped commercially or sent through the mail.

Helping Law Enforcement

FSC also assists law enforcement agencies with special needs that cannot be handled by standard crime laboratories." We're not in the business of routine police lab work," Andresen cautions. However, for cases that are particularly difficult, FSC may be a valuable resource capable of providing a conclusive analysis. In this respect, law enforcement agencies benefit from Livermore technologies that were developed initially to support counterterrorism efforts, detect nuclear proliferation activities, and advance stockpile stewardship.

Under the 1998 "Partnership for a Safer America" memorandum of understanding between the Department of Energy and the departments of Justice, Commerce, and Treasury, the center provides law enforcement agencies such as the Federal Bureau of Investigation (FBI), the U.S. Customs Service, and the Bureau of Alcohol, Tobacco, and Firearms with new *crime-fighting technologies*. This agreement provides a framework for formal working relationships to facilitate the transfer of DOE technology and technical expertise to law enforcement.

FSC deputy director Pat Grant notes that supporting law enforcement increases the center's expertise and shortens the turnaround times for sample analysis. "Anytime we analyze questioned samples important to a real-world investigation, we are honing our skills. It's a much more interesting and stimulating experience than participating in an exercise."

Shrinking Instruments

Some of the center's most enduring accomplishments are new tools it has developed for intelligence, law enforcement, and health professionals working in the field. These compact, battery-powered tools provide mobile chemistry laboratories. Because they eliminate the need to ship samples back to a standard laboratory for analysis, the portable technologies greatly speed decision making.

For example, FSC scientists have miniaturized and modernized *thin-layer chromatography* (TLC), a well-established laboratory procedure that identifies compounds belonging to the same general chemical class. FSC chemists made TLC technology suitable for field use with a portable system that fits inside a suitcase and weighs about 23 kilograms. Although the portable system uses minimal equipment and chemical reagents, it is highly specific and sensitive. The kits can be used to analyze two sets of samples simultaneously, with each set containing about 10 samples. Depending on the compounds being analyzed for, the entire process takes 10 to 20 minutes to complete.

TLC works by separating compounds over the distance they move up a glass plate. Tiny amounts of samples are placed just above the bottom edge of a TLC plate, the plate is placed in a small solvent reservoir, and the solvent moves up the plate by capillary action. A commercial digital camera captures the resulting patterns of dark spots that develop, which are analyzed on a notebook computer using a software program originally developed for the analysis of DNA. Based on the distance the samples have traveled, together with their colour and intensity, the computer program identifies the compounds and their relative concentrations.

The center's portable TLC kits are tailored to detect chemicals indicative of chemical weapons, high explosives, propellant stabilizers, or illegal drugs. Each specialized kit includes solvents and developing reagents that are specific to the compounds of interest.

The TLC system was originally developed for the U.S. Army to quickly detect propellant instabilities within the nation's munition storage depots. *Propellants* (especially high explosives) require stabilizers to prevent them from spontaneously igniting. Because stabilizers are depleted by long exposure to environmental conditions, the Army needed a way to quickly determine the safety of large numbers of munitions. The center's TLC system requires only 50-milligram samples of explosive, instead of the gram quantities typically required by other methods, and 15 minutes for each group of 20 samples, allowing many more samples to be analyzed and at much lower cost than is possible using traditional methods. "Army personnel without a degree or extensive training in chemistry can do this work," says FSC chemist Jeff Haas.

Over a few days in 1998, the portable system successfully characterized the contents of more than 1,200 unearthed mortar rounds discovered in a shallow excavation site at an Army base in Massachusetts. The system is now deployed at several other Army facilities as well as by National Guard units.

The system is also used in instances where analysis speed is essential. In light of repeated success by a variety of users, the center is transferring the portable TLC technology to private industry for commercialization and widespread availability to federal and state law enforcement, customs, and environmental agencies.

Advanced Tools for Field Use

While TLC is effective for identifying classes of chemicals that are specifically targeted, the task of completely characterizing samples in the field requires a more sophisticated instrument such as the gas chromatograph -mass spectrometer (GC–MS). An essential tool in every major analytical laboratory, a GC–MS can detect ultratrace quantities of organic compounds weighing a billionth of a gram or less. The gas chromatograph first slowly heats a sample to about 250°C. As the sample's volatile constituents travel down a long capillary column, they separate according to their vapour pressures and chemical affinities. As they flow into the mass spectrometer, the compounds are bombarded with an electron beam that fragments molecules into ions that constitute a unique fingerprint of that compound for positive identification.

FSC staff scientists have shrunk the standard 114-kilogram laboratory GC–MS to about 28 kilograms; it now fits inside a wheeled suitcase. The self-contained portable device, comparable in sensitivity and selectivity to a standard unit, contains a power generator, vacuum pumps, and laptop computer. The result is an instrument that significantly improves on-scene investigation and evidence collection.

Because of its ability to analyze samples to parts-per-billion sensitivity within 15 minutes, this portable GC–MS can be used to support nonproliferation activities, incident response, and law enforcement investigations. For example, the instrument can precisely identify compounds indicative of the manufacture of chemical warfare agents and illicit drugs. The instrument is currently being manufactured under license to industry.

Identification with Lasers

Although many tools used by FSC personnel depend on analyzing tiny amounts of chemicals that are found in a vapour phase above a liquid or some solid materials, most solid objects, such as human hair or clothing, do not have a significant vapour pressure and thus do not lend themselves easily to GC–MS analysis. However, center personnel can vapourize these solid samples with an extremely fine laser beam to generate wisps of product that contain identifying compounds.

The technology is called imaging laser-ablation mass spectroscopy. The process combines a laser for vapourizing extremely small amounts of material, an ion trap and time-of-flight mass spectrometer for analysis, and a high-powered microscope for viewing. In this way, forensic scientists can collect and rapidly identify suspect chemicals.

The process can be used on almost any solid material—dirt, pieces of glass, paint chips, clothing fibers, strands of hair. The samples are placed inside an ion trap mass spectrometer, irradiated with a laser, and identified within a few minutes by the mass spectrometer. The process allows an investigator to "walk down" a hair shaft by drilling consecutive holes on the same hair with the laser and analyzing each volatile sample.

"Because hair grows at a standard rate, the results can reveal a history of drug use or exposure to compounds used in biological or *chemical weapons* manufacturing," says FSC chemist Greg Klunder. He points out that the method could also be applied to samples of clothing or soil sticking to the shoes of someone suspected of developing chemical weapons.

A similar instrument still under development is capable of detecting chemicals in air and is well suited for high-speed aircraft sampling of exhaust smoke from chemical facilities. Potential applications include identifying hazardous spills, monitoring industrial stacks for certain compounds, and surveying the environment from a remote location to detect chemical releases from a suspect facility.

Wands of Collection

One of the center's most important developments has been the solid-phase microextraction (SPME) collection kits that use optical fibers as "*chemical dipsticks*" for safe and efficient sampling. "The technique has revolutionized the collection of forensic samples in the field," says FSC chemist Pete Nunes.

The technology uses commercial hair-size (100-micrometer-thick) fibers to capture organic vapours. The fiber, residing inside a syringe, is coated with a chemical polymer that, when exposed to the ambient environment for a suitable amount of time, can collect thousands of different compounds by acting as a chemical sponge. The polymer coatings are specific for different types of compounds such as chemical warfare agents, high explosives, or illegal drugs.

The collection technique requires no solvents, sample workup, or additional equipment typically associated with obtaining evidence. The fibers can be inserted directly into a portable or stationary GC–MS for immediate analysis.

Nunes says that because the fibers are fragile, they had never been taken into the field. To overcome their fragility, an FSC team developed rugged aluminum transport tubes, with each tube securing one syringe and fiber. A group of five tubes is contained in each kit. The hermetically sealed tubes prevent any possibility of cross-contamination and support chain-of-custody requirements. A sampling port in the bottom of the tube permits assaying the contents in a glove box before the tube is actually opened.

SPME sampling is being put to good use by FSC weapons scientist David Chambers to monitor nuclear weapon warheads safely. This activity is part of the NNSA's Stockpile Stewardship Program to maintain the safety and reliability of the nation's nuclear stockpile.

Chambers uses SPME's coated fibers to collect volatile and semivolatile molecules that are formed or outgassed from the nuclear and thermal breakdown of organic polymers and high explosives. Signs of outgassing can indicate problems such as corroded metal parts that need to be replaced. By monitoring for the presence of these chemical vapours, scientists are alerted to problems that may be developing inside the weapon.

The center has provided the FBI and other agencies with SPME field kits for the safe and rapid collection of chemical warfare agents. The kits are equally well suited for drug detection and arson investigations. FSC has also developed a new SPME transport tube that is smaller and lighter so that it can fit inside a shirt pocket. Both versions are being licensed to industry for sale to government agencies.

Always On Call

Although the Forensic Science Center was highlighted in a Tom Clancy novel, it is not fiction. It is a rich resource for the national security and intelligence communities and has proved itself a valuable ally to federal and state agencies alike. Just as they have for the past 10 years, FSC personnel will be on call for the next case and the next sample.

6

Chemical Security

The LLNL Chemical and Biological National Security Program (CBNP) provides science, technology and integrated systems for chemical and biological security. Our approach is to develop and field advanced strategies that dramatically improve the nation's capabilities to prevent, prepare for, detect, and respond to terrorist use of chemical or biological weapons.

Recent events show the importance of civilian defense against terrorism. The 1995 nerve gas attack in Tokyo's subway served to catalyze and focus the early LLNL program on civilian counter terrorism. In the same year, LLNL began CBNP using Laboratory-Directed R&D investments and a focus on biodetection. The Nunn-Lugar-Domenici Defense Against Weapons of Mass Destruction Act, passed in 1996, initiated a number of U.S. nonproliferation and counter-terrorism programs including the DOE (now NNSA) Chemical and Biological Nonproliferation Program (also known as CBNP). In 2002, the Department of Homeland Security was formed. The NNSA CBNP and many of the LLNL CBNP activities are being transferred as the new Department becomes operational.

LLNL has a long history in national security including non-proliferation of weapons of mass destruction. In biology, LLNL had a key role in starting and implementing the Human Genome Project and, more recently, the Microbial Genome Program. LLNL has over 1,000 scientists and engineers with relevant expertise in *biology*, *chemistry*, *decontamination*, *instrumentation*, *microtechnologies*, *atmospheric modeling*, and *field experimentation*. Over 150 LLNL scientists and engineers work full time on chemical and biological national security projects. Critical shortfalls exist in our ability to prevent, prepare for, detect, and respond to *chemical* or *biological terrorism*. The LLNL CBNP emphasizes collaborative demonstration programs with end-users as part of a spiral development strategy. These programs provide near-term capabilities, opportunities for dialogue among scientists, engineers and end-users, focus for R&D investments, and paths for pilot-to-regional-to-national systems.

Current and emerging collaborative demonstration programs include

1. Biological Aerosol Sentry and Information System (BASIS) is a "*detect to treat*" environmental monitoring system originally designed for the Salt Lake City 2002 Winter Olympics. BASIS is a joint project of Lawrence Livermore and Los Alamos National Laboratories with significant participation by law enforcement and public health organizations. BASIS successfully deployed to the Olympics and has also been deployed to several other sites. In its first year of continuous operation, it has performed over 70,000 diagnostic tests of complex environmental samples with no false alarms.
2. Laboratory testing of sentinel populations for early detection of bioterrorism (SENTINEL) complements BASIS-type environmental monitoring by performing surveillance of the population through direct high-throughput testing of clinical samples of opportunity. LLNL has demonstrated 1,000 samples (10,000 assays) performed in an 8-hour shift with 2 technicians. SENTINEL is an emerging program with the influenza-like-illness programs and the Veterans Administration to directly detect pathogens and toxins in samples. Preliminary data by LLNL and its corporate collaborator Source Precision Medicine, indicates that the strategy might also be applied to *presymptomatic detection* of host response biomarkers.
3. Local Integration of NARAC in Cities (LINC) provides responders and local government with modeling and prediction tools for decision support. Composite views of plume prediction with important local features including schools and fire and police stations are available to the users. Both local and reach-back capabilities are provided. The first pilot city for LINC evaluation began in September 2002 and is Seattle, Washington.
4. *Bio-Forensics* is a joint LLNL, Northern Arizona University, and Los Alamos National Laboratory project to make specific forensic tools and data available to the broader community. The focus is on supporting law enforcement and the CDC PulseNet Laboratories

for food borne illnesses. Round robin comparisons of different methods and assays will precede the principle deliverables of 1) a database for a variety of end-users and focused on law enforcement and 2) strain-sensitive markers and validated assays for Salmonella and E. coli for CDC PulseNet.

5. PROTECT is an Argonne, Sandia and Lawrence Livermore National Laboratories program for protection of key facilities focused mostly on chemical attacks. LLNL is supporting PROTECT through NARAC and biodetection. NARAC is doing modeling and predictions for outside facility and scenario studies including operational support of deployed systems.
6. OPCW Certified Laboratory is in support of the US State Department's selection of LLNL as the second US designated laboratory for the Office for the Prohibition of Chemical Weapons (OPCW). We have implemented all the technical, safety and procedural systems required and been ISO-17025 approved. Final OPCW designation is pending. The first, and currently only, US OPCW Certified Laboratory is at ECBC in Edgewood, Maryland. The ECBC group has provided significant assistance to LLNL in this process.
7. Restoration of Operations will demonstrate strategies for decontamination and restoration of operations for major transportation facilities. The activity builds on LLNL restoration planning for CW attacks on transportation facilities, decontaminant reagents including L-gel, sampling strategies to support decontamination, high throughput sample processing, accelerated viability testing, and published studies to establish "How clean is clean enough?" Lawrence Livermore and Sandia National Laboratories jointly execute the project with a focus on airports and establishing "*templates*" for restoration strategies.
8. Model Cities is a tri-Lab project to better understand geographic and other local or regional factors that influence prevention, preparation and response. The goal is to create common "*templates*" that can be applied in many locations and in combination to create more comprehensive regional plans. The initial test beds for this concept have been the other demonstration projects (e.g., BASIS and LINC) and a tri-lab demonstration in Albuquerque, New Mexico in December 2002. Integration and evaluation of multiple detection schemes for wide area, special facility, and epidemiological surveillance were accomplished.

The demonstration programs help focus our science and technology (S&T) investments. The S&T is managed in four areas (i) Decontamination and restoration; (ii) Modeling and prediction; (iii) Instrumentation; and (iv) Applied science. Some of the current S&T activities include:

1. *Decontamination* and *restoration* goal is to provide the S&T and systems approach to quickly restore civilian facilities to operation. Decontamination in a civilian setting requires fundamentally different technology from most military applications. Rapid and effective means of decontamination are needed for equipment, facilities and large urban areas. LLNL developed the L-gel decontamination technology. Several new decontamination chemistries are in development and testing including vapourous hydrogen peroxide. In addition, appropriate protocols for efficient restoration are being investigated.
2. *Modeling* and *Prediction* goal is to develop predictive urban environment modeling tools for local and other users for response, planning and vulnerability assessments. Advances in computing algorithms and hardware now make it possible to model air flows over very complex terrain. LLNL is developing tools for modeling such flows in urban environments including around buildings and in subways to determine in advance how to best respond and to permit real-time prediction of agent dispersal during an actual event.
3. *Instrumentation for Chemical* and *Biological Detection* goal is to provide highly sensitive and accurate instruments for early warning, treatment triage, and detection of contaminated areas. LLNL is developing and integrating instruments with substantial increases in detection performance. The focus of chemical instrumentation is miniaturization of laboratory-quality instruments for field detection of CW agents and related material. LLNL has licensed several *chemical instruments* to industry including miniature GC-MS, *thin layer chromatography*, and an integrated optic capillary electrophoresis system. LLNL technology for rapid DNA detection was licensed to industry and enabled a successful product that has been applied to counter terrorism. LLNL has prototyped a new instrument that is capable of 100 simultaneous assays; detection of viruses, toxins, spores, and vegetative bacteria; and capable of autonomous operation for several days at a time. Prototypes of this instrument have been tested with aerosolized live agents and

were deployed in a limited capacity in 2002. LLNL has licensed this technology and will assist our corporate partner to enable and accelerate access to this technology as a commercial product. Several next generation instruments are part of our R&D portfolio and address significant current shortcomings including cost per assay, *operational complexity*, and real time response.

4. *Applied science* goal is to provide biological and chemical support for detection and other countermeasures. LLNL invented and transferred to industry specialized solid-phase absorbants that greatly simplify field collections of CW-associated materials. The availability of DNA and RNA sequence information has enabled rapid development of biological signatures that are highly specific and sensitive. Techniques are also being developed for ligand signature discovery as well as sub-species level bio-forensics. LLNL has invented several high throughput approaches for vetting signatures (both nucleic acid and ligand) including computational screening of potential signatures, automated strain panel testing, complex environmental sample testing and, more recently, pathogen-associated function and host-associated response using *genomic* and *proteomic tools*.

In the following pages, the reader will find a series of Science & Technology Review reprints representative of CBNP activities. Many of the point of contacts have changed—feel free to contact members of our team or me for additional information. The LLNL CBNP is organized into four areas managed by Associate Program Leaders. Because of the wide range of expertise and facilities needed to fulfill our mission in Chemical and Biological National Security, the CBNP also relies on a multidisciplinary team with a number of key assignments.

Abraham Lincoln faced significant challenges to our homeland. His words remain powerful and, unfortunately, relevant today. Our program is fortunate to have a team willing to commit their careers and more to help our country meet today's challenges and preserve what we all hold so dear.

7

L-Gel Decontaminates Better than Bleach

The recent cases of anthrax spores deliberately spread through the mail reminded all Americans, and especially managers of federal and state agencies responsible for public health and safety, about potential terrorism with chemical and biological weapons. The *anthrax* cases have also underscored the need for safer and more efficient methods to decontaminate offices and homes of deadly biological agents.

During the late 1990s, scientists at the Department of Energy national laboratories foresaw the need for a safe, reliable, and easily deployable decontaminating agent that could be used for civilian defense against biological and *chemical terrorism.* DOE managers agreed with the scientists and asked them to use their expertise in chemistry, biology, and environmental protection to develop new decontamination products and procedures.

Lawrence Livermore responded to this request with a team formed from the Environmental Protection Department and three directorates—Chemistry and Materials Science; Nonproliferation, Arms Control, and International Security; and Biology and Biotechnology Research. The team of diverse experts developed a compound called *L-Gel* (the L is for Livermore), which combines a mild, commercially available oxidizer with a silica gelling agent to create a substance that coats walls, ceilings, and other materials like a paint, effectively decontaminating the coated surface.

The material is nontoxic, noncorrosive, easy to manufacture, easily deployable, and relatively inexpensive (about $1 to cover a square meter). Tests at Livermore's laboratories and field trials at both federal and foreign facilities have shown that L-Gel has been extremely effective at decontaminating all classes of chemical warfare agents as well as surrogates for biological warfare agents.

Livermore technology transfer specialists are currently engaged in negotiations with several companies to license the manufacturing and marketing of L-Gel. If negotiations proceed apace, government agencies could have the material by the end of the fiscal year (September 30) to respond to any terrorist incident involving chemical or biological agents.

Different Needs for Civilians

According to *L-Gel development* leader Ellen Raber, a geochemist and head of Livermore's Environmental Protection Department, several decontaminating agents are effective against either chemical or biological warfare agents. However, these materials, which are mainly strong chemicals, were developed by the military for battlefield use, and they pose environmental and health risks when used in civilian settings. At the minimum, they can damage everyday materials such as furniture and office equipment.

Other methods that have been used in civilian settings have serious drawbacks. For example, solutions of *laundry bleach* work well as decontaminants but are very corrosive. Incineration and irradiation have obvious practical limitations in office settings or face public resistance. *Chlorine dioxide gas*, used late last year to decontaminate the Hart Office Building that houses members of the U.S. Senate, is a laborious process and poses a safety risk to workers. It also requires the gassed building to be neutralized before people can reenter.

The Livermore team focused on finding an effective decontaminating agent and application system that is safe to use, does not damage commonly used materials and surfaces, is friendly to the environment, and is effective against both chemical and biological warfare agents. "We wanted something that was less corrosive than bleach, that is easy to apply, and that does not leave workers with a huge cleanup job," Raber says.

Raber points out that speed of decontamination, which is all-important in military applications, is less important in civilian applications, where decontamination times of one to several hours may be adequate. More important in a civilian scenario are ease of application, minimal training required for use, moderate expense, and environmentally acceptable by-products.

The team also recognizes that the new product needs to be effective in three potential settings of a terrorist incident against civilians: an outdoor location such as a stadium, a semienclosed place such as a subway station, and an enclosed space such as an office building. Using the decontaminating material on interior surfaces can have quite different requirements from those appropriate for outdoor use, where natural attenuation from environmental conditions (for example, ultraviolet radiation from sunlight) might well be adequate for effective decontamination.

START WITH OXIDIZER

The development effort began with Livermore scientists Ray McGuire and Don Shepley evaluating several acidic oxidizer solutions that could degrade chemicals into nontoxic, environmentally acceptable components. (Oxidizing solutions do not completely destroy chemical agents but rather break key chemical bonds to render the toxic compound inactive.) The oxidizers considered could be deployed in liquid spray systems or incorporated into compatible gels for clinging to surfaces such as ceilings and walls.

McGuire chose an acidic rather than a basic oxidizer solution, primarily to aid the decontamination of VX, a potent nerve agent. *Acidic oxidizer* solutions are also known to be effective at decontaminating certain *biological warfare agents*, including bacterial spores, which are extremely difficult to kill because of their hard, multilayered coats. The coat allows a spore to remain in a dormant state for many years until, under the right environmental conditions, it transforms into a live organism.

"*Anthrax* is the most difficult biological agent to kill because of its resistant outer coat," says Raber. An oxidizer in acidic solution breaks down the proteins that are found in anthrax coats. Once the oxidizer gets through to the nucleus, its molecules destroy strands of the anthrax DNA or RNA.

The goal was to find the most effective oxidizer at the lowest effective concentration. The oxidizers that were evaluated included *potassium permanganate*, *peroxydisulfate*, *peroxymonosulfate*, *hydrogen peroxide*, and *sodium hypochlorite*. The oxidants were evaluated in laboratory tests on chemical warfare surrogates for such agents as VX, sarin (used in the Tokyo subway terrorist incident), and sulfur mustard (used during World War I).

Livermore bioscientist Paula Krauter evaluated the same group of oxidizers on *surrogate biological agents* and toxins that would likely be used in terrorist attacks. Bacillus subtilis was used for spore-forming agents such as anthrax, Pantoea hericola was the surrogate for plague, and ovalbumin was the surrogate protein for botulinum toxin.

The initial laboratory tests showed that *potassium peroxymonosulfate* was more than 99 percent effective at oxidizing both chemical and biological warfare surrogates that were placed on common materials such as carpet, wood, and stainless steel. The results led to the selection of *Oxone*, a commercial product manufactured by DuPont, which contains *potassium peroxymonosulfate*—its active ingredient—in a water solution. Previous research at U.S. military laboratories had demonstrated the effectiveness of Oxone in decomposing both VX and mustard-type agents, but the compound had not been previously tested on biological agents.

Gel Adds Staying Power

The team recognized that spraying water-based solutions of Oxone would not be effective in all cases. Consequently, McGuire and Mark Hoffman investigated carrier materials that would thicken the oxidizer so it would better cling to walls, ceilings, and other surfaces to increase contact time with the biological or chemical agent.

Hoffman chose colloidal amorphous silica as the carrier material for several reasons. First, unlike crystalline silica, which is toxic, colloidal amorphous silica is safe to use and is found in many household paint formulations. Also, *silicon dioxide* colloidal particles are commercially available, don't require manufacturing in a special facility, and, because they are chemically inert, are compatible with oxidant solutions. When mixed with the oxidizer, the gel can be applied with simple delivery systems, such as paint sprayers. After application, it thickens and tends not to sag or flow down walls or drip from ceilings. Finally, *silica gel materials* can be easily vacuumed up after they have dried.

Livermore chemists have extensive experience with colloidal silica gel. From the late 1960s to the late 1980s, the chemists developed a series of extrudable high explosives based on the gelling of energetic liquids. Although this research did not advance to the explosives production stage, the development effort provided useful experience for working with silica-gel materials. It was a logical step to adapt this work to the gelling of aqueous oxidizers for candidate decontaminants, says Hoffman. "Our research with high explosives gave us a good feel for working with silica gels."

Hoffman selected Cab-O-Sil EH-5 fumed silica as the gelling agent. The final formulation was named L-Gel 115, which is a formulation of aqueous Oxone solution gelled with 15 percent EH-5 silica gel. The viscosity can be varied, depending on the application. Under development is a second formulation, called L-Gel 200, which contains 10 percent t-butanol cosolvent to promote penetration on surfaces with heavily coated paint or varnish.

Field Tests Prove Effectiveness

The final L-Gel 115 formulation was subjected to a series of tests at Livermore facilities using surrogates of potential terrorist chemical and biological agents. The tests involved placing surrogate chemical and biological agents on various common materials—varnished wood, painted steel, glass, fiberglass, and carpet—adding L-Gel to the surface, allowing the gel to dry for 30 minutes to several hours, and then determining the percentage of surrogate that had been decontaminated. L-Gel proved greater than 99 percent effective on all surfaces and for all agents.

The Livermore biological researchers also tested L-Gel on safe strains of the deadly biological agents *Bacillus anthracis* (anthrax) and *Yersinia pestis* (plague). These strains—Sterne and Strain D27, respectively—could be safely used in experiments because they are nonvirulent, that is, they do not contain the genes that create the lethal toxins present in the real organisms. The researchers used the agar plate resistance test, a standard technique to measure the efficacy of antibiotics. In this test, about one million cells (or spores, in the case of *B. anthracis*) were combined with liquid agar, then poured onto a petri dish containing nutrients for cell growth. The strains were also tested against dilutions of L-Gel, which proved more than 99.9 percent effective in killing the cells and spores.

L-Gel also was tested against surrogate spore-forming bacteria in two field exercises. In December 1999, researchers Krauter and Tina Carlsen participated in biological warfare field tests that were conducted by the Soldier Biological and Chemical Command at the U.S. Army Dugway Proving Ground, Utah. The tests compared the ability of several decontamination materials to inactivate surrogate organisms placed on six 40-square-centimeter panels of acoustic ceiling tile, tightly woven carpet, fabric-covered office partition, painted wallboard, concrete slab, and painted metal. Each panel was contaminated with about 10 billion spores per square meter.

After L-Gel was applied, the panels were swabbed about 24 hours later. The number of live spores on most test panels was reduced by an average of 99.988 percent.

In October 2000, Krauter and Hoffman participated in a biological warfare agent room-decontamination exercise that was conducted again at the Dugway Proving Ground. The tests used full-scale, mock offices constructed in an abandoned building. Flooring was divided into quarters consisting of carpet, vinyl tile, varnished oak, and painted concrete. Walls consisted of stucco, wood paneling, plasterboard, and carpet, and the ceiling was constructed of suspended ceiling tile. The room was contaminated with 4 grams of spores. After application of L-Gel, about 400 samples were collected from multiple locations in the room. L-Gel reduced the number of spores by about five orders of magnitude and, in these experiments, did not damage office surfaces, with the exception of bleaching some rust on ceiling supports.

L-Gel was also independently tested on real chemical warfare agents at four locations from October 1998 to October 2000. The tests were conducted at the Military Institute of Protection, Brno, Czech Republic; Edgewood Chemical and Biological Forensic Analytical Center, Maryland; the Defense Evaluation and Research Agency, United Kingdom; and the Soldier Biological and Chemical Command at Dugway. Field tests showed that L-Gel was a more effective decontaminant of real VX, GD (nerve agent), and *sulfur mustard* than the current military standard, *calcium hypochlorite*, on such materials as acrylic-painted metal, polyurethane-coated oak flooring, and indoor–outdoor carpet.

Two of the field trials also demonstrated that the L-Gel 200 formulation has improved penetration and thus promotes solution and oxidation in thickened chemical agents. L-Gel 200 was tested on real chemical warfare agents such as thickened distilled mustard and thickened soman (persistent nerve agent) as part of the Restoration of Operations series of experiments at Dugway Proving Ground. The agents were applied on steel test panels, Air Force air–ground equipment paint, and Navy shipboard coating.

Meets Safety Standards

With L-Gel's excellent performance demonstrated in both laboratory and field trials, it was time to partner with one or more commercial firms that could manufacture the material quickly and efficiently. Fortunately, says Raber, "L-Gel is simple to manufacture.

It's comparable to mixing paint." L-Gel is relatively noncorrosive (its pH is about 4, similar to that of vinegar or lemon juice), and Environmental Protection Agency testing shows its residual materials to be nonhazardous. It also meets the Department of Transportation's nonhazardous and noncorrosive requirements and is stable during shipping.

L-Gel is premixed and then shipped and stored as a semisolid resembling Jello at room temperature. If unopened, its shelf life is expected to exceed a year. It is reliquefied to the consistency of house paint by vigorous shaking by hand or a power stirrer. It can be applied with any type of commercially available spray device, whether airless or compressed-air units, with any stainless-steel atomizing nozzle.

Although L-Gel clings to walls and ceilings, it does not harm most painted surfaces or carpets. Decontamination takes about 30 minutes. When dry (in about 1 to 6 hours), the gel residue, unreacted oxidizer, and decontaminated chemical or biological agents can simply be vacuumed up and discarded as nonhazardous waste. For outdoor use, no cleanup is required.

Raber says L-Gel compares favourably to other decontamination methods that have been used recently to kill *anthrax spores*. The tried-and-true method is a bleach solution. However, bleach is extremely corrosive to metal surfaces and must be used with care by cleaning crews.

A foam developed at Sandia National Laboratories in New Mexico has also been effective for decontaminating *chemical* and *biological agents*. This material is sprayed on surfaces like a firefighting foam. Most of the foam dissipates, and the residual material is then washed off. It has been used to clean offices of Congress and at ABC News. Raber suggests that L-Gel and the Sandia foam could work in tandem, with L-Gel sprayed on walls and ceilings and the *Sandia foam* applied to large pieces of equipment and floors.

Chlorine dioxide, used to decontaminate U.S. Senate offices, is a gas that kills bacteria but also is hazardous to human health and thus must be applied by trained personnel. Afterward, its vapours must be sucked out of rooms and then filtered through an *ascorbic acid bath* to decompose it. Raber notes that gases and *aerosols* have clear advantages for decontaminating ventilation systems and hidden spores, and research needs to continue to find an environmentally safe gas or aerosol that is effective for these applications.

Irradiation, popular in Europe, kills bacteria and spores and is effective in decontaminating mail, food, and other objects. However, the method requires large machines, which are essentially small accelerators, and is not currently viable for large-scale room decontamination.

In the News

News about L-Gel has spread rapidly, and Raber has been interviewed by several newspapers, television stations, and National Public Radio. She has also received a large number of inquiries from emergency response groups across the country interested in additional information and samples.

The developmental work for L-Gel 115 is complete, and Raber's team has begun to develop a new formulation to decontaminate ventilation systems. "Right now, we don't have an easy way to decontaminate air ducts," she says. The team is working on an encapsulation method to aerosolize L-Gel (make it into tiny droplets) so that it could be blown into ventilation systems. In the meantime, licensing of L-Gel manufacture is well under way, and Raber is hopeful that major organizations will soon have an important yet nontoxic new weapon to counter any biological or chemical attack.

Detection of Biological Agents

OR years, experts in terrorism have been warning that a terrorist attack with biological agents is not a question of "if" but "when." As recent events have proved, when is now. For almost a decade, researchers at Lawrence Livermore, working on the when-is-now premise, have been developing systems that can rapidly detect and identify biological agents, including pathogens such as *anthrax* and *plague*. Among such systems are the *Handheld Advanced Nucleic Acid Analyzer* (HANAA) and the *Autonomous Pathogen Detection System* (APDS).

Although HANAA and APDS are of different sizes and made for different situations, they have a common purpose: to get results, fast. Lawrence Livermore biological scientist Richard Langlois explains, "There are any number of laboratory tests available right now to analyze pathogens. They all require getting a sample and then transporting it to a laboratory for processing. Our systems use new instrumentation and methods that provide faster and more timely results, on the spot. Faster results mean the responders can act quickly and begin treatment earlier."

HANAA in Hand

About the size of a brick, the HANAA biodetection system can be held in one hand and weighs less than a kilogram. The system was designed for emergency response groups, such as firefighters and police, who are often first on the scene at sites where bioterrorism may have occurred. Each handheld system can test four samples at once—either the same test on four different samples or four different tests on the same sample. HANAA can provide results in less than 30 minutes, compared with the hours to days that regular laboratory tests typically take.

The process of detecting and identifying what's in a sample works like this. The operator prepares the samples by putting them in a liquid buffer and adding chemicals. A tiny disposable plastic tube holding about 0.02 milliliter of the prepared liquid is then inserted into the system. Many copies of a sample's DNA are needed to analyze it and identify its makeup. HANAA uses a technique called the *polymerase chain reaction* (PCR), which amplifies agent-specific DNA fragments to a detectable level. In PCR, an aqueous sample is heated close to the boiling point and then cooled many times (40 times in HANAA). Every time the DNA is heated, the two intertwined strands of DNA unwind and come apart. As the sample cools down, the DNA makes a copy of itself. Thus, at the end of each cycle, the amount of DNA is doubled.

To detect the DNA in a sample, a synthesized DNA probe tagged with a fluorescent dye is introduced into the sample before it is inserted into the heater chamber. Each probe is designed to attach to a specific organism, such as anthrax or plague. Thus, the operator must have an idea of what substances might be involved. "The system doesn't test for all unknowns," says Langlois. "A responder has to decide what kinds of pathogens to test for ahead of time and set up the system accordingly." If that organism is present in the sample, the probe attaches to its DNA, which is then amplified during the PCR process, releasing the fluorescent tag. HANAA measures the sample's fluorescence and the presence (or absence) of the targeted organism.

One of the big breakthroughs for the handheld system involved the design of a small silicon heater chamber for the heating and cooling cycle, a concept developed at Livermore by Allen Northrup, a former Laboratory scientist. "The commercial thermocyclers used for standard laboratory tests are pretty big, ranging from the size of a microwave oven to a large desk," notes Langlois. "A typical large thermocycler takes about 3 minutes to cycle through one heating and cooling cycle, so a complete analysis requires 2 to 3 hours." In the HANAA system, the thermal cycling process occurs in tiny silicon heater chambers, micromachined by Livermore's Center for Microtechnology. Each chamber has integrated heaters, cooling surfaces, and windows through which detection takes place. Because of the low thermal mass and integrated nature of the chambers, they require little power and can be heated and cooled more quickly than conventional units. The mini-chambers typically cycle from about 55°C to 95°C and back to 55°C in about 30 seconds.

Using this technique, the HANAA system could, in principle, detect as few as 10 individual bacteria in one-hundredth of a milliliter in less than 30 minutes. The system has the potential of saving many lives by saving time—*anthrax*, for example, is highly treatable if detected early.

The Laboratory has a cooperative research and development agreement for HANAA with Environmental Technologies Group (ETG), a chemical and biological detector company and subsidiary of Smith's Industries, based in Baltimore, Maryland. ETG expects to have a commercial version of HANAA available early this year. Ron Koopman, special projects manager for the Chemical and Biological National Security Program at Livermore, notes that HANAA is essentially ready to go at this critical juncture because of the forward-thinking efforts begun in the previous decade. "A number of people recognized the vulnerability of the country to bioterrorism a long time ago," he says. "In 1996, although bioterrorism seemed far away and was something we hoped would never happen, the Laboratory and members of the defense community decided to invest in the research, just in case. Thanks to that investment, we now have something to put in the hands of people to protect us all, something that can help during the current crisis and in the long run."

A Bio "Smoke Detector"

Whereas HANAA can be hand-carried to sites at which an attack is suspected to have happened, the APDS is stationed in one place for continuous monitoring and is designed to work much like a smoke detector, but for pathogens. When fully developed, the APDS could be placed in a large area such as an airport, a stadium, or a conference hall. The system will sample the air around the clock and sound an alarm if pathogens are detected. "The important point here is that the system would be fully automated," stresses Langlois. "The system will collect and prepare the samples, do the analysis, and interpret the results, all without human assistance."

Livermore is testing the second APDS prototype, which is about the size and shape of a *lectern* or *mailbox*. The APDS-II consists of an *aerosol collector*, a sample preparation subsystem, and two subsystems for detecting and analyzing the samples: one based on PCR and the other based on flow cytometry, which uses antibodies to identify pathogens. "The final system will double-test each sample to decrease the likelihood of false positives and increase the reliability of identification," explains Langlois.

The aerosol collector, which was designed by Vern Bergman and Don Masquelier at Livermore, gathers an air sample every 30 minutes—the length of time it takes to complete a sample analysis. A built-in fan pulls in the air, which passes through a glass tube containing water. The water traps any particles in the air, and the resulting fluid is pumped to the next stage for sample preparation and testing.

The flow-through PCR subsystem for the APDS includes a Livermore-designed thermocycler—much like the thermocycler in HANAA—along with a sequential injection analysis system. This analysis system performs all the necessary PCR sample preparation functions, such as mixing the sample with PCR reagents, delivers the resulting liquid sample to the thermocycler, and decontaminates the thermocycler chamber and fluid delivery tubes to prepare for the next run.

For the flow-cytometry subsystem, small "*capture*" beads that are 5 micrometers in diameter are coated with antibodies specific to the target pathogens. The beads are colour coded according to which *antibodies* they hold. Once the pathogens attach to their respective antibodies, more antibodies—those labeled with a fluorescent dye—are added to the mix. A labeled antibody will stick to its respective pathogen, creating a sort of *bead sandwich-antibody*, *pathogen*, and *labeled antibody*. The beads flow one by one through a flow cytometer, which illuminates each bead in turn with a laser beam. Any bead with labeled antibodies will fluoresce. The system can then identify which agents are present, depending on the colour of the capture bead. "Right now, we use seven bead types to detect four agents simultaneously with controls," says Langlois. The next step is to increase the number of detectable pathogens to 20 or 30. Ultimately, the researchers expect to be able to test for a hundred pathogens simultaneously in a single assay.

Langlois and the APDS team hope that, within the next year or two, the system will be ready to put in place wherever needed. Ultimately, notes Langlois, numerous detector systems could be linked together in a network connected to an emergency response center to protect a complex of buildings or a city.

The Faster the Better

From handheld, immediate testing to autonomous and continuous testing, HANAA and APDS are two of many systems Livermore is developing to help the nation fight bioterrorism. With HANAA, emergency responders can get answers on the scene in less than half an hour. With APDS, no human direction will be necessary, and the system will perform on its own, completely self-contained, monitoring 24 hours a day, 7 days a week. "What ties these approaches together is the ability to analyze a sample quickly—within 30 minutes or less—and do it on site," concludes Langlois. "Getting the answer quickly is important. In the case of a biological attack, the sooner we know what bioagent we're dealing with, the sooner treatment can start for those affected. Systems such as these have the potential for saving many lives."

Lethal Agents

Consider this: a ballistic missile carrying a chemical or biological agent is traveling fast toward its target—military or otherwise. What are the implications of intercepting or destroying that missile in the upper atmosphere? Part of the answer to that question depends on knowing what conditions would allow lethal amounts of the liquid agent to reach the ground.

For instance, consider the chemical nerve agent VX, an organophosphorous compound that disrupts the body's nervous system. Lethal doses—ingested, inhaled, or absorbed through the skin—cause rapid death. It is estimated that a lethal dose is contained in a 2- to 3-millimeter-size drop. A warhead holding 400 kilograms of VX contains about 62 million lethal doses. If the warhead were to reach its target—say, a port or air base—it would saturate the target and cause an "*area denial*," that is, make the target site unusable until cleaned up. But what if it were to be intercepted tens of kilometers above the ground? What would happen to the VX?

The extreme conditions experienced by a single liquid drop during its reentry into the atmosphere lie in a regime for which no experimental data exist. To better understand the physics of what happens at these altitudes, physicist Glen Nakafuji, analyst Roxana Greenman, professor Theo Theafanous of the University of California (UC) at Santa Barbara, and research colleagues are studying how liquid breaks up and evolves in rarefied (thin) atmospheres.

To do so, they are using unique hydrodynamic and shock-physics experiments coupled with advanced chemical-kinetic and hydrodynamics computer codes. The experiments and codes simulate the supersonic, rarefied flow environments that reentering droplets of a chemical agent would experience. Nakafuji is the principal investigator for the project, which is funded by the Laboratory Directed Research and Development (LDRD) Program.

Thin Atmospheres, High Velocities, Surface Tension

A number of complicated factors determine how a body of liquid breaks up and how the individual drops or streamers break apart and shape and reshape themselves. The factors include the pressure of the surrounding atmosphere, the velocity at which the liquid is traveling, and the physical properties of the liquid. "At altitudes of tens of kilometers," explains Nakafuji, "the agent disperses and expands in an atmospheric pressure that can be ten thousand times less than that at sea level. Pieces of liquid float out, stretch, and tear in milliseconds, then fall in an expanding cloud into the atmosphere." From there, the mass of drops falls through the air, moving at supersonic velocities through increasing atmospheric pressure. "Originally," notes Nakafuji, "people in the field theorized that the liquid would aerosolize into droplets on the order of 10 micrometers in diameter and disperse. Initial experiments indicate that this may not be true." So the question remains open: Would a given liquid break up into these small-size droplets or not?

"There's a huge gap in experimental data for the behaviour of liquids in this sort of environment," notes Nakafuji. "We know how various liquids break up at sea level, where the atmosphere is dense, and the air molecules—which can be represented as individual particles—are constantly bouncing off each other, pressing together, and acting more like a fluid than individual particles." However, higher up in the atmosphere, the molecules are fewer and more widely dispersed, acting more like individual particles at altitudes above 30 kilometers. "You add to this the fact that the liquid agent is not in free fall but is experiencing atmospheric drag, and the problem becomes very complex," notes Nakafuji. "Yet this is the situation we're faced with in examining the physics of droplet breakup."

Of Weber Numbers and Bag Breakups

The physics of a liquid drop breaking up has much to do with the nature of the fluid (its density and viscosity, for instance) and the forces acting upon it. The ratio of external aerodynamic force—which tends to pull the drop apart—to the liquid's surface tension—which tends to hold the drop together—is a dimensionless quantity called the Weber number. Drops of different Weber numbers break up in different ways. Drops with higher Weber numbers (above 100) tend to have more catastrophic breakup and result in smaller drops. At very high altitudes, where external aerodynamic forces are small, the Weber number remains relatively low, below 100. When the team conducted experiments on drops with a range of Weber numbers characteristic of high altitudes, interesting findings emerged. For instance, drops 3 to 4 millimeters in diameter tended to oscillate before breakup. For drops with Weber numbers between 12 and 100, the experimenters observed a phenomenon called "*bag breakup*," in which a round drop deforms into a shape resembling a bowler hat, with a flat rim and curved crown. As the drop falls, the bag portion, which corresponds to the crown of the hat, oscillates in and out. When the original drop disintegrates, large drops form from the rim, and smaller ones form from the bag. "This happens in tens of milliseconds—much slower than anyone expected," says Nakafuji. "Previously, it was observed that such bag breakup would occur in hundreds of microseconds to 1 millisecond, tops."

ALPHA Goes with the Flow

These experiments were conducted in the ALPHA facility, a one-of-a-kind experimental system designed and built by the Livermore–UC Santa Barbara collaboration to examine liquid fragmentation. The facility is essentially a large, vertical wind tunnel, consisting of a cylinder about 3 meters long and 10 centimeters in diameter, that can be pumped down to pressures of 10 to 30,000 pascals. The methodology for re-creating a drop falling through the upper layers of the atmosphere is as follows. An injector releases liquid through a laser beam. The drop breaks the beam, which makes it act like an optical trigger and causes a diaphragm to burst. Air rushes up the cylinder past the drop, in effect simulating the fall of the drop through the atmosphere, and a high-speed camera records the behaviour of the drop. "We have the capability to get air moving at velocities of Mach 5—about 1.5 kilometers per second," says Nakafuji. The air flows past the drop at a nearly constant velocity for about 200 milliseconds before its speed begins to ebb, long enough to watch a drop fall, reverse direction, rise, and then burst. This past spring, the group tested a drop 1.5 centimeters in diameter—the largest drop yet tested anywhere. "We don't test actual agents," Nakafuji emphasized. "We use glycerin and other kinds of fluid, and extrapolate to agents from there."

Besides examining whether assumptions made at sea level about the breakup of liquid hold true in rarefied environments, the team is also exploring the different break-up modes and whether the dynamics of these modes differ from the dynamics seen for bag break-up. The researchers' efforts have been rewarded. They have documented dynamics that have never before been seen or predicted. "For instance, before the bag breaks, it oscillates at some frequency," explains Nakafuji. "What we saw for the first time—and which no one had expected—is that after the drop turns and begins to move upward, the oscillation frequency doubles. We are now trying to understand this."

Getting Details, Drop by Drop

Ultimately, the team would like to understand and be able to predict the dynamics of specific liquid drops in any rarefied environment. "We'd like to be able to calculate the onset of breakup—when a drop will break up, the configuration the liquid will take, which drops are stable, and which are not," says Nakafuji, adding, "We've definitely made strides in that direction, to the point where we can now accurately predict whether a drop will break up under certain conditions."

The present goal is to obtain critical hydrodynamics and chemical data to validate computer models of these simulations. Working toward this end, the researchers have successfully used the Laboratory's ALE3D code to predict the drag on rigid spheres in subsonic and supersonic rarefied flows, validate a surface-tension model, and test a deformable drop simulation.

"Using experiments and simulations, we are pinpointing the ranges of drop stability and getting a better handle on the physics of liquid breakup," explains Nakafuji. "In the final analysis, we want to be able to predict the rarefied atmospheric conditions under which a given chemical agent will break up into lethal-sized stable droplets. This is a critical question, one whose answer could affect us all."

8

OFFENCE IN GULF

Since its remaining in 1996, the US Army's chemical crops has had the responsibility of preparing the US armed forced to survive and sustain military operations on a nuclear, biological and chemical (NBC)-contaminated environment. From 1946 to 1969, the Chemical Corps' mission, organization and goals remained fairly consistent as those of a technical support branch of the Army. Most chemical Corps officers had master's degrees and doctorates in chemistry, chemical engineering, and biology—and rightly so, given their positions at chemical depots, laboratories, and division and corps headquarters. These were the only positions for active duty chemical officers, as brigade and lower combat units still relied on officers who were not Chemical Corps branched to execute NBC defense programs as an additional duty. Virtually all combat positions were gone, since chemical mortar units, chemical defense companies and battalions had been inactivated and formed as reserve units after 1955. A successful career Chemical Corps officer relied on laboratoıy and depot positions at Edgewood Arsenal, Fort Detrick, Dugway Proving Ground, Rocky Mountain Arsenal, and similar noncombat positions to help him rise to the position of Chief Chemical Officer. This created a "*white lab coat*" image of the "*Chemical Corps*," which persisted from a prior to the Korean War into the late 1970s.

This technical bent may have been what eventually doomed the chemical corps. In October 1972, General Creighton Abrams, Army Chief of Staff, ordered the formation of a special study group, to determine how to disestablish the Chemical Corps, as part of the Army's restructuring plan after Vietnam. This group recommended putting a smaller Chemical Corps under the Ordnance Corps, as a special weapons branch. While Congress did not grant this disestablishment, General Abrams froze recruitment and career progression in the Chemical Corps. The Chemical School shut down at Fort McClellan, Alabama, and moved to Aberdeen Proving Ground, Maryland, as a technical subelement to the Ordnance Corps for special weapons (*chemical munitions*).

Chemical defense training and leadership in the Army vanished for nearly a decade, for all practical purposes. Then the emergence of chemical warfare threats in the Arab-Israeli War brought it back from the edge of extinction, as the US military examined the Soviet's growing offensive chemical warfare capability. The Secretary of the Army reinstated the Chemical Crops in 1979, and the NBC defense program was running smoothly again by 1982. The Chemical Corps restructured its cotrine, force structure and equipment modernization program in a crash effort to regain an NBC defense capability for the armed forces. The new doctrine stressed a three-tiered approach, of contamination avoidance, protection and decontamination. This doctrine emphasized that combat forces should continue the mission even if contaminated, highlighting the need to accept NBC warfare as an environment or condition, not as a separate mission in itself. This was a major change from the past, when combat units had expected to be completely decontaminated before continuing operations.

Table 8.1. Changes to chemical crops doctrine

	Pre-1980	Post-1980
Doctrine and training	Chemical crops concern	Army-wide concern
Operational emphasis	Minimize chemical casualties	Minimize mission degradation
Degree of risk	Zero risk	Take intelligent risks
Control of chemical defense operations	Centralized under division NCB element	Decentralized, flexible down to brigade level
Decontamination operations	Complete decontamination of troops and equipment	Partial decon-enough to continue the mission

Chemical staff specialists slowly joined every level of command from company through corps, developing an in-house expertise on NBC defense doctrine, intelligence, training and logistic in every unit. It would not be until the mid-1980's until all divisions could claim they had chemical-biological (CB) defense experts from company through division headquarters, but the shift from being seen as technicians toward becoming true combat supporters had been made. The Army activated twenty-eight active duty chemical defense companies between 1979 and 1989, revitalizing the Army's divisions with dedicated chemical defense specialists.

While this gave the US Army an immediate credible defensive capability, its leaders had risen in an Army without chemical defense units; learning how to properly employ them would come slowly. Decon companies served as "*car washes*" more often than they were realistically exercised. Likewise, many smoke generator platoons received missions as artillery smoke markers rather than large area smoke obscuration. Change would come slowly to some divisions, more quickly to others.

A series of studies called Combined Arms in a Nuclear/Chemical Environment, or CANE, conducted in the mid to late-1980s, emphasized the psychological isolation and physical degradation felt by soldiers as they attempted to perform individual and group combat operations wearing protective clothing and masks. These studies also quantified the increases in time to mount an offensive, the overall decrease in combat strength and the increased difficulties leaders faced trying to command their forces in a chemical environment. While these findings were generally understood, this was the first time anyone had attempted to quantify and assess these effects. The Chemical Defense Training Facility (CDTF) opened on March 3, 1987. There, potent nerve agents were introduced into various training rooms; students garbed in full protective clothing and masks practiced using agent detectors and decontaminating equipment in a toxic agent environment. As of the summer of 1997, over 40,000 students had passed through the facility without one accident. This facility continues to be invaluable as a confidence builder for chemical defense personnel, teaching them the effectiveness of their equipment and training.

The equipment modernization plan shot forward, fielding M8 and M9 chemical detector paper and M256A1 chemical detector kits, giving all soldiers, not only the specialists, the ability to identify chemical agents. The M8A1 automatic chemical agent alarm provided more reliable point warnings than its predecessor, while the new M1 chemical Agent Monitor (CAM) allowed personnel to pinpoint chemical contamination on troops and equipment. There was an improved protective ensemble, called the *Battledress Overgarment* (BDO), offering twenty-four hours protection against liquid agents. New decontamination systems such as the M13 Decon Apparatus, Portable

(DAP), and the M17 *Lightweight Decon System* (LDS) offered battalions the ability to clean themselves during combat rather than moving off the line to a chemical decon company's site. Collective protection systems in vehicles and tanks meant less physical and psychological degradation to the crews, who would not have to wear masks and clothing while in the vehicles.

Other developmental systems in the 1980s were not so quickly fielded. A new protective mask (M40-series), replacing the M-17 series masks, still waited in the wings, leading to the Army's decision to modernize its Vietnam-era M17 masks to the M17A1/A2 masks in 1983-85. The NBC reconnaissance vehicle (the XM93 NBC *Reconnaissance System* or "*Fox*" NBCRS) and a long range chemical agent detector (the XM21 Remote Chemical Stand-Off Agent Alarm [RSCAAL]) had slipped their delivery dates to the early 1990s. Biological agent detectors, miniature chemical agent detectors and decontamination systems that did not use massive amounts of water fell into the "*too hard*" column. Still, there were tremendous stride in one decade, which the Army had yet to absorb. With less than five years to train with these new items, suddenly the call to battle sounded.

Ready for Desert Shield?

In the mid-to-late 1980s, there was a certain quiet pride in being a member of the armed forces. It seemed that the malaise of the Vietnam years and the resulting hollow military of the 1970s had finally faded away, with the unprecedented peacetime buildup that occurred in the *Department of Defense* (DoD) during the Reagan-Bush administrations. With the actions in Grenada and Panama under their belts, modern combat equipment, and a new joint philosophy termed "*Air-Land Battle*," the call of an Army career attracted the top talent from the pool of American citizens. When the call went out to mobilize for deployment to Southwest Asia, there was a mixture of dread and eagerness: dread because no logical military individual seeks out the battlefield to test his or her skills on other human beings, and the fear of death always dampens excitement. Yet this is what the men and women of the armed services trained to do—to work as a team to carry out the Commander-in-Chief's orders and to act in the interests of national security. The question of whether they could do the job for which they had been trained sat in the back of their minds, even as they deployed into the combat theater. Confidence in themselves and their equipment, excellent training and leadership would tell over time.

These thoughts and fears existed in the minds of every chemical soldier in the Army as well. On the one hand, no one knew more than chemical personnel that the potential danger of an NBC agent environment was real. These individuals had donned protective gear and trained in the CDTF at Fort McClellan. Although some in the military might not think so, even chemical soldiers dislike having to train in full protective posture with chemical soldiers dislike having to train in full protective posture with chemical protective clothing, mask, boots and gloves. Yet they understood and respected the threat, knew how to survive in an NBC environment, and most important, understood that they could operate in a toxic environment. Many chemical soldiers looked forward to using their unique knowledge to help their comrades survive and sustain combat operations.

Because the US military had not suffered the effects of NBC warfare since World War I, many combat arms units (*infantry*, *armor*, *artillery* and *aviation*) had relegated their chemical soldiers to secondary positions within their commands (such as administrative clerks, supply assistants, training officers). Many had ignored the need to integrate NBC training and equipment in the years since the *Chemical Corps* had returned from the dead. Now as the call to deploy went through the ranks, concerned voices spike out. Where are those chemical agent detectors? How exactly do we build these collective protection shelters? What do you mean, we don't have enough mask filters and agent detector batteries for thirty days? When was the last time I checked the fit of my protective mask?

The flurry of individual and unit NBC defense training that began at US bases in August and carried over Saudi Arabia was evident to CNN cameras and other media. What wasn't as public was the feverish twenty-four-hour work being conducted at Aberdeen Proving Ground—Edgewood Area, Maryland, site of the Army's Chemical Research, Development and Engineering Center (CRDEC); at Natick, Massachusetts, home of the Army's Natick RD&E Center (NRDEC); at Rock Island Arsenal, Illinois, home of the Armanent, Munitions and Chemical Command (AMCCOM); at Fort McClellan, Alabama, within the US Army Chemical School (USACMLS); at Dugway Proving Ground, Utah, home of the Joint Test Center; at Pine Bluff Arsenal, Arkansas, the long-standing depot for chemical-biological defense equipment (and in the past, both biological and chemical agent weapons); at Fort Dtrick, home of the US Army Medical Research and Development Command (MRDC) and, of course, at the various staff sections working for the services and Joint Chiefs of Staff (JCS) in the Pentagon. This is their story, and the story of the Army's chemical soldiers—a story of sacrifice, hardships, unending optimism and faith that their skills would find a use in a military that had stopped believing in NBC warfare.

Tales from the Soldiers—Operation Desert Shield

I was at Fort Leavenworth, Kansas, attending the Combined Arms and Services Staff School course along with about thirteen hundred other company-grade officers on August 2, 1990, when we heard the news about the Iraqi invasion into Kuwait. Officers soon began disappearing from the two-month course to mobilize with their units. When the 82nd Airborne Division began airlifting its troops to Saudi Arabia a few days later, may first thoughts were, "Those guys are in trouble. If they get hit by chemical agents, the entire division will lock up in protective postures and freeze in place like a deer in the headlights." I had visited the 82d Airborne Division in 1987, where a brigade chemical officer had explained that the 82d ABN DIV's soldiers trained with masks only for riot control situations. "The 82d believes that none of their missions will call for deployment into an area where we will see the actual employment of CB agent weapons. We'll bring protective masks into areas where military or police forces use riot control agents. We're into low intensity conflict scenarios," he explained.

This attitude was typical of most "*light infantry*" fighters in the 1980s, and the Army's generals knew that this was the case in August 1990 as well. I remember thinking that this was the reason why there was so much public footage of soldiers training in the desert with protective equipment, and why President George Bush, Secretary of Defense Richard Cheney, and other political figures were so quick to warn Saddam against the use of chemical agents. Other soldiers told me of their brushes with CB defense preparations during the mobilization and deployment to the Persian Gulf.

Colonel Mike Ahern, Division Chemical Officer, 2d Armored Division

"I had arrived at Division (Fort Hood) only about three weeks prior to Saddam's invasion of Kuwait. 2AD [2d Armored Division' had already been earmarked for inactivation. Its remaining ground brigade, the 'Tiger Brigade,' was then attached to the 1st Cav [Cavalry] Division for deployment to the Gulf. Other units form the division base were also included, such as the Division's 44th Chemical Company. The only role that I and the 2AD division chemical section played was the important (but not very glamorous) work that everyone was doing—refresher training for the troops deploying, and a huge effort to get serviceable masks, protective clothing, and NBC supplies on hand and issued to the troops. Our unreadiness in the area of supplies, which were supposed to be on hand but were not, and the masks, which were supposedly serviceable until needed for a real war, was my real heartburn. We also conducted some NBC staff exercises for the deploying troops, and then after they'd gone, kept busy by continuing to keep our own battle staff expertise up by participating in numerous Corps-level CPXs [command post exercises].

"It wasn't a real fun time when so many of our Dragon soldiers [Chemical Corps soldiers] were going off to war and we in 2AD were not. I think every single one of us was looking for a way to go over, but the Division Commander (Major General Phil Mallory) was striving to keep the division staff intact as a trained and ready battle staff that could be deployed as a replacement or augmentation to a Corps or Division HQ if needed. I think we all realized the sensibility of this as the Division continued to down-size, but it sure didn't make us any happier."

Lieutnant Colonol Milke D'Andries, Product Manager for NBCRS, Office of the Project Manager for NBC Defense Systems

"I had left the M43 Apache Protective Mask team to join the PM NBC office in mid-July 1990, where I was to take over the Fox project. Because of my past experience both on the mask team and as an aviator, I agreed to be available for all major meeting concerning the M43 mask up to August.

"An example of these meetings included briefing the status of the M43 Apache Protective Mask to a quarterly general officer steering committee for fielding the Apache helicopter at Fort Lee, Virginia. HQ DA [Headquarters, Department of the Army] had stated that the Apache helicopter could not be fielded without a compatible protective mask for its pilots, which brought much attention to this particular mask program. When the Scott Aviation M43 production contract was canceled, we were left without a production source until Mine Safety Applications picked up the contact. Earlier in the year, I had explained that this contract transition would delay the mask until the summer of 1990. I also explained a skin irritant problem for some pilots as a technological challenge—the labs couldn't use silicone rubber for the

M43 as they were planning for the M40/42. The mask production needed to use a blend of butyl and natural rubber to avoid chemical agents absorbing and off-gassing through the thin rubber facepiece. The general officers tasked our mask team to explain this in depth at their next quarterly meeting.

"As mentioned earlier, I left to move into the Fox NBCRS office. I planned on attending an IN-Progress Review meeting at General Dynamics Land Systems in Detroit on August 6, and then flying to Fort Hood, Texas, to brief the Apache general officer steering committee on August 7. To assist in technical expertise, CRDEC had added a civilian member—Rick Decker—who would meet me in Austin. During the drive from the Austin airport to Fort Hood (a two-hour drive), we recognized that we were walking into an unfriendly meeting. The commander of the 6th Air Cavalry Combat Brigade (stationed at Food Hood) was planning to blower was too heavy and they didn't like the skin irritant problem. The program Manager for Apache knew that the aviators hated the mask, and the mask was two of the Safety Center also planned to tell the panel that the irritant was a hazard to flight safety. Our briefing on the skin irritant tissue was not positive-we had planned to tell the aviators that there was no alternative but to use the butyl-natural rubber blend.

"When we arrived to meeting at Fort Hood's officers club, we say lots of stars (Major General Arwood, ODCSLOG; Major General Greenburg, AMCCOM; Jim Morgan, PARC from Rock Island Arsenal), FORSCOM's aviation officer, and the brigade commander of the 6th ACCB) laying in wait for the CRDEC mask team This was not a friendly audience. We told each other (in the manner of individuals resigned to a sure fate), 'If you see them measuring us and carrying hammers and nails, RUN!' and 'We should tell the CRDEC office that if they can't find us tomorrow, to look for our bodies in the Texas desert! The meeting opened with administrative comments and the meeting agenda, which showed the mask briefing in the morning.

As the meeting opened, one officer rose to suggest that the group take a break to review President Bush's address about the crisis in the Gulf. We had missed much of the news about the Iraqi invasion. The group moved into a bar where there was a television. President Bush announced his act of drawing a 'line in the sand' and the deployment of US troops to Saudi Arabia. CNN followed up the President's address with a report on the 82nd Airborne Division's deployment, Air Force and Navy deployments. CNN also reported that the Iraqi military was loading '*gas bombs*' on their aircraft. The mood at the briefing immediately turned somber. Rick Decker ran to the phone to call Mine Safety Applications [MSA, the industry partner] and the CRDEC lab to establish how many M43 masks he could build immediately. As the brief resumed, the general officers had forgotten about the skin irritant problem. They had forgotten about the heavy motor-blower problem and the two-year program lapse. All they wanted to know was how many makes could be built and how soon. Rick replied that they could engineer 243 masks in four weeks using test articles and spare parts at Edgewood, but he couldn't promise that these masks would last for their expected full seven-year life.

"Since we were the only chemical defense specialists at the meeting, the Army aviators asked us where they could find additional M8A1 alarms for aviator units. We received permission from Jim Morgan to incentivize MSA by giving them a bonus for delivering masks sooner than contracted. Major General Greenburg pulled me aside, saying 'You tell me who you need me to kick in the butt, and I'll use my size 9 shoes. And I'll make my personal plane available to ship any M43 spare parts or masks.' The general officers loved us. We left the meeting after lunch, but not before the 6th ACCB commander stated darkly, 'You guys got lucky.' Not only did we survive the program, we came back as heros."

Colonel Rick Read, Chemical Section, Office of the Deputy Chief of Staff for Operations and Plans

"The first week after the invasion, I got into the office about 0630 or 0645 one morning, and the phone rang—it was the Army PAO. He said, 'I need you to get down here right away. You need to go over to CNN studios here in Washington. They need somebody to brief them up on NBC.' I said, 'What? Who's cleared this?' It's already cleared, DCSOPS said you can go.'

"We had a mannequin that we kept inside the door dressed in MOPP [Mission Oriented Protective Posture] gear. So we grabbed this mannequin, and we were going to take him with us along with the mask and a detector kit and a few other odds and ends we had there. As we picked him up, the mannequin disassembled in the middle. We had these big old grocery carts that people used to get supplies from self-help. They loaded this thing in so that the top of the torso was sticking out at one angle and the legs out the other. We're pushing this thing down, charging down the halls and quarters of the Pentagon, took the elevator downstairs to the second floor, ran into PAO. We raced out the door, piled into a waiting CNN van and roared across town.

"At the CNN building, I entered the elevator, standing there in Class A's [service-dress uniform] with that damn mannequin. People were staring at me like I was crazy. When I got upstairs, they ushered me back into the Green Room, where Harry Summers and the president of STI, Inc., were waiting 'OK, Colonel, here's what we're going to do. Colonel Summers is going to go on as an NBC expert. You need to make him an expert before he goes on camera. And then the second speaker will talk about his company's atropine injectors.'

"After Summers came back from makeup, we chatted a little bit. He said, 'OK, take me through this. I can't remember much of this tuff, it's been years.' We talked about the nomenclature of the mask, the purpose of the suit, and the M9 paper and the way it changed color. When the time came, he charged out on the floor. I watched my 'student' perform on the monitor, and he did a fairly credible job. He did the pitch, every body liked it, and I took it all back to the Pentagon. NO sooner did I get back (about noon), the PAO called again. 'That worked well this morning. We need to you bring it all back downstairs this afternoon.' What? What's going on?' We have got Sam Donaldson coming over. He wants to do a stand-up piece.' So we trotted back downstairs to a room that was set up, and put the mannequin up. It was interesting times. That was the kind of stuff that was going on.

Master Sergeant Gregory Drake, S-1 [Personnel] NCO, 210 Field Artillery Brigade, 2d Armored Cavalry Regiment

"I rarely heard a soldier complain about the requirements to have his helmet and protective vest on at all times, and just as seldom would I find a soldier without his load-bearing equipment, M-17 protective mask, weapon and ammunition. Spare chemical suit, water, and rations were part of every vehicle's load plan. Due to the increased threat of chemical weapons deployment by the Iraqi forces, soldiers took chemical protective measures very seriously. Everyone knew what each level of MOPP was, and how to use the individual detection kits. Pyridostigmine Bromide tablets were taken without fail (with NCOs checking as part of their nightly ritual), and M8 chemical detection alarms were deployed and checked almost hourly. Some vehicles and more than one M-11 decontamination device, and no one was without a healthy supply of DS-2 [decontaminant]".

Special Frank Clark, 220th MP Company, Colorado National Guard, at the 402d Enemy Prisoner of War Military Police Camp

"We were activated 2 January 1991 and spent our prep and training time at Fort Carson. There we had daily training and reinforcement in NBC training along with mission-specific training. We worked with the individual detection kits, M8 chemical detection units. Spent lots of time talking about MOPP, about nerve agent antidotes, etc. Another interesting fact was that we couldn't be deployed until every protective mask passed a 100 percent function check and visual check. Some masks had to be turned in because of potential problems.

"Late in January we were finally deployed to Southwest Asia. At Fire Base Mike, chemical preparedness was taken seriously, as at the airports. But within the time of about a week, this went downhill fast. After the first few Scud attacks, we were no longer forced to MOPP up and actually slept through half of them. I usually put my mask on just to be on the safe side; usually the all-clear was given only minutes after a Scud attack. As far as I know, there were no chemical alarms set up in the area of Fire Base Mile. The lack of detection equipment worsened as we moved forward. Out company had very little chemical detection equipment, and its use was even more inconsistent. Chemical monitoring might have been done diligently by the front line and infantry, but we were right behind them (within twenty miles of the border) before the ground ware, and were even Scud'ed at the 402d [location], but no chemical precautions were taken on encouraged. This posture and attitude was prevalent throughout the desert during my time there."

Lieutenant Colonel Stephen Franke, Assistant Army Attache, American Embassy, Saudi Arabia

"I was assigned as to DAO's Defense Attache System as an Assistant Army Attache. I became intimately familiar with Saudi Arabian Ministry of the Interior and Municipality of Riyadh. They were the main Saudi Arabian government bodies responsible for civil defense and counter measures/ recovery against (dreaded) chemical warfare attack by the Scud SSM [surface-to-surface missiles]. While assisting them, I accompanied the Saudi police and civil defense guys to Scud impact sites, helped carry bodies, assessed damages, showed that the US shared concern and the danger, and interviewed witnesses and survivors.

"On a side and somewhat still-humorous note, I remember the panic and indignation by the resident expatriate British community because their embassy wouldn't get gas masks for their horses! Those valiant horsemen swore up and down that since the British had gas masks for their military horses in WWI, then Her Majesty's Government certainly must have a stock back in the United Kingdom, or they could get some made and delivered posthaste to Saudi Arabia. Her majesty's ambassador was most firm, clear, and not delicate in his negative reply."

TALES FROM THE SOLDIERS—OPERATION DESERT STORM

First Lieutenant Russel Baggerly, Pier Operations Officer, 24th Transportation Battalion, 7th Transport Group, 22d Support Command

"It was January 16th, the deadline had passed and the air war finally started. Almost at the very moment we sat that Peter Arnett was foolishly not keeping his head down, came the wail of Damman's air raid sirens. 'Scud warning!' said the radio and we scrambled to get into mission-oriented protective posture (MOPP). I gathered with the rest of the off-shift soldiers in a nearby warehouse, and then realized that due to the heat, and my almost constant sweating over the last few months, I had loss enough weight that my mask didn't fit anymore. Air bubbled through the sweat pooled in the chin cup of my mask. Trying in the best traditions of the Officer Crops to stay calm, because, "panic is contagious," I tried to set the example while I desperately held the chin of my mask firmly against my face and sat with the soldiers. I also tried to remember first aid for NBC casualties. OK, it's atropine for blood agent, no, wait first the little one, then the big one, no... shit.' I remember thinking. 'This isn't how I thought I'd get it.' That Scud supposedly whistled overhead for a not-even-near miss in the gulf, and the sirens sounded the all clear.

"Later, after our 'fifty-seventh' Scud warning we got a bit nonchalant abut the whole thing. When the siren went off, we would run to the railing of the barge to watch the fireworks. Some of the ships reacted to the Scud warnings by hitting every fire hose on the ship and 'showering' themselves to 'wash off' the chemical agents they feared. To us it was funny, the sirens blew, and the ships disappeared behind a curtain of water. Not that were not afraid, but what do you do?"

Captain Andrew Entwistle, commander, 45th Ordnance Company, XVII Airborne Corps

"When it finally came, the message that awakened me was all that I'd expected. 'It's started. Have your guys take their pills, get into MOPP and be ready to go to the bunkers.' Turning on the portable radio we listened with the rest of the world as Bernard Shaw of CNN witnessed what we could not. I paused in dressing, thinking aloud to LT McPeak: 'This is history, happening right now. You just tore open a brand-new protective suit because you really might need it. We're taking these PB tables for the first time ever in the field. None of this stuff has ever happened before and we don't know tonight how it will end, or even if either of us will ever see it end.' Our eyes met, and we finished dressing in silence. The Scuds did not come, and at dawn we held stand-to, marvelling at the streams of aircraft filling the sky.

["On the third day he was awakened.] 'Scud launchers are up, some pointed this way. Take the pills and head for the holes.' Each soldier carried a chemical suit tightly rewrapped since its first exposure. We'd been told that this could preserve it [after being worn once], but we'd never heard that before and few of us believed it, especially later, as the number of 'reusable' days was increased almost daily. Inside the commo shack, panic broke out with the whooping of an M8 alarm set on the perimeter. I could hear it as they screamed to me over the commercial walkie-talkie, and I thought about those letters I dreaded. It never occurred to any of us at that moment that we hadn't seen any type of delivery system, or that no one else's alarm was sounding. We were not going to die! Screaming at the top of my lungs, I raced around the perimeter. The company exploded into action, heading for MOPP level 4 in record times that will never be broken. A soldier without his gear bolted for his tent barley touching the ground. Someone yelled that I had not yet masked, that they'd carry the word around. Precious seconds burned as I desperately tried to force a bootie on backwards, but I got it on somehow. Masked and ready, we waited.

"And waited. Around the perimeter, soldiers reviewed their lessons: 'One sign of being gassed is sweating... I'm sweating!' Through sheer willpower mouths dried out, heads pounded, and the twitching began. The pills made many nauseous, but they couldn't be sick in the mask, and if they could not take the mask off.... A soldier fainted and panic nearly overtook us. There's no telling what our self-inflicted body count would have been had not the sun finally topped the horizon, revealing the tents of the chemical platoon, 50 yards away. Wandering to the four-holers in their t-shirts and flip-flops, they could not imagine what the idiot commanding the 45th Ord was doing practicing NBC in the dark. I started at them, waiting for the first to writhe and fall. None did. Suddenly, things were very clear to me. I had read about, and scoffed at, the self-perpetuating panic of Orson Welles's *War of the Worlds*. Now I scoffed no longer, and was deeply ashamed that I had been so easily stampeded. I decided to prolong the charade just a bit longer, for not to practice the M256 detector kits now would have been to admit utter defeat. We had 220 volunteers for the unmasking procedure, and a few minutes later retaped our chemical suits for what would be the last time of the war.

Captain Shirley DeGroot, Group Chemical Officer, 171st Corps Support Group

"It was the last week in January 1991. I was assigned to the Headquarters Company, 171st Corps Support Group. We were the forward support group with a mission of supporting the Division Support Command, 24th Infantry Division, and all the XVIII Airborne Corps-level troops within the 24th ID area of operation. Our Group had bout 2,000 soldiers in it, and I was the only chemical officer, so I was quite busy during Desert Shield coordinating the NBC training and contingency planning for thee soldiers. In the midst of all this, I was asked by the Group Commander and the HHC Commander to give a few NBC common task refresher classes to the troops of the HHC before we deployed forward to locate near the 24th ID.

"One of the classes I naturally selected for a unit about to get a scenic, motor-coach tour of southern Iraq was 'Treat Self Using the Nerve Agent Antidote Kit,' as there was at least a minor threat that the Iraqis might utilize a semi-persistent or non-persistent nerve agent on our advancing forces. One of the training aids required to give this class is a 'Dummy' Nerve Agent Antidote Kit (NAAK) that soldiers can use to simulate injecting themselves with the antidote. Since the HHC deployed to Saudi Arabia during September 1990 in a bit of a hurry, there were not any of the bright blue training aids available (training items being something that didn't get packed in the rush to deploy).

As the Chemical Officer, I had custody of the 'live' antidote kits until they were issued to the individual soldiers. As is usually the case in the Army, some of the 'live' kits had been roughly handled during shipment to Saudi, and a few of them had accidentally fired their antidotal contents into the protective packing around the auto-injector. Because there weren't any 'dummy' kits, my Assistant Instructor, Sergeant Bob olive-drab, just like everything that's an operational item in the Army. We syringes 'FOR TRAINING USE ONLY.' Now we were ready to give the class.

"On the appointed day, Sergeant Brasco and I gathered the personnel from Headquarters Company into the Mess Tent for NAAK class. As an aside, it never failed to amaze me how popular NBC training was in Saudi Arabia. Having been anything, up to and including volunteering for KP, to get out of having to practice NBC skills. But NBC training was always a number-one attraction during the Gulf War–amazing what a marvelous training motivator a bit of poison gas can be. To myself 'Gee, I sure wish I'd arranged for another two or three Assistant Instructor task at hand, the soldiers quieted down; soon I had their complete attention as I case of nerve agent poisoning. The demonstration completed, I split the HHC into small groups, each with a homemade training auto-injector, to practice the skill. Sergeant Brasco and I floated, supervising the practice and testing those soldiers who had mastered the task.

"We were about halfway through the practice period, when I was approached by a lieutenant colonel who had arrived late. He was in a harried state anyway about the upcoming operation and was quite concerned about missing the class; he asked me to catch him up to speed on what to do. The office had secured an antidote kit, so I told him we'd go over the main points of the task immediately. First, I would explain the symptoms and the procedure, then I would demonstrate it, then he would practice the task on his own, and when he felt confident, I would test him. Agreed. I talked the officer through what would happen if he was exposed to the agent. Then I grasped the antidote kit and held it in the proper position in my left hand, extended out form my body at 90 degrees. With my right hand, I demonstrated how you 'clear the area,' which means you pat your posterior to ensure you're not preparing to inject the antidote into your wallet or other obstruction. Then, I explained, you grasp the auto-injector in your right hand and swing it down onto the hip that you've cleared, like so....

"I ripped the auto-injector from where it had fired into by buttocks. My tardy colonel had somehow taken his 'live' auto-injector out from his protective mask carrier to use as his training aid. Of course, in being Captain Helpful and volunteering to demonstrate the task, I got the full dose of atropine in my behind. The runny nose I had been suffering from for several days cleared (or should I say dried) up immediately. Knowing that I was in for a very pleasant 'trip' in a short while, I ordered Sergeant Brasco to take charge of the class. I reported to my supervisor, the Group Operations Officer, and said that I'd explain more fully in the morning, but that I was going to go lie down on a cot for a while. What followed was the best night's sleep I had during the entire six months of my stay in Southwest Asia. I awoke the next morning with the war's greatest hangover –not even the morning after an epic New Year's Eve party complete with home-distilled, white-lightning brand hooch could compare to how bad I felt following my NAAK class.

"I had a meeting with 1st Corps Support Command's Chemical Officer that next day. Major Fred Evans was mildly amused at my predicament, and especially at the enormous quantities of water I kept tossing down by dry throat. His only comment was, "Well, you're not a real chemical officer until you've fired up with an auto-injector.' My only regret is that I didn't have the presence of mind to ask Major Evans exactly what the circumstances were when he'd become duty-qualified."

Colonel Bob Thornton, VII Corps Chemical Officer

"On the night prior to the ground war's initiation, the television show 48 *Hours* had sent a video tape to Lieutenant General Franks on a story they had done on the VII Corps's preparation for combat. The only VCR in the Corps Main Command Post was in the Chemical Section, so the general's aide told us the general was going to come down to view the tape. A few minutes later General Franks arrived, and after watching the ten-minute segment, with all of us crowded around him, he sat back and quietly reflected a few moments. Finally, still looking at the darkened screen, he solemnly remarked as if to himself, 'You know, if we've done our job right, we won't lose a lot of people tomorrow.' With that, he rose, spoke a few brief words of encouragement to the chemical staff, and departed for the forward deployed Tactical Command Post, about to begin the attack."

Captain Nick Swanye, Commander, Headquarter and Headquarters Battery, 212th Field Artillery

"I was a commander of an artillery unit in Saudi. We were attached to the 24th ID and did the left hook into Iraq, stopping just west of Basra. We returned via the same route. During the four-plus months we were waiting (near Nayiria on the pipeline road) for the war to start, we had our brand new M81A1 alarms on 24/7 [twenty-four hours a day, seven days a week]. They never went off.

"A brigade HHB does not have any organic decon equipment. We were having problems with our CUCV [Commercial Utility Cargo Vehicle] RATT [Radio TeleTypewriter] rigs getting stuck every 100 meters, so I took three 2 ½ ton trucks and mounted RATT rigs on them. There was room left, so we added a three-hundred-gallon fiberglass tank up front. We filled it with water and bleach. I bought gas-powered pumps, high-pressure hose, and made nozzles for them. They worked great for putting out tent fires (using straight water), and with the bleach mix we figured they were better than nothing for decontamination.

"On the first day of the war, I was the lead vehicle. We crossed into Iraq near the west end of the neutral zone. I had wired an M8 [chemical alarm] onto the roof of my 'humvee' to monitor for agents (this is not a recommended solution because the new alarms are so susceptible to dust). Within four hours of crossing the border, the alarm was going off so frequently that we shut it off. Our chemical officer said it was due to the dust (which was so thick, visibility was down to twenty-fifty feet). Our entire brigade, and the 24th ID, stayed in MOPP-1 from day one of the air war until the day we crossed back into Saudi Arabia (10 March). My unit never entered Kuwait, and departed, for the most part, by 10 April.

Purpose

The primary goal of this book is to identify the chemical-biological warfare (CBW) challenges learned from the Persian Gulf War. During the months of Operation Desert Shield, the media, the political leadership and the military leadership examined the threat of CBW against US and allied forces in minutia. Many articles and stores examined the chemical attacks during the Iran-Iraq War in the 1980s, the US military's defensive equipment and training (or lack thereof), and the real threat of chemical or biological agent attacks against US forces.

Coalition nations' politicians and military leaders warned Saddam both publicly and diplomatically about the consequences of such actions, while praying for enough time to bring their soldiers up to speed on survival skills. When the air campaign began in January 1991, NBC munition production and storage facilities were the number-two target on the priority list, right after Iraqi command and control sites. As Scuds landed on Saudi Arabia and Israel, chemical detection teams raced out to the impact areas to determine whether CBW had been initiated.

When the ground offensive kicked off, commanders donned their chemical protective suits and, as they crossed into Iraq, prayed silently that no CBW munitions would be used. As most accounts of the Persian Gulf War will state, the politician and military leadership claims that the combination of their defensive preparations against NBC agents, a massive conventional offensive against Iraqi NBC munition production and storage sites, and highly mobile divisions moving quickly against Iraqi forces kept Saddam from employing NBC munitions against the coalition.

In the aftermath of Operation Desert Shield/Storm, the US military is dangerously close to ignoring the fact that lightning has struck the same spot several times. As it did in World War I and World War II, the US army went into Southwest Asia initially unprepared to survive and sustain its forces in an NBC-contaminated environment. In all three instances, the military developed a capability that enabled it to fight on a potentially NBC-contaminated battlefield, although not necessarily in the timeframes one would optimally choose.

The following chapters will reveal that it took six months of production and six months of training to prepare for NBC warfare, none of which would have been possible had the Army's Chemical Corps not worked hard for ten years prior to 1990. Because of the efforts of chemical soldiers throughout Southwest Asia and the continental US, the coalition would have survived any NBC munitions attacks—in February 1991. Had Saddam ordered the attack to continue into Saudi Arabia before November 1 and used NBC munitions as he had in the Iran-Iraq War, the coalition would have suffered massive casualties General Norman Schwarzkopf has since stated that this was one of his worst fears.

Why then, in all the books and articles written after the war, does no one acknowledge that the Chemical Corps might have been doing something to prepare the armed forces for this effort? This book attempts to show that effort did take place, and was successful in preparing the US Central Command (CENTCOM) for the real threat of NBC warfare. All the concerns about the US military's vulnerability were reported accurately by the media, by political and military leaders before Congress, and were accepted as true statements. But that doesn't explain two things—why did DoD, and more importantly, the military leadership, allow this vulnerability to develop over the years? And what did the Army Chemical Corps do to ensure American soldiers, airmen, sailors and Marines were prepared to overcome these deficiencies prior to the ground offensive. The general officers in Desert Shield/Storm, who had to face these questions, are retiring and leaving DoD. Chemical warfare specialists who understood offensive chemical munitions employment have long since left, and only a few remain form the US biological warfare program.

We are quickly losing the resident expertise that understands how future adversaries might employ chemical and biological warfare munitions. On top of this, the Army is being downsized, chemical defense companies are being moved out of the divisions, Dugway Proving Ground and Fort McClellan are on the Base Realignment Committee list, and the chemical defense community grows smaller every year. Until we get a grasp on this issue and make reasoned decisions based on costs and benefits, the US military remains in grave peril from the NBC warfare threat.

This declaration is not intended to overstate the issue. Only if CB weapons were used on civilians and population centers, would they truly be "weapons of mass destruction." On the military battlefield, these weapons, shorn of the ridiculous air of menace given to them by politicians and the media, are merely another tactical-operational factor like enemy attacks or unforeseen terrorist attacks; military forces can and to take steps to minimize the effects of chemical-funds in planning, defensive equipment and training, the immediate threat of mass casualties is avoided, and chemical-biological weapons become merely "*weapons of mass disruption*" instead of destruction. We have the specialists and the right doctrine (both then and now). It's really that simple—if the military invests in equipment and training, they maintain a viable combat force. If they do not, their troops become as vulnerable as unprepared civilians.

The saying is that every military force prepares to fight the last war. In that case, in the early hours of the next conflict the US Army will prepare for CB warfare just as it has in the past, by checking its CB defense "insurance policy" and determining whether or not it has done enough in CB defense equipment and training to protect its investment—the men and women of the US armed forces. When military and political leaders see that the same challenges still exist, they will wave their arms around, push bushes of money at the Army, and improvise a solution as the US military has always done when faced with the threat of CB warfare. But I do not think that next time we will have a six-month grace period to build up the necessary stocks and training expertise.

Tension Rise in the Gulf

The FDA formally approved the Army's New Drug Application for the CANA autoinjectors in December 5. It seemed like the CANA would be available in limited quantities in time for the air war. All of the soldiers might have them by the ground offensive, if the production lines kept to schedule and training programs to use the CANAs were accomplished as planned. The forecasted numbers for biological vaccines were less clear. The FDA and DoD had wrangled over the question of biological vaccine and chemical agent pretreatment *Investigational New Drug* (INDs) for months. As General Sir Peter de la Billiere would point out later, there really was no need for trial-tested decision, in the end. He noted, "We should be entirely blameworthy if we didn't use it [the vaccines] and Saddam delivered biological." To supplement the troops' ability to resist infections, the Armed Epidemiological Board agreed to the CINCCENT Surgeon's recommendation to issue antibiotics to all troops. At a special Biological Warfare Defense Review hosted by ODCSOPS on December 18, Major General Louis Del Rosso reviewed the biodetector employment scheme and the biodefense vaccine plan. The results went the next day to Secretary Cheney, who approved the immunization plan for anthrax and botulinum toxin, the immunization team travel, the use of antibiotics and other treatments.

General Powell authorized a warning order to CENTCOM on the biological vaccine distribution. CENTCOM was to initiate plans to receive the bio detection teams, 500,000 individually packaged antibiotic kits plus enough bulk-packaged ciprofloxacin and doxycycline for one million troops for thirty days, 3,500 doses botulinum toxin vaccine, and 100,000 doses of anthrax vaccine. This would require additional refrigeration and vaccination teams to distribute the doses.

Finally, the FDA published regulations on waivers of informed consent. OASD(HA) submitted the waivers for informed consent for the topical skin protectant, the PB tablets, and the botulinum toxoid. On December 31, DoD and FDA officials agreed that the botulism vaccine would be administered by trained individuals with a health care background, and that the inoculated soldiers would be briefed orally at a minimum, and if feasible in writing. DoD pointed out that this information sheet would not be available to all troops, depending on where receive a verbal brief. The FDA granted the informed consent waiver, concurring that obtaining the informed consent during wartime was not feasible in a specific medical alternatives to PB tablets or tablets or botulinum vaccine. Time was running out —if Saddam was planning to launch BW-armed scuds, the coalition needed time to distribute the vaccines and begin the inoculations.

The House of Representatives held hearings within the Armed Services Committee on December 10, 1990, to discuss the "Crisis in the Persian Gulf." The committee heard conflicting views on the potential effectiveness of Iraq's CB arsenal. This began with the CIA assessment from Director Judge William of various chemical agents loaded into munitions. Intelligence sources had identified these munitions entering Kuwait, including stockpile of at least 1,000 tons of various chemical agents loaded into munitions. Intelligence sources had identified these munitions entering Kuwait, including stockpiles of CW warheads for FROG-7 missiles. General Ed Meyers, former Army Chief of Staff, admitted that chemical defense was one of the major problem areas of the military. Admiral Elmo Zumwalt, former Chief of Naval Operations (once involved in decisions about employing Agent Orange in Vietnam), cautioned the committee to take the threat of CB weapons seriously, given evidence that the Iraqi threat of CB weapons against Tehran had had a significant impact for the ending of the Iran-Iraq War. General George Crist, the former CENTCOM Commander-in-Chief, echoed the assessment of skilled Iraqi chemical warfare operations, adding his opinion that CB warfare should be expected against US troops. Edward Health, former British prime minister, had met Saddam to arrange for the release of British hostages in Iraq. He recalled the president's determination to use CB weapons if the allied coalition used nuclear weapons against Iraq.

Several other military experts countered these views with far more dismissive attitudes. Colonel (Ret.) Trevor DePuy, a noted military analyst, argued that historically an antagonist armed with chemical weapons had never used them against a force that could retaliate in kind of worse. Colonel Michael Dunn, commander of the Army's MRICD, stressed that the Iranian chemical agent fatalities during the Iran-Iraq War were about 3 percent for mustard gas and 5 percent for nerve gas. His naval medial colleague, Commander That Zaddowicz, echoed the assessment that poison gas was not a "particularly effective or efficient way to make war." Julian Perry Robinson, Seth Carus, and Professor Matthew Meselson, all civilian experts in CB warfare, downplayed the effectiveness of the Iraqi stockpile. They felt that given the level of chemical defense equipment and training of the allied coalition, the (relatively) small Iraqi chemical stockpile would be operationally insignificant.

Two other testimonies, given by Brad Roberts and Lieutenant Colonel John Pitman (Former division chemical officer, 24th IN DIV), pointed out that no one was considered CB weapons as an overwhelming decisive capability for Iraq; nor was it a war-winning factor against the coalition. These weapons could, however, be used as a force-multiplier during specific military operations. For instance, chemical agents could protect weak flanks of the armies, upset logistical operations in the rear areas (slowing the tempo of combat operations), disrupt assembly areas or planned drop zones for airmobile forces, affect aircraft pilots' vision (by low levels of nerve agent causing miosis over several days), and so on. This would enable temporary tactical advantages to the side using chemical agents, allowing attackers to overwhelm disorganized defenders fumbling around in their protective clothing. Using chemical weapons in conjunction with other conventional weapon systems was a lesson the Iraqis had learned in their struggles against the Iranians.

Notably absent from the train of experts invited to the Congress were the many former Chemical Corps chiefs of latter years, such as Major General (Ret.) John Stoner, Major General (Ret.) Jack Appel, Major General (Ret.) Pete Olenchuck, Major General (Ret.) Jim Klugh, Brigadier General (Ret.) Pete Hidalgo or chemical general officers still on active duty (Generals Gerry Watson, Walt Busbee, and Bob Orton). In part, this may have been due to Congress's exposure to senior chemical officers testifying in the 1950s and 1960s on issues such as the potentially devastating effects of NBC warfare, the military's need for chemical binary weapons, and the public concern over the chemical demilitarization program.

As a result of the overselling of the need for a chemical Corps in the past, on one in Congress (except for a select few) believed these general officers would be able to express their expert opinions without personal bias.

More Chemical Defense Equipment Arrives

The Marine Corps decided to purchase a number of ETGI's *Individual Chemical Agent Detectors* (ICADs) pack-sized individual alarms allowed Marines more freedom of movement, but possibly less warning time, thus representing a higher chemical agent casualty risk in favor of increased operational capability. Congress questioned why the Army had not invested in the ICAD program, which appeared on the surface like a good idea, a low-unit cost, lightweight chemical agent detector. Rather than try to explain the Army's concerns that the ICAD was a high-risk detector prone to false alarms, ODCSOPS ordered one thousand for ARCENT forces.

The Canadian CAMs were distributed as planned in December 1990. There would never be enough CAMs to go to every line company, as had been intended. IN fact, the 500 CAMs had to be split among the four services (despite their previously expressed disinterest in the CAM). The immediate scheme of issue gave medical units and decontamination companies the first priority for CAMs, which pretty much consumed the Army's share in a very short period for time. The Chemical School sent over a CAM new equipment training team from December 11 to January 15; it trained 670 operators in all four services. All units were running short of the unique lithium batteries required to power the CAMs. This was in part due to attempts to convert them to automatic chemical agent detectors by jamming on the power switch, and in part due to using the same battery for the hand-held Global Positioning Systems that proved so valuable in the desert. Complicating the issue was the fact that the Canadian and British CAM loan did not include lithium batteries. Because US industry was unable to "*ramp up*" the production of the expensive and complex lithium batteries quickly, CRDEC developed an alternative battery pack for training, using D-cell sized alkaline batteries. These would not last as long, but could somewhat alleviate the units' shortages. Two thousands battery packs were shipped by the end of December, with another 3,000 on the way in January and February.

The issue of maintaining what was already a small stock of protective masks kept chemical soldiers busy inspecting their units' masks. Ever since the XVIII ABN Corps had requested maintenance support on the heat stress problems of the M24/25 masks (and related issues for the M17 masks), Pine Bluff had been accelerating its efforts to repair and rebuild all the masks it could. VII Corps had a requirement for 5,000 masks, yet came into the theater with less than two hundred masks in reserve. Representatives from both corps NBCCs met with representatives of CRDEC, AMCCOM, Depot Support Command, and Pine Bluff to discuss requirements for repairing and supplying protective masks. Pine Bluff officials observed early on that it would be more cost-effective to check and repair the masks in theater than to ship them back to CONUS (given that most masks until HQ AMC established on November 17 the US Army Support Group-Forward (USASG) in Dhahran, Saudi Arabia, to keep up with the constant demand for logistical support for all Army equipment. A group of

Pine Bluff Arsenal technicians volunterred to join the USASG. They packed and palletized their test equipment and repair parts, shipped the equipment to Dhahran, and were operational by December 10.

The original intent of the Mask Maintenance Facility was to inspect, repair and test theater M17-series masks assets turned in as unserviceable by the units. Upon successfully repair and tests, the facility would return them to theater stocks for reissuing. This would entail about an eight-day turnaround on most masks. It was not originally meant as a casual "*drop-in*" service shop for passing soldiers. While this facility did provide some immediate relief to the mask shortage, walk-ins increased through December and into 1991. The problem was that soldiers wanting to have their masks inspected had not allowed their units' chemical officers and NCOs to inspect them first. Many of the masks were rigorously challenged at the Mask Facility, as the Pine Bluff Arsenal personnel held the inspected masks against new inventory acceptance standards. During the first three days of operation, 160 M-17 series masks were tested. More than 40 percent failed standard quality assurance tests, most problems centering on the voice meter assembly or one of its subcomponents, which a soldier's unit NBC or supply NCO might have been able to fix at their level. As more soldiers heard of the high number of "rejects" by word-of-mouth, the number of walk-ins increased, as many soldiers questioned their masks' fitness. None of these masks were shipped back to Pine Bluff Arsenal, which meant that these rejects would shorten the already low supply. The facility's intentions were good, but it was sending the wrong message to the soldiers.

In response to the increased concerns, CRDEC released a number of protective mask fit validation systems (PMFVS), the XM41, a spinoff of a commercial mask testing device. The PMFVS compared the pressure inside and outside the mask through a series of tubes, electronically compared the two, and digitally displayed a confidence factor that would judge the mask's fit on an individual. The marine Corps and Army were both very interested in this system and purchased 128 PMFVSs starting in the late November to test soldiers' masks prior to their deployment. Teams deployed to the division deployment sites in the US and in Europe to test and validate hard-to-fit individuals. The PMFVS teams deployed to the USASG mask maintenance facility in December to augment their staff. The personal who could not use an M17 mask were fitted with one of the 426 M40 masks available; if that didn't work, they didn't deploy.

Chemical Defense Unit Preparations

The 2d Chemical Battalion held a smoke demonstration at Kind Fahd International Airfield (KFIA) on December 13-15.CENTAF had always been concerned about the chance that an Iraqi air attack might sneak in with CB munitions. The AirBase Operations office at Eglin AFB suggested using fixed smoke generators to obscure the airport; they would act as survivability countermeasure to keep Iraqi pilots from acquiring and hitting targets with chemical (and conventional) munitions. The 2d Chemical Battalion controlled the 761st and 59th Chemical Company's smoke generator platoons to generate both a covering smoke haze over the airfield and a smoke curtain before the airfield. Seventy-two smoke generators gushed thick white smoke from thirty-six High Mobility Multi-purpose Wheeled Vehicles (HMMWVs). Smoke screens, rolling horizontally over the ground, would work best early in the morning or late in the evening, while smoke curtains, rising vertically from the generators, would be better in the midday heat.

CENTAF tested the smoke screens with A-10 aircraft from the 354th Tactical Fighter Wing acting as the Iraqi air force. The smoke generator platoons had fifteen minutes warning to make smoke, on the first morning run, the A-10s found that was the only thing that their weapon systems would lock onto was the control tower, jutting out of an immense sea of white smoke. On the second run, the low-flying A-10s came up against the smoke curtain, which was located just before the pilots' munitions release point. The A-10s had to climb to get over the curtain (not knowing what was on the other side) and ran directly into the sights of an air defense Stringer missile team. The one-to-two-second disruption gave the Stringer teams time to lock on and "kill" the attacking A-10s before they could lock onto the airfield targets. The smoke demonstration worked so well that the 59th Chemical Company had to leave its smoke platoon in place the airfield for the air war's duration.

Colonel Bob Thornton arrived at VII Corps HQ early in December to assume the corps chemical officer position, having been heavily involved in the Chemical School's preparations for the military operations between August and November. The VII Corps NBCC deployed to Saudi Arabia on December 18 after the 2d ACR had arrived and the VII Corps COSMOS was unloading. Along with the COSCOM came the 51st and 11th Chemical companies, which had originally been designated to arrive earlier in XVIII ABN Corps's deployment. VII Corps would have immediate reconnaissance and decontamination support for its deploying forces, which were very vulnerable as they arrived at the jam-packed ports and airfields.

Decontamination units no longer held the urgent priority that they had had in August. Now the Army needed smoke generators to cover the breaching of the beams and minefields. ODCSOPS called on three mechanized smoke generator units to provide front cover for the armored and mechanized divisions that would lead VII Corps into Iraq. ODCSOPS tagged the 46th Chemical Company from Fort Hod, the 84th Chemical Company from Fort Polk, and the 172d Chemical Company form Fort Carson to mobilize and support smoke operations in Southwest Asia. They were scheduled to arrive by the end of January. These smoke generators units would require a substantial among of fog oil, having one-third more capacity than the HMMWV version. Obtaining fog oil for the smoke generators was one of the few material success stories of the Chemical Corps. Military supplies of fog oil were delivered in fifty-five gallon drums, and because no other military unit within CENTCOM required for oil, divisions were not used to procuring and prepositioning large quantities, and there would be no difficulty in supplying smoke generator units with all the fog oil they could haul. Local procurement of fog oil began on December 18.

Saudi Arabia had formally invited Czechoslovakia to send the previously mentioned "*anti-chemical*" detection unit on November 7. Its deployment of sixty-one vehicles and 170 personnel began on December 11 with the assistance of US military transport in Germany. The Czech detection unit, as noted, would be stationed in CENTCOM's rear support area (around KKMC) About 160 kilometers from the Iraqi border. By December 14, it was in-theater, setting up shop. The hospital near Hafar al-Batin, and one each with the Saudi 20th Mechanized Brigade and 4th Mechanized Brigade. Each platoon carried an AL-1 Mobile Laboratory, three ARS-12M decontamination vehicles, and one UAZ-469 NBC recon jeep.

As the CENTCOM force doubled in size, managing the logistic became twice the headache. Unit requisitions and supplies became misplaced or lost, or were given to the wrong units in the constant loading and unloading of ships and planes. Often, if a unit received supplies that did not belong to it, its logistics cell would hoard the CB defense supplies rather than returning them to the already over burdened supply channels. This resulted in the original unit sending another requisition to AMCCOM, and another shipment being shipped out. This shortage of items in the first place. VII Corps did not have the luxury of making local purchases to augment their CB defense supplies; the local supplies of HTH bleach, for instance, had long been depleted by XVIII ABN Corps. There were several orders for drums of HTH due in over the next few months. At least the mechanized nature of VII Corps meant that it did not require the use of local water haulers, also all taken by XVIII ABN Corps.

Just after Christmas a special Fox briefing was given to the division and corps commanders during an operation plan update. The two corps agreed to transfer the two borrowed VII Corps platoons back to their original units after the New Year, equalizing the distribution of Fox assets at three platoons each (with the 3rd ACR returning to Saudi Arabia on December 27-28), but depriving the 24th IN DIV and 1st CAV DIV of their assets. Of the remaining twenty-five vehicles, the Marines would take ten, leaving fifteen for the Army. ARCENT had evaluated the proposed two-corps attack plan with the intent of evaluating the CBW threat and companies. Their proposal was to equip the incoming 1st IN DIV with one platoon and use the second platoon for ARCENT rear area reconnaissance, leaving three for floats. ARCENT's staff argued that if the theater rear area were attacked with persistent chemical agents, the results would impact on both corps' sustainment and operational temp. As a result, the 490th Chemical Batalion would man the last Fox platoon under ARENT Support Command. This would leave a total of four Foxes as theater floats.

Other options were to field the second platoon to either the 24th IN or the 1st CAV DIVs. The 24th IN DIV claimed that its soldiers had worked closely with its attached Fox platoon. While their chemical company had not deployed their recon platoon to Sonthofen for formal training, they had acquired adequate "*on-the-job*" training to operate their own Fox platoon. Giving the 24th IN DIV an organic Fox Corps's vulnerable rear area. If the XVIII ABN Corps did not receive the additional Fox platoon, it would have to decide whether the 5/25th would support the 24th IN DIV, the rear area, or both. Major General McCaffrey asked for a waiver to allow his division to receive the Foxes without training.

As for the 1st CAV DIV, it had become the theater reserve for the ground offensive. Because the 1st CAV DIV would have a prominent role in feinting up the Wadi al-Batin and might be called on to counterattack the Republican Guards, there was an argument that they should get a Fox platoon (either from XVIII ABN Corps or ARCENT's second platoon option). These foxes would help the two combat brigades negotiate their way through chemically contaminated areas much faster than the M113 APCs currently in the 68th Chemical Company's recon platoon. Both the ARCENT G-3 and Lieutenant General Gary Luck, XVIII ABN Corps commander, disagreed with giving up one of XVIII ABN Corps' Fox platoons. They argued that the Foxes should not serve in a reserve role but rather be in general or direct support of front line units (similar to the use of artillery). In addition, the 1st CAV DIV's chemical company had never received the Fox recon training nor had they the benefit of Chemical School trainers and would not have been able to operate and maintain the new systems properly.

General Schwarzkopf sided with ARCENT's recommendation, stressing the need for school-trained chemical recon platoons. The division and corps commanders discussed the allied nations' needs for reconnaissance vehicles. The British force had eleven Foxes, eight of which were outfitted for NBC recon, and three for electronic warfare. The French and Arab forces had decontamination assets but no NBC recon vehicles. One section of the 82dABN DIV's Fox platoon (now the 92d Chemical Company recon platoon) would be under the operational control of the French division (as would one brigade from the 82d) as of February 16, through the initial ground offensive. CENTCOM considered giving two Foxes to the Egyptian forces next to the Marine divisions, but no division commander felt comfortable giving these assets up. It was decided that if chemical agents were used against the Arab military forces, the nearest Fox platoon to the area would assist them in marking the contaminated areas.

These discussions demonstrated the blind faith and lack of understanding by the senior leadership regarding the role of NBC reconnaissance systems. These commanders saw the XM93 NBCRS as a lucky charm against chemical contamination, rather than realizing that their predecessors the M113-euipped chemical recon platoons, had the same essential capabilities with trained chemical soldiers and tested equipment (albeit in a slower-moving package). While the XM93 NBCRS had several important features that made it superior to the M113, commanders overemphasized the system's potential and ignored the lack of crew experience operating and maintaining the NBCRS. They wanted the latest, state-of-art system to minimize the effects of CB munitions against their operations, and who could blame them?

After Christmas, the 2d Chemical Battalion staff worked with the two corps to identify ways to support the planned movement west. The commander's intent was to hold the enemy's attention to the area of the Wadi al-Batin and eastward while the forces moved west. A ground maneuver force from the 1st IN DIV, mixed liberally with realistic tank and APC decoys, would move near the front lines east of the wadi. The 59th Chemical Company would provide large-area smoke to cover the force and decoys, confusing the real size and location of the force. Their deception operation would begin between January 5 and 10 and continue until the XVIII ABN Corps had enough time to move safely past the wadi.

As the end of the year approached, all the services continued high-level defense exercises. ARCENT's divisions conducted large-scale decontamination exercises, mass chemical agent casualty exercises, and the command post exercises. CENTAF tested disaster preparedness plans at its air bases, and readied its decontamination equipment. NAVCENT exercised its chemical agent casualty handling process through the two medical ships, and practiced decontamination training in shipboard and in the ports. The marines conducted a division-wide decontamination exercise to assess the effects of a large-scale CB agent attack and their ability to defend against it. SOCCENT prepared its teams to hunt for chemical and biological weapons bunkers and the mobile Scud delivery systems hidden in the Iraqi desert.

Into the New Year—Preparations Mount

The vaccination teams arrived in the Gulf on January 2, followed closely by the advance liaison for the Biological Detection Teams. CPTs Plume and Minor arrived in Dhahran on January 3 with XM2 samplers and a metrological sensor, ready to set up operations and test their equipment. One of their primary goals was to establish background readings prior to employing the biodetectors. After getting established in the theater, the biodetection teams found that they had to rent vehicles to get around. Auto rental prices and skyrocketed, but they were able to rent a number of British Land Rovers to augment their transportation. The Army's 966th Medical Laboratory established its forward base at KKMC, bringing advanced laboratory equipment and supplies for the Naval Forward Laboratory and for the KKMC site.

When Lieutenant General Calvin Waller, Deputy CINC for CENTCOM, was briefed on the final biological defense concept on January 10, he formally approved deployment of the point detection systems. The stand-off biological detection systems would not be deployed. The SRI ground infrared stand-off system had failed its testing at Yuma and Dugway, and it was scrapped. The LANL aerial laser stand-off system was ready to be mounted on a C130 aircraft and deployed to Saudi Arabia, but there was a concern about the availability of hanger space there. Due to the crowded airfields throughout the theater, General Schwarzkopf had laid down the law on any additional planes due in after January 1. If the aerial stand-off system was to enter the theater, CENTCOM had to make room for two fixed-wing aircraft and one helicopter to support the system. Unwilling to give up any aircraft spaces prior to the air offensive, Lieutenant General Waller refused the stand-off system, preferring to rely solely on the point biodetectors.

Some military and civilian personnel in CONUS fought that decision into mid-February, stressing the need to deliver anything that might aid the biodetection effort. However, one aerial stand-off system would only cover a very small area of the overall theater, and definitely could not stay airborne continuously. Combined with its inability to positively identified suspected biological agent clouds, the eye-laser hazard out to ten kilometers, and the lack of tested doctrine, it was better left behind.

The first thirty soldiers from Fort Lewis arrived at CRDEC on January 15 to initiate their training on XM2 samplers and XM21 RSCAALs. The remaining soldiers would arrive four days later to train on the PM10 samplers. All would have less than two weeks training prior to deploying to the desert, becoming the only force that could positively indicate to CENTCOM headquarters whether the force was under biological agent attack or not.

As the order to move west arrived, the 2d Chemical Battalion received orders to switch its support to VII Corps (as the main effort) effective 10 January. Several other chemical units arrived in January, adding to the strength of the force. The 457th Chemical Battalion would support XVIII ABN Corps, taking the 59th Chemical Company (after the deception operation was executed), the 327th and 340th Chemical companies under its control. The 413th Chemical Company joined the 490th Chemical Battalion, while the 323rd chemical company reported to 2d Chemical Battalion upon its arrival.

The order moving the 2d Chemical Battalion to VII Corps also initiated the return of two VII Corps recon platoons to their original parent companies. All the Fox platoons commenced to play "musical chairs" as they rotated to new commands. The Foxes in 1st CAV DIV returned to the 22d Chemical Company in 3rd AR DIV (due to the 3rd

AR DIV's expected arrival in theater). The 24th IN DIV gave up the 5/69th Recon Platoon to its original division, the 1st AR DIV. The 5/25th Recon Platoon rotated from the 2d Chemical Battalion to the 24th IN DIV. The 101st ABN DIV transferred the 7/92d Recon Platoon to the 82d ABN DIV. The 101st would have no replacement, given its planned air assault mission, but would retain the 761st Chemical Company (Smoke/Decon). The remaining twenty five Foxes earmarked for CENTCOM had not yet arrived. With the British, Israeli and Turkish armies and the Marine Corps all demanding their Foxes, Thyssen-Henschel had a very busy month.

Serious logistics issues still remained on the eve of the air war. The Mask Maintenance Facility had the entire theater stockage at Dhahran, 2000 M17A2 masks. In the forward logistics bases of VII Corps 800 kilometers away, the entire corps stock consisted of 147 M17 masks. This would maintain the normal wear and tear of combat, but would quickly be consumed if chemical warfare broke out. XVIII ABN Corps was not much better off in its mask status. Both corps had a zero balance of extra M256A1 detector kits and had just received the British CAMs. XIII ABN Corps received 260 CAMs, while VII Corps received the balance of the 500-CAM order. As it appeared, each combat division would have less than fifty CAMs each, with six detectors given to each brigade. The medics and decontamination companies would have a few extra CAMs, given their potentially larger exposure to chemical agents.

New BDOs began arriving as the four new suit contractors delivered the first 8,000 of their emergency contract. Roughly 100,000 protective suits had been delivered over the past six months under the old contract (in place before the war), which helped divisions to start reaching for the recommended goal of three protective suits per soldier. It appeared feasible that at least two suits would be available to each soldier in CENTCOM, and five suits for each decon company soldier. The Marine Corps was still unsatisfied with the shortfall of BDOs and ordered an additional 135,000 lightweight Saratoga suits from a US clothing Corps also finalized a procurement contract for 100 M21 RSCAALs from Brunswick in January (none of which would be delivered before the ground offensive).

By the end of January, one thousand M17 SANATORs would be in the Gulf—one-third distributed to Marine Corps units, and two-thirds sent to the Army's two corps. Air Force and Navy facilities units continued to rely on the larger M12A1 decontamination apparatus as did many Army units; but M121 decon systems were increasingly breaking down due to the heat, and spare parts were not readily available for the ancient system. The M17 SANATORs would ease the challenge of having to maintain the M12A1s. DS-2 decontamination solvent eventually became plentiful, and thousands of gallons were stockpiled in the Gulf. The German government made another equipment gift, this time of 150 Karcher decontamination apparatus that closely resembled the M17 SANATOR. Half of these went to VII Corps, and half went to XVIII Corps. When Army units discovered that the M1 CAM gave a false alarm when used near the M258A1 or M290 decon kits, the Medical Research and Development Command released its M291 personal decon kit for production. Many of these kits were in the Gulf in time for the beginning of ground combat. The Navy complained of another problem with the CAM—it was false-alarming due to the organic compounds in the fire-fighting form abroad the ships. It continued to ask for the CAMs, however, to allow a detection capability for their port facilities.

Military and political leaders still had concerns over bombing the biological and chemical weapons production sites. While DIA suspected that Iraq's last major chemical agent production run had ended in October, there was evidence of increased activities in mid-December through mid-January. Late that month, trucks carrying suspected Scud warheads were observed entering and leaving the Muthanna facility, whose activity had increased significantly. This might confirm program. These sites had to be hit soon to knock out Iraq's production capability, but predictions of possible contamination were still sketchy.

DNA had successfully developed ANBACIS-II into a highly sophisticated contamination prediction package by January 1991. It detailed weapon effects with a real-time satellite weather input and digital raster maps, together with a user-friendly, interactive graphical interface. Given the appropriate weapon data and release height, it could draw map overlay contour with different agent dosage levels. By incorporating the ANBACIS-II software into Crays, DNA teams could develop a contamination prediction. The target analyst could then print the footprint on a transparency, place it on the appropriate map, copy the two together, and end up with a complete contamination prediction, ready for transmission. The only drawback was that the model could not determine the effects of terrain on the CB agent cloud, resulting in flat-earth predictions; this would not become a critical issue in the desert, but it meant the predictions would not be 100% accurate.

Since the ANBACIS-II system relied upon the DNA Crays for computational power, Major General Wilson devised an operational plan for the NBCCS to the their resources from Southwest Asia. He purchased twenty-one STU-III phones and facsimile machines, and proposed to set these up at the CENTCOM HQ ARCENT main and alternative HQs, and corps and division HQs. When the NBCC reported an NBC attack, they would fax the information to the waiting DNA teams in their Ops center. The team would develop the information, copy the map, and fax a complete contamination prediction directly to the requester within ten minutes, worst case. Because the analysts had pre-determined 11,000 footprints of various weapons releasing either chemical or biological agents, the actual time of the analysis could be cut down even further. The DNA Operations Center would run three shifts of operators twenty-four hours a day, with a minimum of six computer operators available on each shift to conduct multi-tasking simultaneous calculations as needed. They would use ten Sun Computers interfaced with the Crays.

DNA displayed their capability to the CENTCOM J-3 on January 11. The only catch was that Major General Moore, CENTCOM's J-3 operations officer, did not think CENTCOM needed the ANBACIS-II system. The Air Force was completely comfortable in manually charting contamination predictions, by the official but "*safe-sided*" Allied Technical Publication-45 prediction method. On the other hand, many people inside and outside Southwest Asia were questioning exactly how for would CB agents travel downwind if a CBW production facility more accurate ANBACIS-II plot. CENTCOM NBCC and DNA's Operations Center assisted Air Force planners by providing advice on the potential for bombing missions on all the CBW production and storage sites creating a downwind collateral CB agent hazard.

The British Ministry of Defense and the US DoD both publicly announced the beginning of the biological vaccine program at the end of December. Only 8,000 individuals could receive the botulin toxin vaccine. The anthrax vaccine situation was similarly perilous: because of the limited supply and inability to find additional sources of vaccine, only 150,000 military personnel in the Gulf would receive this vaccine. If it had had until May 1991, the entire US force would be protected, but time had run out. The question was, which part of the theater would be protected? CENTCOM had to decide whom to vaccinate, as Washington officials did not want to make the call. War game studies postulated a special forces/terrorist attack with biological agents in riyadh and Dharan, while others thought the front lines the obvious target. CENTCOM staff recommended that the special operations forces, the armored units that would lead the assault, and the important rear area targets (such as the CENTCOM headquarters staff) should receive the vaccines.

This decision became a very serious and stressful one for the division commanders. No one wanted to choose who should and who should not receive the vaccines. Who was to say who the more critical individuals truly were? The final decision for the anthrax vaccinations would be to prioritize the areas at risk, starting with Riyadh, Dhahran, and Bahrain, where the most critical command and communications and supply bases lay. KKMC and the major logistics bases (Alpha through Echo) were next, followed by HQ VII Corps, HQ XVIII ABN Corps, and 1st CAV DIV (in order of mission priority). Major General Binford Peay, commander of the 101st ABN DIV, later told Colonel Read that the decision to use this limited amount of vaccine was one of the greater mistakes of the war. In this view, there should have been enough vaccines for everyone or for one, sharing an equal risk among all troops. Lieutenant General Franks and other commanders shared this view as well.

Now that the medial community was free to implement its vaccination plans, the anthrax vaccinations began, starting on January 5. By January 13, half of all forces received their first anthrax vaccine shots. Each soldier was to read a statement detailing the purpose of the vaccinations, warning them that the fact that they were receiving the shots was classified SECRETE. While some would later interpret this as covering up experimental vaccine testing on troops, the true intent of the classification was to conceal the extent of the vaccination program from Iraqi intelligence sources. The safety test on the botulinum vaccine was still not completed, however. The FDA would not complete the tests until January 24, 1991, nearly a week after the air campaign had begun. While it was known that the vaccines were in short supply, both the US and British defense departments refused to detail publicly how much they had or who would be receiving the vaccines. The PB tablets received FDA approval on January 8. All military individuals in the Gulf, and also government civilians and even news media crews, began receiving the PB tablets before the air war began.

Battle Plants Finalize

The *Operation Desert Storm* operation order was published on January 13. It made several assumptions about Iraqi CB weapons employment. The Marine Corps divisions would initiate the assault at 04000 hours local time, attacking into Kuwait. The Tiger Brigade would hold the left flank of the 2d Marine Division (MARDIV), with the 1st MARDIV on the right flank. Their objectives were to hold down the Iraqi divisions within Kuwait and keep the attention of the Republican Guards on the first day of battle. Since their M60A3s could not use the mine plows designed for the M1 tanks, they would have a more difficult time penetrating the minefields. This would make the Marines Prime targets for chemical munitions effects. The Marines counted on the Army MLRS battery and air support to suppress any artillery fire during the mine-clearing operations. Their Foxes would mark contaminated areas to allow the following troops to avoid most of the hazard As the Tiger Brigade moved to replace the British 7th AR BDE as the Marine Corps heavy armor attachment, it brought along one decon platoon of the 44th Chemical Company.

The XVIII ABN Corps would initiate its attack at 0538 hours, just as the night began yielding to the dawn. The French 6th AR DIV had the main air base near as-Salman as an immediate objective (Objective, White, or Rochambeau to the French). Although there were no air units there, it had been identified as a potential mobile Scud firing site, and intelligence was calling it a major chemical weapons stockpile. This airfield had been a major concern throughout the war as an arming point from which Iraqi planes could hit KKMC. The 101st ABN DIV would conduct the largest airmobile operation in history, leapfrogging forward to supplies from Kuwait. The 761st Chemical Company would join them to compensate for their lost recon assets. The 24th IN DIV had several objectives in and around an-Nassariyah, including several suspected CB munitions stockpiles. Its intermediate objective was to take the ground around the Iraqi 26th Division (Objective Grey), which was suspected of holding a chemical stockpile. The final objectives included Tallil and Jalibah air bases, which military intelligence had identified as significant chemical stockpiles. Because of the increased chance that 24th IN DIV units would cross chemically contaminated areas, it received the 327th Chemical Company for direct support, and an additional decon platoon from the corps's 101st Chemical Company for its DISCOM. 3rd ACR would protect the right flank of the corps and conduct chemical reconnaissance along with its screening mission.

While the French expected the possibility of a chemical attack at as-Salman, Major General McCaffrey was convinced that his division could be attacked several times with chemical munitions. When his division hit the Europe valley, it would threaten the Iraqi army's main supply route to Baghdad. It would be within range of several Iraqi helicopter landing pads and other air fields, all of which could deploy Iraqi helicopters and aircraft with chemical weapons. He and his division chemical officer, Lieutenant Colonel Schubert, concluded that it would be counterproductive to dwell on the threat. They knew their soldiers had the capability to protect themselves and that at some point they might be called upon to use that defensive capability. There was not much they could do about it other than trust in their soldiers' training and defensive equipment. Of all the CENTCOM divisions, McCaffrey's troops were perhaps the best trained and prepared for the potential chemical attacks.

VII Corps would initiate the breach operations (the XVIII ABN Corps area of operation was beyond the border berm obstacles) at 0538 hours. The 1st IN DIV would break and penetrate the berm on the right flank, allowing the British 1st AR DIV to pass through it and protect the right flank of the corps. One hour later, the 2d ACR would breach the berm on the left flank, followed by 1st AR DIV and 3rd AR DIV. Once they secured their immediate security area past the berm, they would pause to allow the "wheel" to develop prior to continuing the attack the next day. This was the most vulnerable point of the offensive. If the Iraqis reacted quickly enough, they could catch the 1st IN DIV and 2d ACR in the middle of their berm breaching operations, and attempt to slow VII Corps down with a chemical attack. If there was one thing the Iraqis knew how to do well, it was slowing down an enemy offensive with chemical munitions.

Two scenarios were envisioned. First the Iraqis might react to the breach by a local counterattack against the VII corps while it was passing through the berms at the fourth hour of the attack. This would include coordinated nerve or mustard agent attacks with artillery, Scuds, and aircraft. Based on computer war gaming, this might slow the VII Corps attack by as much as thirteen to eighteen hours. This would allow time for the Republican Guards either to assault the vulnerable flanks of the Marine divisions or attempt to position themselves to seal the breach. The other scenario envisioned a larger last-ditch Iraqi counterattack between twenty-four and thirty-six hours after the breach. Then the Republican Guards, as the theater strategic reserve, might reorient themselves against the western attacks and employ persistent chemical attacks to halt the coalition's advance. The first scenario seemed the more likely.

The 1st CAV DIV, with its two combat brigades, would act as the CENTCOM theater reserve. It would remain near the Wadi al-Batin to keep Iraqi forces concerned about an attack up the wadi into the Republican Guards (where the Iraqis expected the main attack) and then commit to either VII Corps or the MARENT effort, on CENTCOM's call. To keep the Iraqi military's attention, the 1st CAV DIV would feint at the wadi's defenders. While the 1st CAV DIV did not expect to be a primary target of initial chemical weapons attacks, to be an effective counterattack force it required the capability to maneuver through wide contamination areas created by Iraqi artillery, aircraft and Scuds. The 44th Chemical Company headquarters, one decon platoon and one smoke platoon remained with the 1st CAV DIV, as well as its own 68th Chemical Company.

To support the operations plan, ARCENT moved the 2d Chemical Battalion to support VII Corps, as the main effort, and attached two mechanized smoke companies to the battalion to aid in the breaching. For the breach itself, the 2d Chemical Battalion would operate directly in support of 1st IN DIV. The 457th Chemical Battalion would support XVIII ABN Corps largely by protecting the rare logistics supply dumps and supply routes that would lead into Iraq. The 490th Chemical Battalion would continue protecting ARCENT's rear area and would borrow the ARCENT maintenance float Foxes to provide a limited reconnaissance capability. The 457th was at a disadvantage compared to the other two battalions, having just arrived in the first week of January. While both the 2d and 490th Chemical Battalion had had several months to settle into the theater, the 457th would have to adjust very quickly prior to the ground offensive. Fortunately, the 59th Chemical Company, as one of its attached units, would help the battalion staff adjust to the theater's administrative and logistics procedures. Each chemical battalion would have at least one reserve decon company for general support in its for its larger mission of theater rear area support. All decon companies coordinated with engineers to dig sumps for the thorough decontamination sites.

Because CENTCOM and ARCENT NBCCs were more focused on supporting battle plans, the logistics flow of chemical defense equipment (especially Foxes and protective clothing), and chemical soldier personnel shortages, they could not directly support the changing task organizations. The arrival of the additional reserve chemical decon companies and staff detachment to support VII Corps caused real confusion at the divisions, and what was available for future operations.

While serious logistics issues continued to threaten the Army's ability to sustain operations in an NBC-contaminated environment, chemical specialists could see the light at the end of the tunnel. It was beginning to look like CENTCOM would survive a short-time, limited chemical war. Now it was time to see if all the preparations had been time and energy well spent.

Operation Desert Storm Begins

United Stated Resolution 678, cast on November 29,1990 set January 15 as the deadline for the removal of Iraqi forces out of Kuwait; otherwise the coalition could use "*all necessary means*" to oust the Iraqi occupation. Despite several meetings between UN and Iraqi delegations through December, it appeared the Iraqi forces were in Kuwait to stay. Congress finally voted to support the UN measure on January 12, 1991. CENTCOM forces were not fully ready for NBC warfare, although individually the troops were as finely honed as they would be. By this time, CENTCOM had thirty-six Foxes in theater. Although the ANBACIS-II system had been proven functional, none were set up in the theater to warm against the threatened attacks. Concerns remained over the shortages of chemical protective suits and masks in theater stockpiles. There were insufficient stocks for the thirty days of conflict planned, if CB agent warfare continued throughout the conflict. Hospitals on land integrated their few collective protection system into their units positions, while the two Navy hospital ships prepared for chemical casualty treatment.

The political rhetoric increased on all levels to convince Saddam Hussein against using CB agent munitions. During a visit to the Gulf in December, Defense Secretary Cheney warned that if Saddam Hussein was "foolish enough to use weapons of mass destruction the US response would be absolutely overwhelming and it would be devastating". White House Chief of Staff John Major assured reporters during a trip to Saudi Arabia on January 6 that the UK would not consider nuclear weapons in response to Iraqi CW attack:" We have plenty of weapons short of that. We have no plans of sort you envisage." In Saudi Arabia, British embassy officials began distributing protective masks out to British civilians in the area. In Israel, government officials accelerated the distribution of protective masks, atropine kits, and instructions on how to construct temporary collective protection shelters at home. Isreaeli officials made clear to Washington that they would have to respond to any Iraqi chemical strikes against their cities, and that response would not be limited to conventional arms.

Secretary of State James Baker met with Iraqi Foreign Minister Tariq Azia in Geneva on January 9 to allow Saddam one more chance to back out of a conflict. Secretary Baker hand-delivered a letter from the president for Saddam Hussein. In the letter, President Bush warned of the consequences of not pulling out of Kuwait and engaging in other unconventional warfare. "Let me state, too, that the United States will not tolerate the use of chemical or biological weapons or the destruction of Kuwait's oil fields and installations. Further, you will be held directly responsible for terrorist actions against any member of the coalition. You and your country will pay a terrible price if you order unconscionable acts of this sort."

The deadline came and passed. At 2230 hours on 16 January (Kuwaiti time), the air phase began as air crews readied their planes for combat operations over Iraq. Tomahawks leapt out of their tubes on Navy warships at 0130 hours. At 0238 hours, Apache helicopters form the 101st ABN DIV destroyed Iraqi early warning radar stations. The strategic air campaign had begun.

Phase I/II: Strategic Air Campaign/KTO Air Supremacy

The final, approved air campaign plan focused on five military objectives. These included isolating and incapacitating the Iraqi regime's leadership and communication systems gaining and maintaining air supremacy to permit unhindered operations, destroying Iraq's NBC warfare production and storage capability, destroying major parts of key military production and infrastructure, and rendering the Iraqi forces in the KTO ineffective. In the case of Iraq's NBC warfare capabilities, targets included the nuclear research and production facilities and reactors, the biological research and development center at Salman Pak and suspected biological storage sites, the chemical research and development centers at Samarra and chemical storage sites, and operational delivery systems such as Scud launchers and aircraft mounted with spray tanks.

The biological and chemical targets were hit on the first day of bombing, as they were considered more of a threat than the nuclear targets; the coalition hit the nuclear facilities on the second day. Later press releases had revealed that three primary nuclear sites, ten biological sites, and eighteen chemical sites had been attacked. Nuclear targets included the two small reactors at Tuwaitha (including the rebuilt Osirak nuclear facility), a centrifuge production facility at Taji, north of Baghdad, and a nuclear weapons R&D establishment in Iskandariya. The Tuwaitha reactors had been hit by both Air Force fighters and Navy Tomahawk missiles, two nuclear research sites in the north, one near Mosul, the other near Arbil, were hit later in the month by F-117s and cruise missiles, causing 95 percent destruction of the buildings. A fourth nuclear weapons plant, which processed uranium near al-Qaim, was damaged heavily by missiles and bombs.

Biological targets included the main research facility at Salman Pak and support facilities at Samarra, al-Fallujah, Akashat and Badush. Fighter-bombers hit several refrigerated bunkers suspected to be biological weapons storage sites. Chemical targets focused on the major chemical weapons plants located at Samarra, northwest of Baghdad. The Muthanna complex at Samarra was hit by at least sixteen cruise missiles fired by Navy battleships, in addition to follow-up bomb runs by Air Force. The three Habbaniyah chemical agent precursor facilities at al-Falujah, heavily bombed, were destroyed. Secondary targets included subsidiary facilities such as the ethylene oxide plant near Barah (used in the production of thiodyglycol, a mustard precursor), two phosphorus production sites at Akashat and Al Qaim, and suspected chemical munitions storage sites.

General Schwarzkopf told reporters that all Iraq's nuclear facilities had been destroyed and that half of the nation's chemical and biological munition production sites either destroyed or heavily damaged. In addition, eleven CB weapon storage sites had been destroyed. "We're going to continue a relentless attack on this very, very, very heinous weapon system," he stated. Allied bombing and wreaked considerable damage: six of the ten building at Samarra were destroyed; all the buildings in the three Habbaniyah precursor chemical facilities were seriously damaged; one bunker of the eight targeted was destroyed, while the remaining seven were only superficially damaged; of the twenty-two S-shaped chemical bunkers at thirteen other locations, sixteen bunkers were destroyed, and the rest were seriously damaged.

The four biological agent facilities at Salman Pak, Taji and Abu Ghurayab were attacked on the first day of bombing. Eleven of the thirteen main buildings were destroyed, and the remaining two were severally damaged. All of the nineteen suspected BW storage bunkers were destroyed. In addition, CENTAF targeted the Baghdad power grid. When it was knocked out, the nearby refrigerated bunkers had lost power, and presumably their suspected biological cultures had died. The strikes on the nuclear facilities were reportedly devastating; in General Powell's words, "I think I can confirm for you that the two operating reactors they had are both gone. They're down. They're finished.

The battle damaged was not however, as extensive as CENTCOM's initial assessments had estimated. In truth, only about 60 percent of Iraq's weapons of mass destruction program had been destroyed. The bombings hampered only the production capability, sparing the munitions that had already been manufacture. Later *battle-damage assessment* (BDA) reports in February brought this fact to light, initiating a second wave of bombing against the NBC warfare sites. In later congressional testimony, Lieutenant General Horner admitted that the seemingly inflated estimates of 75 percent of higher given during the air campaign had represented the assessments on "known" targets. In truth, actual BDA assessments were not available for days later (and in some cases, weeks) and the assessments had been made on percentage of sorties and target hits. After the war, UN inspection teams got a look at the real size of the Iraqi NBC munitions program, much of which was untouched by the air campaign.

Saddam had anticipated the fierce air attack and after the raid on Osirak developed considerable deception capabilities and defensive counters to the coalition's air campaign. The DoD Report to Congress noted that Baghdad was more heavily defended than Murmansk, one of the main ports of the Soviet Navy, with at least twice the defensive density of the most heavily defended targets in Cold Ware-era Eastern Europe. While the reactors could not be hidden, much of the secondary equipment and research and development was concealed. Much of Iraq's nuclear program was spread across the entire country, including 2,000 foreign-trained scientists, 18,000 Iraqi engineers, a network of Jordanian front companies to procure foreign equipment, and had thirty-nine facilities at nineteen locations. Components of the centrifuges were manufactured at Za' Faraniyah, south of Baghdad, assembled at Tuwaitha and moved to locations in north Iraq. The components for the high-explosive trigger were built and assembled at A1 Atheer, a facility that claimed to manufacture composite materials. It was the target of the last bomb dropped by an F-117A1 in the conflict, late in the war. Most of these facilities escaped damage.

Tuwaitha had been especially well protected. As mentioned earlier, it was surrounded by SAM batteries and anti-aircraft guns, as well as protected by sand berms. Several F-117s had bombed the nuclear reactors and laboratory on the first day, but Lieutenant General Horner wanted the installation flattened. A flight of F-16s flew out to level the remaining buildings. As they approached the facility, the Iraqis put out several smoke pots, effectively concealing the buildings from view. The lack of visibility, combined with the anti-aircraft fire and SAMs lofting skyward, prevented the F-16s from bombing the targets without risking collateral damage. CENTAF would have to rely on the Tomahawks and F-117s to knock out Tuwaitha.

The biological R&D center at Salman Pak was hit hard-but not before its valuable equipment had been moved to a complex at Al Hakam, a facility southwest of Baghdad whose cover was research on the production of animal feed. The Iraqis had kept the program safe by arranging equipment and supplies ordered overseas to be delivered to facilities at Taji and Latifiyah, and then moving them to al Hakam. This fooled American intelligence into targeting the facilities at Taji and Latifiyah instead of al Hakam, which remained a secret until the end of the war. This could be one of the reasons the "infant formula factory" at Abu-Ghurayd was bombed early in the air war, without any evidence being found later of biological manufacturing equipment, biological munitions or biological agents. The fighters hit BW support facilities at al Fallujahm, Akashat and Badush. The twenty-one suspected refrigerated bunkers did not hold biological agent munitions; instead, as UN inspectors learned after the war, these air-conditioned bunkers protected conventional munitions and electronics from the desert heat.

The targeting of the Abu-Ghurayd "*infant factory*" had resulted from DIA analysts tracing potential biological warfare agents supplies and equipment sent to the factory vary a period of years. Over the previous six months, there had been to milk transport or other commercial activities at this facility, although there had been a large presence of Iraqi military personnel. While this did not confirm it as a biological agent production site, it was enough to put it on the "suspect" list. In December 1990, Iraqi forces began painting a mottled camouflage pattern on two other confirmed biological sites' roofs and applied the same to this factory's roof. This caused analysts to immediately shift the target from "suspected" to "confirmed." This combined with the presence of military guards at a nearby garrison and a barbed wire fence surrounding the facility, seemed to contradict Iraqi claims that the factory was an innocent non-military target.

Despite these points this event shook many onlookers in the Arab world as well as in Washington. A French contractor who had built the factory in the 1970s stated that it was constructed as an infant formula factory. It had subsequently closed in 1980 and had just reopened in 1990 due to the UN embargo. Two New Zealand dairy experts who had worked until May 1990 in a cheese-manufacturing building a half mole from the target, also indicated that the plant was innocent. Both their cheese factory and the baby formula factory were enclosed within the industrial park, which included a pharmaceutical plant, a milk sterilization plant and a housing complex. This event, combined with the bombing of a civilian-filled bunker, would result in new orders that air targets in an around Baghdad had to be reviewed and approved by General Powell specifically.

The chemical weapons targets were much more in the open, built on the same design as large manufacturing plants for pesticides and fertilizers, and thus more vulnerable to the bombers and Tomahawk missiles. The main complex at al-Muthanna, near Samarra, had been hit hard, but its heavy equipment had been already dispersed to other locations in the country. The three precursor facilities were put out of operation, but as later inspections would reveal, only tow facilities had really been in operation; the munitions themselves had been dispersed to more than twenty locations including storage sites and air bases. The mobile Scuds built at Taji were moved out into the desert as CENTAF attacked the permanent Scud sites in the west. Subsidiary chemical facilities at Basra, al Qaim, Mosul and Akashat were hit. Despite the destruction of 75 percent of the chemical munition manufacturing capability of Iraq, this still left before the ground war 46,000 chemical munitions, 97,000 unfilled munitions, 750 tons of bulk nerve and mustard agents and unknown tons of anthrax and botulinum toxin.

Saddam's Response

Iraq's military countered with salvos from mobile Scuds in the early hours of the second day of the coalition's air campaign. Twenty-eight fixed-launch sites in western Iraq had been knocked out early on the first day, but the mobile Scud teams were trained to "*shoot and Scott*' from one pre-surveyed launching point to the next. These points allowed the Scud teams to fire their rockets at cities and known target points using map coordinates, without having to verify if a target was there or not. Estimates on the number of mobile launchers averaged approximately thirty-six, twenty-two of which had been bought from the Soviets and the remainder built in Iraq. Contrary to what one might expect in the desert, there were a number of ravines, wadis, and other natural and man-made features which allowed the mobile Scuds to hide between missions. In addition, East German launcher decoys distracted allied planes from the real launchers. As a result, on the morning of January 18, the first of eighty-six Scuds against Israel and Saudi Arabia was launched.

In the first week and a half, Iraq fired twenty-five Scuds against Israel (Tel Aviv and Haifa) and twenty four against Saudi Arabia (Riyadh and Dhahran). The first eight fired against Israel on that Friday morning (six against Tel Aviv) caused the most concern for the coalition, which feared the threat of Scud-delivered nerve agents. As the warning sirens wailed just after 2:00 a.m., Israeli citizens scrambled to don their protective masks and enter their "*safe rooms*," sealed against any intrusive chemical vapors with plastic sheets and masking tape. In the United States as families watched the evening newscasts, moderators interrupted their field correspondents in Tel Aviv to tell them to don their own protective masks, even though the masks muffled their report's on the events.

As the missiles struck, Israeli and US officials immediately began to fear the worst. Reconnaissance teams raced to the impact sites with CAMs and other detection equipment. NBC news correspondents came on-air with the first reports from Israeli police confirming nerve agents, with CBS and CNN adding their reports of suspected nerve agent detection. As more detailed reports came in, it appeared that the CAMs had falsely identified the nitrous acid rocket fuel in the Scuds as nerve agent; further tests from M256A1 kits confirmed that the warheads had actually been conventional high explosives. The news was not enough to save three Israelis who had suffocated in all-prepared protective masks, or the dozens that fell ill from injecting themselves prematurely with atropine autoinjectors. Ironically, not one death resulted from the Scud warheads.

The second danger arising form the Scud attacks was the Israeli retaliation that Saddam had hoped to provoke. If Israel attacked Iraq, Saddam could hope for sharp dissent among the Arab allies within the coalition. In fact, as the attacks took place, reports of Israeili fighter-bombers on standby and Jericho rockets being prepared for launch soon surfaced. Devensive flights circled Jerusalem, searching for inbound Iraqi fighters. When the first reports of chemical agent from the Scuds came in, White House officials were convinced that the Israelis would retaliate. US officials were able to talk the Israeli government out of a retaliatory attack, promising to deploy two Patriot batteries to Israel.

In the next few days, Scuds flew against Saudi Arabia. Satellite warnings of the launches gave a five-to-eight minute warning to soldiers and civilians in Riyadh and Dhahran. Patriot batteries had been stationed in Riyadh and Dhahran during the deployment of the American forces. These batteries had been primarily designed for anti-aircraft roles, and secondarily for intercepting a stable ballistic missile warhead reentry. The erratic path of a disintegrating missile and its warhead were hard for the Patriot's radar to lock-on to. This led to operational decisions to err on the side of safety; for instance, on the third night of Scud attacks, thirty-six Patriot PAC-2 missiles rose to meet six incoming Scuds.

Contractors from Raytheon continued refining the target acquisition software in an effort to better predict interception patterns. The Pentagon reportedly asked Raytheon to investigate the possibility of putting chemical-neutralizing agents on the Patriot missiles to counteract any chemical agents that might escape from an exploding warhead. There is no evidence that this project came to fruition. Initially, disintegrating Scuds were interpreted as successful Patriot strikes, accounting for claims of a more than 90 percent. Still, it was used, as the Israeli military attache in Washington stated, not because it was the best weapon against Scuds but because it was the only weapon available.

The US military did not react well to the Scud attacks. The two Army corps NBCCS had expected some form of Iraqi retaliation, and warned their corps rear areas to assume MOPP-1 with the beginning of the air war, since most logistics bases were at known Saudi fixed sites they could be easily targeted, using a simple map. The forward combat units would not be as vulnerable, since the Iraqis had little intelligence information as to where they were, but most of them assumed MOPP-0. As the Scuds flew, radio messages warned of the launches through the chain of command. Because CENTCOM could not predict exactly where the Scuds were headed and what was their intended target, everyone assumed that their unit wast at risk. Practically every soldier in the theater ripped open his or her protective clothing packs and went to MOPP-4, gulping down PB tablets on the way to the trenches. Without any local chemical agent alarms sounding or munitions landing near their locations, soldiers everywhere had masked and suited up, expecting their areas to be hit by chemical agents. It was a massive overreaction that no one had anticipated. Added to the Scud scare, false alarms from individual M8A1 detectors were now causing panicked stampedes for their suits, The next morning, many units realized that their newly opened chemical suits would expire in fourteen to thirty days (depending on which suit one owned—at least a third had been the older CPOGs). This left most individuals with only one suit for future chemical attacks. Commanders immediately reduced the MOPP levels to zero (removing all protective clothing) and told their units to discontinue taking PB tablets.

The big problem was that the supply of suits could not support the anticipated combat usage. Many soldiers thought that since they had opened their suit's protective packaging, they required replacement suits in unopened packages prior to the next Scud attack. In addition to troop requirements, the numerous Third World civilians driving much of the ARCENT's truck fleet deserted, in fear of exposure to chemical attacks. The only way they could be coaxed back was to give al their own chemical protective suit to keep in the truck cab with them. Other Third World nationals, serving as cooks, security guards and other positions soon began eying the Us troops' masks slung at their waists. Based on the high use of protective suits during the Scud alerts and calculated projections, CENTCOM would be out of suits by April.

When the logisticians brought up these concerns, CENTCOM NBCC called the Natick labs to find whether these expiration dates were firm and hared, or what level of protection could be expected if the suits were repackaged and resealed to be used again. All the scientists had done previously was guarantee the BOD suits up to twenty-two days extendable to thirty days; they had no data on when suits would actually expire if unused. The older CPOGs caused more concern, as they were not designed to be extended past fourteen days. These expiration dates were determined based on the concept that soldiers would be constantly moving and fighting, wearing down the suits over that time period through physical wear and tear (not because of expiring charcoal liners). Even if the CPOGs were used past fourteen days, they were certainly still better than a sweat-soaked T-shirt in protecting against chemical agents. A quick review of protective suit qualities seemed to indicate that if the suits were repackaged and not damaged or water-soaked, they might provide the protection against a teen-gram per square-meter challenge for a longer period of time than expected. However, no one was willing to swear to exactly how much longer or what level of protection was provided.

As the soldiers repacked and resealed their protective clothing packs, there was a nagging suspicion in many of their minds that the "studies" were not telling the whole truth. During peacetime training, had not chemical officers and NCOs stressed the need to retain fresh suits? Many soldiers suspected that the leadership was fudging the data to cover for the extreme shortages of protective suits. In Major General McCaffrey's words, soldiers half-expected that some magic preserving fluid leaked out if one had torn or punctured the protective suit airtight bags, making the concept of repackaging the suits illusory. The number of walk-ins to the mask Maintenance Facility in Dhahran soared after the first Scuds fell, as soldiers ran into confirm their protective mask fits yet again. As later Scuds fell and the chemical agents did not emerge, soldiers gradually relaxed from jumping into MOPP suits every time an alert sounded.

While the *Scud attacks* alarmed many in the theater, it did have two positive aspects. First, the missiles had been armed with high explosives, not CB agent warheads. Just as with the World War II V-2 rockets, these missiles relied on shock and explosive power for terror and did not disseminate CB agents. Whether or not Saddam was reserving CB warheads for later was unknown. Second, this allowed the divisions to work out several operational issues. This "*rehearsal*" allowed the divisions to send out chemical recon teams and Fox vehicles to sample for CB agents at impact sites, to practice plotting and communicating predicted contamination hazard areas, to operate chemical agent detectors, to determine how to sleep in protective clothing, and how entry/exit procedure into collective protection shelters should work. This threat also emphasized the need for quick turnaround reports on Scud impact areas and predicted contamination hazard areas.

ARCENT NBCC changed its procedures so as to provide Scud warnings to subordinate units only after the Scud azimuth had been determined, and then only to sectors that were targeted. Cooperation between the ARCENT Air Defense Officer NBCC would result in a quick report of at what height and what slant angle the Scud exploded, allowing them to identify the target area accurately. The two corps NBCCs designated high-risk areas that would "*MOPP up*" in the event of future Scud launches. The main and rear headquarters, the Corps Tactical Operations Centers, units in Dhahran, and the main logistics bases would go to MOPP-2 (suits and boots, no masks). No other units would assume MOPP status unless their detectors went off or there were other indications (munition explosions, agent symptoms, etc.). These steps would reduce the number of suits expended. Lieutenant General Franks was unwilling to allow his soldiers to take an unknown risk if there were protective suits available, however. Efforts redoubled to draw protective clothing from Pacific and European war reserves and CONUS stocks. Chemical officers soon were tracking the individual flights bringing protective suits into Dhahran. All Scud intercept areas were scanned by Fox vehicles, in addition to CAMs and M256A1 kits.

The threat of potential CB agent Scud warheads kept strong political pressure on CENTCOM to step up anti-Scud efforts. SOCCENT created a special 877-man Joint Special Operations Task Force of aviation and ground forces, which worked in conjunction with British special operations teams under CENTCOM to hunt Scuds. These teams searched out Scud launchers and called in Air Force support to destroy their targets. The SOCCENT task force claimed a dozen launcher kills; many of these were later found to be decoys. The Air Force responded by launchers. Many of the targets attacked by F-15s turned out to be decoys or mistaken targets. Throughout the great Scud-hunt, CENTCOM could not state conclusively that one Scud launcher had been destroyed. The number of launches apparently did decrease between January 28 and February 10; only eight Scuds (five against Israel, three against Saudi Arabia) were launched during this period. This was more the result of the Iraqi crews running from the coalition's air superiority and SOCCENT teams than from the effective elimination of Scud launchers.

The threat of CB agent munition attacks would keep Iraqi delivery systems a high priority target. Air bases at Tallil, Al Jahrah, Shaibah, al-Taqaddum and Balad were reported as storing chemical warheads. American intelligence had received a report that the Iraqi military had prepared to launch three remotely piloted MiGs equipped with spray tanks from Al Rashid Air Base in southern Baghdad. An F-117 nailed one MiG, but poor weather prevented attacks on the other two. A salvo of six cruise missiles were fired from the cruiser USS *Normandy* in the Red Sea against this target to destroy the planes before they were launched. This demonstrates the level of concern within CENTCOM, expending over $10 million worth of missiles to take out tow aircraft capable of chemical agent delivery. The mere threat posed by potential CB agent weapons platforms redirected a substantial portion of CENTCOM's air and sea assets from conventional interdiction and air superiority missions to these special search and destroy missions.

Iraqi soldiers began walking toward allied lines to surrender as soon as the air offensive began. To allow a capability to control these prisoners firmly, President Bush granted CENTCOM's request to use riot control agents (RCAs—specifically, CS and CN grenades), under strict guidelines (only for defensive purposes, only within the theater of operations, and only during the period of hostilities). Because of the media's exaggeration of the use of tear gas in Vietnam, CENTCOM's staff was told not to discuss publicly the concept of operations or any operational maters concerning the use of tear gas in theater.

As the air effort shifted toward targets within the KTO, military officials sought to reassure the American public as well as their own forces that the CB warfare threat had been neutralized. In Riyadh, CENTCOM spokesman Brigadier General Richard Neal told the press that the targeting analysts had used "*special bombs*" on the chemical weapons plants and storage facilities in order to produce a minimum impact on the environment. In Washington, Lieutenant General Kelley told the media that "there is very, very, very little NBC production going on in that country—it ranges from zero to may be ten percent of what they had before the war." Several days later, Kelly assured the press that some chemical weapons in storage would have lost their potency over the last month because of Iraqui's poor manufacturing capabilities. He assessed the Iraqi CW threat as nowhere near as significant as it was at the outset of Operation Desert Shield.

That did not reassure any of the commanders. Random reports of CB munitions attacks kept coming into CENTCOM HQ. Early in the morning of January 17, CENTCOM-12 (Intelligence) passed a Saudi report of a chemical rocket launch on the border (later discounted). A pilot stated he had flown through a cloud of anthrax while returning from a raid; this claim was discounted by CENTAF an hour later. Incoming Scuds all had to be physically verified as having had high explosive or chemical warheads. An early morning British report on January 19 detailed a mustard agent attack at al-Jubayl, disproved by later tests. Many troops were calling in chemical agent alarms based on one detector's alarm, often without using manual and more sensitive backups such as the CAM and M256A1 kits to confirm the presence of absence of agent. When soldiers conducted second checks at the reported sites, all the alarms were proven false.

On January 19, Czech chemical units and French units reported to the Saudi military traces of nerve agents—air readings of 0.05 and 0.003 mg/m3 lasting for about an hour at two sites 25-30 kilometers northeast of Hafir at Batin. ARCENT dispatched a Fox team to the location; it arrived four hours later. Its crew could not verify any chemical agents, nor did it find any sign of munitions (Scuds, artillery shells, or aerial bombs). Some staff officers immediately speculated that it could have been traces of agent released from the bombing of Iraqi chemical weapons manufacturing sites, or the suspect CW bunkers at An Nasiriyah. Two days later, the Czech team reported low-level traces of nerve agent in the air near KKMC in the French sector; again, US chemical teams were unable to confirm their readings. On January 24, Saudi officials called a Czech unit to investigate a small area of what appeared to be wet desert soil several kilometers to the north and outside of KKMC. The contaminated area measured only about sixty centimeters by 200 centimeters. Using two separate protocols, the team determined that the area had been contaminated with the mustard agent. The Czech units filed a situation report with Saudi forces; however, there is no that any other units were called to provide independent confirmation. Since there were no CB agent casualties or expended weapon systems in the area, no contact reports form other coalition forces (Egyptians, Syrians, British) and no enemy activity (other than Scud launches), CENTCOM NBCC decided the events were false alarms, at worst non-incidents. Once the media got wind of this event, they immediately began speculating about CB agent originating from the bombed munition production facilities and weapons strong sites.

The CENTCOM and ARCENT staff studied the Czech reports, but the "*bombed facilities*" story did not pan out. KKMC is hundreds of miles from the bombed facilities. It would be physically impossible for liquid agents to travel that distance through the air in any lethal amounts. Any vapor traces of chemical agents would have evaporated long before reaching KKMC. CENTAF had been careful to attack CB agent storage and production sites prior to dawn, allowing the rising sun to begin its evaporative effects immediately. M8A1 alarms and numerous M256A1 kits (and similar sensitive detectors of others nations' force) used to detect agents in between KKMC and the bombed facilities (where, in theory, agent concentrations should have been higher) were all reporting negative results. No CENTCOM units had reported any immediate ill effects from low levels of CB agents. The weather between January 18 and 24 had included winds pushing northward, and rainstorms, which should have prevented any vapor clouds from retaining any integrity over one hundred-plus miles.

The lack of any evidence of CB agent exposure did not stop the spread of fears as the Scud launches continued, although they were not as great as in the initial two weeks of the air campaign. Rumors continued to run wild; statements such as "a guy in the mess hall said he talked to an MP who talked to a truck driver who saw some dead camels and said they had died of poison gas. Pass it on," ran through the theater. To paraphrase a saying, no one wanted to be confused with facts.

Scud attacks accelerated the pressure to deploy the biological detection teams and to field ANBACIS-II computers in theater. On January 19, Lieutenant General Waller formally agreed to implement DNA's ANBACIS-II system, and he approved the biodetection team concept. DNA teams began installing equipment at fifteen ARCENT and six CENTAF locations beginning on January 22, to be completed by the end of the month. On January 23, CENTCOM NBCC discovered that not all the first wave of the 9th Chemical Company was inbound. Because of airlift constraints, only five biodetection teams (instead of the planned seven) could enter the theater as the first increment of three deployments. The personnel arrived at Dhahran on January 26, with equipment (seven XM2 sampleres, four PM10s, five XM21 RSCAALs and eight HMMWVs) arriving on January 29. Five more XM21 RSCAALs were sent to MARCENT. The five Army area-sampling chemical-biological detection teams deployed on February 1 to al-Jubayl, Ras Safania, Riyadh, KKMC and Dhahran to begin immediate monitoring operations using XM2s and XM21s. The XM21 RSCAALs, not reliable during the hotter parts of the day, would operate between 0100 and 07000 hours, the most vulnerable windows for chemical agent attacks. The terms would take two biological agent samples daily, at 0600 and 1800 hours, likewise anticipated windows for biological agent attacks.

Phase-III: Battlefield Preparation

For vehicles shipped to the theater were tracked throughout their journey by the PM NBC Defense Office, both ODCSOPS and ODCSLOG at the Pentagon, the USAREUR Chemical officer, and the CENTCOM, ARCENT, corps and division NBCCs. Lieutenant Colonel Willhoite and Major Newing were briefing Lieutenant General Gordon Sullivan (Vice chief of Staff of the Army) and Dennis Reimer (DCSOPS) regularly on the Fox program. This personal involvement increased after the Scud attacks. In some cases, chemical offices were tracking airplane tail numbers and vehicle bumper numbers to monitor the progress of "their" vehicles. 3rd ACR's 89th Chemical Company accepted five Foxes rolling off the lines in Kassel just prior to Christmas, repressing the first of the second batch of thirty vehicles, and returned with them to Saudi Arabia. There were an addition twelve

Foxes due in by the end of January, raising the total to forty-eight. The first ten of those would go to the 1st IN DIV. Thirteen more might make the deadline of mid-February. Originally the schedule had called for the last five to be delivered in the late March, but the PM office had been able to convince Thyssen-Henschel to accelerate the deliveries. Four more vehicles would pass to 1st DIV, six vehicles for ARCENT's Support Command, and one to replace the "Nunn" vehicle standing in for the 92d Chemical Company's loss, leaving the last two to be added to the theater "float" (for at total of four reserves). If everything went according to plans, CENTCOM would receive sixty-two Fox recon vehicles, including the one that had broken its axle in November, leaving a final tally of sixty-one NBCRS in theater for the ground offensive.

The 1st IN DIV was the last Army heavy division to receive Foxes. The division's brigades wanted its Foxes up front to monitor whether the Iraqis used chemical weapons while they were working through the border berm and minefields. As they represented the corps's main effort, their sense of urgency increased. In the event that the 1st DIV Foxes did not arrive on time, the division was to receive four Fox vehicles from 3rd AR DIV on the morning of January 21. The 3rd AR DIV had received its platoon back from 82d ABN DIV, but the entire division force would not close into the theater until February 6. The deal struck was that two Foxes would be returned to 3rd AR DIV after the breach operations and that the remaining two Foxes would return once the British 1st AR DIV passed through 1st IN DIV lines.

Problems surfaced regarding the GDLS maintenance contract support. The British, Israelis and now Turkish militaries had received their Foxes, and this began to put a strain on the maintenance system for spare parts. Because most of the recon platoon shad been careful not to overtax their vehicles, the operational readiness of the US Foxes remained above 95 percent. The contractors, however, had never been told about the possibility that they might have to go into Iraq to maintain the Foxes. As the coalition bombings began and the offensive intent of the coalition became, clear many contractors left Dhahran. GDLS had to hire new contractors under terms that included the offensive plans. (This should reflect on the future need to pay more attention to the role of contractors in an armed conflict). While the Navy and Air Force were more accustomed to this procedure, the Army had not as much experience; Navy and Air Force contractors, however, were never involved on the very edge of the battlefield, as the Army contractors would soon be.

On the morning of January 29, three Iraqui heavy divisions advanced against the Marine Corps lines in what was later called the "*Khafji offensive.*" According to later analysis, this was not just a preemptive probe or quick attempt to bloody the Americans but a major attack designed to test the coalition front. The early attacks on the west side of the advance included an artillery barrage against the frontier observations points. Some explosions sounded more faint than others. Because both Army and Marine Corps troops had been warned that munitions exploding with a "hollow" sound were potential chemical munitions, the chemical agent alarm quickly ran up the chain of command. Fox vehicles scurried from one site to another, confirming the lack of any agent. Fierce air attacks and aground marine Corps/ Arab coalition counterattack to retake Khafji on January 31 drove the Iraqi units back. Later, after the attack had been blunted, the Marines discovered there had been no chemical munitions used. This battle was seen by some to be indicative of the battle ahead, although CENTCOM missed much of the significance of the attack at the time. Attempting to stage a major mechanized attack, the Iraqi forces had been unable to coordinate a multi-divisional movement under a sky they did not own. This was not the way the battle against the Iranians had taken place.

The Khafji battle was significant in that no chemical munitions had been used. If the attack had been just a probe, that in and of itself would not be surprising. Iraq had always saved its chemical munitions for major assaults or defense missions, during the Iraq-Iran war. Later analysis showed the Iraqi attack to have been much grater than just a probe. As part of a major attack, the lack of chemical munitions use meant one of three things: either Iraqi forces did not have the chemical munitions nearby; or they were unwilling to use chemical munitions because of threat of massive conventional retaliation; or their forces were not well enough trained to incorporate chemical weapons into the offensive. Then again, the Iraqi force in Kuwait could have had the chemical munitions nearby but had thought they would not need the munitions for a short, swift assault. Or it the results were encouraging, no one was ready to discount the possibility of chemical attacks once the CENTCOM forces moved into Iraq.

Moving CB Defense Units into Place

The two corps began their movements west after the air war began. The 82d and 101st ABN DIVs, as the extreme left wing of the attack, moved forward first, followed by the 24th IN DIV and 3rd

ACR. VII Corps would follow as soon as the XVIII ABN Corps had cleared the KKMC area, to avoid a potential traffic jam. This was an extremely vulnerable time for both corps. XVIII ABN Corps was lined up along Tapline Road, a single hardtop road that paralleled the border. As 113,000 troops and thousands of vehicles headed west along the road, the nervous division NBCCs could only hope that the Iraqis did not get any reports of the movement. A few Scuds or FROGs spilling persistent agent on the Tapline Road would have disrupted the movement plan considerably, which would have been worse than the few casualties that might result. The 1st IN DIV task force in the al-Batin area, with its decoys and large-area smoke, mesmerized the Iraqi forces into looking for a straight-up-the middle attack into Kuwait. Only one Iraqi division deployed west of the wadi after the deception operation.

XVIII ABN Corps would also lose a degree of its rare area chemical defense during the movement. While the corps NBCC had kept the rear area reasonably well informed with warning messages, once the corps was spread out and moving, radio communication with the numerous support units became very spotty. The majority of the chemical agent detectors and decontaminants were in the combat divisions, and the promised NBC protective covers for protecting the corps logistics had never materialized. VII Corps would be in a similar situation, but being more mechanized, it could count on speed and heavier protection for some degree of contamination avoidance. Both rear support areas would have to augment their decontamination companies and medial units with other rear-area support troops to ensure quick evacuation, decontamination and treatment of chemical casualties. The last Reserve chemical defense company, 340th Chemical Company (Decon), arrived in theater 30 January and moved to Logbase CHARLIE to join the 457th Chemical Battalion.

Once the VII Corps HQ began moving west, it decided to use the movement from the tactical assembly areas to the forward assembly areas as a rehearsal for the attack into Iraq. Each division assumed the planned distance and spacing, moving along axes that mirrored those that would be used in the actual attack. During this movement the units were confronted with exercise scenarios that caused them to use the Fox NBCRS platoons to negotiate simulated contamination. The divisions discovered during this rehearsal that a large maneuver formation traveling in column had to plan its actions to execute upon encountering a contaminated area. There had to be a quickly executed process wherein in the NBCRS vehicles would discover the contamination, mark it, and guide the following units around the area without losing their momentum. For the upcoming offensive, VII Corps decided to include military police in the forward units, so that once the NBCRS had marked the contamination, the MPs could guide the rest of the column around it (until the agent evaporated). This would allow the NBCRS vehicles to resume their point recon mission quickly. Another potential problem was that the warning markers dropped by the NBCRS were too small and too spread out; they would never be noticed in the dark hours of the mourning. Fox crews would now attach chemical luminescence lights to the NBCRS markers to make them more visible in the dark.

On February 3, a second increment of soldiers, representing seven biodetection teams, arrived at Dhahran International; their eight HMMWVs with ¾-ton trailers, fixed-site biodefense teams had been trained primarily on the PM10 commercial biodetectors. With the additional teams in theater, CENTCOM NBCC made plans to move the five area sampling teams to Logabases Alpha, Charlie, Echo, Al Quaisumah (near Hafar al Batin) and Ras Safaniya, focusing on the vulnerable forward deployment and logistics areas. Two fixed site teams would deploy to the Riyahd and Dhahran/Dammam areas, with the remaining three moving to Jubayl, KKMC, and Log Base Bastogne. Because the commercial biological detectors were experimental prototypes, heavy, more fragile and highly dependant on logistics and maintenance support, they were not stationed directly on the fluid front lines.

Initial operational tests of the biodetectors resulted in a report of anthrax at Dhaharan late on February 4. Team 6 using an XM2 sampler and registered the detection downwind of sheep pens, leading medics to believe it was a false positive report. In addition samples taken west and upwind of the sheep pens were negative. False positives occurred when the biodetector detected a potential positive biological agent that was later proven absent at the forward labs. Of course, these tentative results, reacting to indigenous biological organisms, were better than false negatives (nor reacting to a real BW agent).

Once the Navy Forward Laboratory matured the biological sample into a more definable culture, it proved the report to be wrong. The samples were evacuated to Fort Detrick to be sure; there the results were confirmed as relating to an organism similar to anthrax but definitely hot lethal or a manufactured agent. The biodefense teams had not correctly established the natural background of biological organisms in theater; also, the SMART tickets were reacting to filter paper fibers in the liquid samples, lending to false positives. Changes in sampling and evacuation practices would lessen the chance of future alarms.

The ANBACIS teams ran tests from mid-January through mid-February, using several possible scenarios of Iraqi chemical weapons attacks. The included 122 mm rocket attacks, MiG-23 aerial attacks, FROG and Scud rocket attacks, using all known chemical agents. The DNA Operations Cell in the United States returned contamination hazard footprints to CENTCOM with fifteen minutes. This quick turnaround ensured the most accurate prediction capability against any possible CB agent attack the Iraqis might deliver, throughout the theater and at all hours.

Concerns over protective clothing shortages had climbed to a pitch as the fourteen-day shelf life CPOGs "expired" at the end of January. CENTCOM and its units had been flooded with messages form CRDEC, NRDEC, AMC, DLA, medical offices and the Pantagon on what the overgarment were life extension policy should be, in the absence of any official guidance or clarification. Not all of this advice was good; Lieutenant General Yeosock told Lieutenant General Reimer that he was well aware of the situation and did not need more message traffic to confuse the issue. ODSCOPS finally laid down the "final world" and instructed CENTCOM that ODSCOPS, as the point office for chemical defense equipment procurement, would release the official policy and that only this policy would apply. This policy confirmed that CPOGs that had been exposed to the air and resealed in their packages would still have an effective protection capability when used again. The important factor was the number of days that the troops actually wore the overgarments, not the number that the suit had been removed from its airtight bag. Reports that 130,000 BDOs were due in from Korea via air and the promised BDOs from Europe were enroute by sea gave ARCENT some hope of resolving the CPOGs issues. If these suits could be distributed to the troops by mid-February, many commanders would breathe much easier.

There still were no confirmed guidelines on the handling, decontamination and transportation of contaminated human remains. The issue of contaminated casualties had been worked on throughout the DoD and up to President Bush, with the intent that no American remains be left behind because of CB agent contamination. Scientists at Dugway Proving Ground and Quartermaster School had developed a theoretical procedure, but they had not tested it. Decon personnel would use wire-mesh litters to dip the contaminated body in a high-bleach solution to clean the body, and then use two body gags to seal the remains. Medical units at Dover AFB had monitoring and transportation procedures in place and were prepared to accept the contaminated casualties. Lieutenant General Franks saw no reason to alarm the troops and commanders on this aspect of chemical warfare. He reviewed and approved a message on handling contaminated remains, a message that would have been distributed in the event of a chemical attack.

In Washington, the political leadership expressed its concerns as well. Colonel Read presented a special brief to Paul Wolfowitz, Under Secretary of Defense for Policy. Paul Wolfowitz had participated in all of the high-level discussions about the CB agent threat and asked ODCSOPS how the first few days of the ground offensive would look if Saddam chose to use CB agent munitions. Colonel Read explained the expectation that CENTCOM forces would under attack as they broke through the berms, by both Iraqi artillery and possibly aircraft using chemical munitions. Iraqi military forces would use previously identified target points, since their observation of CENTCOM forces would be severely limited.

Colonel Read described how CB agent attacks in the Corps' rear areas would slow down the force's logistic and resupply. He discussed how the Fox vehicles would locate and mark contaminated areas, allowing following units to bypass and avoid them. If divisions could keep moving and avoid heavy engagements, they would avoid becoming targets for Iraqi CB weapons. Heavy casualties might be minimized by closing quickly with the enemy. The question came up again about the possibility of contaminated casualties. One solution was to leave the bodies in Saudi Arabia, seal the bodies in airtight coffins, or cremate the bodies to avoid the problems associated with transporting contaminated bodies to their families. This was unacceptable to both the civilian and military leadership in Washington—one way or another, all US troops were coming home.

".....And then We are Going to Kill it"

Final combat preparation against Iraqi CB agent use would include massive conventional attacks against any rebuilt airfields, facilities or delivery systems that might be able to employ CB agents. NBC weapons production and storage sites, such as a newly discovered BW facility at Latifyah (west of Baghdad), received another barrage of aircraft delivered munitions and Tomahawks. Despite coalition emphasis on degrading Iraqi artillery, three were still more than enough artillery tubes and rocket launchers available to Iraqi forces to fire high-priority chemical agent delivery missions. Operational intelligence assets had pinpointed most of these. Artillery batteries and naval battleship guns pounded anything in range of the Iraqi border that might be able to deliver CB agent munitions.

This still left the threat of Scuds and Iraqi aircraft. Saddam Hussein had built up an air force with over 600 combat aircraft. Approximately 100 of these flew to Iran before the air war, and another thirty-three aircraft had been destroyed by the air offensive. This left over 500 aircraft capable of delivering CB agent munitions. If the command and control structure could still operate, and if the munitions. If the command and control structure could still operate, and if the munitions produced prior to the air campaign had been transported to the air bases, there was the possibility that Iraq could employ CB agent munitions against the coalition. CENTAF's air offensive had destroyed the ability of the southern airfield to support CW strikes against CENTCOM forces, but other airfields still existed. The limited number of CW warheads designed for Scuds and the intense coalition air superiority would mean only a limited capability but could not necessarily prevent any "*leak through*" of aircraft of Scuds in a saturation air attack.

Logistically speaking, the coalition was about as ready as it would ever be. When Defense Secretary Cheney and General Powell asked the corps commanders what would prevent them from being able to launch offensive operations by February 21, Lieutenant General Frank's reply was, "having two chemical overgarments for every soldier crossing the line of departure." Supply centers continued distributing the protective that shipment through out CENTCOM. Orders had gone out that no soldiers would turn in uncontaminated suits used in January's Scud scare, unless a second set had been issued to all soldiers. LTC Merryman described the search for additional protective suits as similar to a 90 percent-off suit sale at Macy's. All the soldiers would have at least two unused protective suits, including the resealed suit opened in mid-January. The protective mask shortage had not improved; VII Corps would go in with less than 150 spare M17- series masks immediately available for replacements. The M291 skin decon kit had gone out to most of the soldiers, not necessarily in bulk, but enough to handle the first few chemical attacks.

Media attention fell on the absence of the new M40 protective masks, in part due to Scott Aviation's observations that the M40 mask could have been available had the government stayed with it as the prime contractor (now Mine Safety Applications [MSA] and ILC Dover). Although ILC Dover had conducted a large portion of the R&D on the mask, the production contract had been awarded to Scott Aviation as the low bidder in May 1987. Scott Aviation delivered only 3, 358 make out of a contract target of 300,000, which initially resulted in a stop-work order in 1988, and eventually the termination of the contract "for the convenience of the government" in January 1990. In September 1988, AMCCOM awarded Mine Safety Applications (MSA) and ILC Dover short-term M40 production contracts (120,000 each by September 1989) in an effort to get at least some masks out to the major Army units. Both still faced some technical and production problems, such as difficulties developing the proper to August 1990.

Scott Aviation's president stated on ABC's *prime Time Live* that had the Army stayed with his company, the deployed soldiers might all have superior M40 masks, Brigadier General Dave Nydam, also interviewed on the show, countered that accusation by pointing out that Scott Aviation had failed to meet Army production deadlines and had failed first-article test requirements. The M-17 series mask, while initially designed in the 1960s, was improved in 1983 to the M17A2 model and was more than adequate to protect the soldiers against Iraqi chemical agents, especially since all soldiers had repeatedly checked their mask fits before and during the conflict. The public debate caused a flurry of calls from worried spouses to their soldiers in the field, asking, if they were sure their protective masks were safe and had been checked This drop in morale and confidence concerning their masks was not what the soldiers needed at this point.

Since the Gulf war, much has been made of the Manley report, which sites that the M17A2 protective mask had a 26-40 percent failure rate. These numbers arose from a classified Marine Corps' protective mask fit validation study, which people have misinterpreted as a report that identified the M17A2 as a defective mask. The study actually stated that if an untrained individual attempted to fit an M17-series mask to his or her face, there is that chance the mask would not fit perfectly. If an individual has an NBC specialist fir him or her, this percentage becomes practically negligible, as hundreds of thousands of military personnel who have ever been inside a CS-chamber will attest. For months soldiers had their unit NBC specialists on hand to check their masks, in addition to the Pine Bluff mask facility, banana oil checks, the PMFVS device, and other tests to verify everyone's fit. No field commander was taking any changes that troops would die unnecessarily. At the time, this validation study was classified because of the chance that Iraq might misread the study as pointing out a vulnerability, and might attempt to exploit the opportunity by initiating chemical warfare.

Final Preparations

The 1st DIV had become increasingly concerned over its lack of Foxes, especially after seeing the Marines accept their ten Foxes first in the late January. When the first two NBCRs vehicles were ready in January (alone with the USMC allotment of ten), VII Corps NBCC tasked the 1st IN DIV to send its Property Book Officer, the platoon leader and some personnel form the chemical recon platoon to fly to Rhein-Main AFB (the deployment site had moved from Ramstein) to sign for them. While 1st IN DIV had looked forward to receiving the vehicles, the division staff was reluctant to send the chemical recon platoon to travel to Germany to sign for and transport the vehicles back personally. With the 1st IN DIV's critical breaching mission only weeks away, the division did not want to part with half of their NBC recon assets; and they instead requested that logistics channels deliver the Foxes to KKMC. In the interest of time, the VII Corps NBCC sent one of its captains to Kassel to sign for the vehicles in early February.

The 12th Chemical Company crew members traveled to Dhahran on February 11 to accept the two Foxes, only to discover they had not yet arrived. The Foxes had left on the evening of February 13 on a specially chartered C-5A cargo plane, but a Scud scare during the flight caused the plane to turn back to Germany. The plane finally delivered the two Foxes to Saudi Arabia on February 15. Yet there was one problem: due to the shortage of radios caused by wartime requirements, they arrived without vehicle radios and combat vehicle crewman helmets. These vehicles had to stop by the GDLS/PM NBC Fixed Fox Facility to receive final equipment. This allowed the 1st IN DIV to return two borrowed Foxes to the 3rd AR DIV, with a promise to return the other two after the breaching operations on the first day of the ground war. In the early hours of February 19, VII Corps NBCC called to inform 1st IN DIV that the last four Foxes had arrived at KKMC. The 1st IN DIV had its Fox-equipped recon platoon barley a week before the ground offensive started.

Resolving the 1st IN DIV issue still left the last nine Fox vehicles of the sixty-Fuchs loan to go. The 490th Chemical Battalion sent a team to Germany on February 17 to escort the nine vehicles to Dhahran. By February 21, they were ready to return to Saudi Arabia, delivering three vehicles each on the 21st, 24th and 25th, but the Air Force was not ready to delivery. Last-minute theater airlift priorities had prevented their immediate return although they had been third priority for in-bound logistics (first being Patriot missiles, second being 120 mm tank ammunition).

On the eve of the ground offensive, there were a total of fifty-one operational Fox vehicles in the US forces, not including the one "*Nunn*" float VII Corps had twenty four of the vehicles on-line, while XVIII ABN Corps retained seventeen. The ARCENT Support Command would not have its planned Fox reconnaissance vehicles, but it could still rely on chemical troops in APC recon vehicles. MARCENT had the other ten vehicles, split between their two divisions. The XM21 and biodetection sampling teams increased their vigilance to cover the division marshaling areas. While the greatest concern was focused on the threat of Iraqi chemical strikes against CENTCOM forces in the breach operation, there was equal interest in the possibility of chemical Scud attacks and Iraqi air attacks against the rear area supporting the offensive operations. ARCENT NBCC counted wells burning constantly in Kuwait presented new problems to the Marines and VII Corps. In addition to posing health problems because of the hydrogen sulfide fumes, the heavy, oil-laden smoke clogged the M8A1 filter paddles responsible for filtering particulates from the air sampling mechanism. The limited air flow caused increasing number of false alarms, until many units simply turned off the detectors rather than constantly checking for chemical agents.

A staffer in CENTCOM headquarters brought up the question of what would happen if the units captured biological munitions. Up to his time, no one had considered what exactly combat units should do with munitions filled with biological agents. Normally one would call the Explosive Ordnance Division Disposal (EOD) teams to disarm munitions, but were not special circumstances present here? While the US had established ways to demil biological munitions at US production sites in the 1970s, there was no mobile capability to do this in Southwest Asia. The Joint Staff began working on procedures to permit a field destruction capability for biological weapons, in the event that CENTCOM might capture armed biological munitions.

With all the divisions in place on February 20, deception operations continued. The mechanized smoke generators of the 68th and 44th Chemical Companies set up a smoke screen to support the 1st CAV DIV Battlefield Deception Teams, who set up loudspeakers and pop-up replicas of M1A1 tanks and M2 Infantry Fighting Vehicles (IFV) around the Wadi al-Batin. Under Operation Knight Strike, Task convince the Iraqi force that the main attack would follow on that terrain. Division artillery "prepared" the Iraqi side as the engineers moved up to it. Two mechanized smoke generator platoons obscured the engineers as they blasted eight lanes through the berm, allowing the task force to move into the wadi with relatively good cover. This was the first smoke operation conducted on enemy territory since Vietnam. As the smoke generators moved forward with the task force, the American forces came under heavy fire dug-in Iraqi positions. One smoke generator crew noticed a M163 Vulcan air defense team (4-5th Air Defense Artillery) that had been hits by an Iraqi rocket-propelled grenade. Two chemical soldiers, Specialists John Benavides and James Santos, stopped to render first aid to the wounded. As the probe withdrew, artillery-fired smoke covered the units. The two specialists encountered injured soldiers in a Bradley IFV, and once again stopped to render assistance.

This type of smoke support was just what the Chemical School had intended with its conception of smoke generators on M113A2 chassis. In contrast, the 1st IN DIV attempted to conduct a fake breach on the same day, a bit west of the 1st CAV DIN attempt, without breaching the berm. This lack of smoke support would affect the 1st IN DIV's concept of the first day's operations. Because of difficulties in employing smoke during simulated combat operations at the National Training Center, Major General Tom Rhame chose to exclude the two smoke generator companies from the breaching operation. He felt that the breach operation was already difficult enough without smoke; that the Iraqi opposition would not offer stiff resistance; and that the attached US units were not prepared to conduct the operation effectively under obscured conditions. Intelligence reports had noted Iraqi armor units puling away from the 1st IN DIV sector, leaving the Iraqi infantry units there vulnerable to a hard-hitting combined arms force. The 1st Brigade commander, comfortable in the knowledge that nothing the Iraqis had would penetrate the front armor of an M1A1, suggested that this tanks, outfitted with mine plows, could punch through the minefields before the Iraqis could react. His plan would not require the extensive smoke and engineer support at the onset of the battle.

The 2d Chemical Battalion commander, Lieutenant Colonel Mike Kilgore, worked out an alternative plan with Major Polley, the division chemical officer, that would employ the smoke generators on the east flank of the division. They could obscure the flank of the division as it breached the berms and assist the 2d Brigade's initial attack on the Iraqi recon assets. The 2d ACR and 3rd AR DIV planned to obscure their breaches west of the 1st IN DIV position. They had smoke platoons from the 172d Chemical Company that would drop on obscuring haze over the engineers prior to their blowing lanes through the berm.

In addition to working out the smoke plan, the 2d Chemical Battalion planned two through decontamination sites south of breach and one north of the breach. Engineer support from the 7th Engineer brigade (ENC BDE) would dig the sump pits necessary to collect the contaminated run-off of the washes. Both of the rear decontamination sites took over a square kilometer of land, with two decontamination platoons ready for action. Logistically, the battalion moved 600 barrels of fog oil up to the line and 20,000 gallons of water to the decon sites. At the other two chemical battalions, similar decontamination preparations were underway. If Saddam was going to try to stop the CENTCOM's offensive, the breach was the most logical place to use chemical agents. Once the offensive moved past the breach, the maneuver forces would rely on their own operational capabilities of maintain the momentum. The decontamination companies would move behind them and prepare thorough decon sites closer to the battle as the combat units moved forward.

Biological Warfare Scares

Just as the units were lining up against the border, a new threat emerged Reconnaissance elements of the 115th MP Company reported finding groups of dead camels and goats along Main Supply Route Yugo, near Qaryat al Alya, and on Main Supply Route Cadillac during the week of February 16-21. Along both MSRs the MPs had noted a number of green plastic grain-feed bags, around which the dead animals were clustered. Although the nearby villagers seemed unconcerned, CENTCOM immediately suspected biological agents. On February 23, soldiers noted a large number of dead sheep near Logistics Base Alpha. That same day, the XM2 sampler at Logistics Base Alpha, in the vicinity of Sodowiyat on the Tapline Road, had a positive hit for anthrax on one air sample, while an XM2 sampler at al-Jubayl reported a positive hit on botulinum toxin. The PM10 samplers at Dhahran and Riyahd both reported anthrax samples. Army veterinary and bio-medical sampling teams rushed out to sample all these areas, while the divisions sat poised on the front lines. Subsequent analysis at the forward labs yielded negative reports on all four, but positive confirmation would require laboratory analysis at Fort Detrick and a twenty-four-hour turnaround, more than a day later.

What had happened was a series of unfortunate coincidences. The locals had a practice of isolating sick and weak animals from the herd and killing them with poisoned feed. The animals had died at their owners' hands. There were no reports of mass illnesses nearby in either the military or civilian communities that would indicate a large area biological attack. These alarms, coming so close to the initiation of the ground offensive, could have been either a brilliantly timed stroke by Saddam or a false alarm. There were no immediate ways other than the troops' health and the forward laboratories to tell one way or another. While no one could rely 100 percent on the biodetection teams, they were the only indicators against the one threat capable of stopping the offensive. This brought home the message that a more credible and responsive, real-time biological warfare agent detection system was needed. Meanwhile, the reports compounded fears throughout the leadership on the eve of the ground offensive. The two corps issued orders to increase MOPP status and start taking PB tablets prior to H-hour.

Phase IV: Offensive Ground Campaign

The Marines had conducted deception operations, artillery raids and cross-border screening operations for several weeks prior to the ground offensive. Over the past few days, their task forces had been successful in penetrating the first obstacle belt and establishing firing positions within Kuwait. Finally, at 0400 hours on February 24, the 1st MARDIV moved from its firing positions within Kuwait into the obstacle belts. The Marines had donned their Mark-IV protective suits and boots (MOPP-2) in order to prepare for the possibility of chemical mines or chemical artillery projectiles. The combat engineers had cleared three of the four lanes, mostly with three-shot line charges followed by M60 tanks with track-width mien plows. At about 0730 hours in lane 3, one mine exploded with a suspiciously low sound. Fearing the worst, the engineers reported a possible chemical mine had gone off. Major General James Myatt immediately ordered the division go to MOPP-4 (full protective posture) until a Fox could confirm the report. Although the Fox vehicle seemed to confirm a mustard agent in the area, the M256A1 kits and M8 paper did not detect vapour or liquid agent traces. A second Fox further upwind detected no agents. The false alarm had cost the Marines only twenty minutes, but that was twenty minutes of lying still, vulnerable in a narrow lane, waiting for the "all clear" to move forward.

During this time the 1st MARDIV's Fox's report of confirmed mustard agent had been intercepted by one of the JSTARS planes and flashed to the Joint Chiefs of Staff. The PM NBC Defense offices secure phone began ringing that Sunday morning, with the Joint Staff questioning LTC D'Andries as to how reliable the report might be. By the PM office's estimate, the MM-1 was a well-engineered piece of equipment, but there were too many variables (environmental interferrents, operator interpretation, level of training etc) for them to determine whether or nor this was a valid detection. The foxes used the MM-1 for ground contamination detection only, relying on CAMs on board and M8A1 detector for air contamination detection. The PM NBC Defense office advised the Joint Staff to allow the Marines at the site to make the call. By the time this communication had taken place, the 1st MARDIV was back on the move.

The 2d MARDIV crossed its line of departure at 0530 hours, engaging in the same obstacle clearing. It encountered no chemical mines but kept expecting heavy artillery as it struggled through the lines. The MLRS battery and Marine artillery kept up a constant counter battery fire to limit any Iraqi artillery fire. A second chemical alarm went off that afternoon, without accompanying explosions or incoming artillery—again a false alarm. The constant smoke from the oil fires kept the skies dark, and it also kept the M8A1 and ICAD chemical agent detectors false-alarming. It would be enough to keep the nervous Marines jumping throughout their push towards Kuwait City. As they pushed toward A1 Jaber Air Base outside of Kuwait near midnight, several Marines mistook low-lying artillery smoke for chemical attacks. After masking and checking their M256A1 kits, they noted the negative results and moved on. Iraqi EPWs captured nearly confirmed the lack of any chemical weapons at Al Jaber. Next to the Marines, the Egyptian army had its scares as well. One soldier put on a mask in the breach site. Men behind him took that as a sing of a chemical attack, masked and froze in place, waiting for confirmation. No casualties—again, a false alarm had interrupted the battle's forward momentum.

XVII ABN Corps had initiated its attack at 0400 hours as the western hook into Iraq. Most of XVIII ABN Corps remained at MOPP-

0 (sits nearly, not worn), anticipating little resistance this far west, and counting on speed to avoid enemy targeting. As the French fought elements of the Iraqi 45th Division no chemical attacks occurred. The 101st ABN DIV got its airborne assault off two hours late due to weather but encountered no problems establishing forward Operating Base (FOB) Cobra.

As the reports from MARCENT and XVIII ABN Corps came in to CENTCOM, it appeared that the Iraqis did not intend to retaliate with chemical weapons as had been anticipated. Indeed, the few Iraqi artillery responses seemed to be hitting pre-planned fire zones rather than where the soldiers were actually moving. After conferring with Lieutenant Generals Luck and Franks, General Schwarzkopf made the decision to push the schedule ahead. The 3rd ACR led the 24th IN DIV north at 1400 hours, five hours ahead of schedule due to success on the left flank. Both units anticipated chemical attacks as they crossed the line of departure in MOPP-1 (suits on). As the units moved forward, the chemical attacks did not occur, nor were the chemical munitions stockpiles at the intermediary points as intelligence had warned them they would be.

The VII Corps had the main Army breach operations on the first day of the ground offensive. Initially, the corps MOPP level was MOPP-2 (suit and boots), but Lieutenant General Franks gave latitude to the division commanders as to what levels to set within their own units. The 2d ACR led the way on the left flank at 0538 hours. Its goal was to conduct a movement to contact and fix the Republican Guard, and allow the following divisions to pass through to continue the fight. The 2d ACR assumed MOPP level 1 after crossing into Iraq proper, and it would continue that level until assuming the corps reserve (when it would downgrade to MOPP-0). The two forward cavalry squadrons each had a chemical reconnaissance squad of two Foxes attached, while the third Fox squad remained under the ACR's general control for rear-area operations or to assist the forward squads.

The foxes would mark contaminated areas and find bypass for the following cavalry regiment, and the 1st AR and 3rd AR DIVs. Initially, smoke operations had been planned to cover the initial breach of the border berm and then toe screen the flanks of the ACR. Due to the heavy winds and inclement weather (setting a ten-year record for rainfall in the region), smoke operations were not carried out. VII Corps deliberate decon support to the 2d ACR. The initial breach found no chemical mines and no artillery attacks to oppose VII Corps's entry into Iraq. The 1st AR DIV and 3rd AR DIV rolled north behind 2d ACR on their way toward al Busayyah, at 1400 hours.

1st IN DIV had the same experience as 2d ACR. It had decon platoons of the 181st Chemical Company standing by, two platoons with the engineers and two in the rear area where all the VII Corps supplies would soon run through. After the 7th ENG BDE breached the berm in twenty-four lanes, two combat brigades rolled through to clear and secure the far side.

Because there was no resistance or artillery fire at the breach, the division was able to move quickly through the berms into Iraq proper. MG Rhame had successfully gambled on not having smoke support; had there been Iraqi artillery and a counterattack, things might have gone the other way. More importantly, there were no chemical artillery or air attacks. After securing the Iraqi security zone, the 1st IN DIV received orders at 1500 hours to continue exploiting the offensive. Because the British division had not practiced passing through the 1st IN DIV at night, VII Corps decided to hold off on its passage of lines until the next day.

As the end of the first day approached, CENTCOM checked on the suspected anthrax cultures, now twelve hours old. The Theater Army Medical Laboratory found no signs of any anthrax but was waiting the full twenty-four hours to make a solid confirmation. The real damage was rumors flying through ARCENT that a solid confirmation. The real damage was rumors flying through ARCENT that biological agents were being used in theater.

British representatives joined up with CENTCOM's NBCC to ask questions about the anthrax alert. Evidently, General Powell had relayed the report of a possible agent attack through Number 10 Downing Street, to British commander of forces in Saudi Arabia. The story was complicated by the fact that six British soldiers sharing the same tent had come down with flu-like syndromes. CENTCOM NBCC assured them that the report was negative and offered to sample the soldiers' blood to make sure. The absence of Iraqi chemical attacks during the initial breach was still mystifying, but it was gratefully accepted.

Day-Two

On G+1 (twenty-four hours after the battle, began, February 25), the Marine divisions continued forward. The Tiger Brigade led the 2d MARDIV north toward Kuwait City, while the 1st MARDIV drove toward the Aahmad Al-Jaber Air Base, in fierce fighting. The Marines' M60A3 tank optics relied on ambient light and had difficulty piercing the black oil fire smoke, but the Tiger Brigade's M1 tanks had no such difficulties. Egyptian and Syrian forces drew up behind 2d MARDIV, while the Saudi and Kuwaiti task forces moved up the seacoast. Around 1800 hours, a chemical alert caused the Marines to check with their M256A1 kits, which turned up negative twenty minutes later. While there had been no more reports of chemical mines, radio traffic intercepted from Baghdad to the Iraqi 3rd Corps granting permission to initiate chemical attacks. These attacks never came in part perhaps to the propaganda warning that any leader authorizing such attacks would be treated as a war criminal, or perhaps because the coalition attacks were so successful and quick.

To the west, XVIII ABN Corps had completed its wheel. The 3rd Brigade, 101st ABN DIV assumed the flank guard for the 24th IN DIV, northwest of Nasiriyah and just a few miles north of Tallil air base. The 24th IN DIV took operational control of the 3rd ACR and began its drive east toward the two airbases that might still hold chemical weapons. Early that morning it had secured Objective Grey, where it had expected to find chemical munitions (and once again had found none).

VII Corps continued to attack the Republican Guards. The 2d ACR shifted southeast to make room for 1st AR DIV's advance and began the move east, with 3rd AR DIV training. The 1st AR DIV drove to within artillery range of Nasiriyah before pausing for the night. The British 1st AR DIV had passed through 1st IN DIV that afternoon and moved west against the Iraqi forces in the Wadi. 1st IN DIV began to reconsolidate and move up to the 3rd and 1st AR DIVs to begin a concerted strike east. As the two armored divisions moved closer to the Republican Guards, the commanders called for an increase in the MOPP level to MOPP-2 (suit and boots).

As the 1st IN DIV prepared to move out, there was a change of mission from VII Corps. The 2d Chemical Battalion would move with the 42d Field Artillery Brigade and catch up the 3rd AR DIV. As of 1500 hours, the 2d Chemical Battalion was detached form the 1st IN DIV to join the 3rd AR DIV, the VII Corps main effort. The battalion would support 3rd AR DIV with one smoke generator company and one of the two decon platoons from 323rd Chemical Company. The other smoke generators company had decon platoon would join 1st AR DIV. As the chemical units moved out, the field artillery unit promptly outran them, leaving the 2d Chemical Battalion moving along with the British 1st DIV to catch up to the battle.

The thousands of enemy prisoners of war (EPWs) revealed the Iraqi military's unprepared state. It had been so used to being the stronger side that its defensive equipment was not exactly first-class. Many of the soldiers had thin butyl-rubber fabric overgarments, more a cloak than a protective suit. There was a variety of masks—some Yogoslavian, some Russian some East German, some US and British, and some an Iraqi knock-off of the M17 masks. Geneva protocols dictate that EPWs are allowed to retain their protective masks as a basic survival measure, but there was concern regarding those prisoners without masks. Had Iraq initiated chemical warfare, would the coalition be expected to provide masks for EPWs, when their own stocks were so low? The laws of war seemed to call for this measure. Fortunately, the issue never presented itself—had chemical warfare occurred, CENTCOM would have been in a real moral quandary. Iraqi soldiers' decon kits and detection kits were equally heterogeneous, coming from Poland, Russia, Czechoslovakia, and other former Warsaw Pact countries. Some of the Iraqi prisoners of war told their captors of markings that would identify the chemical munitions; three red rings denoted nerve agent; three green rings choking; and three yellow rings, blister. A blue flare was used by the Iraqis to warn of a nearby friendly chemical strike. This intelligence data turned out to be deliberately erroneous—all the chemical munitions found later were unmarked.

Four of the last nine Fox vehicles had arrived that afternoon at KKMC. One fox went to 3rd ACR, and two foxes were dedicated as ARCENT ORFs. One would be operated by 409th Chemical Battalion troops to provide rear-area reconnaissance against any Scud or aircraft attacks against the vulnerable ARCENT Support Command, with five Foxes on the way. So far, the rear area had remained safe. With the absence of any Iraqi chemical attacks in the breach, most units downgraded their MOPP status to MOPP-1 or 0. As long as the coalition force kept moving tight against the enemy, Iraqi targeting for chemical agents would be difficult.

Day Three

The inhospitable terrain and poor weather on G+2 (February 26) kept progress in the west difficult. The 101st and 82d ABN DIV consolidated their positions in the Euphrates Valley and far left flank of the army. The 24th IN DIV began its roll down Highway 8 toward Jallibah around 1400 hours and ran into two Iraqi infantry division and a Republican Guard division. During a four-hour fire-fight, the 24th IN

DIV destroyed fifty-seven tanks, four artillery battalions and routed the divisions. It stopped south of the two airfields (Tallil and Jalibah).

The Marines circled the outskirts of Kuwait City, fighting off counterattacks as they pushed closer to the city limits. Early that morning, a Fox vehicle reported a lewisite detection. CAMs nearby registered mustard agents, but second readings form the Fox's mass spectrometer and M256A1 its showed no agent present. Air analysis showed high levels of petroleum products due to the burning oil wells, which may have caused false alarms. The 2d MARDIV and Tiger Brigade circled northwest around the city, while the 1st MARDIV attacked and secured the international airport. That night the division had to fight off an Iraqi counterattack to take the airport. With battleship fire support the division fought back and finally secured the airport at 0300 hours the next morning.

VII Corps had consolidated its "first," as Lieutenant General Franks called it, and the 1st and 3d AR DIVs attacked east to engage the armored Republican Guard divisions. The superior optics in the M1A1 tanks cut through the thick black smoke caused by the oil well fires now encountered by VII Corps forces. In the greatest tank battle of the war, 800 American tanks faced off against 300 Iraqi tanks and crushed two Republican Guard division. 1st IN DIV attacked south of the armored divisions to consolidate the eastern flank, as the British division continued to attack east toward Kuwait City. This afternoon was the moment of the 2d ACR's now-famous "*Battle of 73rd Easting*" in its four-hour attack against two Iraqi armored divisions. General Schwarzkopf released 1st CAV DIV to VII Corps, which immediately committed the division forward. The 2d Chemical Battalion, its two smoke generator companies and decon company had just caught up to the action at 1800 hours of the second day. Their third day was spent reorganizing, refueling and re-supplying for the final push in the 3rd AR DIV's support command area. By the time 2d Chemical Battalion caught up to the 3rd AR DIV tactical units on the fourth day, the cease-fire had been announced.

Four more Foxes arrived at KKMC, adding to the 490th's rear area recon capability. One more would arrive early morning of February 27, filling out the rear area recon platoon. This represented the last of the sixty German gift NBCRSs to CENTCOM. Because it was still unclear whether or not Saddam's forces would attack using chemical weapons in a last desperate attack, these Foxes were not too late to be employed.

Day Four

On the fourth day of battle (G+3, February 27), the coalition forces were involved in some brisk engagements with small Iraqi units, but the majority of the enemy force was fleeing towards Basrah. The Marines and Arab forces consolidated their positions around Kuwait City, and the Kuwaiti units officially liberated their capital. Having refueled over the night, the 24th IN DIV occupied the Tallil and Jalibah air fields. Again while Tallil and Jalibah may have held chemical munitions for the Iraq-Iran war, none were found this day. No chemical munitions were found in the Kuwait Theater of Operations by any US forces. Conjecture was that either the air offensive had prevented Iraqi supply convoys from moving munitions to delivery systems in the forward areas, or that Saddam had never given the authorization to do so.

VII Corps was still engaging enemy armor trying to escape north towards the Euphrates. All five divisions and an ACR were now attacking in synchronization against the Republican Guards. The five Iraqi heavy divisions were broken. Offensive operations were ordered halted at 0800 hours on the fifth day, February 28. This gave just enough time for VII Corps to mount one last morning attack to destroy the remaining Iraqi divisions west of Basrah. As the new defensive positions tool hold, CENTCOM began its humanitarian efforts and clean-up operations.

Although this is not a confirmed view, one reason why the coalition forces may not have pushed through and past Basrah was the threat of Iraqi chemical munitions. The Iranians had repeatedly attacked Basrah during their conflict with Iraq, only to be met with stiff defensive positions, massive chemical agent munitions attacks and armored counterattacks. Basrah is the second-largest city in Iraq; its impending fall might have been a tripwire for CB agent munitions releases. Since most of the CENTCOM combat divisions were in and around the Basrah/Kuwait City region, it would have been relatively easy to target US forces, had the coalition divisions pushed the issue.

Post-Combat Operations

One chemical incident occurred immediately after the ground war, on February 28. Private First Class David A. Fisher, a cavalry scout from the 3rd AR DIV, had been exploring enemy bunkers in northern Kuwait for intelligence material and assisting in the demolition of enemy fighting vehicles. During his exploration of one empty bunker, he came into contact with the walls of the interior. Eight hours later, during a radio watch, he experienced blistering and pain along his arms. On March 2, his arms featured more small blisters and reddening. The medics classified him as a possible blister agent casualty and evacuated him to a chemical decon station at C company, 45th Support Battalion.

The doctors identified four blisters about an inch in diameter and confirmed the mustard agent through later analysis of urine and skin samples. Colonel Mike Dunn, commander of the MRICD, personally evaluated and confirmed the results. A Fox from the 3rd AR DIV chemical company arrived, whose detectors confirmed the agent as well. Tech Escort Unit teams evacuated PFC Fisher's ballistic protective vest and coverall sleeve to CRDEc, but the scientists could not detect any agent by that time. Evidently the amount was so small, that it had evaporated.

Because there was no positive information on the marking of chemical munitions, every time CENTCOM units found a weapons cache they treated the site as a potential source of CB agent munitions. In the cases of the larger caches, this called for a Fox vehicle and one or more XM21 RSCAALs to monitor the munitions until it was confirmed safe. Until this time no one had envisioned using the Foxes in this role. While commanders may have thought that the state-of-the-art Fox had the most sophisticated chemical agent detector (the German MM-1 mass spectrometer), it was designed to detect ground contamination, not to operate as a mobile air monitoring systems (but its presence made people more confident). The Marines and SOCCENT both called for Fox vehicles to confirm reports of chemical munitions and suspected chemical weapons bunkers in and around Kuwait City, none of which were positive. The fox vehicles and XM21s were also stationed downwind of munitions demolition sites, with decon units under the 2d Chemical Battalion on stand-by in Kuwait in the event that chemical agent munitions were missed and EOD teams required their assistance.

Two biodetection teams deployed forward to Kuwait City on March 3, collecting eight soil samples in southern Iraq and assisting the FMIB search for chemical munitions within Kuwait. Although no chemical munitions were found, they remained in Kuwait City to assist the FMIB by providing technical information on Iraqi chemical defense equipment. CENTCOM terminated the vaccination program on March 3. The two teams redeployed back to KKMC by March 17, and all teams were back in Fort Lewis by the end of the month.

The corps NBCCs continued to track down reports of possible chemical storage sites throughout the Euphrates River area. Because the demilitarization line ran just south of the river and south of many of the towns and villages, the Army would have to wait for the UN teams to conduct a full inspection of the area. The reserve and active chemical decon companies moved south to support "car wash operations," as the divisions began to load their vehicles on ships and aircraft to re-deploy back to Europe and the United States. This mission eventually diminished, as the engineers established nearly 100 wash points in Kuwait City, Dhahran, al-Damman and al-Jubayl.

As the 1st IN DIV packed its vehicles and equipment for redeployment, it received word from VII Corps that its Foxes had been nominated to stay behind in Saudi Arabia as prepositioned stocks. Given all the difficulties it had seen in obtaining the Foxes, the division bitterly fought the issue, from the chemical company commander all the way to MG Rhame himself. All was to avail. ARCENT had to select someone's six Foxes, and the 1st IN DIV was at the bottom of the priority list. 3rd ACR also had to turn in its vehicles, as it was not their turn to receive the Foxes by the official fielding schedule. The 1st CAV DIV finally received their Foxes from ARCENT as it was returning to Fort Hood. As the units began to deploy back home, the 11th ACR, whose chemical company had just completed its training at Sonthofen (the last US platoon to do so), arrived to assure the peacekeeping role in Kuwait.

UN Inspection Teams

The United Nations Security Council passed Resolution 687 on April 13, 1991; it required Iraq to register its NBC weapons and ballistic missiles, and to destroy, render unusable to remove these weapons and all production and research facilities. The resolution further required that Iraq disclose all its holding and programs, permit on-site inspections, and to permit the destruction of the weapons. In May 1991 the UN set up a special commission (UNSCOM) established by the Secretary General. The UNSCOM teams had a charter to conduct the inspection for weapons of mass destruction throughout Iraq.

The nuclear program exposed by the UNSCOM inspections proved to be much larger than had been previously believed. During the air war, the nuclear site target list had grown from four to eight potential sites; UNSCOM discovered a total of thirty-nine nuclear facilities at nineteen locations across Iraq in its over thirty nuclear inspections. While Iraqi officials had cooperated with the chemical and biological inspections, there was no end of interference with the inspectors for the nuclear sites. Iraqi officials were particularly resistant to granting any access to documents related to the nuclear program. One UNSCOM inspector believed that the Iraqis deliberately gave in on the chemical facilities only in the knowledge that they could rebuild and re-supply these production sites quickly. The nuclear weapon production equipment and material were not so easily replaced, and therefore the UNSCOM teams found significantly more resistance.

The inspection teams found no evidence of biological agents in any bunkers, or of manufacturing equipment at any of the suspected locations. Two inspections for biological agents were conducted by the end of 1992. The UNSCOM team that inspected Salman Pak identified research equipment that could have been used either for offensive or defensive programs, with offensive programs as the primary purpose. During the second inspection, the UN teams singled out the single-cell protein facility at al-Hakem as a potential next step in the Iraqi biological warfare program and recommended continued monitoring of the site. Ten suspected biological agent storage sites were inspected. As mentioned earlier, the Iraqi military had used the suspected refrigerated bunkers for conventional munitions and electronic components rather than for storing biological munitions. The Special Commission found no conclusive evidence of an offensive biological warfare program at that time. Later evidence, however, told a different story.

Based on Iraqi declarations through August 1995, the total capability of Iraq's BW program was formidable. It had manufactured 11,800 liters of botulinum toxin 8,825 liters of anthrax spores, 2,200 liters of aflatoxin and 340 liters of clostridium perfringens toxin (gas gangrene). In 1990 the Iraqi military had tested both anthrax and botulinum toxin in live agent weapons tests. During December 1990 Iraq had deployed 150 filled bombs (100 botulinum toxin, fifty anthrax) and twenty-five Scud missiles with biological agent warheads (thirteen botulinum toxin, ten anthrax, two aflatoxin) to forward storage locations. Three 2,000-liter aerial spray tanks had been stored for the purpose of anthrax dispersement, ready for use in the early months of 1991. In September 1995 Iraq admitted to conducting biological warfare research, development and storage at Al Fallujah, Muthanna, Salman Pak, Al-Kindi and Al Hakam. The Iraqi government had claimed to have destroyed all biological agents and their delivery systems prior to June 1991.

The first inspection of chemical munitions sites was UNSCOM-2 which focused on the primary declared site at the Muthanna facility near Samarra. This inspection, carried out June 9-14, 1991, was not a thorough, detailed investigation but a broad-brush attempt to get an idea of the scope of effort necessary for future inspection. The second chemical team, consisting of twenty-two people from eleven nations, assembled in Bahrain to prepare for the inspection. On August 15, its members entered Iraq to begin their inspection work. They began with one day at each of the three "*precursor*" facilities at al-Fallujah, followed by two days at the Muthanna facility, and one day at the al-Taqqadum air base, south of Baghdad. The team was to identify any chemical agents that had been produced, what precursors were used, the industrial site capability, where the munitions and bulk agent were stored, and any other pertinent CBW activities. Muthanna and the three precursor facilities had been elaborately defended, but the overwhelming air superiority of the coalition effectively had destroyed all four sites.

The Muthanna State Establishment facility featured two pilot plants and a destruction site in addition to its manufacturing capabilities. The main complex was quite large, measuring over twenty-five square kilometers. It had been legitimately producing pesticides after the Iran-Iraq cease-fire in 1988; after the ware had ended, it was no longer cost-efficient to maintain a chemical warfare production line, and the Iraqis changed the production to pesticides to support the state's agricultural business. It changed back to its original purpose in August 1990 and was producing chemical agents in October and December. These production runs were necessary to replace nerve agent munitions which, due to poor quality, were degrading in effectiveness. In addition to basic chemical munitions R&D, it produced mustard gas, tabun, sarin and nerve agent GF. The plant also filled chemical munitions manufactured at other facilities. It appeared that the initial estimates of poor quality control in the production of nerve agents had been correct. The Iraqis had developed the ability to make 70 percent pure nerve agent at best, with an average standard of 55 percent. The effectiveness of their nerve agent would have significantly degraded if stored over forty-five days.

The largest precursor site, Habbaniyah 2 at al-Maamoun, had produced a wide variety of precursors, including several industrial chemicals (chlorine, hydrochloric acid, caustic soda and sodium hypochlorite) as well as the chemical agent precursors (thionyl chloride, difluoro and dichloro-methyl phosphine oxide, phosphorus trichloride, methyl phosphite). The second plant, Habbaniyah 1 at al-Farouk, formulated pesticides, produced plastic bottles, and stored the precursors. The teams found twelve tons of di-isopropylamine, twenty-five tons of dimethylamine hydrochloride, forty tons of thiodiglycol, and fifty-five tons of 2-chlorobenzaldehyde (the last chemical being a precursor for CS agent). Enough precursors existed to manufacture 500 tons of VX nerve agent. The forty tons of thiodiglycol included a large shipment originating from Baltimore, Maryland, that had been sent through Jordan to Iraq prior to the Kuwaiti invasion (but during the embargo against Iraq).

The last facility, Habbaniyah 3, had no chemicals, as its production had been suspended at the end of 1987. Ironically, it was the most thoroughly bombed of the three sites. At the Al Taqqadum air base the inspection team found 200 mustard bombs, a few of which were leaking. The bombs were not marked, nor were they stored in any special fashion. This was also the case for chemical munitions later found near al-Nassariyah in October 1991. It seems that the Iraqi army had special escort units to accompany movements of chemical weapons from production and filling to the storage areas, and from these storage areas to the delivery systems. This negated the need to mark munitions, since most were made to be employed shortly after production.

The majority of the chemical munitions examined in August were degraded and tactically insignificant. Few of the GB/GF-filled 122 mm rockets were functional, their chemical agents having lost much of their lethality. The "*binary*" munitions were not truly binary, as the US military had designed its weapon systems. These munitions required an individual to mix the chemicals manually and then rush the weapon to the delivery system. Once made the chemical agent immediately began to degrade, making it essential to use the weapons at that time or not at all. Records showed that the Iraqi Ministry of Defense had ordered 8,320 rockets filled with about fifty tons of binary mix in December 1990. It should be emphasized that although the UNSCOM team found these weapons degraded in August 1991, they were most likely potent and very much a threat to the coalition in the summer and fall months, the Iraqis declared that they had destroyed.

In addition to what was found, the Iraqis declared that they had destroyed 19,000 122 mm rockets, 800 aerial bombs, and forty-five binary agent-filled al-Hussein missiles warheads prior to the inspection.

They also revealed 82 mm/120 mm CS-filled mortar shells and CS-filled RPG-7 infantry rockets. Notably absent from this list is any record of chemical-filled land mines.

Of the more than 350,000 mines removed since the end of the war, no chemical land mines have been discovered (contrary to Marine Corps's reports). By the end of 1992, UNSCOM had completed fifteen chemical inspections and three biological inspections in Iraq. Technical escort units transported all chemical munitions that were safe to move to al-Muthanna and its chemical destruction facility. All chemical munitions discovered were destroyed by late 1993 by incinerating the mustard agents and hydrolyzing the nerve agents.

Upon returning to Bahrain on August 23, the inspection team made the following conclusions. The Iraqi military command had expected the ware to be a sequel of the earlier Iran-Iraq War. Its production sites had been well protected; there had been good communications and unrestricted movement during that war; and the leaders assumed that this would be the case again. The Iraqi leadership had not accounted for the incredible accuracy of allied air attacks and the total loss of airspace control. Its production sites proved to be much more vulnerable than airspace control. Its production time had not allowed them to build up a sufficient stockpile prior to the destruction of those facilities in the air campaign. The neutralization of their air force, a prime delivery system, and the destruction of the transportation infrastructure meant that the only real chemical delivery capabilities that Iraq had at the beginning of the ground offensive were artillery and rockets, which were thoroughly targeted.

There were a number of GB/GF-filled warheads for the al-Hussein missiles still available, which could have been used against Israeli or Saudi cities or to harass and delay the supplies and troops at Dammam, Dhahran or KKMC. There was, however, no effective means for Iraq to carry out a protracted CBW campaign against the coalition forces, whatever the desire to do so. Iraqi EPWs stated that the massive artillery suppression had stopped them from even planning a coordinated chemical strike, since they could not hope to mass the amount of chemical munitions on target to be militarily effective. However, their few weapon systems still could have severely disrupted the coalition offensive because of the psychological impact on military leaders and troops. This assumption that the Iraqis could disrupt combat operational temp and cause massive casualties had kept US forces on edge for six months as they prepared their chemical defense plans.

MG McCaffrey offered two insights as to why there was no chemical warfare in a talk to chemical officers at Fort McClellan. First, every time a chemical officer had the opportunity, he or she had shown reporters, congressional delegations and other visitors how prepared their units were to survive and sustain combat operations in a CB-contaminated environment without any substantial effects to their combat strength. Not only did they state that opinion, the soldiers and leaders of the 24th IN DIV believed it. They did not state that it would make life utter misery—but they would be alive.

General Powell shared this same confidence, that while the soldiers were threatened by biological agent weapons, and the cities by Scud chemical warheads, the soldiers could have performed well under chemical warfare conditions. This preparedness may have convinced those in Baghdad that chemical weapons would only anger the Americans, not stop them. This point did not alter Saddam's use of the chemical weapons arsenal as a strategic bluff, one card to force the CENTCOM coalition to spend six months preparing for what they thought would be a grueling and high casualty battle.

Second, McCaffrey remained unconvinced that Saddam would not have ordered the use of CB agent munitions despite the US defense preparations. The Iraqi soldiers had protective masks, overgarments and decon kits ready for something. US national policy still asserted the right to retaliate in kind, despite a commitment by the current administration to demilitarize the chemical arms stockpile. It could be that they did fear the possibility of US retaliation with chemical weapons, or the threat of British, French or Israeli retaliation with nuclear weapons. Steady diplomatic pressure, combined with strong psychological warfare against using CB agent munitions, may have had an effect on the Iraqi field commanders. Iraqi political and military leaders were never quite sure what the coalition nations meant when they talked about retaliation. Later statements from Iraqi commanders stressed their fear that the United States would retaliate with nuclear or chemical weapons. Their forces were not prepared to defend against chemical weapons, and this concern kept CB agent munitions from being used.

Other possible explanations exist. Iraqi forces did not face the situations that had prodded them to use chemical agents against Iran. CENTCOM stopped prior to taking Basrah, as opposed to Iran's attempts to capture one of the major cities in the country. There was no drive against Baghdad to spur last- second desperation tactics. Also, the continually declining quality of nerve agent might have played a part in the decision not use chemical munitions, especially as the production lines were shut down. There was no capability after January 1991 to replenish the stocks, and it may be that Saddam was reserving his few Scud CB agent-filled warheads, artillery shells and spray tanks for a coalition attack against Baghdad.

The US military had received an unexpected reprieve from a test of its chemical defense capability. Nonetheless, US forces should not have had to build up their readiness to desperately in the last half of 1990. Chemical soldiers met to discuss how these lessons might be captured and what was needed to improve US armed forces' defensive capability for future battles.

9

MICROFLUIDIC DEVICES

The microchip revolution made possible today's miniaturized electronics industry. In like manner, the microchip is changing laboratory instruments that analyze fluids. Large and costly instruments are being replaced by microchip-based systems known as microfluidic devices. These miniature systems move fluids through a maze of microscopic channels and chambers that have been fabricated with the same lithographic techniques used for microelectronics.

Microfluidic devices are fashioned from silicon, glass, plastics, and ceramics into 2- or 3-square-centimeter slices with cover plates. In them, red blood cells, bacteria, *biological macromolecules* (such as proteins and DNA), *polystyrene beads* (that bond to targeted macromolecules), and other materials can be manipulated in channels with characteristic length scales on the order of 100 micrometers. The devices integrate sensors, actuators, and other electromechanical components to dispense with myriad moving parts and the people required to operate and service them.

Microscale instruments and processing are the future of medical research and the chemical and pharmaceutical industries. Microfluidic devices hold the promise of a small analytical laboratory on a chip to identify, separate, and purify cells, biomolecules, toxins, and other materials. They would perform these tasks with greater speed, sensitivity, efficiency, and affordability than standard instruments.

They might also be used in the future for detecting chemical and biological warfare agents, delivering precise amounts of prescription drugs, keeping tabs on blood parameters for hospital patients, and monitoring air and water quality.

For more than a decade, Lawrence Livermore researchers have been working on several aspects of microfluidic devices. The Laboratory's Center for Microtechnology has more than 30 experts in electronics, biology, optics, and engineering who are developing microfluidic components for transporting, sensing, separating, mixing, and storing fluids and their constituents. Current Livermore projects include the design and prototyping of devices for the human genome program, chemical and biological warfare agent detection, and medical analysis.

First Complete Model Designed

To help guide the design of microfluidic devices at the Center for *Microtechnology* and elsewhere, a team of Livermore researchers is developing a complex, three-dimensional simulation tool. The team consists of chemical engineers David Clague and Elizabeth Wheeler, postdoctoral mechanical engineer Todd Weisgraber, and University of California (UC) at Berkeley student Gary Hon. In this work, they collaborate with other Livermore researchers from several disciplines as well as colleagues at universities. The team has been funded for the past three years by the Laboratory Directed Research and Development (LDRD) Program through Livermore's Center for Computational Engineering and, more recently, by the Defense Advanced Research Projects Agency (DARPA) of the Department of Defense.

The team's computer code has drawn increasing interest because it provides an accurate representation of the behaviour of suspended particles, especially polystyrene beads and biological macromolecules, as they travel inside a microfluidic device. The simulation capability incorporates into a single numerical code complex channel geometries and such parameters as fluid flow rates, particle interactions, and external forces. "We want to predict the complex interplay of the forces involved in microfluids to give designers a way to accurately predict how beads, cells, and macromolecules will behave," says team leader Clague.

Clague notes that suspended particles traveling within *microscopic channels* are subject to a number of physical forces that influence their transport and separation from each other and the channel walls. The forces, such as subtle electrical attractions and repulsions, can be used to achieve the movement and manipulation of suspended particles in ways that would not work in traditional bench-scale laboratory instruments. The Livermore simulation capability provides a new tool to assist microfluidic device designers who want to engineer systems that will reliably move, separate, concentrate, and identify suspended particles of interest.

With effective simulation, the designers can see the effects of design decisions before they build a prototype. For example, a designer may want to position selected biological macromolecules in the central region of a microchannel for capture by an electric field and therefore must determine what field strength will be required. Or a designer may want to see how restricting a channel with a tiny post might affect the fluid flow rate and the mixing behaviour of particles as they are forced to "*slalom*" around it.

The program uses a form of the Boltzmann transport equation called the *lattice Boltzmann equation* (LBE) to represent the behaviour of fluids and suspended particles within microfluidic devices. (Ludwig Boltzmann was an Austrian physicist whose greatest achievement was the development of statistical mechanics, which explains how the microscopic constituents of matter—atoms and their properties—determine macroscopic properties such as thermal conductivity or viscosity.) In recent years, the LBE method has gained popularity and usefulness in simulating the flow of complex gases and liquids. It is based on a statistical description of the fluid on a cubic lattice in which each lattice site represents up to several thousand individual fluid molecules.

In the team's numerical model, spheres represent polystyrene beads and biological macromolecules within the lattice. The spheres can be assigned different sizes, densities, and electrical properties. Because of their size, the spheres can occupy several lattice sites. The code tracks the spheres as they move on the lattice and calculates the extent to which the spheres interact with each other, the channel walls, the fluid, and external forces that may be applied to manipulate them. The simulation tracks the time evolution of both the fluid and suspended spheres. The *algorithms* (mathematical routines) used by the program tend to be readily applied, allowing calculations in a straightforward manner and making it easy to incorporate new forces.

A Natural for Parallel Computing

Because the LBE method is naturally suited for parallel computing, the simulation capability is designed for large computers, preferably supercomputers that use tens to hundreds of microprocessors together. Simulations representing time scales on the order of tens of seconds of continuous suspension require a few days of computer time. The team uses several Livermore machines for their simulations, including the Compass Cluster and two massively parallel supercomputers: Blue, the 740-gigaops unclassified portion of Blue Pacific, one of the Department of Energy's Accelerated Strategic Computing Initiative supercomputers, and the 680-gigaops TeraCluster2000. The TeraCluster2000 is the preferred computing platform; simulations on it use up to 50 microprocessors working simultaneously.

One important advantage of the code is its flexibility. The simulated suspended particles can be assigned different physical and electrical attributes, including electrostatic forces that cause fluids containing biological macromolecules to act far less predictably than ideal species, which would consist of hard, inert spheres. External forces such as gravity, alternating current, or direct current can be simulated. These forces can be turned on and off to isolate their specific effects on particle behaviour. Livermore engineer Peter Krulevitch, a microfluidic device project leader, says that until now, no program was capable of simulating all the forces acting on fluids containing particles. "The problem has just been too complex," he says.

The LBE method contrasts with traditional fluid modeling based on finite-element analysis and boundary element methods, which typically deal with pure fluids. Results from the Livermore code, however, can be handed off to larger-scale computer-aided design simulation tools that use standard finite-element analysis.

Mike Pocha, a Center for Microtechnology section leader, notes that device designers can build prototype devices—a long and painstaking process—and determine their capabilities or, preferably, simulate them first and then build a prototype guided by the simulation results. Going from concept to manufacturing a prototype is increasingly more time-consuming and expensive as microfluidic devices get more complex, says Clague. "With a more comprehensive simulation tool, researchers will be better able to predict what will happen to the suspended species in these complex microenvironments. Ultimately, such a capability will speed the design effort and reduce costs."

The physics involved with the operation of microfluidic devices is complex and varies, depending on the fluid, the molecules suspended in the fluid, and the extent, if any, of external fields. In building the code, the team has steadily added capabilities that more completely represent the physical forces at work in *microfluidic devices*. After every addition of a new feature, the team makes sure the results are in excellent agreement with existing theory and, where possible, with published alternative numerical methods.

LDRD Laid the Groundwork

One of the team's first accomplishments under LDRD funding was simulating hydrodynamic forces acting on a stationary sphere. These forces are dependent on the velocity of the suspending fluid and the proximity of the suspended particles to channel walls. The LBE method naturally takes into account the entire spectrum of fluid and particle behaviour, including inertial effects and hydrodynamic interactions between suspended particles. In other words, the simulations account for the minute disturbances propagated within a fluid by the particles that *"feel"* each other's presence and, as a result, change their trajectories and the properties of the fluid.

The *hydrodynamic forces*, including inertial effects, are particularly well captured. The first is the *drag force*, which is a result of the fluid exerting a force on a suspended particle because of differences in fluid and particle velocities. The second force is a *lift force*, which is caused by small inertial effects and gradients in fluid velocity. The lift force is exerted perpendicular to the flow, causing the species to migrate to the center of the channel. Also coming into play is a particle's density, which affects its buoyancy within a fluid and the extent to which it can be lifted.

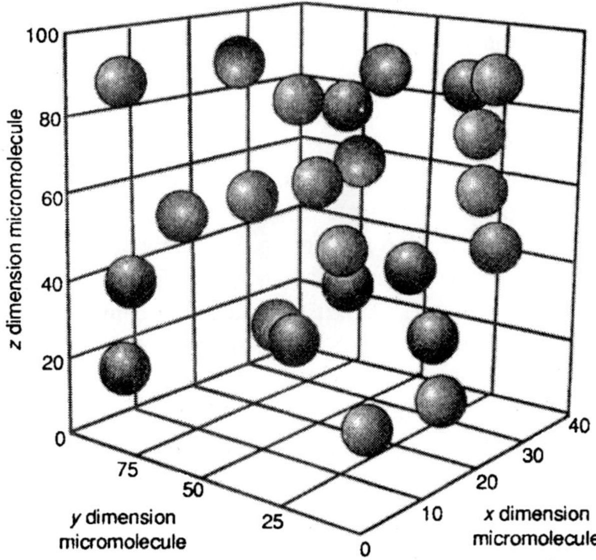

Fig. 9.1. Simulations using the lattice Boltzmann equation method are based on a cubic lattice, here with dimensions of 40 by 100 by 100 micrometers. Spheres represent polystyrene beads and biological macromolecules within the lattice.

Fluids normally flow through microfluidic channels without turbulence so that suspended particles typically mix only by diffusion. One of the key parameters used to characterize fluid flow is the Reynolds number, which defines flow conditions and measures the relative importance of inertial effects to viscous effects. Most fluid flow in small channels occurs at a low (but finite) Reynolds number. However, even at small Reynolds numbers, researchers have found that there are small lift effects. The Livermore simulation capability takes into account these inertial effects for predicting the extent of lift as a function of Reynolds numbers.

The code also simulates the effects on particles that are near channel walls. Much like the effect of a boat's wake, the motions of molecules cause disturbances in the fluid that bounce off the channel walls and reflect back on the particles. Close to the walls, particles experience forces retarding their motion, and even closer to the walls, they experience large resistive forces known as lubricating forces.

Adding Real Effects

If the simulation is to be accurate, it must also account for non-Newtonian characteristics that are exhibited by biofluids containing human cells, bacteria, and *biological macromolecules* such as proteins and DNA. These materials do not behave like electrically neutral and perfectly round spheres. Instead, they have widely varying shapes, densities, and often electrical charges that are asymmetrically distributed.

More importantly, these materials tend to have elastic character, which gives rise to unexpected effects. Strands of DNA, for example, can be long and gangly with a preferred, three-dimensional shape that orients itself in a particular manner to its neighbours. If forced to travel through a narrow channel, the strands deform but then exert a small force in an attempt to recover their favoured configuration, much like a compressed spring reverts to its normal shape. If there is a sufficient concentration of such strands, this restoring force can have a profound effect on fluid behaviour.

Depending on their concentration, particles interact with each other and with the channel walls. Under certain conditions, they can coagulate with each other or stick to walls because of *van der Waals* and *electrostatic forces* (electrical attraction and repulsion forces between species). The simulation team is incorporating these and other forces associated with biological macromolecules into the models, including *hydrophobic* (water hating) and *hydrophilic* (water loving) interactions. Clague explains that some proteins have hydrophobic regions that cause the proteins to aggregate when they are in close proximity to other proteins; therefore, these unique forces must be taken into account.

Last August, the team began work for DARPA, the advanced research arm of the Department of Defense and a major backer of *microfluidic technology*. One of DARPA's goals is to develop devices called *BioFluidic Chips* (*BioFlips*) that will identify biological macromolecules and microbes based on certain electrical or chemical properties. Soldiers would use *BioFlips* devices both to detect chemical and biological agents and to monitor their own general health. As part of the microfluidic development effort, a program called Simulation of Biomolecular Microsystems (*Simbiosys*) is funding the development of advanced computational tools for the *BioFlips* design effort. The Livermore team's simulation work is part of the *Simbiosys* program.

Focus on Dielectrophoresis

The team's work for DARPA builds upon LDRD research, particularly with regard to simulating the coupling of hydrodynamic and dielectrophoretic forces. Dielectrophoresis (DEP) is an efficient and increasingly popular method for separating molecules in microflows. DEP electrodes generate nonuniform, alternating current electric fields that induce electrical polarization in target species. On an absolute scale, the force is quite small, but in microfluids, the force can be quite effective in manipulating and positioning biological macromolecules with electrodes using less than 10 volts. The degree of induced polarization is dependent on the electrical properties of the molecule, the surrounding fluid, and the magnitude and frequency of the applied electric field.

"Different species typically have their own unique dielectric response fingerprint that can be exploited by DEP," says Clague. As a result, DEP can be used to select from among a number of different particles suspended in the same fluid. The selected particle will either be drawn toward or repelled from the region of high field intensity (toward or away from the DEP electrode located within a channel wall). The first instance is referred to as *positive DEP*, and the second is referred to as *negative DEP*.

DEP forces can be switched on and off to selectively capture cells, bacteria, spores, polystyrene beads, DNA, proteins, and other matter. Once captured, the molecules can be held in place or, with the removal of the force, sent on their way to a different location for analysis. For example, DEP can be used to selectively capture a suspected pathogen. The pathogen would then be shuttled to a different area where its DNA would be extracted and analyzed.

The DEP simulation work involves close collaboration with pathologist Peter Gascoyne at the University of Texas M.D. Anderson Cancer Center in Houston, Texas. Gascoyne and his colleagues, in a project sponsored by DARPA, are developing an instrument that uses DEP to separate cells and identify them based on their dielectric properties. A *prototype* has been used on whole blood samples to separate malignant cells from normal cells.

An important group of simulations is focused on examining the interplay of suspended particle concentration, flow rates (and inertial lift effects), and DEP forces with the effects from different kinds of suspended particles. Preliminary simulations show that the *hydrodynamic interactions* between particles can screen and thwart DEP forces; therefore, concentration effects become very important. The suspended particles that are not screened encounter a positive DEP force and are pulled to the electrode surface, where they are held motionless.

The team is continuing to enhance the numerical model to investigate the forces influencing DEP manipulation of molecules suspended in flowing fluids. One research avenue they are taking is to give biological macromolecules more realistic characteristics. For example, the team has explored replacing the simulated spheres with more accurate bead-and-spring representations of long-chain polymers such as DNA fragments. Also under development are representations of cell properties unique to organelles and membranes, which can significantly influence the response. Finally, the team is working on the inclusion of electrostatic and *van der Waals forces* as well as *hydrophobic* and *hydrophilic interactions*.

The team has collaborated with UC Berkeley researchers on developing arrays of 50-micrometer-diameter needles. The goal is to deliver drugs more efficiently, but interactions between particles cause the microneedles to become clogged. The Livermore team's simulation work is targeted at obtaining a better understanding of the problem. This work complements a DARPA-funded project at UC Davis, where researchers are developing microneedle arrays for drawing body fluids painlessly to *monitor soldiers*' health on the battlefield.

Clague expects the simulation program to become increasingly useful as applications for microfluidic devices expand. By providing a tool that allows microfluidic device designers to turn the variety of physical forces at play on and off, the team hopes to make possible the discovery of new ways to manipulate suspended particles. Such detailed and accurate simulations speed the design and development of novel *microfluidic devices*. As a result, the simulation effort may well have an important role in saving soldiers' lives and in developing new medical devices that could help drive down national health care costs.

10

ZEROING IN ON GENES

Almost every cell in the human body contains the same set of genes. But not all of the genes are used, or expressed, by those cells. For example, some processes that are particular to cells in the liver are completely unused in brain cells. Ever since genomic research began, scientists have been searching the tangle of DNA for the expressed genes, the ones that really matter.

If one thinks of the nucleus of a cell as a library, then the chromosomes in the cell are bookshelves and the genes are the books on each shelf. Almost every cell in an organism contains the same libraries and the same sets of books. The books represent all of the information (the DNA) that every cell in the body needs so that it can grow and carry out its various functions. Two challenges complicate the process of locating our genes: Not all of the genes are expressed in any one tissue, and less than 10 percent of our DNA is actually used to make genes. Only occasional passages in the library's written material are important. A team at Livermore led by molecular biologist Allen Christian has developed Gene Recovery Microdissection (GRM), a process that can weed out the unexpressed genetic material from a piece of DNA. With GRM, scientists can isolate all of the genes in a chromosomal region that are being used by a specific tissue at any point in time. GRM can be used for any plant or animal species. A variant of this method can also be used to clone all of the DNA of any organism, including bacteria, even those that cannot be cultured.

"It's not always necessary to sequence the entire genome of a species to locate its gene," says Christian. "With GRM, we can focus on particular regions of a genome that are of interest."

Amplification Twice Does the Trick

The product of gene expression is messenger RNA (*ribonucleic acid*), or mRNA. Typically, before work begins to isolate expressed genes, the mRNA molecules are converted into more stable complementary DNA molecules called cDNA, which has exactly the same sequence as the mRNA but is easier to handle in the laboratory. Then the cDNA is combined on a microscope slide with chromosomes. The cDNA molecules hybridize to the chromosome regions corresponding to the genes of which their parent mRNA is a product. Using tiny glass needles and microdissection, scientists can isolate regions of the chromosomes of interest and, with them, the hybridized cDNA molecules. Finally, amplification by *polymerase chain reaction* (PCR) is used to produce many copies of the molecules in preparation for DNA sequencing.

The basic technique of using microdissection to isolate genes has existed for about five years. But no commercially available gene libraries have been generated because of inefficiencies in the hybridization and subsequent PCR amplification processes. Because genes are typically represented only once in a chromosome, a maximum of one cDNA molecule will be present for each expressed gene following microdissection. Successful hybridization, dissection, and PCR amplification of a single molecule is virtually impossible. Gene libraries made with this procedure are too incomplete to be useful.

Livermore's GRM process overcomes this inefficiency by combining cytogenetics and genomics with chromosome microdissection. CRM increases both the number of targets available for cDNA hybridization and the total number of cDNA molecules in each region following hybridization.

The trick is to perform PCR amplification in situ, on the slide rather than in a tube, which is the conventional means. And it occurs twice. First, prior to hybridization, random-primed PCR of the chromosomes on the slide produces many copies of the target DNA, significantly improving the chances of cDNA hybridization. Second, following the hybridization, another PCR amplification using primers specific for the ends of the cDNA molecules increases the numbers of bound cDNA molecules. Instead of isolating just one cDNA molecule per expressed gene in a region, the GRM process recovers hundreds or even thousands of cDNA molecules. This simple step makes possible the production of highly useful chromosome-region-specific libraries.

GRM has other advantages. While cells generally contain only one or two copies of a gene, some genes make thousands of copies of mRNA and others make only a few copies. Finding mRNA molecules with a low number of copies amid the "noise" of the more numerous gene products can be difficult with conventional methods of making cDNA libraries. But the hybridization step in GRM results in a balanced library in which mRNA molecules with high and low numbers of copies are equally represented.

Several companies offer processes that provide partial information about gene expression and genomic location. But no other single technique identifies both known and unknown expressed genes and determines the part of the genome that regulates their expression. GRM makes possible in one process what multiple processes could previously handle only in part, and it does so cost effectively. Current estimates are that the costs associated with GRM will be substantially less than those of traditional methods. The process is also significantly faster.

Benefits Abound

GRM was invented to allow researchers to identify cancer genes in chromosomal regions for which no genomic information existed. Initially, these were regions for which scientists had good evidence of their importance in rat mammary cancer but almost no other knowledge. To identify the genes expressed in these regions, researchers needed a quick, simple, inexpensive, and reliable method of identifying and characterizing both new and previously known genes in chromosomes.

GRM focuses on data that current genomic sequencing efforts do not provide, namely, information concerning the expression of genes in specific regions of abnormal cells, such as those found in cancerous tissue. "We are using GRM to learn which genes are expressed in certain parts of chromosomes in cancer cells," says Christian. "We can then compare our data with data from the Human Genome Project and learn how these particular cancer cells differ from normal cells."

GRM will be used to generate chromosome-specific and chromosome-region-specific libraries of genes that are expressed for any tissue, normal or diseased, of any organism that can have its chromosomes spread on a microscope slide. Once these libraries have been produced, they can easily be placed on microarrays and made available to other investigators for more detailed analyses, including gene expression studies. GRM can thus be used to create a systematic approach to identifying genes expressed in virtually every species of interest to humans. This capability opens the door to sequencing many plant and animal species that might otherwise be ignored because of the prohibitive cost of genomic analysis. Agriculture, environmental sciences, and veterinary medicine will all benefit.

GRM technology provides the preliminary step toward a full genomic analysis of an organism, allowing time and money to be saved during the full analysis. This invention will enable scientists to identify genes that are expressed after exposure to drugs, environmental chemicals, or radiation. Toxicologists can study the reactions of cells and organisms to chemical and radiation exposure, furthering basic understanding of the molecular mechanisms involved in responses to adverse environments. Similarly, the pharmaceutical industry will be able to decipher biological responses to drugs.

11

Biomedical Research Benefits

The short history of *accelerator mass spectrometry* (AMS) for biomedical research at Livermore has been sweet indeed. Just 10 years ago, Livermore scientists first used AMS to determine how low doses of a suspected carcinogen affect the DNA of mice. A remarkably sensitive measuring technique, AMS can seek out one carbon-14 isotope from among a quadrillion other carbon atoms. It achieved a tenfold improvement in detecting damaged DNA over the best methods then available, thus enabling studies to be conducted directly with humans. Ever since, Livermore has been expanding the development of AMS for biomedical and pharmaceutical applications and is today a recognized leader in the field.

Livermore researchers are continuing to study the effects of carcinogens on humans and animals. Perhaps not surprisingly, they have discovered that humans and animals metabolize these substances differently, with resulting differences in the way DNA is affected. AMS is being used in collaborations with researchers from around the world to begin to solve many challenges in biomedicine—from examining the way we metabolize vitamins to developing a new cancer diagnostic test. AMS has even proved invaluable for learning how pesticides move through ant colonies from workers to the queen.

When Livermore proposed that the *National Institutes of Health* (NIH) establish a National Research Resource for AMS at Livermore, University of California (UC) and Department of Energy scientists provided key testimony to demonstrate the value of AMS. Along with all the other evidence, their testimony must have been persuasive. Last November, Lawrence Livermore joined an elite group of research facilities when NIH awarded the five-year grant. There are other NIH Research Resource facilities for various types of mass spectrometry, but this is the first for AMS. An NIH review of Livermore's proposal had this to say:

> An overwhelming case was made for the need for an AMS resource and a number of outstanding collaborative projects have already been initiated.... At the present time, the LLNL Resource is clearly the most advanced site in the U.S. to explore the use of AMS in biomedical research.

Chemist John Knezovich, director of Livermore's Center for Accelerator Mass Spectrometry (CAMS), is pleased with progress to date. "CAMS is unique in this country in concentrating on biological AMS. Beyond integrating the Laboratory's scientific expertise in both AMS and biomedical research, CAMS provides a major facility that is enabling research projects from all over the world."

He adds, "A big plus is that in addition to the large, multipurpose AMS machine that we've had for years, a much smaller one will soon come on line that is dedicated to biological studies using carbon-14. And, we have begun to use yet another new spectrometer for biological samples that have been tagged with tritium, a new tracer element for AMS. On top of that, we have added a heavy-isotope line to our large AMS machine for studies of *plutonium*."

An important aspect of Livermore's work to date has been in establishing AMS as a routine biomedical research tool. An AMS experiment no longer requires a large and expensive staff of physicists and technicians. Livermore scientists have led the technological advances necessary to make AMS a more effective, dependable, and economic tool for the biomedical, pharmaceutical, chemical, and clinical communities.

Established in 1989, CAMS was designed to diagnose the fission products of *atomic tests*; monitor the spread of *nuclear weapons* to other countries by detecting telltale radioisotopes in air, water, and soil samples; and use isotopic tracers to study climate and geologic records. It still does all these things today—and much, much more.

Sensitivity is the Key

So what is the value of AMS to you and me? AMS is an ideal method for tracing the passage of chemicals through humans without disturbing normal metabolic processes. Perhaps researchers want to know how the human body metabolizes a drug or vitamin. The molecules of the substance are manipulated slightly to "*tag*" them with a *radioactive isotope*, typically carbon-14, though other radioisotopes may be used as well. Rare radioisotopes of elements found in organic materials are used as tracers because they can be incorporated into biomolecules and because they are present naturally at low levels, so tagged molecules can be detected easily.

A collection of human subjects swallows or otherwise ingests the substance. Then, using AMS to measure the number of carbon-14 atoms in samples of urine, feces, saliva, or blood over the next hours, days, and weeks, researchers can trace how much of the substance is absorbed, how it travels through the body, what organs it affects, how much of it is lost through excretion, and so on. The first experiment to trace the vitamin folic acid in a human followed a single dose of just 35 micrograms for a remarkable 200 days.

Information this detailed has never before been available using healthy human subjects. Less sensitive measuring techniques, such as scintillation counting, require ingesting large doses of both the chemical being studied and the radioisotope, something few people want to do. Sometimes, such studies are done with volunteers. Usually, however, scientists have used animals for their research. Then considerable extrapolating has been required: from large doses to small doses and from laboratory animals to humans.

Now researchers can use much smaller, more realistic doses on human subjects. They can measure the true effects of a typical dose of, say, *vitamin A* or *aspirin*. AMS, the only method that can trace these low doses over such long time periods, has been described as the most significant new tool for nutritional studies since the 1930s.

And the amount of radioactivity taken in with the chemical being studied is less than one would encounter during a single day's exposure to background ionizing radiation from walking around in the sunshine. (Cosmic rays contain a small amount of radioactivity that we are exposed to every day.) An airplane flight exposes us to far more ionizing radiation than participation in one of these experiments.

Biochemist Ken Turteltaub, one of the developers of AMS for biological applications, is sold on the process. He says, "With accelerator mass spectrometry, we can address problems that cannot be solved otherwise."

Grant Recognizes Achievement

The Livermore team spent five years building and demonstrating the capabilities that led to the NIH grant to Livermore. Today, Turteltaub is the grant's principal investigator, assisted by fellow biochemist Karen Dingley and a team of CAMS scientists. As an NIH Research Resource for biological AMS, Livermore is charged with providing biological researchers throughout the country with access to carbon-14 AMS analysis in their research, developing new methods and instrumentation for the use of AMS in biomedical research, demonstrating new applications, and educating the biomedical research community on AMS. All of these functions have been under way at Livermore for many years, which makes award of the grant particularly gratifying as recognition of a job well done.

All NIH Research Resource grants focus on collaborative work in order to educate the biosciences community. For this grant, Turteltaub and his cohorts are working to expand support for the use of AMS and to export its use to as many researchers as possible.

In work that is just beginning, they are also developing new experimental methods so that AMS can be applied to as many types of biological research as possible. They are developing the sample preparation and analytical methods necessary to reduce handling, automate processes, and increase sample throughput. The team will explore new spectrometer components that allow the direct interface of bioanalytical instrumentation to the spectrometer for simplified, rapid, on-line analysis. Finally, further development of the small carbon-14 spectrometer will help to bring AMS machines to more bioanalytical laboratories.

Measuring Damage to Molecules

Turteltaub, Dingley, and other researchers at Livermore are already involved in several collaborations with researchers in the U.S. and England to examine the effects of substances produced by cooking meat. Both 2-amino-1-methyl-6-phenylimidazo [4,5-b]pyridine (PhIP) and 2-amino-3,8-dimethylimidazo[4,5-f]quinoxaline (MeIQx) are *heterocyclic aromatic amines* that have been shown to cause cancer in laboratory animals when administered at high doses. The team has used AMS to establish whether DNA and protein adducts (damage) can be detected in laboratory animals and humans when they take in a smaller, more typical dietary amount of these substances.

In numerous experiments using *carbon-14*-tagged PhIP and MeIQx molecules, the team has confirmed not only that adducts can be detected at low doses, but also that humans may be more sensitive to these substances than mice or rats. These results are important because researchers in the fields of *toxicology*, *pharmacology*, and nutrition currently make two basic assumptions: that data obtained from high-dose experiments can be accurately extrapolated to more typical environmental levels and that animal models are valid. While all the data are not yet in on the veracity of either assumption, AMS provides the sensitivity and precision needed to address each of them thoroughly.

Dingley performed the first AMS experiments using biomolecules labeled with *tritium* (hydrogen-3). With tritium-labeled PhIP and *carbon-14*-labeled MeIQx, she found comparable sensitivities at low doses. (The lowest doses were equivalent to the amount of PhIP you would take in when eating a single well-cooked hamburger.) These experiments demonstrated the feasibility of using tritium AMS for biomedical studies as well as the feasibility of using both tracers in experiments to study how two substances, given at once, may affect each other.

Tritium is widely used in biological tracing and has some advantages over *carbon-14*. It is relatively easy to label a molecule with tritium, whereas *carbon-14*-labeled molecules must be custom synthesized, which can be expensive. While the use of detection techniques other than AMS requires relatively high tritium dosages and large samples, AMS eliminates those disadvantages. In fact, Livermore's experiments have demonstrated that AMS could be used to detect tritium in biological samples with a 100- to 1,000-fold improvement over scintillation and other decay counting techniques.

From Ants to Elephants

AMS is ideal for measuring extremely small samples, certainly the case when ants are the subject of study. CAMS worked with UC Riverside to follow the path of *carbon-14*-tagged food and insecticides through colonies of Argentine ants housed at the university. Once native to Brazil and Argentina, the Argentine ant is now the most prevalent pest around homes in California, the Caribbean, the Mediterranean, and South Africa. No available control strategy works effectively because each colony is home to several queens, any of which can regenerate the colony if other queens are destroyed. Learning how nutrients make their way to the queens is essential to finding an effective control method.

Work on nutrient dynamics was part of the largest AMS collaboration in place before the new NIH Research Resource was established. It involves CAMS and four UC campuses. Several campus—lab collaborations are ongoing at Livermore and other laboratories managed by UC, and the UC Office of the President has described this one as the most successful of all. Livermore's principal investigator for the Consortium for Ultra-Low-Level Tracing is physicist John Vogel, assisted by Bruce Buchholz, who was trained as a nuclear engineer.

Vogel has been involved with CAMS from the start and has been responsible for many of the technological advances that have helped to establish AMS as an increasingly routine biomedical research tool. His work with UC Davis on nutritional studies has earned him the rank of adjunct full professor of nutrition. "One never knows where a career will go," he chuckles.

The CAMS–UC Davis experiment that followed a single dose of *folic acid* for 200 days was no fluke. Many over-the-counter products that we take with barely a thought stay in our bodies for a remarkably long time. A similar experiment followed a single dose of beta carotene in blood, urine, and feces samples for 3 months. The three primary "*pools*" of beta carotene or retinol, the *vitamin A* that *beta carotene* metabolizes to, are clearly visible, first in the intestine, then in blood plasma, and finally in a circulating form with a 38-day half-life. The existence and equivalence of the slowly changing pool that starts 9 days after dosing would be undetectable without AMS.

Metabolic studies of vitamins and other nutrients are of more than passing academic interest. At present, little is known about vitamin metabolism except that it seems to vary widely among individuals. Folic acid, one of the B vitamins, is required for the production of red blood cells, DNA, and RNA. A deficiency can cause anemia and is related to heart disease and certain birth defects. A deficiency in beta carotene can cause blindness, a serious problem in less developed parts of the world. In fact, a new variety of carrotyorange "*golden*" rice, rich in beta carotene, has recently been developed in Switzerland for use in undeveloped countries.

Dr. Andy Clifford, professor of nutrition at UC Davis, has headed all of this important nutrient metabolism work with CAMS. As a result of his research to date, he has been awarded follow-on grants from NIH to conduct definitive AMS studies in humans. His experiments are now under way using healthy human volunteers aged 18 to 60.

CAMS researchers are working with clinicians at UC San Diego to develop a diagnostic technique sensitive enough to detect the growth protein that cancerous tumours produce. Most of this protein stays at the site of the *tumour*, but a very small amount leaks out into the blood. Different kinds of tumours—ovarian, prostate, breast, liver, and so on—produce slightly different kinds of growth proteins. A blood test that could detect the protein would be an effective tool for an early diagnosis. The test could also be used to determine whether follow-up treatment was working; ideally, the protein level would drop to zero over time.

Yet another current study is of very large animals—elephants—but small samples. A hormone imbalance in bull elephants can produce raging behaviour known as *musth*. The only way to obtain a sample from an enraged elephant is from its feces. But most of that is undigested fiber, leaving researchers with little usable material from which to measure the *carbon-14*-tagged hormone precursors that the elephant has ingested. AMS comes to the rescue again.

Science in Revolution

For all this work to date, biological AMS is still very new. Knezovich acknowledges this, saying, "We at Livermore are still doing lots of missionary work, educating the research community about this powerful technology. But the NIH grant makes clear that the biological research community is convinced of the worth of AMS."

Livermore's AMS experts are part of an apparent revolution in which biology may be replacing physics as the haute discipline. Research in biosciences now accounts for more than 40 percent of federal funding for basic research, fueled in part by an aging population and increased needs for health care.

As the use of AMS for biological research grows and matures, related applications will quickly be found. CAMS has already participated in a study of the effects of atrazine, a commonly used herbicide, on a group of volunteers in California who wore a skin patch of atrazine for 24 hours. Radioactivity in their urine was too low to be counted efficiently with liquid scintillation counting. But with AMS, uptake and elimination could be followed easily. Samples were even chromatographically separated to determine how the subjects metabolized the compound during exposure, a day after exposure, and several days after exposure. These biomarkers provide the data needed to develop an assay for occupational exposure to this chemical.

From agriculture to nutrition, from toxicology to chemotherapy—the potential uses of AMS for our better health are almost endless.

12

SMALL SCIENCE

Finding the best ways to detect *biological warfare* agents is one of Lawrence Livermore's missions today. Detecting large quantities of a biological pathogen is not difficult. The challenge is in detecting a few molecules of a toxin or a few bacteria or viruses to provide the early warnings of a *biological attack*.

Physicist Christine Orme and colleagues in the Chemistry and Materials Science Directorate are helping to understand some of the fundamental issues that underlie biodetection as well as fulfilling other Laboratory goals. They are performing research at minute scales in a field known as *nanoscience*, which takes its name from nanometer, a billionth of a meter. The team is examining, on an atom-by-atom and molecule-by-molecule basis, the organization of materials on surfaces and learning how that organization affects material properties. "One of the keys to working in nanoscience is controlling the surface and then being able to detect what is there," says Orme.

At the *nanoscale*, experimental results can be viewed only with the most powerful imaging tools. The *atomic force microscope* (AFM) has been used since the mid 1980s to produce topographic maps of *nanostructures*. Today, Orme's colleagues are developing new microscopic techniques based on use of the AFM that give even higher resolution and supply more than just topographic data. They are also refining the spectroscopic techniques that identify chemical bonds and supply fingerprints of molecules.

The current research builds on pioneering Livermore work in crystal growth and thin multilayers, both of which depend on a keen understanding of material behaviour at the atomic level. Livermore has a long-standing effort in crystal growth and characterization, born out of the need for large, ultrapure crystals in Livermore's lasers. Multilayers—exceedingly thin alternating layers of materials—were first demonstrated more than 50 years ago. But improved fabrication technologies developed by Livermore's Troy Barbee have prompted their use as highly reflective mirrors for telescopes as well as in a variety of optical applications, including electron microprobes, scanning electron microscopes, and particle beamlines in accelerators.

Seeing Is Believing

In atomic force microscopy, an extremely sharp tip senses the atomic shape of a sample while a computer records the path of the tip and slowly builds up a three-dimensional image. The AFM tip is positioned at the end of an extremely thin cantilever beam and touches the sample with a force of only 1/10 millionth of a gram, too weak to budge even one atom. As the tip is repelled by or attracted to the sample surface, the cantilever beam deflects. By imaging a larger or smaller area, researchers can vary the level of magnification of an AFM image. The AFM can also be adapted to sense a range of forces including attractive or repulsive interatomic forces, electrostatic forces, and magnetic forces.

But even the sharp tip of the AFM is sometimes not tiny enough for the small scale at which the research team is working. Physical chemist Aleksandr Noy is growing *carbon nanotubes* that can be used to replace the standard AFM tip. The figure above compares a typical AFM tip and a carbon nanotube tip. Carbon nanotubes are built of carbon hexagons that are arrayed in a configuration resembling chicken wire. They are 1/50,000th of the width of a human hair but a hundred times stronger than steel at one-sixth the weight. Noy can make many kinds of nanotubes—single wall, multiwall, thick, thin, single isolated, or large arrays. The smaller, lighter nanotube tip tracks the shape of an object more accurately to provide more detailed information about its surface.

Noy used the nanotube-tipped AFM to image the *cucumber mosaic virus* and reveal its structure fairly clearly. AFM images contain less information than structures revealed through x-ray diffraction techniques, but Noy's image was captured in minutes, whereas the same structure took over a year to resolve from diffraction data. "In principle, this technology could be used to image a single virus," says Noy. "Emergency workers could compare its image with a computerized database of known virus structures to identify it very quickly."

With the nanotube tip on the AFM, a team led by Noy also obtained the first unambiguous visualization of a DNA repair protein bound to DNA. By incorporating a synthetic mutagenic molecule into DNA and tagging a repair protein with a *fluorochrome*, they will be able to study the repair process *in situ*. Another imaging technique being used by physicist Thomas Huser and others is *confocal microscopy*. It is based on a *fluorescence microscope* augmented with a pinhole that limits the volume being probed to get rid of extraneous background "*noise*." Its beam can be focused to 500 nanometers. The confocal microscope efficiently collects fluorescence emitted from fluorescent molecules that have been excited by laser light. With this spectroscopic technique, Huser has been able to detect single molecules.

The confocal microscope is ideal for studying conjugated polymers, a new material that may be used to fabricate the next generation of *light-emitting diodes* (LEDs). Known as 2-methoxy, 5-(2'-ethyl-hexyloxy)-p-phenylene-vinylene, or MEH-PPV, the polymers are composed of a chain of benzene rings that emit light when linked by electrodes to which voltage is applied. The advantages of these polymers over the inorganic semiconducting materials of today's LEDs are many: They are easier to process on a large scale, they can be used to create ultrathin and flexible devices, and their power consumption is lower. Last year's Nobel Prize in Chemistry was awarded for the development of conjugated polymers.

Huser has learned that the physical configuration of the MEH-PPV molecules affects their fluorescence. "The *photoluminescence* of conjugated polymers depends strongly on how they are shaped," says Huser. When they fold up into a well-organized pattern in toluene, their shape enhances efficient energy transfer within the molecule. As conjugated polymers begin to be used as LEDs in electronics, some LED applications will take advantage of the high-energy-transfer configuration while others will benefit from the less ordered pattern for low energy transfer.

In experiments, Huser exposed MEH-PPV to two solvents, toluene and chloroform. In toluene, the MEH-PPV molecules curl up tightly because, says Huser, "they don't like toluene. They try to avoid it." Spectrographic data collected every 5 seconds show a slight flicker as the molecules die off with exposure to oxygen and the light they emit shifts from red to blue. In chloroform, the polymer spreads out. There is no blue shift, the light spectrum is broader, and the light intensity simply decays slowly with time.

Huser recently began experiments with the confocal microscope to examine the dynamics of single molecules of DNA. Fluorescent labeling of DNA, RNA, enzymes, and proteins is common laboratory practice to illuminate the interactions and functions of these important biomolecules.

At the same time, Noy has built a whole new microscope system that combines the topographic capabilities of the AFM and the spectroscopy of the *confocal microscope*. He will be using this system to obtain even better information about DNA repair as well as new information on how DNA is packaged.

Identifying a Single Molecule

Another tool for identifying molecular species is *Raman spectroscopy*, a form of light scattering similar to fluorescence. Although Raman-scattered light is much less intense than fluorescence, the technique is a powerful analytical tool because the changes in wavelength of the weakly scattered light are characteristic of the scattering material. Raman spectroscopy can identify *chemical bonds* and obtain the unique *fingerprint* of a molecule. Every molecule has a unique Raman spectrum, but not every molecule fluoresces. Raman spectroscopy is one of the few optical techniques that can identify a molecular species and determine its chemical bonding by observing its distinct molecular vibrational frequencies.

To increase the brightness and thus the resolution of Raman-scattered light, Huser has introduced nanometer-size gold crystals to the tip of a *scanning probe microscope* in a technique known as *surface-enhanced Raman spectroscopy*. The gold is negatively charged and attracts positively charged materials such as amino acids to adhere to kinks in the crystals. Electron density waves radiate from the corners of the gold crystals and increase the Raman signal by a factor of a quadrillion. At the same time, the scanning probe produces an image of the physical structure of the sample. The combined data allow for identification of single molecules. Unlike fluorescence, which fades with exposure to oxygen, the increased energy from the gold particles persists.

"Being able to characterize materials and chemical bonds at the level of a single molecule is a whole new capability for Livermore," says Huser. It is possible to perform Raman spectroscopy on single DNA molecules or proteins and to look for differences between individual cells. Using this technique, scientists also can detect and identify the by-products or precursors of chemical agents such as the nerve gas sarin. This capability is important in the development of sensors for chemical warfare agents.

Controlling Biomolecules

Some *nanoscience* projects require the careful design of surfaces to collect and organize atoms, molecules, nanocrystals, colloids, cells, and spores. These surfaces are known as *templates* or, as Noy describes them, "*landing pads*" for toxins, proteins, and other biomolecules.

Livermore is exploring several techniques for creating templates. Physicist Jim De Yoreo is developing one method based on dip-pen nanolithography, which dips the tip of the AFM into an "*inkwell*" of organic molecules to "*write*" on an inorganic surface. As the tip moves across the surface, it makes a pattern that has almost no topographic relief but exhibits chemical contrast with the surrounding region. It is even possible to create multiple ink patterns with this method. The feature size is controlled by such factors as tip coverage, humidity, and contact time with the substrate, or, in the case of lines, tip speed across the substrate. Examples of patterns created using a gold-coated mica surface for the substrate and 16-*mercaptohexadecanoic acid* for the ink are shown in the figure at right. This method has been used to deposit patterns of antibodies that would attract toxins and viruses, a first step in the development of *nanostructured biosensors*.

Another major area of research at Livermore's Biology and Biotechnology Research Program (BBRP) and elsewhere is in proteomics, the study of proteins. Cells produce particular proteins either all the time or as needed to prompt gene expression, that is, to turn a specific part of the genetic code on or off. Without proteins, our DNA could not operate properly. One of the best ways to examine the structure of a protein is to crystallize it and then subject it to x rays to obtain its unique diffraction pattern. During the crystallization process, molecules come together and separate (in a process known as *nucleation*) until a critical size is reached. Reaching that critical size can take a long time, and sometimes it does not happen at all. One goal of current proteomics work is to speed up the nucleation process and make it more likely that proteins will crystallize.

Dip-pen lithography, using a chemical that would prompt protein nucleation, is an option. "But," says Orme, "the size scale is a challenge. Proteins are extremely small, typically from 1 to 10 nanometers."

"If we make the pen's lines smaller, they won't be visible," adds Noy. So he and researchers in BBRP are developing a fluorescent ink for drawing lines with the density of a single molecule. In initial tests, a single-molecule line of the *human chorionic gonadotropin* (HCG) antibody has been successfully drawn. The next step will be to attract the HCG protein.

Nanolaminates, the next generation of multilayers, are also being explored as a way to accelerate the nucleation and growth of ordered proteins. Nanolaminate structures have been successfully synthesized with layers that are the same small size as typical proteins. The alternating layers have different surface charges, which prompt the proteins to adsorb in ordered rows. In the example, a nanolaminate was dipped into a solution of the protein ATCase. The nanolaminate was then removed, rinsed, air-dried, and imaged with AFM using a carbon nanotube tip. The resulting extremely high resolution of the image makes nonspherical proteins individually distinguishable on silica stripes. An image of the same deposition onto a homogeneous silica surface is very different, lacking any linear order. This set of experiments was the first step in accelerating nucleation and growing protein crystals that are suitable for x-ray diffraction.

Mimicking Natural Growth

Nanoscience is finding another application in the hands of Orme, De Yoreo, and colleagues whose research on the growth of calcite crystals sheds new light on the formation of bones, eggshells, and seashells.

The natural growth of organic crystals is known as *biomineralization*. *Biomimetics* is the term for mimicking nature's building methods to make a synthetic material. "We can only learn to make better bones and teeth if we first understand how the materials grow and interact with biological molecules," says Orme. "While there is a big step between this fundamental research and synthesizing materials that are truly similar to the real thing, we are part of the process to create better materials that affect health."

Pure calcium carbonate in the mineral form called *calcite* grows only in a symmetrical, six-sided rhombohedral-shape crystal. But that does not explain the intricate shapes found in nature, such as that of seashells. Researchers have known for a long time that organic molecules can influence the shape of a growing mineral crystal by attaching themselves to it. But it took experiments at Livermore to demonstrate the process in detail, showing how amino acids work at the molecular level to change a growing crystal.

In the experiments, the team added aspartate, one of the more abundant amino acids found in the proteins of shellfish, to calcite crystals growing in solution. *Aspartate* is typical of many amino acids in that it exhibits handedness, or chirality. As the researchers monitored crystal development, they found that the left-handed and right-handed form of the molecule attached more strongly to opposite atomic steps. The results were crystals that were mirror images of one another. The figure below illustrates how a chiral amino acid influences a growing calcite crystal. By knowing which steps the amino acid interacted with and using the symmetry relations of the crystal and the amino acids, the team was able to predict the binding position of the amino acid to the calcium carbonate step.

Comparable experiments are just beginning on calcium phosphate, the material used by animals to grow bones. Ultimately, experimental results may be put to myriad uses, from potential laboratory growth of human and animal bones to prevention of scale formation in pipes to the manufacture of toothpaste—any situation in which calcium-based crystals grow naturally or are used.

Fundamental Science at Work

A nanostructured device is also finding its way into tests for the Yucca Mountain project, the nation's candidate for a repository for long-term storage of nuclear wastes. Tests of corrosion-resistant materials are being developed that use patterns formed by "writing" with voltage rather than with chemical inks. A voltage is applied between the AFM tip and a metal or semiconductor substrate to grow oxide patterns under the tip. In the figure below, an oxide greeting is written into a titanium film. The dot on the "*i*" is made larger and broader by applying a higher voltage. If the *nanopatterns blur* or dissolve during testing, the change provides a very sensitive indicator that the protective oxide film is changing.

This project is typical of so much fundamental research performed at Livermore. Using funding from the Laboratory Directed Research and Development (LDRD) Program, the oxide templates were originally developed to nucleate calcium phosphate minerals and to control protein deposition onto medical implants. Now, the Yucca Mountain project is putting the template to practical use. Much of the other work at Livermore to grow and image nanostructures also started as basic research, funded either by LDRD or by the Department of Energy's Office of Basic Energy Sciences, before finding a range of applications—including sensors that may someday be a lifesaver.

13

Artificial Sleep

"*Domestic security*" has created a science-fiction reality with the aid of electricity, sound waves, gas and foam. It paints a picture of civil conflict which, despite a 30 year old tradition in the use of hi-tech weaponry such as pepper gas, computer searches, computer intelligence networks, police round-ups, is still seen by most as some fantastic script for a Hollywood film and bearing no relation to reality.

A read through *PE 166 499*, an evaluation of technical and scientific means of crowd control, published by the EU programme STOA and later texts shatter all illusions.

The tools of crowd control are today already considered to be "*intelligent*", this overutilized terminology omits an explanation of exactly how a shift in technology from the conventional to the non-conventional will replace "*physical crowd control*" with "*direct mind control*" and what the effects of such weapons will be. Methods of the media age such as beaming and acoustic modification and avant-garde biochemistry have found their home in police arsenals. Immaterial or molecular carriers, which boast the ambiguous title "*agents*" will, in the future, be at the forefront of curbing civil unrest, such chimerical machinery will be deployed to confuse and perturb. The literary style of the ten year-old *International Convention on the Use of Non-lethal Weapons* already establishes the likeliness of these new developments to a work of art.

The paper is the militaristic philosophical demon-child of futurologists Alvin and Heidi Toffler, conceived during a lull in armament policy at the end of the Cold War. The spurious text was drawn up with the help of Chris and Janet Morris, two American

Quakers and a former Green Beret Commander and Viet Nam veteran John B. Alexander. Its novel-like proposal for a clean-handed democracy, free of bloodshed, yet armed to the teeth with hi-tech weaponry stealthily circumvents all of the conventional arms restrictions and at the same time poses as a humane strategy for the optimization of police efficiency in street combat.

The technological and biological machinery outlined in their paper employs temporary or partially reversible effects such as sleep, pain, blindness, paralysis, vomiting and spontaneous defecation amongst others.

M2 Technologies Inc., the company owned by Chris and Janet Morris offer "*tuneable*" weapons capable of delivering such effects in their virtual shopping mall: high-energy microwaves and DNA-mapping chemicals as "*Law Enforcement applications*" or nanoparticles as the future of self defence.

Despite the efforts of some who try to dispute the classification of such apparatus as "*weapons*" or interpret their use as less harmful in order to banalise any implications of brutality, one thing remains clear: such weapons, especially police-weapons, whether lethal or not, are intended to be directed against persons.

The fact that cultural assets, public housing and military infrastructure remain unscathed by the use of these devices is a convenient side effect which is often used to reinforce the case for their existence, it is however just that: an unintentional side-effect. The name says it all: Lethe is the goddess of final oblivion; she comes for mortal souls, not buildings or machines.

Low intensity warfare confines itself, in the main, to mass control (*monitor everything*), group control (*blanket arrests*) and prison control (*selective suppression*). A new approach no longer calls for the incapacitation of the subject's body but an interruption of thought and motor functions.

Recent studies conducted by *Bradford University's Peace Studies Department* and SIPRI (*Stockholm International Peace Research Institute*) or conferences such as *Futuresonic*, which took place in October 2002 in Manchester, UK have focused on the implications of this chemically induced sleep as a means to influence behavioural change, something which has become the ambition of hi-tech political control. The biotech industry is thus alchemising new generations of highly specific designer pharmaceuticals, hypnotics and anaesthetics, developed and tested on computer displays. They offer the solution to containing unruly masses:

programmable lapses of sleep and unconsciousness, the future of law and order in the 21st century state.

The use of *non-lethal weapons* as a proven means of countering terrorism is being increasingly propagated, genetically modified gases, which can single out the DNA of certain ethnic groups, are being put to the test. The effect of these gases is so exact that a person with only a minimally differing gene makeup to the desired target will go unharmed.

A substance of this description has been sitting in a biotech laboratory in Nes Tziyona near Tel Aviv since January 2003 awaiting its first assignment somewhere in Iraq. The factory in Nes Tziyona was in fact the consignee of the cargo of Sarin carried by the El- Al plane which crashed into a building in Amsterdam in 1992. This pathogenic substance is a modern-day variation of the ethnic bomb, coined the "*pigmentation weapon*" by the South-African biochemists who developed it many years ago. The *Human Genome Project* has taken the worldwide arms market by storm due to recent success where its awesome gene mapping capabilities have been unleashed.

Researchers, politicians and police spokesmen in both Eastern and Western Europe are arguing the case for the use of hi-tech weapons, the terminology leaves nothing to the imagination: "*mood management*" and "*mass incapacitation*" form the core of the sales policy of such technologies whose consistency with existing laws is as questionable as their ethical justification. In future control scenarios the objective is to directly influence the "*suspects*" central nervous system without harming the person's body, an effect which is, in general, forbidden by European laws and is underscored by the NLW convention, hence a "*complete liquidation*" of the target groups (protesters, militant inciters, terrorists) is to be avoided. In this context the terms "*psychoelectronics*" and "*nanotechnology*" are mentioned with irritating frequency. A "*relatively reversible effect*" is the object of such developments and how this is achieved can be found in reports commissioned by the STOA programme of the EU Parliament in Brussels. The relationship with its namesake, the Greek school of philosophy, is so remote that it invokes suspicions of a ruse.

STOA simply stands for *Scientific and Technological Option Assessment* and is an organ, which deals with practically any matter from fisheries to ecology to human rights. In October 2002 the *Omega Foundation* an NGO from Manchester, England completed a revision of their colossal report *An Appraisal of Technologies of Political*

Control. With contributions by international specialists and experts in the current political landscape this report scrutinizes recent events in Moscow and the preparation for the invasion in Iraq.

Politician's will never get to read the full version of the facts delivered in the round 1,000 page STOA study which deals with themes ranging from the "*Trojan vehicle*" to a veritable "*Pandora's box*" of new substances to "*hypno-politics*" as they will be presented with a slender "booklet" version of the original, incapable of providing the scope of the parent study. Ultimately many of the astonishing facts unearthed by the interim reports will be omitted. ...

In order to use the information included in the report for the debate over perspectives for our future, it seems essential to create extended platforms for further "*translation*" of the report. Only then will the investigation, provided by Steve Wright, the founder of the *Omega Foundation* and his specialists, furnish a solid basis for a criticism of the ideologies behind "*domestic security*". A translation of its contents is a necessary addition to the report which EU unfortunately publishes in a shortened version without the photos and illustrations of the original.

Without such clarification its pages tell a very benign, consumer-friendly story, for who would have guessed that the apparently harmless phrase "*border control technologies*" is a covert for the rebuilding of the Iron Curtain in the form of an electric frontier. How does it feel to be struck by 50,000 volts of electricity from 200 meters away carried by ions in the air which have been charged by a UV laser? And the development of an explosive device containing 5,000 microscopic hooks attached to thin cables, which penetrate a person's body and hold them paralysed, still fully conscious, until the battery is depleted, does this mark the long-awaited humanization of the notorious border land mine?

On the 19th of April 2003, with the heavy artillery of the Iraq conflict still ringing in the air, DPA announced that one of the war-waging parties, Great Britain, has armed its police force with devices, which have enjoyed a long test phase in the USA. Five selected districts in the United Kingdom will now be the testing ground for the Taser M26, a pistol, which from a distance of seven meters, shoots hooks attached to conductible cables delivering a charge of 50,000 volts that induces muscle laming in order to facilitate handcuffing the suspect. However the article neglects to mention how the "*shaped pulse*" electric power affects the delinquent's psyche after having been shot at a hundred times or over a period of hours, a core features for incapacitation, advertised in the company's shiny Hollywood-style DVD manual.

After having witnessed the building site fences erected to cordon off inner-city security zones in Genoa and Barcelona in 2001 and 2002, who would have believed that "*area denial devices*", the mobile barriers of the future, are not, in fact, cemented into the ground but are highly-adhesive substances, which cling to the body of the target. How does a bystander feel who mistakenly becomes the target of "*sticky foam balls*" that pin him to a wall, leaving him helpless until the next riot squad arrive with the appropriate solvent to set him free? The US Marine Forces have already been using these glue canons for several years. Similar "*kinetic impact*" weapons can be found in the arsenals of almost all EU member states. Even though most of these countries do not have a policy of turning these weapons on people, rather they are used for sealing rooms and escape routes in order to confine suspects, this does not rule out a political change of heart and their subsequent use against soft targets.

What does it say about the state of our culture, when, despite society's current preoccupation with hygiene, methods of control are being proposed which, by means of a specially confectioned gas, can induce spontaneous defecation in a large congregation of, say 4,000 people? A sense of shame becomes a means of control. The internal paper of the US *Joint non-lethal Weapon Directorate,* published by the NGO *Sunshine.org* through the Freedom of Information Act, discusses "crowd control by means of olfactory stimulants", which are artificially manufactured malodorous substances: yet their use seems almost superfluous given that the above mentioned application produces the same effect as a side effect for free. Priority is given to the use of bacteria-filled projectiles, which, when dispersed, serve to neutralize a "*fractious mob's*" sense of smell.

Who would have believed, in spite of recent developments in art and media, that the participants in futuristic new media expositions are being selected from the ranks of the police force? What does a spectator at a public rally feel when he is harassed by "*sonic hallucinations*" projected from several hundred meters away and only audible to the target person, confounding his thoughts as an ethereal "*voice in his head*" fills his mind with misinformation? Doesn't that appear to be the technical solution for inducing paranoia to people?

Who, after having seen Bill Viola's meditative installation with sleeping heads, would wish for its transmutation into a 3-D video projection to be shown openly in public spaces as a living simulation beamed onto a layer of transparent gas?

Apparently the technocrats of domestic security do not see the roots of democracy in the Athenian Polis, rather in the war between the Greeks and the Trojans. The "*mobile tactics*" in literature on non-lethal warfare and suppression of civil disturbances tell explicitly of Trojan technology, for example riot vehicles, which from the exterior, have the appearance of ambulances but are, in fact full, of "*cyber-cop*" apparatus. From these rolling Trojan horses, then, security forces can shoot into a heterogeneous crowd of protesters and single out citizens of a certain gene makeup, who collapse unconscious or are seized by pain and sent writhing to the ground while others walk away unharmed. After the first cinema showing of the action film *Copkiller*, cinemagoers spoke excitedly for weeks of a scene in which ex-Sex Pistol, Johnny Rotten puts his head in a microwave. 20 years later, who is talking of the microwave canon, jointly developed by German research institutes and the German army, capable of jamming signals to enemy aircraft? A photo of this sophisticated blue aircraft, tells nothing of the hidden capabilities of this microwave technology which is also available in a convenient hand-held version, which, when used on a living object, can raise body temperature to 42°C within seconds. Needless to say this device has also found its place in the ranks of non-lethal weapons. All of these various systems are mentioned in the EU report as possible options, some in their research and some in their test phase. An explanation to their ultimate application has been hitherto refused.

Camouflage

The European automotive industry uses the term "*Trojan vehicle*" to describe cars especially adapted for the police and special response units. Their exact sales description is, ironically, DOV(e): "discreet order vehicle". A whole host of companies are involved in the development of the "*non-aggressive*" four-wheeled combat machines, they include: *Sicherheits-Transport* from Austria, three French companies; *Saviem*, *Panhard* and *Renault*, *Bonowi Mercedes Benz*, *Rheinstahl* and *Thyssen* all from Germany, Italian partners are *Fiat* and *Iveco*, *DAF Special Products Division* from the Netherlands and a British firm called *Trojan Vehicles*, a subsidiary of *Rolls Royce Aircraft*. In total there are more than twenty companies involved in the production of DOV(e)s, which one would instinctively imagine to be painted white like the bird of peace, which lent them its name.

DOV(e)s celebrated their debut in *Nonlethal Weapons: Terms and References*, first published in 1998 by professor Robert J. Bunker of *California State University* in San Bernardino. This work was compiled with the help of the aforementioned John B. Alexander who is a US delegate to a NATO advisory group and has an e-mail address at America Online under the pseudonym "*Apollinair*" (without an 'e'!).

One of Apollinaire's theories was that an artist must lose his humanity in order to adapt to his environment. The validity of this theory is underscored in the pages of Alexander's two books *Future War: Non-lethal Weapons in 21st Century Warfare* and *The Warrior's Edge*. Doubtless, this type of publication promotes the increasing impetus for a revolution in the responsibilities and combat tactics of the police and military alike and their joint application of research in this field. This anti-democratic process is laid out in exemplary fashion in Alexander's blueprint for police technologies of the future.

His article *The New Mental Battlefield* written in 1980 already describes how psychological warfare can be used in battle. As a colleague of General Burt Stubblebine of *US Army Intelligence and Security Command* (INSCOM) Alexander became renowned for his piloting of research programmes, which explored "*human potential*" in ways never before witnessed. It seems that the collection of data on extra-sensory techniques (comparable to PSI technology) is the most prominent part of these programmes. Neither the CIA nor DIA (*Defence Intelligence Agency*) admits authorship of these programmes; the blame is constantly being passed from one to the other. The *Science Applications International Corporation* (SAIC) has also been drawn into the cross-fire.

The SAIC is a hi-tech arms developer involved in the conception of various weapon prototypes. In recent years it has been working on a "*mobile robot infantry*" designed for use in situations of urban disorder.

After leaving the army, Alexander also worked at this American elitist research institute in Los Alamos, where he fostered his concept of non-lethality and promoted his ideas to politicians, academics and the heads of the military and secret services. Later he took a position in a private research institute in Las Vegas called *The International Remote Viewing Association* of which he is also a board member. This institution is a metamilitary sectarian union whose speciality is nurturing "*mental capacity*" as a means of transmitting and recording information outside of the sense organ. In this capacity, Alexander is also advisor to the White House.

Alexander and his co-author Bunker envisage the use of DOV(e)s as follows: "Mobile tactics is a procedure used against rioters in which an anti-riot team is embarked on vehicles, rapidly driven near rioters, whereupon they quickly disembark and rush towards the crowd, followed by another team, which repeats the procedure and exploits the momentum gained by the original team."

In the same encyclopaedia entry a description of the weaponry is offered: "*Operational Nonlethal Weapons, Western.* Weapons that are explicitly designed and primarily employed so as to incapacitate personnel or material, while minimizing fatalities, permanent injury to personnel, and undesired damage to property and the environment. Unlike conventional lethal weapons, that destroy their targets principally through blast, penetration and fragmentation, non-lethal weapons employ means other than gross physical destruction to prevent the target from functioning. Nonlethal weapons are intended to have one, or both, of the following characteristics: a they have relatively reversible effects on personnel or material b they affect objects differently within their area of influence."

For two decades long-standing readers of Virilio have believed that close contact battle will have disappeared and have been replaced by the battle of video based camouflage bombers and cinematic perception machines. They stand corrected. The task is tough and physical, like the battle of Troy.

Deceive

These inconspicuous tactical vehicles are intended to increase mobility and efficiency in extinguishing civil rebellion. They serve as sophisticated, modern-day battle steeds for the "*cybercops*" of the anti-globalization era. They are agile riot tanks, which show up on the prying camera lenses of journalists as ambulances or fire engines. Taking on the outer appearance of civil vehicles enables the unhindered transportation of malign, ultra-modern weapons to the nucleus of unrest where their force can be unleashed from behind the protection of the armoured "*rescue*" vehicle.

The concealed potential of these vehicles is not limited to their appearance, even the technology on board has, apart from its non-lethal characteristic, a secondary sinister dimension: an effective combat weapon has to be "smart".

Such labels are best seen in an older context, one that began with the New York Times' christening of Hiroshima as "*ground zero*" in

1946. The current media rhetoric has not only grafted the name "*ground zero*" onto site of the disaster in Manhattan in 2001, but similar to the bombing of Hiroshima, has not delivered any real images, which document the aftermath of the event.

This is known amongst vigilant observers of the media coverage of the Iraq conflict as "the CNN effect". Television audiences worldwide could engage in a first person perspective of computer-coordinated missile raids on Iraqi targets as if they were sitting on the bomb itself, able to accompany it until its impact somewhere along the "*axis of evil*". Satellite images then gave spectators an after-impression of the raids, there was not a single picture of dead bodies or bloodied remains only images of demolished buildings.

Such "*intelligent*" bombs, equipped with video imaging capabilities belong to the family of "smart" technology. Killing is no longer messy it is refined, even clever. They withhold the after-effects of devastation, they spare us the horrific pictures of the real damage, which they inflict and at the same time pretend to deliver more coverage of such atrocities than ever seen before. It is a linguistic irony that the word "smart" was chosen to describe such weapons due to its meaning of "ingenious" for it has another meaning which is often overlooked in this context: that is to say "causing sharp, stinging pain".

The term "*non-lethal*" refers to nothing more than the reduced likelihood that a target will be killed by the impact of a certain weapon. Ballistic science has addressed this problem by marginally reducing the kinetic energy of firearms, by using softer forms of ammunition or decreasing the concentration of paralysing agents in chemical spray canons. The "*CNN effect*" delivers a feasible, consumer-friendly alternative to images of atrocity, a group of "*anarchists*" who collapse, anaesthetized under the effect of a sedative is well within the bounds of acceptable news and considered fit for broadcast. "*Sedated*" gives the impression of a temporary, reversible condition; something *one can live with*. "*Sedate*" is already a part of our vocabulary it gives a notion of fogginess, obscurity, dimness, stupor all of which are transient states that subside with the passing of time.

By this logic, then, the "enemy" is only in a state of senselessness, not dead, and legal implications of guilt could, in turn, be interpreted very differently. A television audience no longer needs to feel uncomfortable and can watch the investigation of such a case without feeling uneasy: they can watch in peace. Conversely, shocking images in the press or on television of the dead body of a young man lying on the ground at a demonstration at a G8 summit in Genoa would not be welcomed. Bleeding civilians belong in the hospital, not on the covers of magazines or on television screens. Likewise, riot weapons and vehicles are not to be shown as such; instead they should look like commonplace automobiles thus drawing no suspicion.

Select

Another aspect in the coming development phase of "*mass incapacitation tools*" is research on the susceptibility ot human genes. Widely accepted research results like those of the global gene databank of the *Human Genome Project* tell us that the margin of discrepancy in our gene structures and distinction in the human species is greater than ever. These results provide a means to distinguish between ethnicities thereby enabling specific treatment of a particular race.

The intended applications describe in the STOA report are listed as: "behavioural change, race-specific crowd control and border control". The seeds of research sown in 2000 are now ready for harvesting. The "*Selfish Gene*" is superceded by the "*Criminal Gene*" in the dawning of a neo-Lombroso era. Future scenarios of civil uprising such as anti-globalization rallies and blockades of nuclear waste transporters will no longer be a disarray of storming riot police and fleeing protesters. Armour-plated doves of peace will arrive on the scene where crowd control specialists will, with the help of non-lethal spray canons, cover the mob in a cloud of genetically adapted barbiturates, which paralyses Friesians or inflicts Pakistanis with excruciating pain as never felt before.

Spray

In 2001 the French newspaper *Liberation* published a photograph of a naked protester in Genoa. The image was crowned with a quote from the French philosopher Miguel Benasayag, which reads "*Resistance is Creation*".

In a thick cloud of riot gas, the man stands bare, God's creation ... wearing a gas mask! He is holding his arms upwards in a v-shape. In the foreground there is a lamp post which lends several interpretations to the image. Did the photographer see Jesus at the foot of the cross? Do the thrown-up arms and the naked body signify that the man is surrendering to the overwhelming might of the police? Is he euphoric with defiance, intoxicated like the partygoers at countless raves? Does the V-shape of his arms mean victory or capitulation? Or is the V-man a hired provocateur?

The escalation in police violence and the fatal shooting of a protester by a young Carabiniere at the G8 summit riots in the summer of 2001 have fixed people's attention on police practices and equipment. Pictures from Northern Ireland spring to mind where 50 children are said to have been killed by rubber bullets. Then all eyes turn to Zurich as rubber ammunition ricochets off the walls of buildings in the Swiss city. The police, whose very name is derived from the etymological root of a word meaning both "citizen" and the ruling hand of public security, has suddenly become the symbol of an excess of power, and thus altogether contradicts its own heritage. The Medieval Latin word *policia*, meaning state administration, is a derivative of the Greek *polis,* meaning city and is also a metonym for "*executive organ*", i.e. the police as the upholders of public order. Even in its first ten years of existence the doctrine of police armament often came into disrepute predominantly because of the use of non-lethal weapons.

European attempts to classify gaseous substances, sprayed into crowds from road vehicles or helicopters as "*humanitarian weapons*" date back to the 1960s. Jean Louis Braus' book on narcotics *L'Histoire de la Drogue*, first published in 1968, contains a chapter entitled *Police Drugs and Psychochemical Weapons* in which French officer R. Nardi is cited "psychochemical weapons have, above all, the characteristics of moral, humanitarian arms that do not inflict pain upon their targets but render them incapable of resistance for a limited duration." The seductive effects such a description could have are difficult to resist at a political level.

The current EU report on the "*technologies of political control*" points to countless historical precursors, which enable a fair evaluation of the juristic, medicinal and human rights dimensions of political control. Some of the most unsavoury examples drawn upon by *The Omega Foundation* in their investigations for the STOA are the research programmes conducted since 1995 by the American *Defence Intelligence Agency* (DIA) that are remnants of older, widely discredited CIA projects from the 1950s, likewise mentioned in the report. The critical studies published by the EU do not portray the events in Genoa as an inadvertent escalation of violence, rather as a dystopian example of a hi-tech future gone wrong.

Awaken

The film *Minority Report* from 2002 offers this vision on the big screen. A new model of crime prevention is proposed: superhuman children who can telepathically communicate with each other whilst in the "*immersed ambience*" of an alimentary fluid. One look at the film's police agents, armed to the hilt with NLWs, their *vortex ring guns* and iris scanners emits an unambiguous resonance about the ultimate consequences of therapeutic freezing.

In 1950 the way in which natural scientists and engineers viewed the world was shaken by Richard Feynman's lecture *There is Plenty of Room at the Bottom*. From that day on the human race has lived with a new and radical concept of the dimensions of scientific possibilities and with it came a new idea of the frontiers of human life, which could be traversed by science in the name of progress. Size is, and always has been, the biggest obstacle for evolution but "deep below", 10^{-9} meters below to be exact, there is always *plenty of room* to breathe.

Thanks to the ability to inspect the body at an atomic level, the complete decryption of what scientists believe to be the brain's mechanistic makeup no longer poses a problem. The body, seen through "the eyes of a neutron" is considered a loosely knit garb of billions of molecules, if at some stage a stitch is dropped, all that is required is the correct needle to pick it up again. Since the 1950s researchers at the CIA and their colleagues at the DIA have been constantly preoccupied with possible methods of embroidering new stitches into the brains existing pattern. The name of these secret service research projects *Mind Kontrol* (with a 'K'!) leaves little room for speculation.

Not only the more indiscrete projects like *Pandora* have proved themselves as magnets for attention, even the more cryptic of programme titles like *MK Ultra*, *MK Delta* and *Artichoke* were soon to attract notoriety as human experimentation programmes. This research reduces human thinking, in the main, to nothing more than the result of electromagnetic activity, which as the fundamental ideology of the programmes would suggest, is subjected to various forms of influence and control in the shape of transmitters, electrodes and drugs.

Remote Control

As a result of the *Mind Kontrol* and other espionage research programmes a veritable zoo of paramilitary mutations has been born over the last five decades.

Bull

The *Yale* professor Jose Delgado, author of the classic *Physical Control of the Mind: Toward a Psychocivilized Society* has become a living legend. In the same year as the publication of his book he performed an extraordinary experiment, which would demonstrate the awesome power of mind control. Armed with nothing more than a black cigar box he stands face to face with a menacing, fully-grown bull, its massive skull tilted forwards ready to attack.

The cigar box has two buttons; with one the professor can send FM radio waves to the bull's brain stimulating it to charge. The other sends an electronic charge to an electrode implanted in the bull's brain, which instantaneously reduces it to a docile lapdog. As the doctor finally pushes the second button he is almost caught under the hooves of the stampeding bull. The device, which was financed by the *Office of Naval Research*, has been appropriately coined the *Stimoceiver*. Delgado formulates his thoughts on *psychocivilisation* precisely: "*human beings can be controlled like robots by push-buttons*".

Dog

Project Artichoke saw the metamorphosis of a dog into a bomb for use in the "*War on Terror*". A brain wave stimulator provides a means of remote control so that the dog may be guided over several kilometers to a specific target. The operator is able to send a charge to electrodes implanted in the dog's cerebellum and thus steer the canine bomb towards its target. Once the dog has located the enemy the operator can then remotely detonate the plastic explosives in the dog's stomach.

Cat

Even more perfidious is the transformation of a cat into a reconnaissance device, which was also conducted by the animal-lovers at the CIA in their project *MK Ultra*. In this instance an electronic signal converter is surgically implanted into the cat's inner ear, this constantly transmits the signals, which the cat's ear receives. The feline microphone can pick up interesting conversations as long as the speaker is a cat-lover and the cat is able to remain in his proximity.

Mouse

The *Osmo Mouse*, the world's first *cyborg* needs no introduction, it was designed as a prototype pilot for future space exploration not as a weapon. The success of the *Osmo Mouse* has inevitably paved the way for a series of follow-up programmes, which have military applications in sight. NASA commissioned psychiatrists and drug specialists Nathan S. Kline and Manfred E. Clynes to find a way for astronauts to physically and psychologically endure the long periods of motionlessness during the flight time in space. Their proposed solution does not adapt the surrounding environment to the organism rather it does exactly the opposite. Scientists replaced the mouse's tail with an osmotic pump, which slowly releases small doses of psycho-pharmaceuticals causing chronic behavioural change. Even fully paralysed the mouse is in high spirits due to the precise dosage of medication.

Cockroach

In the middle of the 1990s an international research team headed by Isao Shimoyama of Tokyo's *Tsukuba University* ventured further along this path. The team developed a microscopic remote controlled robotic surveillance camera the problem of weight and power supply was addressed by mounting the camera under the shell of a cockroach. The Kafkaesque biomachine is naturally equipped with all of the faculties that a robot would have to learn: it instinctively scuttles away when exposed to light, it will naturally find protection in cracks, it can suspend itself from ceilings and has more strength than a robot and a comparably infinite energy reserve. The most significant advantage is that it costs nothing and shortage is not a problem. Shimoyama's cockroaches are remotely controlled with the aid of transmitters they will react instantly to any command signal. The bugs can, theoretically, carry out their directives in coordination with other "customized" insects of the same species as an absurd ballet of insectile machines. The Japanese government was so enthused that they awarded the team a research "prize" of five million US dollars, a sum, which resembles an investment payout rather than a financial reward.

Bacteria

According to an account by *The Sunshine Project* the Pentagon has presented the Department of Justice with three bills, which will legitimize the use of bacteria for "the War on Terror". These microscopic battalions will engage in low-level combat breaking down the asphalt of Iraqi airport runways or eating up the fuel tanks of Taliban jeeps. However there has been no mention of how the bacteria are then to be contained once they have accomplished their mission. The same is true of the nanotechnologically generated polio viruses successfully completed in 2002.

Humans

In 1970 the invention of Rubenstein and Aldrich's "Schwitzgebel machine" read like something from the pages of Nazi pulp fiction.

The two researchers developed a radiotelemetric device that was capable of recording all of the physical and neurological signals emitted by a target situated miles away. Tests proved that fundamental bioelectric behaviour in humans could be directly manipulated, although almost twenty-five years old this experiment has not been forgotten. Sooner or later video footage was to find its way into the public eye, the tape was the testimony of a patient's devotion to her psychiatrist. The patient in question suffered from a behavioural disorder so the psychiatrist saw it his duty to develop a means of appeasing her suffering.

The doctor was able to stimulate a particular part of the patient's brain with an electrode, which instantly transformed her outbreaks of aggression into bouts of tenderness. In 1977, as soon as the *New York Times* reported that experiments with the patient were underway at Canada's *Allan Memorial Institute* the CIA tried to procure all existing research papers of similar projects, which had not yet been disclosed to the public. These cover-up attempts, however, backfired as a quantity of documents about *Mind Kontrol* unexpectedly strayed into public.

Spy

Fans of Orwell's *Room 101* will no doubt be aware that since the summer of 2002 prominent middle-European executives can check in at London Heathrow's express check in counter if they have previously undergone an iris scan. A new breed of patient is voluntarily signing up for the surgical implantation of subcutaneous alarm chips or the installation of minuscule telephone systems in the inner ear. Doctors and political activists alike regard the incorporation of the "*electronic tag*" as a real-life horror scenario, so much so, that they have been fighting their surgical development for over twenty years. Just one of a thousand examples of perversions of this technology was launched by *Siemens* in the same year. The market had already been primed for the *ID-Mouse*, a metaphorical expansion of the mutant enclosure at the already heavily overpopulated zoo.

With the *ID-Mouse* computer networks users have the power to access a server literally *at their fingertips*. A fingerprint enables them to submit their access credentials and to be located by others via computer address or mobile telephone tracking. Far fetched? The information epidemic began years ago, for years already e-mail attachments have incubated "parasitic" information about the sender, which, unbeknown to him, attaches itself to the host and lies dormant until ready to "hatch". Likewise verbal communication, it has long been known that, with aid of encoded calls, any analogue telephone can be used as a microphone without the need of bugging the receiver or the room in which it stands.

It is also a fact of modern-day life that already thousands of people all over the world are consuming so-called "*smart drinks*", which are alleged to biochemically enhance the brain's capacities and retard the natural ageing process-*Sleeping Beauty* from a test tube. The image of nanotechnology and neurological research as the medicine of the future, as the gift of science and salvation in times of a frightening evolutionary standstill would appear, for the most part, to be a misconception. The Trojan horse of tomorrow will be built from "*atomic Lego*", a neatly packed *gift* in its truest Germanic sense.

14

TYPES OF WEAPONS

The proliferation of *nuclear*, *biological*, and *chemical weapons* is widely recognized as the most serious threat to the national security of the United States and other nations. Official and public attention to proliferation issues, however, has varied over the years from near hysteria to apathy. During this first decade of the twenty-first century, concern is very high, with passionate international debates over which strategies can best prevent the spread and use of these weapons.

To inform these debates, this second edition of *Deadly Arsenals* revises and updates all the chapters, figures, and tables from the first edition published in 2002. This edition includes new chapters on Iraq, Iran, Libya, North Korea, and new information and analysis on other countries, which are needed to capture the dramatic developments of the past three years. All the parts of the book emphasize factual and historical analysis of weapons programs. The book is intended to serve as a proliferation atlas and ready reference for students, experts, and concerned citizens alike.

One significant change in the new edition is that it no longer employs the term "*weapons of mass destruction.*" Though used widely by officials and the media, this phrase conflates very different threats from weapons that differ greatly in lethality, consequence of use, and the availability of measures that can protect against them. *Chemical weapons* are easy to manufacture, but they inflict relatively limited damage over small areas and dissipate fairly quickly. *Biological weapon* agents can be made in most medical laboratories, but it is very difficult to turn these agents into effective weapons, and prompt inoculation and quarantine could limit the number of victims and the areas affected.

Nuclear weapons are difficult to produce, but one weapon can destroy an entire city, killing hundreds of thousands instantly and leaving lingering radiation that would render large areas uninhabitable for years. A failure to differentiate these threats can lead to seriously flawed policy. For example, the repeated use of the term "*weapons of mass destruction*" to describe the potential threat from Iraq before the 2003 war merged the danger that it still had *anthrax-filled shells*, which was possible, with the danger that it had nuclear bombs, which was highly unlikely. Similarly, saying that Syria has weapons of mass destruction merges the danger that it has chemical weapons, which is almost certainly true, with the danger that it has a nuclear bomb, which is certainly not true. The first threat is real, but its elimination requires an entirely different set of policies than does the second. The term also blurs the possible responses to threats, justifying for some the use of nuclear weapons to prevent a potential *chemical weapons* attack. This study disaggregates these threats, considering weapons and programs as they actually appear.

Twentieth Century's Deadly Legacy

Nuclear, *biological*, and *chemical weapons* were twentieth-century inventions. There is nothing new, of course, about mass destruction. From ancient times, a military campaign often meant the slaughter of tens of thousands of soldiers and civilians. As the Industrial Revolution mechanized warfare, the industrialized nations sought ways to more efficiently kill armored troops or unprotected populations dispersed over wide areas and to annihilate military and economic targets. Military researchers produced weapons that could deliver poison gas, germs, and nuclear explosions with artillery, aerial bombs, and, later, missiles.

Poison gas was used for the first time during *World War I*, as both the Central Powers and the Allies tried attacks with *chlorine gas*, mustard gas, and other agents to break the trench warfare stalemate. Japan inaugurated biological warfare in its attacks against the Chinese at the beginning of *World War II*, but all the belligerent nations had biological weapon research programs, and Germany invented and used *nerve gas* to kill millions of Jews and other prisoners in its concentration camps. *Nuclear weapons* were used for the first and last time at the end of that war, when the United States struck Japanese cities.

Global arsenals peaked during the Cold War years of the 1960s, 1970s, and early 1980s, when both the NATO nations and the Warsaw

Pact perfected and produced tens of thousands of nuclear, biological, and chemical bombs. Since then, the absolute numbers of these weapons have decreased dramatically.

Even before the end of the *Cold War*, the United States and the Soviet Union, which had the vast majority of global holdings, agreed to reduce their nuclear arsenals and to eliminate all their chemical and biological weapons. As the threat of global thermonuclear war receded, officials and experts agreed that the acquisition of those weapons by other nations or groups posed the most serious remaining threat. In January 1992, for example, the U.N. Security Council declared that their spread constituted a "threat to international peace and security." In 1998, the U.S. Defense Intelligence Agency concluded in its annual threat assessment, "The proliferation of nuclear, chemical, and biological weapons, missiles, and other key technologies remains the greatest direct threat to U.S. interests worldwide." In early 2001, President George W. Bush said, "The grave threat from nuclear, biological, and chemical weapons has not gone away with the Cold War. It has evolved into many separate threats, some of them harder to see and harder to answer."

Weapons and Trends

The nations of the world confront serious and immediate threats from the global presence of thousands of *nuclear weapons* and *chemical weapons*. They also face the possibility that some nation or group still has or soon could have biological weapons. A wide variety of delivery mechanisms for these weapons exists, including *ballistic missiles*, *cruise missiles*, *aircraft*, *artillery*, *ships*, *trucks*, and *envelopes*. There is also now the added danger that terrorist organizations could kill thousands with these weapons or by sabotaging critical urban and industrial infrastructures.

Although a terrorist attack on these infrastructures using conventional weapons is the most likely threat—as seen by the terrorist attacks on September 11, 2001, in New York and Washington and on March 11, 2004, in Madrid—the explosion of a *nuclear weapon* would be the most devastating. This calculation of "*risk times consequences*" should force us to focus most of our attention on this catastrophic possibility while not neglecting the threats from chemical and biological weapons and doing all we can to prevent conventional attacks.

The development of accurate threat assessments and effective national policies requires understanding the technologies of the various types of weapons, the history of their spread, and the successes and failures of nonproliferation efforts. The sections below give a brief overview, with greater detail provided in the country chapters that follow. It is followed by a global assessment of the current threats and of past and proposed nonproliferation policies.

Nuclear Weapons

Nuclear weapons are the most deadly weapons ever invented—the only true weapons of mass destruction. A single, compact nuclear device can instantly devastate a midsized city. *Nuclear weapons* are also the most difficult of the three types of weapons to manufacture or acquire. Today, only eight nations are known to have *nuclear weapons*. Five *nuclear weapon* states are recognized by the Treaty on the Non-Proliferation of Nuclear Weapons (NPT) and enjoy special rights and privileges under international law. In order of the size of their nuclear arsenals, they are *Russia*, *the United States*, *China*, *France*, and *the United Kingdom*.

The members of this group acquired their arsenals during the 20 years after *World War II*, and the group remained remarkably stable from 1964, when China tested its *first nuclear weapon*, until 1998, when *India* and *Pakistan* both detonated nuclear devices and declared their intention to deploy weapons. India and Pakistan have not yet openly deployed any weapons, but both are capable of configuring aircraft and missiles with tens of weapons over the next few years, if they so desire. *Israel* is widely believed to have approximately 100 nuclear weapons but neither acknowledges nor denies their existence. India, Pakistan, and Israel are not parties to the NPT.

Apart from these eight countries, two others may be actively pursuing nuclear weapons programs. *North Korea* acknowledges a program and may have accumulated enough material to construct as many as nine weapons. The 1994 agreement that had frozen the nation's plutonium program broke down in 2002, and it soon announced its withdrawal from the NPT. In January 2005, North Korean officials declared publicly for the first time that they had nuclear weapons. *Iran* is slowly but steadily pursuing an open civilian nuclear power program and may be covertly developing expertise for nuclear weapons. Iran is a member state of the NPT and, as such, any nuclear weapons program is illegal and, if proved, could subject it to additional sanctions or even military action through U.N. resolutions.

Since the signing of the NPT in 1968, however, many more countries have given up nuclear weapons programs than have begun them. There are fewer nuclear weapons in the world and fewer nations with nuclear weapons programs than there were 20 or 30 years ago.

In the past 20 years, several major countries have abandoned nuclear programs, including *Argentina* and *Brazil*, and four others have relinquished their nuclear weapons to join the NPT as non-nuclear-weapon states. *Ukraine*, *Belarus*, and *Kazakhstan* gave up the thousands of nuclear weapons deployed on their territories when the Soviet Union dissolved, thanks in great measure to the dedicated diplomacy of the George H. W. Bush and Bill Clinton administrations. Similarly, *South Africa*, on the eve of its transition to majority rule, destroyed the six nuclear weapons its apartheid regime had secretly constructed. President Nelson Mandela agreed with the decision, concluding that South Africa's security was better served in a nuclear-free Africa than in one with several nuclear nations, which is exactly the logic that inspired the original members of the NPT decades earlier. (Africa is one of several areas of the world that have established nuclear-weapon-free zones, where the use or possession of nuclear weapons is prohibited anywhere on the continent.) *Iraq* gave up its nuclear program after the 1991 Gulf War and subsequent U.N. disarmament efforts, though the United States led a coalition of nations to invade Iraq, claiming that the country still had major programs for nuclear, biological, and chemical weapons. *Libya* gave up its nuclear and chemical weapons programs and long-range missile program in December 2003 after negotiations with the United States and the United Kingdom. *Algeria* showed some interest in nuclear weapons over the years but turned away from these programs in the 1990s and is no longer considered a high-risk state.

Radiological weapons, although not as destructive as nuclear explosive weapons, also pose a serious danger, particularly as a terrorist threat. These are weapons that use conventional explosives, such as dynamite, to disperse radioactive materials, including the highly radioactive waste material from nuclear power reactors or other nonweapon sources. They may be attractive weapons for terrorists owing to the relative ease of their acquisition and use and mass disruption potential. A terrorist act involving the dispersal of radioactive materials would contaminate a wide area, making the treatment of casualties more difficult, exposing many people unhurt in the initial explosion to death and injury from radioactivity and rendering large areas uninhabitable, pending sizable removal and cleansing operations. As with chemical and biological agents, the invisible and uncertain danger from these weapons would cause widespread fear and horror. There is also the risk of a "*reverse dirty bomb*" that brings the conventional explosive to an existing radioactive source (e.g., storage pools for spent-fuel rods from civilian nuclear reactors), triggering an explosion that could be many times more deadly than the accident at Chernobyl.

Biological Weapons

Biological weapons are weapons that intentionally use living organisms to kill. They are second only to nuclear weapons in their potential to cause mass casualties. Although instances of the deliberate spread of disease go back to the ancient Greeks and Assyrians, the efficient weaponization of biological agents did not occur until the twentieth century. With the exception of the Japanese attacks in China before and during World War II, these weapons have not been used in modern warfare.

During the Cold War, the United States and the Soviet Union perfected biological weapons, each developing arsenals capable of destroying all human life and many food crops on the planet. In 1969, President Richard M. Nixon announced that the United States would unilaterally and unconditionally renounce biological weapons. He ordered the destruction of the entire U.S. biological weapons stockpile and the conversion of all production facilities to peaceful purposes. He reversed 45 years of U.S. reluctance and sought the ratification of the 1925 Geneva Protocol, which prohibited the use of biological and chemical weapons in war (and which was subsequently ratified under President Gerald Ford). Nixon successfully negotiated the Biological and Toxin Weapons Convention (BWC), signed in 1972 and ratified by the Senate in 1975, which prohibits the development, production, stockpiling, acquisition, or transfer of biological weapons. This treaty requires all signatories to destroy all their biological weapons and biological weapon production facilities. The treaty has no verification mechanism, however, and the states that are parties to it have been trying to negotiate a verification protocol and additional measures to strengthen it.

It is often difficult to get a complete picture of which countries or groups have biological weapons or programs. Milton Leitenberg points out that official assessments rarely distinguish between *suspected*, *capability*, *developing*, and *weapon*. Worse, nations with such capabilities or programs are often lumped together in lists with countries that have chemical weapons programs or capabilities. This book differentiates the distinct programs and threats. National programs are distinguished by whether they have produced actual weapons, have only research and development programs, or have the basic capability to produce agents. The chapters on specific countries provide the full details of each program.

When the BWC originally entered into force in 1975, 4 nations were thought to have biological weapons: the United States, the Soviet Union, China, and South Africa. By the spring of 2005, 169 nations had signed the treaty; however, seven nations are suspected of having some level of offensive biological warfare research programs: China, Egypt, Iran, Israel, North Korea, Russia, and Syria. U.S. officials have publicly identified many of these nations on several occasions, including at the 1996 and 2001 review conferences for the BWC and in annual reports to Congress. These nations are all suspected of pursuing offensive biological weapons programs prohibited by the BWC, though not all the countries, such as Israel, are members of the BWC. Almost all the programs are research efforts, and only one nation—Russia—is believed to have produced and stockpiled weapon agents; four others—Iran, North Korea, Israel, and China—may have done so.

Biological weapons production

Although the *Soviet Union* claimed that it had ended its extensive bioweapons program when it signed the BWC in 1972, President Boris Yeltsin in 1992 disclosed that work had, in fact, continued at substantial levels. There is still considerable uncertainty surrounding Russian weapon facilities, and the possibility exists that agents and weapons remain in Russia.

Biological weapons programs

Israel is believed to have a sophisticated biological weapons program; it may have produced anthrax and more advanced agents in weaponized form as well as toxins. U.S. officials believe that *North Korea* has pursued biological warfare capabilities since the 1960s and may have the capability to produce sufficient quantities of biological agents for military purposes within weeks of a decision to do so. *China* has a large, advanced biotechnical infrastructure that could be used to develop and produce biological agents. Chinese officials have repeatedly asserted that the country has never researched or produced biological weapons. U.S. officials, however, believe that the voluntary BWC declarations submitted by China are inaccurate and incomplete.

Possible biological weapon research programs

Iran may have an offensive biological weapons program, including the capability to produce small quantities of biological weapons agents.

In November 2001, U.S. undersecretary of state John Bolton said that Iran had actually produced agents and weapons, but he had a more cautious assessment in 2004: "I cannot say that the United States can prove beyond a shadow of a doubt that Iran has an offensive biological weapons program. The intelligence I have seen suggests that this is the case." There is considerable evidence that *Egypt* started a program in the early 1960s that produced weaponized agents. In 1996, U.S. officials reported that by 1972 Egypt had developed biological warfare agents and that there was "no evidence to indicate that Egypt has eliminated this capability and it remains likely that the Egyptian capability to conduct biological warfare continues to exist." Egyptian officials assert that Egypt never developed, produced, or stockpiled biological weapons. *Syria* has a biotechnical infrastructure capable of supporting limited agent development but has not begun a major effort to produce biological agents or to put them into weapons, according to official U.S. assessments. *Sudan* is not believed to have a biological weapons program, but U.S. officials have repeatedly warned of Sudanese interest in developing such a program.

Other states of some concern include *South Africa*, which had a bioweapons program that the new unity government says it ended in 1992, and *Taiwan*, which is now rarely mentioned in either official or expert reviews. *India* and *Pakistan* are not believed to have produced or stockpiled offensive biological weapons, although official assessments note that both countries have the resources and capability to support biological warfare research and development efforts. Finally, U.S. officials had long believed that both *Iraq* and *Libya* had biological weapons or programs, but inspections after the 2003 war in Iraq and the 2003 agreement with Libya showed that neither had an active program.

Bioterrorism

During the past several decades, terrorist attempts to acquire biological agents have fallen short of successful weaponization. Almost all threats to use biological agents—including hundreds of terrorist *anthrax* hoaxes against abortion clinics and other targets in the United States—have been false alarms. There have been only two significant biological attacks by terrorists in recent times. Some experts contend that the complexity of a biological weapon design for effective dissemination has by and large thwarted bioterrorism. The Japanese religious sect Aum Shinrikyo, for example, tried for several years, and with considerable funding and expertise, to produce and weaponize botulinum toxin and anthrax. The group's extensive efforts failed, and it resorted to using the chemical agent sarin for attacks in a Tokyo subway in 1994 and 1995. The first successful terrorist incident involving biological agents occurred in 1984 in Dalles, Oregon, when a religious cult, Rajneesh, disseminated salmonella bacteria in ten restaurants, infecting 750 people, but with no fatalities.

When the bioterrorism attack that many had long feared finally came, it was not what the experts had predicted. In the United States in October 2001, someone sent letters containing anthrax to members of Congress and the media. The terrorist either did not realize that sophisticated dispersal mechanisms were required for mass casualties from anthrax or simply did not care. The letters killed five and infected eighteen others. The attack could have been much worse, but this was the first time that a biological warfare agent was used against the U.S. population. Even this limited attack caused mass disruption and cost billions of dollars in decontamination and prevention expenses.

Chemical Weapons

Mass casualties require large amounts of *chemical agents* relative to either biological or nuclear weapons. Still, 5 metric tons of the nerve gas sarin carried in bombs and dropped by two strike aircraft or the warheads of 36 Scud missiles could kill 50 percent of the people over 4 square kilometers. By comparison, a Hiroshima-size nuclear bomb of 12-kiloton yield would kill 50 percent of the population over 30 square kilometers.

Chemical weapons have been used only in isolated instances of warfare since World War I, despite (or perhaps because of) the substantial numbers of weapons that were in national arsenals. The 1996 Chemical Weapons Convention (CWC) started a process of "*deproliferation*," whereby most nations declared their holdings (if any) and began eliminating their arsenals and production facilities. The CWC requires all state parties possessing chemical weapons to destroy them in a safe and environmentally friendly manner not later than ten years after the treaty entered into force, or by April 29, 2007, unless special extensions are granted. The treaty also requires all state parties to destroy or convert all present and past capabilities used to produce chemical weapons by that time. The declarations by the United States and Russia account for the vast majority of known *chemical weapon stockpiles*.

As of the spring of 2005, 168 countries were state parties to the CWC. Four countries—the United States, Russia, India, and South

Korea—have declared their possession of chemical weapons stockpiles totaling more than 70,000 metric tons of agents. Russia's 40,000 metric tons is the largest declared stockpile, and that nation's financial difficulties make complete elimination of its stockpile by 2007 impossible. Eleven nations have declared their possession of existing or former chemical weapon production facilities: Bosnia and Herzegovina, China, France, India, Iran, Japan, Russia, South Korea, the United Kingdom, the United States, and Yugoslavia. Forty-nine of the 64 declared facilities were destroyed or converted, nearly 10,700 metric tons of chemical agents were destroyed, and one-fourth of the 8.6 million chemical weapons declared by the four possessor states was eliminated through treaty procedures between 1997 and February 2005.

The most significant remaining suspected national programs are those of China, Egypt, Iran, Israel, North Korea, and Syria. The other countries sometimes suspected of conducting chemical weapons research include India, Pakistan, Sudan, and Taiwan, but there is no publicly available evidence of such activity.

Suspected chemical weapons stockpiles

U.S. intelligence assessments state that *North Korea* has had a long-standing chemical warfare program, including the ability to produce bulk quantities of nerve, blister, choking, and blood agents. North Korea is believed to have a large stockpile of these agents and weapons.

Israel is also believed to have an active research and development program for chemical warfare agents and to have produced and stockpiled weapons. *Syria* has not signed the CWC, and U.S. officials believe it has a significant stockpile of the nerve agent sarin. A 1990 intelligence assessment reported that Syria had weaponized these chemicals in 500-kilogram aerial bombs and warheads for its Scud-B missiles. *Egypt* was the first country in the Middle East to obtain chemical weapons and the first to use them. It reportedly employed phosgene and mustard gas against Yemeni royalist forces in the mid-1960s. It is believed still to have a research program and has never reported the destruction of any of its chemical agents or weapons. Israel, Syria, and Egypt are not members of the CWC.

Iran's declaration at the May 1998 session of the CWC conference was the first time that nation had admitted to having had a chemical weapons program, apparently developed in response to Iraqi chemical warfare attacks during the Iran- Iraq War. U.S. officials say that in the past Iran has stockpiled blister, blood, and choking chemical agents and has weaponized some of these agents into *artillery shells*, *mortars*, *rockets*, and *aerial bombs*. Iranian officials deny these charges.

China has ratified the CWC and has declared that it does not possess an inventory of chemical agents. U.S. officials, however, believe that China has a moderate inventory of traditional agents, an advanced chemical warfare program and a wide variety of potential delivery systems.

Libya gave up its offensive chemical weapons capability with the 2003 negotiations and has joined the CWC. *Iraq*'s chemical weapons program ended after the 1991 Gulf War, but it has not yet joined the CWC. *Albania* discovered and declared a small cache of chemical weapons in 2004, pledging to destroy them by 2006.

Chemical weapon research programs

Sudan may have an active interest in acquiring the capability to produce chemical agents but is not believed to have done so. Sudan is a member of the CWC. *Pakistan* sometimes appears on a list of countries with chemical "*capabilities*" because it has the ability to manufacture chemical weapons should it choose to do so. Though Pakistan has imported a number of dual-use chemicals, they are probably for the development of commercial chemical industrial activities and not for a dedicated warfare program. *India*'s declaration under the CWC in June 1997 was the first time that nation acknowledged it had a chemical warfare production program. Though it has pledged to destroy all agents and production facilities, India's activities and exports of dual-use equipment and chemical precursors cause some concern. *South Korea* ended its weapons program when it ratified the CWC in 1997 and has been destroying its chemical weapons and production facilities.

Missile Proliferation

Much of the proliferation debate over the past few years has centered not on the weapons themselves but on one possible means for delivering them: *ballistic missiles*. It has become common wisdom and a political habit to refer to the growing threat of ballistic missiles. The threat is certainly changing and is increasing, according to some measures. Yet by several other important criteria, the ballistic missile threat to the United States is significantly smaller than it was in the mid-1980s.

In comparison with the high point of deployments in the mid-1980s, there are now dramatically fewer long-range, intermediate-range, and medium-range ballistic missiles. Most nations that have missiles have only short-range, Scud-type missiles, and many of these arsenals are being retired as they age. The number of countries trying to develop long-range ballistic missiles has not changed greatly in 20 years and is somewhat smaller than in the past. The nations now attempting to do so are also smaller, poorer, and less technologically advanced than were those with missile programs 20 years ago.

Only China and Russia have the capability to hit the mainland of the United States with nuclear warheads on intercontinental land-based ballistic missiles. This has not changed since Russia and China deployed their first intercontinental ballistic missiles in 1959 and 1981, respectively. Confusion arises when policy makers speak of missile threats to the United States or to such U.S. interests as forward-deployed troops or allied nations. This merges very-short-range missiles, of which there are many, with long-range missiles, of which there are few.

The greatest programs of concern are those developing medium-range missiles in India, Iran, Israel, North Korea, and Pakistan. None of these nations view their programs as threatening, but their neighbours take a decidedly different view. Though these programs are a cause for serious regional concern and could develop into potential international threats, overall the ballistic missile threat is limited and changing slowly.

Global Nuclear Threat Assessment

On the basis of the proceeding information, it is reasonable to conclude that of all the potential threats, nuclear weapons pose the greatest risks. We can categorize these threats along four axes, though developments along one axis often influence developments along the others. These four categories of threat are nuclear terrorism, new nuclear weapon states and regional conflict, existing nuclear arsenals, and regime collapse. The greatest concerns are outlined here.

Nuclear Terrorism: The Most Serious Threat

Although *states* can be deterred from using nuclear weapons by fear of retaliation, *terrorists*, who do not have land, people, or national futures to protect, may not be deterrable. Terrorists' acquisition of nuclear weapons therefore poses the greatest single nuclear threat. The gravest danger arises from terrorists' access to state stockpiles of nuclear weapons and fissile materials, because acquiring a supply of nuclear material (as opposed to making the weapon itself) remains the most difficult challenge for a terrorist group. So-called outlaw states are not the most likely source. Their stockpiles, if any, are small and exceedingly precious, and hence well guarded. (Nor are these states likely to give away what they see as the jewels in their security crowns.) Rather, the most likely sources of nuclear weapons and materials for terrorists are storage areas in the former states of the Soviet Union and in Pakistan, and fissile material kept at dozens of civilian sites around the world.

Russia and other former Soviet states possess thousands of nuclear weapons and hundreds of tons of inadequately secured nuclear material. Terrorist organizations and radical fundamentalist groups operate within Pakistan's borders. National instability or a radical change in government could lead to the collapse of state control over nuclear weapons and materials and to the migration of nuclear scientists to the service of other nations or groups.

There is also a substantial risk of terrorist theft from the nuclear stockpiles in more than 40 countries around the world. Many of these caches of materials consist of highly enriched uranium that could be directly used in nuclear weapons or further enriched to weapons grade. There are also significant stockpiles of plutonium that could be used in a weapon, though with more difficulty.

New Nuclear Nations and Regional Conflicts

The danger posed by the acquisition of nuclear weapons by Iran or North Korea is not that either country would likely use these weapons to attack the United States, the nations of Europe, or other countries. States are and will continue to be deterred from such attacks by the certainty of swift and massive retaliation. The greater danger is the reactions of other states in the region. A nuclear chain reaction could ripple throughout a region and across the globe, triggering weapons decisions in several, perhaps many, other states. And along with these rapid developments and the collapse of existing norms could come increased regional tensions, possibly leading to regional wars and to *nuclear catastrophe*.

New nuclear weapon states might also constrain the United States and others, weakening their ability to intervene to avoid conflict in dangerous regions—as well as, of course, emboldening Tehran, Pyongyang, or other new possessors.

Existing regional nuclear tensions already pose serious risks. The decades-long conflict between India and Pakistan has made South Asia for many years the region most likely to witness the first use of nuclear weapons since World War II. There is an active missile race under way between the two nations, even as China and India continue their rivalry. In Northeast Asia, North Korea's nuclear capabilities remain shrouded in uncertainty but presumably continue to advance. Miscalculation or misunderstanding could bring nuclear war to the Korean peninsula.

In the Middle East, Iran's nuclear program, together with Israel's nuclear arsenal and the chemical weapons of other neighbouring states, add grave volatility to an already conflict-prone region. If Iran were to acquire nuclear weapons, Egypt, Saudi Arabia, or others might initiate or revive their nuclear weapons programs. It is possible that the Middle East could go from a region with one nuclear weapon state to one with two, three, or five such states within a decade — with existing political and territorial disputes still unresolved.

Risk from Existing Arsenals

There are grave dangers inherent in the maintenance of thousands of nuclear weapons by the United States and Russia and the hundreds of weapons held by China, France, the United Kingdom, Israel, India, and Pakistan. Though each state regards its nuclear weapons as safe, secure, and essential to its security, each views others' arsenals with suspicion.

Though the Cold War has been over for more than a dozen years, Washington and Moscow maintain thousands of warheads on hair-trigger alert, ready to launch within fifteen minutes. This greatly increases the risk of an unauthorized launch. Because there is no time buffer built into each state's decision-making process, this extreme level of readiness also enhances the possibility that either country's president could prematurely order a nuclear strike based on flawed intelligence.

Recent advocacy by some in the United States of new battlefield uses for nuclear weapons could lead to new nuclear tests. The five nuclear weapon states recognized by the NPT have not tested since the signing of the Comprehensive Test Ban Treaty (CTBT) in 1996, and no state has tested since India and Pakistan did so in May 1998. New U.S. tests would trigger tests by other nations and cause the collapse of the CTBT, which is widely regarded as a pillar of the nonproliferation regime.

To the extent that the leaders of a given state are contemplating acceding to U.S. or international nonproliferation demands, these leaders may feel a strong need for equity so that they can show their public that giving up nuclear aspirations is fair and in their interest. It is difficult, if not impossible, to demonstrate either positive outcome when immensely powerful nuclear weapon states reassert the importance of nuclear weapons to their own security.

Risk of Regime Collapse

If U.S. and Russian nuclear arsenals remain at *Cold War levels*, many nations will conclude that the weapon states' promise to reduce and eventually eliminate these arsenals has been broken. Non-nuclear states may therefore feel released from their pledge not to acquire nuclear arms.

The NPT has already been severely threatened by the development in several states of facilities for enriching uranium and reprocessing plutonium. Although each state has asserted that these facilities are for civilian use only, the resulting supplies of nuclear materials give each country a "*virtual*" nuclear weapons capability. This situation greatly erodes the confidence that states can have in a neighbour's non-nuclear pledge.

Additionally, there appears to be growing acceptance of the nuclear status of India and Pakistan, with each country accruing prestige and increased attention from leading nuclear weapon states, including the United States. Some now argue that a nuclear Iran or North Korea could also be absorbed into the international system without serious consequence.

If the number of states with nuclear weapons increases, the original nuclear weapon states fail to comply with their disarmament obligations, and states such as India gain status for having nuclear weapons, it is possible that Brazil, Japan, and other major non-nuclear nations will reconsider their nuclear choices. Most nations would continue to eschew nuclear weapons, if only for technological and economic reasons, but others would decide that nuclear weapons were necessary to improve their security or status. There is a real possibility, under these conditions, of a systemwide collapse.

Successes and Failures of the Nonproliferation Regime

Ever since American scientists detonated the first nuclear bomb at Alamogordo, New Mexico, in July 1945, many officials and experts have feared the future. They have worried that proliferation could run out of control, creating a bleak, dangerous world with dozens of nations armed with nuclear weapons. Several times in the past few decades, the public's fear of nuclear war has moved millions of people worldwide to petition for an immediate change in their governments' policies. More than once, the very fate of the Earth seemed to be at stake, as Jonathan Schell titled his book in 1982.

President John F. Kennedy worried that while only the United States, the Soviet Union, the United Kingdom, and France in the early 1960s possessed nuclear weapons, by the end of the decade 15 or 20 nations would have them. The concern was not that developing countries would acquire the bomb but rather that the advanced industrial nations would do so, particularly Japan and Germany. Several European nations were already actively pursuing nuclear weapons programs. Neutral Sweden, for example, was then developing plans to build 100 nuclear weapons to equip its air force, army, and navy.

Kennedy moved aggressively to counter those trends. He created the Arms Control and Disarmament Agency in 1961; began negotiations on a treaty to stop the spread of nuclear weapons; and negotiated the Limited Test Ban Treaty, which ended nuclear tests in the atmosphere, under water, and in outer space.

U.S. diplomacy and international efforts to create legal and diplomatic barriers to the acquisition of nuclear weapons, which were codified in the NPT in 1968, dramatically stopped the rush toward nuclear weapons status. Twenty years after Kennedy's warning, only China (with Soviet help) had openly joined the ranks of the new nuclear nations, whereas India had exploded a so-called peaceful nuclear device and Israel was building a secret nuclear arsenal. All the other nations that had studied nuclear programs in the 1950s and 1960s had abandoned their pursuits. The treaty did little at that time, however, to constrain the nuclear arms race between the two superpowers in the 1960s and 1970s, which was sometimes known as vertical proliferation.

Throughout the 1980s and 1990s, however, proliferation experts were again ringing alarms. As Leonard Spector said in 1984 in *Nuclear Proliferation Today* (the first book in the Carnegie Endowment's series on proliferation): "The spread of nuclear weapons poses one of the greatest threats of our time and is among the most likely triggers of a future nuclear holocaust.... The spread of nuclear arms also increases the risk of their falling into the hands of dissident military elements or revolutionaries.... The threat of nuclear terrorism is also growing."

Nonproliferation efforts have steadily advanced in the past two decades, but never easily and never without serious setbacks. Though some nations renounced their weapons of mass destruction programs, others started new ones. Often a majority of nations was able to agree on new treaties and new restraints, only to have other nations block their progress or feign compliance.

Since September 11, 2001, few have questioned the need for urgent government action. President Bush said during his meetings with Russian president Vladimir Putin in November 2001, "Our highest priority is to keep terrorists from acquiring weapons of mass destruction.... We will strengthen our efforts to cut off every possible source of biological, chemical, and nuclear weapons, material and expertise." These new efforts can be built on the successes of previous actions.

Although nuclear, biological, and chemical arsenals in the United States and the Soviet Union once grew to enormous levels and the technology of these weapons has become increasingly accessible, the world has not been devastated by a thermonuclear war. Moreover, the number of new prospective nuclear nations has shrunk dramatically during the past 20 years, not increased, and the international norm has been firmly established that countries should not, under any circumstances, possess or use either biological or chemical weapons. Global expectations are that the existing stockpiles of nuclear weapons will be greatly reduced, even if their eventual elimination seems but a distant hope.

Since 1964, only four nations are known to have overcome the substantial diplomatic and technical barriers to manufacturing nuclear weapons. The proliferation of biological and chemical weapons is broader, but it is still mainly confined to two regions of the world: the Middle East and Northeast Asia. Most of the world's biological weapons have been destroyed, and the bulk of the global chemical weapons arsenals will likely be eliminated in the next ten years.

Even with all the serious challenges it has faced, the non-proliferation regime has still had a remarkable record of success. But can it hold? Or are international conditions so different today that the regime can no longer work?

Twenty-First-Century Proliferation

Some argue that with the end of superpower conflict, the world confronts a fundamentally different proliferation problem. Although the regime may have worked in the past, they doubt the holdouts can be convinced to adopt the same norms as those held by the regime founders. This inspection regime had failed to independently detect significant hidden programs in Iran, Iraq, and Libya. Many officials in the George

W. Bush administration believe that the entire process of negotiating and implementing nonproliferation treaties is both unnecessary and harmful to U.S. national security interests. They argue that some of the treaties—such as the CTBT, the Anti-Ballistic Missile Treaty, and the Landmine Treaty—restrict necessary armaments, thus weakening the principal nation that safeguards global peace and security. Other treaties, such as the CWC and the BWC, promote a false sense of security as some nations sign, then cheat on, the agreements.

The Bush administration therefore has implemented a radically new nonproliferation approach. Previous presidents, as noted above, treated the weapons themselves as the problem and sought their elimination through treaties. President Bill Clinton, for example, warned in November 1998 of the threat "posed by *the proliferation of nuclear, biological, and chemical weapons and the means of delivering such weapons*". President Bush framed the issue differently in his 2003 State of the Union address: "The gravest danger facing America and the world is *outlaw regimes that seek and possess nuclear, chemical, and biological weapons*". The Bush administration thus has changed the focus from "what" to "who." This corresponds to a strategy that seeks the elimination of regimes rather than weapons. This action-oriented approach has been detailed in two key documents—*The National Security Strategy of the United States of America* (September 2002) and *National Strategy to Combat Weapons of Mass Destruction* (December 2002)—in which the administration states its view that the threat from weapons of mass destruction emanates from a small number of outlaw states and from the nexus of these states, nuclear weapons and materials, and terrorists.

The first direct application of this theory was the war with Iraq. There had been previous applications of military force to deal with proliferation threats, but this was the world's first nonproliferation war, a battle fought primarily over the claimed need to prevent the acquisition or transfer of nuclear, biological, and chemical weapons.

Three major conclusions can be drawn from the war: In 2003, Iraq was not producing and did not have stockpiles of, nuclear, biological or chemical weapons or any Scud missiles or unmanned aerial vehicles designed to deliver such weapons. All active nuclear, chemical, and biological programs ended between 1991 and 1996.

U.N. sanctions and inspections were more effective than most realized in disarming Iraq after the 1991 War. Inspectors in 2003 were finding what there was to find.

In the year prior to the war, U.S. and British officials systematically misrepresented Iraq's weapon capabilities.

This last finding is contested by officials in the U.S. and British administrations but is widely accepted outside these governments. Further, none of these conclusions appear to have diminished the enthusiasm of the proponents of the Iraq war for applying the Iraq model to other problem states. The new strategy, however, has not yet proved superior to the one it replaced.

Since 2000, proliferation problems have grown worse, not better. Libya has been the only unqualified success, as that nation has abandoned decades of work on nuclear and chemical weapons and missile programs. But Iran has accelerated its program—whether peaceful or not—in the past few years. So has North Korea. That country ended the freeze on its plutonium program, claimed to have reprocessed the plutonium into weapons, withdrew from the NPT, and declared itself a nuclear weapon state. Globally, the threat from nuclear terrorism has grown as U.S. intelligence officials have concluded that the Iraq War made the terrorism problem worse and supplies of weapons and weapons materials remain dangerously insecure. Though U.S. attention focused on the three "*axis of evil*" states, the nuclear black market of Pakistan's A. Q. Khan spread nuclear weapons technology and know-how around the world. It is not clear if this network has shut down or merely gone further underground.

Meanwhile, the United States and Russia have ended the process of negotiating reductions in their nuclear arsenals, and the reductions themselves are proceeding at a slower pace than previous administrations planned. Programs to secure nuclear materials in the states of the former Soviet Union are also slowing down, though only half the materials have been secured. Finally, there is growing concern that the entire nonproliferation regime is in danger of a catastrophic collapse.

Elements of a New Nonproliferation Policy

Some believe that the strategy, or some modified variation, could still prove its worth. Many countries are cooperating in the Proliferation Security Initiative to interdict illegal trade in weapon components. There is a much greater willingness internationally to enforce nonproliferation commitments. The right combination of force and diplomacy could yet result in negotiated solutions to the North Korean and Iranian programs. And prospects for peacefully resolving regional conflicts may have increased through the growing movement for democracy in the Middle East and Central Asia.

A combination of approaches may offer the best chance of success. There is the need for a new strategy that combines the best elements of the United States–centric, force-based approach with the traditional multilateral, treaty-based approach. For example, the European Union has crafted a joint nonproliferation strategy that includes tying all E.U. trade agreements to the observance of nonproliferation treaties and norms. This "*soft power*" approach could meld with the "*hard power*" of the United States to replicate the success of the United States and United Kingdom with Libya. The Libyan model could emerge from and prevail over the Iraq model: Change a regime's behaviour rather than change the regime.

The theory and practical applications of a new approach have been detailed in a 2005 Carnegie Endowment report, *Universal Compliance: A Strategy for Nuclear Security.* This report analyzes how to end the threat of nuclear terrorism by implementing comprehensive efforts to secure and eliminate nuclear materials worldwide and to stop the illegal transfer of nuclear technology. The strategy would prevent new nuclear weapon states by increasing penalties for withdrawal from the NPT, enforcing compliance with strengthened treaties, and radically reforming the nuclear fuel cycle to prevent states from acquiring dual-use technologies for *uranium* enrichment or *plutonium* reprocessing. The threat from existing arsenals would be reduced by shrinking global stockpiles, curtailing research on new nuclear weapons, and taking the weapons off hair-trigger-alert status. Finally, greater efforts would be devoted to resolving the regional conflicts that fuel proliferation imperatives and to bringing the three nuclear weapon states outside the NPT into conformance with a expanded set of global nonproliferation norms.

Tomorrow's solutions, like yesterday's, will not emerge in a diplomatic vacuum. As we struggle to develop new policies, it is worth remembering that the nonproliferation treaties were an integral part of the political and military balance-of- power and alliance systems of the late twentieth century. Alliance security arrangements, including the promise that the United States would extend a "*nuclear umbrella*" over Europe and Japan, undoubtedly made it easier for several industrial nations to abandon their nuclear weapons programs. The Soviet Union simply forced nonproliferation on its alliance system, whereas the United States was not adverse to using strong-arm tactics to compel South

Korea and Taiwan, for example, to abandon nuclear weapons research. Further thwarting proliferation, many developing nations found that their ambitions ran into formidable financial and technological obstacles to nuclear weapons development, missile engineering, and biological agent weaponization. This is still true today and should give pause to those who predict a smooth and rapid rise to nuclear weapon status for new nations.

These financial, technical, and alliance factors were not, however, sufficient barriers to proliferation. These factors were present in the 1960s and 1970s. But before the signing of the NPT, nuclear proliferation was on the rise; afterward, it was on the decline. The critical importance of the NPT and other treaties is that they provide the necessary international legal mechanism and establish the global norms that give nations a clear path to a non-nuclear future. These historic lessons must be remembered anew, lest in our haste to construct new solutions we tear down the very structures we mean only to repair.

15

Droplet-based Micro-electrofluidic Biosensor

Recent events have heightened the need for new technologies for combating *bioterrorism* threats and for monitoring environmental toxins. In a likely scenario, a dangerous pathogenic microbe, such as the variola virus that causes smallpox, may be spread in a densely-populated area such as an airport. It takes 12 to 14 days for the appearance of the first symptoms of smallpox, making it possible for hundreds or thousands of people to be exposed before the attack is detected. It has been recognized that an undetected bio-attack could easily become a national outbreak. Therefore, the real-time detection and identification of pathogenic bio-molecular agents in the field is key to an effective homeland security infrastructure. There is a pressing need for fast, accurate, and reliable biological/chemical sensing and detecting systems for critical locations, such as airports or subway stations. Such systems, capable of continuously sampling and testing air or water samples for biological or chemical warfare toxins and other pathogens, can offer an early warning capability to people before anyone exhibits symptoms.

Bio-molecular detection can be carried out either using immunoassay or DNA-based testing. The former is based on an antibody-antigen reaction. An antibody is a highly selective ligand, which is produced by mammalian immunological systems in response to the introduction of an antigen. Nucleic acid testing based on DNA hybridization or DNA sequencing has been employed for commercial biochips. It uses *polymerase chain reaction* (PCR) to amplify suspect samples, thus making it possible to detect even a single organism.

In recent years, a novel *droplet-based microelectrofluidic system* has been developed to analyze nanoliter volumes of agents in real time. These systems reduce the rate of reagent consumption enabling continuous sampling and analysis for on-line, real-time biological/chemical analysis. By scaling down the concentration of the samples, simple sensing techniques can be utilized to replace conventional, costly, and time-consuming practices involving batch analysis, sample pretreatment and frequent calibration. Advances in this technique make droplet-based microelectrofluidic systems a promising platform in the realm of massively parallel DNA analysis and real-time molecular detection and recognition. The feasibility of performing either protein or DNA real-time reaction on this novel sensing and detecting system has been successfully demonstrated. Furthermore, these droplet-based microelectrofluidic systems offer the exciting possibility to explore a radically different bio-molecular detection approach by decoupling the problem of determining a binary yes/no response from the problem of determining the agent concentration. By placing such droplet-based microelectrofluidic systems at predetermined detection sites, a series of simple bio-molecular tests, based on colorimetric reactions and optical detection, can be performed. For example, the *Coomassie Brilliant Blue* method can detect the presence of a protein, which could be the outer coat of a virus or some other infectious agents, by monitoring the change of colour. This reaction is rapid and the maximum absorbance occurs within 2 to 5 min. This bio-molecular recognition approach not only reduces the detection time drastically, but it also solves the problem of detecting an unknown agent.

As droplet-based microelectrofluidic systems become widespread in safety-critical biomedical applications, system reliability emerges as an essential performance parameter. In order to ensure availability, e.g., as an always-on "*bio smoke alarm*," these microelectrofluidic systems should not only be tested adequately after manufacturing, but also need to be monitored continuously during field operation. Therefore, there is a pressing need for efficient testing methodologies that are applicable to both manufacturing and operational defects for such systems. In fact, the 2003 International Technology Roadmap for Semiconductors (ITRS) recognizes the need for new test methods for disruptive device technologies that underly microelectromechanical systems (MEMS) and sensors, and highlights it as one of the five most difficult test challenges beyond 2009.

In this chapter, we propose a cost-effective test methodology that is applicable both in-field and after manufacturing for droplet-based microelectrofluidic systems. We present an analysis of likely defects in such systems and classify them as catastrophic and parametric faults. We present a novel unified fault detection mechanism for both catastrophic and parametric faults. Fault detection is based on tracking droplet movement through the unused portions of the system. It can be implemented without disrupting the normal mode of operation, and with negligible hardware overhead. Then, we present tolerance analysis based on Monte-Carlo simulation to characterize the impact of variations in physical and fluidic parameters on the system performance. Finally, we present experimental results on a droplet-based micro-electrofluidic system for a real-time PCR application, where three distinct physical defects are evaluated in terms of their detection capabilities.

ELECTROWETTING-ACTUATED DROPLET-BASED MICROELECTROFLUIDIC SYSTEMS

Electrowetting-based actuation of microelectrofluidic systems has recently been proposed for optical switching, chemical analysis, and rotating yaw rate sensing. By varying the electrical potential along a linear array of electrodes, electrowetting can be used to move nanoliter volume liquid droplets along this line of electrodes. Droplets can also be transported, in user-defined patterns and under clocked-voltage control, over a two-dimensional array of electrodes without the need for pumps and valves. The droplet, usually containing biomedical samples, and the filler medium, such as the silicone oil, are sandwiched between two parallel glass plates. The bottom plate contains a patterned array of individually controllable electrodes, while the top plate is coated with a ground electrode. The hydrophobic dielectric insulator is added to the top and bottom plates to decrease the wettability of the surface and to add capacitance between droplet and control electrode.

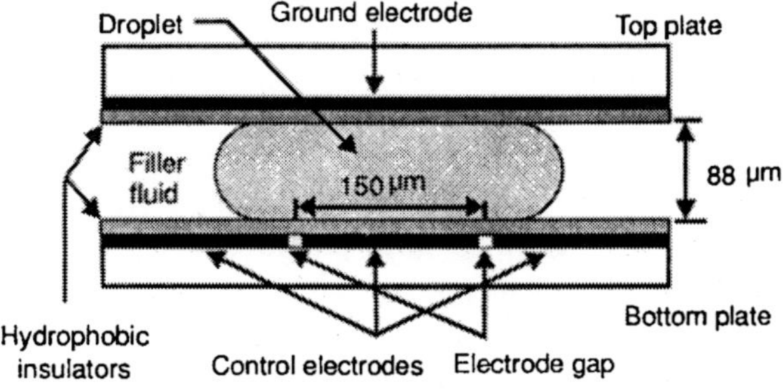

Fig. 15.1. Actuation mechanism for droplet motion.

The basic principle of *microdroplet transportation* is to electrostatically control the interfacial tension at the droplet/insulator interface. A control voltage is applied to an electrode adjacent to the droplet and at the same time the electrode just under the droplet is deactivated. This causes an accumulation of charge in the droplet/ insulator interface, resulting in a surface tension gradient across the gap between the adjacent electrodes, which consequently causes the transportation of the droplet. The velocity of the droplet can be controlled by adjusting the control voltage (0 ~ 90 V), and droplets can be moved at speeds of up to 20 cm/s. Based on this principle, microfluidic droplets can be moved freely to any location of a two-dimensional array. This design is ideally suited for a large-scale integrated microfluidic system, which is expected to be extensively used for biomedical applications, such as DNA sequencing and bimolecular detection, in the near future. The electrodes can be viewed as building blocks in nanotechnology such that huge networks of nano devices can be easily assembled. Each electrode set can be viewed as a pump at the nano/picoscale, and an array of these pumps can be used for biochemical assays.

Fluid droplets are introduced to the device from the input-output (I/O) ports on the boundary of an array. Droplets in the array have identical volumes. Hence, this device is called a unit-flow device. It is desirable to maintain the unit-flow constraint since the rate of chemical and biomedical reaction grows exponentially with the growth of droplet volume. In a unit flow environment, the routes that droplets travel and their rendezvous points are programmed into a micro-controller that controls the voltages of the electrodes.

Related Prior Work

Over the past decade, the focus in testing research has broadened from logic and memory test to include the testing of analog and mixed-signal circuits. MEMS is a relatively young field compared to IC design, and MEMS testing is still in its infancy. Recently, fault modeling and fault simulation in surface micromachined MEMS has received attention. Researchers in Carnegie Mellon University, Pittsburgh, PA, are developing a comprehensive testing methodology for a class of MEMS known as *surface micromachined sensors*.

However, *test techniques* for MEMS cannot be directly applied to microelectrofluidic systems, since the techniques and tools currently in use for MEMS testing do not handle fluids. Hence, they are of limited use for testing microfluidic devices. Most recent work in this area has been limited to the testing of continuous-flow microfluidic systems. Researchers at the MESA+ Research Institute of the University of Twente, Twente, The Netherlands, have applied mixed-signal testing techniques to the problem of testing a microanalysis system. Also, a *design-for-testability* (DFT) technique for flow-FET-based microfluidic systems has been proposed. Similar to MOSFET, a flow-FET has source and drain electrodes over which a relatively large voltage (~100 V) is applied.

Due to the principle of electro-osmotic flow, the electric field moves the charge accumulated between the fluid and the surface of channel, dragging the bulk liquid through the channel. This type of microfluidic systems belongs to the category of continuous-flow systems where fluid motion constitutes continuous streams as opposed to discrete droplets. Testing of discrete droplet-based fluidic systems, both off-line and in-field, has not received much attention to date, as these systems have been introduced very recently.

A Faults in Droplet-based Microelectrofluidic Systems

It is evident that droplet-based microelectrofluidic systems exhibit behaviour resembling analog and mixed-signal devices. Therefore, we classify the faults in these systems as being either catastrophic or parametric, along the line of fault classification for analog circuits. *Catastrophic (hard) faults* lead to a complete malfunction of the system, while *parametric (soft) faults* cause a deviation in the system performance. Aparametric fault is detectable only if this deviation exceeds the tolerance in system performance. Due to their underlying mixed technology and multiple energy domains, microelectrofluidic systems exhibit failure mechanisms and defects that are significantly different from the failure modes in analog integrated circuits.

Catastrophic faults in microelectrofluidic systems may be caused by the following physical defects.

1. *Dielectric breakdown*. The breakdown of the dielectric at high voltage levels creates a short between the droplet and the electrode. As a result, no charge can be stored in the interface. As the electrowetting mechanism depends on the amount of energy stored in the capacitor formed by the electrode and the droplet, dielectric breakdown inhibits fluid motion.
2. *Short between the adjacent electrodes*. As a result of a short circuit between two adjacent electrodes, these electrodes effectively form one longer electrode. Thus, the droplet residing on this electrode

is no longer large enough to overlap with the adjacent electrodes, inhibiting its actuation.

3. *Degradation of the electrode*. This degradation effect is unpredictable and may become catastrophic during the operation of the system. A consequence of electrode degradation is that droplets often fragment and their motion is prevented because of the unwanted variation of surface tension forces along their flow path.
4. *Open in the metal connection between the electrode and the control source*: This defect results in a failure of charging electrode while trying to drive the droplet.

Physical defects that cause parametric faults include the following:

1. *Geometrical parameter deviation*. The deviation in insulator thickness, electrode length, and height between parallel plates may exceed their tolerance value.
2. *Insulator degradation*. This "wear-and-tear" defect may become apparent gradually during operation. If left undetected, it may eventually cause electrode degradation.
3. *Particle contamination*. During in-field operation of a microelectrofluidic system, the droplet or the filer fluid may be contaminated by a particle, such as a dust particle or a foreign fluid droplet. Typically, such particles are then attached to the surface of the insulator of a cell and affect the motion of the droplet.
4. *Change in viscosity of droplet and filler medium*. These deviations can occur during the operation due to an unexpected biochemical reaction, or a defect in the control system causing unwanted temperature variation.

Faults in microelectrofluidic systems can also be classified based on the time at which they appear. Therefore, system failure or degraded performance can either be caused by manufacturing defects or by *parametric variations*. Testing of manufacturing defects, such as a short between the adjacent electrodes or a deviation in the value of the geometrical parameters, should be performed immediately after production. However, operational faults, such as degradation of the insulator or change in fluid viscosity, can occur throughout the lifetime of the system. Therefore, concurrent testing during system operation is essential to ensure the operational health of safety-critical systems.

Unified Detection Mechanism

In the proposed testing methodology, test droplets (e.g., 0.1-M KCL) are released into the microelectrofluidic system from droplet sources and are guided through the system following the designed testing scheme. Both catastrophic and parametric faults are detected by electrostatically controlling and tracking the motion of these test stimuli droplets. This testing method is minimally invasive and easy to implement, which offers an opportunity to eradicate the need for expensive and bulky external devices.

To facilitate a decision-making process, a detection mechanism is needed for both *catastrophic* and *parametric* faults. This mechanism needs to be based on a pass/fail criterion that yields the some response to each of the possible faults to prevent masking among various types of faults. The proposed unified detection mechanism consists of a simple RC oscillator circuit formed by the sink electrodes and the fluid between them as an insulator. The capacitance of this structure depends on the presence of the droplet since the filler medium and the droplet have distinct primitivities. By sensing the capacitance of this structure through a simple frequency counter, one can determine whether a droplet has reached the sink. This mechanism can be electronically implemented and easily integrated on chip. In order to provide a unidirectional and unambiguous detection mechanism, the pass/fail criterion has to be determined based on the presence of the droplet at the sink electrode and this criterion should be applied for all test cases. In this chapter, we associate the fault-free operation with the presence of the droplet at the sink electrode and faulty operation with its absence.

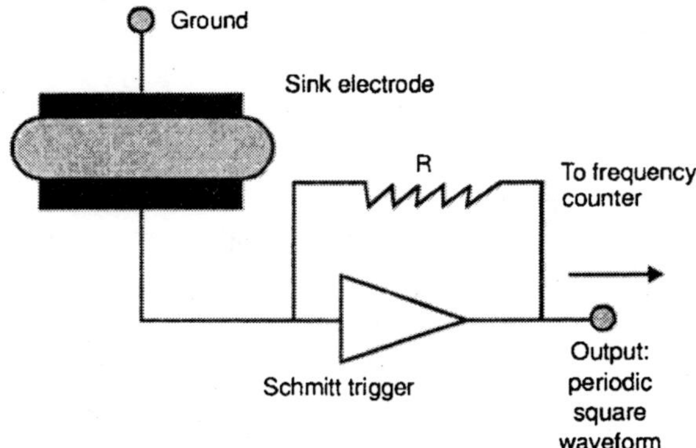

Fig. 15.2. Simple R-C oscillator circuit.

Online Testing of Catastrophic Faults

Most *catastrophic faults* cause a complete cessation of droplet transportation at the system level. Therefore, we can easily detect these faults by using the testing scheme. The fault site in this two-

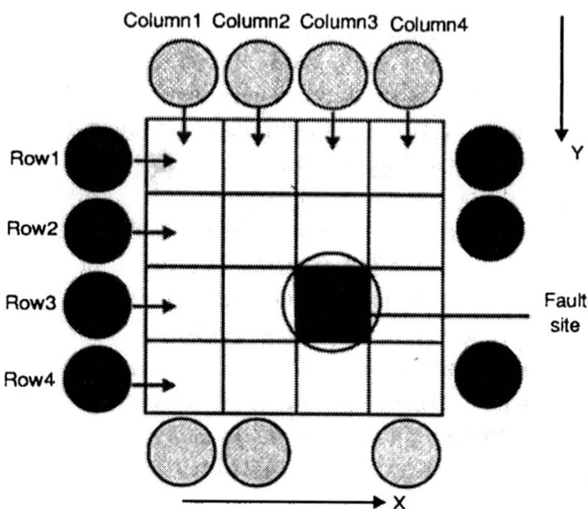

Fig. 15.3. Illustration of catastrophic fault testing scheme.

dimensional array is highlighted. *Droplets* are first driven along one direction, e.g., along the axis, and they are observed at the other end of the array. Each row of the array transports a single droplet of fluid. Due to the catastrophic fault in Row 3, no droplet is observed for this row. As a result, the cells in this row are deemed as candidate faulty cells. Next, droplets are driven along the axis, and due to the fault in the array, no droplet is observed at the other end of Column 3. Thus, we conclude that Column 3 contains a faulty cell. From the information about the faulty row and column, we can uniquely identify the faulty cell in the array.

The above illustration assumes that a catastrophic fault affects only one cell of the array. The testing technique described here can, however, be extended for locating multiple faulty cells, e.g., through the use of multistep adaptive fault location methods. An important advantage of this approach is that it can be integrated into the droplet-manipulation-based microfluidic steps underlying a biomedical reaction, e.g., polymer chain reaction. Concurrent testing can be carried out simultaneously with a biochemical reaction utilizing unused cells in the array, and a degree of fault tolerance can be achieved by reconfiguring the array such that the droplets avoid faulty cells in their flow paths.

Parametric Fault Testing

While catastrophic faults have the highest priority for detection as they result in complete malfunction, *parametric faults* are much harder to detect and may result in malfunction depending on the application domain and specifications. As a result, a viable concurrent testing scheme needs to consider both catastrophic and parametric faults. A large set of parametric faults that can arise from environmental effects, or from the degradation of system materials, may eventually lead to system failure.

The degradation of the insulator thickness and changes in the viscosity of the fluids are examples of such parametric faults that do not necessarily result in imminent loss of droplet movement, but rather result in degraded performance. For example, an increase in the viscosity of the filler fluid might impede droplet motion, resulting in undesired fluid concentrations at the mixers. The identification of such deviations is essential during in-field operation in droplet-based microelectrofluidic systems. The analysis of fault manifestations requires an understanding of the fault-free behaviour and the variations in this behaviour with respect to the variations in underlying parameters.

Fault-Free Model

The behavioural model of droplet-based microelectrofluidic systems is based on the electrowetting actuation principle. We assume that the liquid flow within the droplet can be approximated as laminar flow, which requires that the Reynolds number of the droplet fluid be less than 1000. This assumption is valid because the Reynolds number of a nanoliter of fluid is usually no larger than 100. The principle underlying this model is to balance the work done by the surface tension gradient force with the power dissipation. The power dissipation during the droplet transportation is caused by three factors: the viscosity and the resistance of the filler medium, the friction around the droplet/insulator surface and the internal viscous flow of the droplet. The following analytical model for droplet motion is derived in

$$\frac{\varepsilon_0 \varepsilon_R}{2d} V^2 - F_T = B\left(\frac{\mu_d U}{\gamma_{LM}}\right)^{0.3} \gamma_{LM} + \left(\frac{mL}{h} + s\right)\mu_0 + \zeta U \quad ...(1)$$

where V is the control voltage, U is the transport velocity, ε_0 is permittivity of free-space, γ_{LM} is the liquid-medium interfacial tension constant. Equation (1), covering all the significant physical phenomena in electrowetting, shows that the transport velocity of the droplet is a function of the control voltage and a number of relevant physical and fluidic parameters. We experimentally verified using laboratory apparatus that the analytical model accurately describes physical behaviour. The experimental data obtained from video frame counting matches simulation data for a wide range of values for the control voltage.

Table 15.1. Physical parameters affecting the droplet velocity

Parameter name	*Parameter description*	*Normal value*
d (μm)	Thickness of dielectric layer	1
L (μm)	Electrode length	150
h (μm)	Height between two parallel plates	88
μ_0 (cP)	Viscosity of filler fluid	1.7
μ_d (cP)	Viscosity of droplet	1.9

Table 15.2. Numerical coefficients affecting the droplet velocity

Coefficient name	*Coefficient description*	*Value*
F_T (dyne/cm)	Threshold	2.47
B	Droplet viscous effect	0.55
m, s	Oil viscous effect	28,112
ζ (dyne s/cm^2)	Contact-line friction	0.4
ε_R	Relative permittivity of insulator	1.93

This behavioural model implies that the velocity of the droplet is a function of the environmental parameters, provided that the voltage is kept at a constant value. Thus, a defect involving these parameters results in a deviation of the droplet velocity from the nominal value predicted by (1).

Ideally, at a certain applied voltage, the *droplet velocity* is precisely determined by (1). However, in practice, all the parameters involved in (1) vary with a certain tolerance, resulting in a range of acceptable values for the droplet velocity. A viable parametric testing scheme has to take these variations into account to minimize the likelihood of a false alarm. Such parametric variations dictate certain upper and lower bounds on the droplet velocity in a fault-free system. These bounds can be computed through tolerance analysis.

Since *parametric faults* manifest as deviations in droplet velocity, parametric testing mainly consists of ensuring that the droplet velocity is within its bounds. Direct measurement of droplet velocity requires experimental methods such as video frame counting and capacitive sensing. All these methods, however, require external devices such as CCD cameras or oscillator circuits for capacitance measurement, which add unacceptable overhead and make testing cumbersome, especially in concurrent scenarios.

Fortunately, we can determine whether the droplet velocity is within the predetermined bounds through a nonintrusive and cost-effective test setup, which is based on the readouts of droplet ports, and on adjustments in the duration of each electrode pulse.

Lower-Bound Testing

A *parametric fault*, such as an increase in the viscosity of the filler fluid, may slow the droplet beyond the acceptable value U_{min}. In order to detect such effects, the droplet can be moved between two ports, a source and a sink, such that it can reach the sink only if its velocity is higher than the required minimum. For the droplet to move from the source to the sink, each electrode actuation has to be in the form of a pulse and the duration of the pulse has to be long enough for the droplet to reach the boundaries of the adjacent electrode. This is the boundary condition (corresponding to $U = U_{min}$) under which the droplet can move continuously. If the actual velocity is larger than U_{min}, the droplet will rapidly traverse through the adjacent electrodes, and wait there until the next switching of control signal. On the other hand, if the velocity is less than U_{min}, the droplet cannot keep up with the switching rate of the control electrodes. This implies that when the droplet reaches one electrode, the adjacent electrode has already been deactivated. For example, if the voltage V_3 becomes zero before the droplet reaches X_2, the droplet will be stuck at some point between X_1 and X_2.

As a result, the shortest pulse duration T that allows the droplet with the minimum acceptable velocity, U_{min}, to reach its destination is given by: $T = L/U_{min}$, where L is the electrode length. If the pulse duration is chosen appropriately, the droplets with velocities higher than U_{min} will reach the sink, and the droplets with lower velocities will fail to complete the movement.

Upper-Bound Testing

Upper-bound testing differs from lower-bound testing in the sense that the fault-free case is represented by the failure of a droplet to catch-up with the pulse frequency. However, testing for the upper-bound is more complicated than simply checking whether the droplet fails to reach the target since it violates the unified pass/fail criterion. Moreover, a catastrophic fault that impedes the droplet motion may be perceived as a fault-free operation in this case.

Fortunately, by slightly modifying the lower-bound testing scheme, we can test for the upper-bound of the droplet velocity. In this case, bidirectional droplet movement is utilized, where the source and the sink are the same port. In the first phase of the test, pulses of duration $T = L/U_{max}$ are utilized, where U_{max} is the precomputed upper bound on the droplet velocity ($U < U_{max}$). A droplet with an acceptable velocity will not be able to reach the final electrode; it will be stuck at an intermediate position. In the second phase of the test, which begins right after the final electrode is deactivated, the droplet motion is set in the reverse direction. However, one electrode is skipped so as to keep the droplets that had reached the final electrode from moving. In this phase, the pulse duration is much higher to allow for the slower droplets to continue their motion. This *backward pulsation* will pick up the droplets that may have been stuck at intermediate points and move them toward the sink. Hence, the detection of a droplet at the end of the operation indicates a droplet velocity that is lower than the allowed maximum, i.e., a fault-free operation.

It is evident that this testing scheme can be combined with catastrophic fault testing to form a unified complete test methodology. It only needs to detect the droplet ports without additional testing devices; this feature dramatically reduces the test cost. In addition, its simplicity facilitates concurrent testing.

Evaluation of the Parametric Test Strategy

The parametric testing strategy described here relies on the fact that parametric deviations result in an unexpected deviation in the droplet velocity. Equation (1) guarantees that a high-enough deviation in each parameter will eventually result in the velocity bound being violated. Hence, the minimum-detectable deviations for all the parameters serve as a good evaluation metric in understanding the viability of the proposed testing scheme.

For a certain amount of deviation in a parameter to be detectable, it needs to shift the droplet velocity outside its determined bounds, while other parameters are allowed to vary within their tolerance. Since the droplet velocity for both the fault-free and faulty systems can be expressed in the terms of ranges, the detection of a certain parametric deviation can statistically be assured if droplet velocity ranges for the faulty and fault-free systems are nonoverlapping. However, since most physical parameters exhibit a Gaussian-like distribution, the *nonoverlapping* criterion can be relaxed to include a 10% overlap, leading to a detection probability higher than 99.9%.

Evaluation of Detectability

In order to illustrate the viability of the parametric testing scheme, we have conducted simulation-based experiments and computed the velocity tolerance, as well as minimum-detectable deviation values for each physical parameter.

Tolerance analysis

It is noted that the equation governing the relation between transport the velocity and the control voltage is nonlinear. The simplest and the most popular method for nonlinear statistical tolerance analysis is the *Monte-Carlo simulation method.* Random values for each parameter are generated according to its distributions, and the value of the response function is computed for each set of parameter values. By generating very large samples, the tolerance response can be statistically analyzed.

In our case, it is assumed that all parameters, including geometrical parameters (d, L, h) and fluidic parameters (μ_0, μ_d), follow a Gaussian distribution with a mean value μ and a standard deviation σ. Using a 5% tolerance for each physical and fluidic parameter, Monte-Carlo analysis has been carried out through MATLAB simulations (1000 runs). For high control voltage values, the deviation in droplet velocity is higher as the sensitivity of parameter increases with the square of the control voltage, making this parameter the dominant variable. For a nominal control voltage value of 50 V, the transport velocity tolerance is determined to be 7%.

Minimum detectable deviations

In order to compute the *minimum detectable deviations* (MDDs) for each parameter, a linear search algorithm in conjunction with Monte-Carlo simulations is utilized. Even though linear search is quite inefficient, computational complexity is not an issue here due to the small number of parameters.

In order to determine the MDD for a parameter, p, we start with a deviation Δp that exceeds the tolerance of p. Through Monte-Carlo simulations, the upper and lower bounds on the resulting transport velocity are determined. If the overlap between the fault-free and faulty ranges of the transport velocity is less than 10%, the corresponding deviation Δp is considered to be detected. Since the actual distributions are Gaussian like, such an overlap results in less than 0.1% probability of misclassification in terms of both false positives and false negatives.

Table 15.3 shows the MDD values for the physical and fluidic parameters for a control voltage of 50 V. For this particular setup, the thickness of the dielectric layer (d) has the most impact on the transport velocity. Thus, even small variations in d can be detected using the proposed concurrent detection method. On the other extreme, the viscosity of the droplet μ_d has the least impact on the transport velocity, leading to a high MDD value. It is worthwhile to note that the viscosity of the filler medium μ_0 and the viscosity of the droplet μ_d are closely related, and are affected by the same environmental changes. As a result, a change in μ_d is associated with a similar change in μ_0 and, thus, is detected at a much lower deviation than as suggested in Table 15.3. In addition, by using various control voltage values, the sensitivities of a number of parameters can be adjusted. This multiphase testing scheme deceases the MDD values for all parameters involved.

Table 15.3. Minimum detectable deviations

Parameter	*Nominal*	*MDD*
d (μm)	1	8.5×10^{-2} (8.5%)
L (μm)	150	91 (60.7%)
h (μm)	88	33 (37.5%)
μ_0 (cP)	1 7	0.28 (16.5%)
μ_d (cP)	1.9	11 (5.8×100%)

Experimental Setup

In this section, we apply the previous analysis of detectability evaluation to test multiple parametric faults and present the experimental results for a droplet-based microelectrofluidic system for real-time PCR applications.

Real-Time PCR in Droplet-Based Microelectrofluidic Systems

The *polymerase chain reaction* (PCR) is used to amplify the copies of specific fragments of DNA and is a key technique for DNA-based bio-molecular detection. There are three major steps in PCR, which are repeated for 30 to 40 cycles. First, the target genetic material must be denatured, i.e., the double strands of its helix must be unwound and separated into single stranded DNA by heating it to 94°C. The second step is *hybridization* or *annealing*, in which the primers bind to their complementary bases on the now single-stranded DNA at 54°C. The third is DNA synthesis by a polymerase. 72°C is the ideal working temperature for the polymerase. Starting at the annealed primer, the polymerase can read a template strand and match it with complementary nucleotides very quickly. This step generates two new helixes, each of which is composed of one of the original strands plus its newly assembled complementary strand. Because both strands are copied during PCR, there is an exponential increase of the number of copies of the genes. An experimental investigation has been conducted to determine the suitability of droplet-based microelectrofluidic systems for microfluidic PCR application. Within such electrowetting-actuated systems, real-time PCR assays in 300 nL droplets have been successfully performed. Techniques for modeling and optimization of PCR at the system level have been also described in the literature.

Testing Parametric Faults in PCR Microelectrofluidic Systems

In order to increase the reliability of the real-time PCR application, which is critical to DNA-based bio-molecular detection, the possible faults in such microelectrofluidic systems need to be tested not only after manufacturing, but also during in-field operation. Parametric faults, arising from degradation of system materials or environmental effects, are much harder to detect than *catastrophic faults*. Here we analyze the testing for some parametric faults in such systems in terms of their MDD values. The nominal values of system parameters are except for viscosities of the droplet and the filler fluid (μ_0 and μ_d), which change due to the different application temperatures of PCR.

Insulator degradation

As described already, this "*wear-and-tear*" defect may appear gradually during the in-field operation of a microelectrofluidic system. We can consider this degradation as a global defect and model its effect in the parameters d and h. Thus, the degradation of the insulator (denoted as Δd) causes two inversely-corrected geometrical parametric faults, i.e., decreasing the insulator thickness (d) and increasing the height between parallel plates (h). In order to break the dependency between d and h, we introduce an independent manufacturing variable H to denote the overall height of the two-electrode structure. With this convention, d and h are the independent variables during manufacturing and $h = H - d$. However, after manufacturing, any degradation of the insulator affects both d and h; thus, the dependency needs to be incorporated into the random sampling process for Monte-Carlo simulations. In order to find the minimum value Δd of that causes a fault alarm, the Monte-Carlo sampling needs to be modified as follows.

1. Sample d and H independently, then calculate h as $h_{\text{calculated}} = H_{\text{sampled}} - d_{\text{sampled}}$.
2. Insert the degradation defect Δd into d: $d = d_{\text{sampled}} - \Delta d$; set $h = h_{\text{calculated}} + \Delta d$.
3. Sample all other variables according to their rules.

4. The linear search algorithm is applied to find the minimum value of Δd causing an alarm, and record it.

Monte-Carlo simulations indicate that the minimum detectable degradation of insulator is 0.051 μm (i.e., $\Delta d/d = 5.1\%$). Therefore, even a small degradation during the operation is easily detectable. This approach is also applicable to the analysis of degraded performance caused by the deviation in insulator thickness during the manufacturing process.

Particle contamination

During in-field operation of PCR in a microelectrofluidic system, the droplet or the filler fluid may be contaminated by a particle, such as a dust particle or a foreign fluid droplet. Typically, such particles are then attached to the surface of the insulator of a cell since they are not large enough to move with electrowetting. As a dust particle is likely to be smaller than droplet in size, this defect should be modeled as a point defect, not a global defect. Similar to the insulator degradation case, this defect causes the deviation of two geometrical parameters and . However, the analysis of these two parametric faults is more complicated than a global insulator degradation. Equation (1) of the fault-free model indicates that the surface tension gradient force is proportional to the electrostatic energy ($(1/2)CV^2$), which is stored in the capacitor formed between the conductive droplet and the control electrode when a voltage V is applied. The main contribution to C is from the insulator layer, i.e., $C = (\varepsilon_r\varepsilon_0/d)A$, where ε_r is the relative permittivity of the insulator, and A is the area of the interface between the droplet and the insulator and approximated to be $\pi(L/2)^2$. Here, the effect of the dust particle on the capacitance C can be modeled as $C_{eff} = C_1 + C_2$, where C_2 is the capacitance of the insulator area covered by the particle and C_1 is the capacitance of the remaining structure. We then use an equivalent capacitor model to obtain C_2, which is considered as a series of two capacitors C_3 and C_4, i.e., $1/C_2 = 1/C_3 + 1/C_4 = (2r/\varepsilon_p\varepsilon_0 A') + (d/\varepsilon_r\varepsilon_0 A') = (1/\varepsilon_0 A')((2r\varepsilon_r + d\varepsilon_p)/\varepsilon_r\varepsilon_p)$ where r is the radius of the particle, ε_p is the relative permittivity of the particle, A' and is the area of the interface between the particle and the insulator and approximated to be πr^2. Therefore

$$C_{\text{eff}} = C_1 + C_2 = \frac{\varepsilon_r\varepsilon_0}{d}\left(\pi\left(\frac{L^2}{4}\right) - \pi r^2\right) + \frac{\varepsilon_r\varepsilon_r\varepsilon_P}{2r\varepsilon_r + d\varepsilon_P}(\pi r^2) \quad ...(2)$$

We would like to reflect the charge in the effective capacitive onto one of the variables involved in the fault-free model d. Therefore

$$C_{\text{eff}} = \frac{\varepsilon_r \varepsilon_0}{d_{\text{eff}}}\left(\pi\left(\frac{L^2}{4}\right)\right) \quad \text{and}$$

$$d_{\text{eff}} = \frac{\varepsilon_r\left(\frac{L^2}{4}\right)}{\frac{\varepsilon_r}{d}\left(\frac{L^2}{4} - r^2\right) + \frac{\varepsilon_r \varepsilon_p}{d\varepsilon_p + 2r\varepsilon_r}(r^2)}. \qquad \text{...(3)}$$

In order to analyze the minimum detectable size (r) of this dust particle, Monte-Carlo simulation needs to be modified by taking into account its impact on the overall insulator properties. Thus, the Monte-Carlo sampling procedure needs to be modified as follows.

1. d, L, and H are sampled independently, then calculate h as $h_{\text{calculated}} = H_{\text{sampled}} - d_{\text{sampled}}$.
2. Using (2), calculate d_{eff}; set $\Delta d = d_{\text{eff}} - d_{\text{sampled}}$.
3. Calculate the effective height h_{eff} by $h_{\text{eff}} = h_{\text{calculated}} - \Delta d$.
4. Sample all other variables according to their rules.
5. Apply the linear search algorithm to find the minimum value of r causing an alarm.

The minimum detectable radius of particle is found to be 22 μm when ε_p is set to be 10. Thus, with this methodology, contaminates of size larger than 2% of the droplet size can be detected. The manufacturing defect that causes a bulge in insulator surface can also be analyzed by this method with setting ε_p to be ε_r. In this case the minimum detectable radius of bulge is 20 μm (1.5% of the droplet volume).

Defect in the Temperature Controller

Temperature is a critical factor in the PCR application, as the three steps in one cycle of PCR require distinct temperatures. Error in the temperature may degrade the performance of PCR, even cause the failure. For example, a wrong temperature during the annealing step can result in primers not binding to the template DNA at all. The error in temperature may result from the malfunction of the temperature controller. This defect affects fluidic parameters, i.e., viscosity of droplet μd and viscosity of filler fluid (silicone oil) μ_0, but not geometrical parameters. In order to model the temperature error, the variation of viscosity versus temperature for droplet and filler fluid is analyzed. Here we assume linear interpolations in the temperature range T of 25°C ~ 100°C as follows:

- viscosity of silicone oil: $\mu_0 = 1.0955 - 0.0054T$ (cP);
- viscosity of 0.1 M KCL: $\mu_d = 1.0225 - 0.0080T$ (cP)

where test stimuli droplet is 0.1M KCL and filler fluid is silicone oil. These linear interpolations are applied to (1), and we replace the fluidic parameters and with one temperature variable T

$$\frac{\varepsilon_0 \varepsilon_R}{2d} V^2 - F_T = B\left[\frac{U(1.0225 - 0.0080T)}{\gamma_{LM}}\right]^{0.3} \gamma_{LM} + \left(\frac{mL}{h} + s\right) U(1.0995 - 0.0054T) + \zeta U. \quad \text{...(4)}$$

Then, a similar approach is utilized to obtain the minimum detectable deviation for temperature in each step of PCR. Here we assume a 5% tolerance for each physical parameter as well as the temperature. The experimental results show that the MDD of temperature is 13.8% for the denaturation step, 29.6% for the annealing step, and 19.4% for the synthesis step, making the denaturation step the most suitable phase for detecting defects in the temperature controller.

CONCLUSION

In this paper, we have presented a model for physical defects in droplet-based microelectrofluidic systems and a test development methodology for both operational and manufacturing defects. As microelectrofluidic systems become widespread in safety-critical biomedical applications, dependability emerges as a critical performance parameter. We have developed a cost-effective concurrent test methodology to increase the dependability of droplet-based microelectrofluidic systems. We have presented a classification of catastrophic and parametric faults in microelectrofluidic systems and shown how faults can be detected by electrostatically controlling and tracking droplet motion. A tolerance analysis method based on Monte-Carlo simulation has been developed to characterize the impact of parameter (both *physical* and *fluidic*) variations on system performance. We have also studies the use of droplet-based microelectrofluidic systems for real-time PCR and evaluated some typical defects in terms of their ease of detection. In our ongoing work, we are investigating the diagnosis of parametric faults that affect system performance.

16

BIOWEAPON

MAKING ANTHRAX A WEAPON

How do you turn something that grows in the ground into a weapon of mass destruction?

It isn't easy.

Bioweapons experts say there are vast differences between the anthrax that occurs in nature and anthrax that has been processed for use as a weapon. For one thing, natural anthrax is far easier to obtain than the "*weaponized*" version.

"Naturally occurring anthrax is in the soil, it's all over the place," says Van Blackwood, director of the chemical and biological warfare program of the Federation of American Scientists.

Someone with experience working with anthrax could extract anthrax spores and use those as seed stock to produce millions more. Growing anthrax isn't terribly difficult, Blackwood says, but you have to choose your strain carefully. Some strains aren't infectious to humans. More important, he says, anthrax spores found in nature tend to clump together. That makes them hard to inhale. "They wouldn't go very far down into your lungs or spread readily through a building's ventilation system."

Weaponized anthrax is far more complex to produce because it is designed to be widely dispersed and especially deadly. A bioweaponeer would select the most lethal available strain, grow large quantities of it in a fermenter and then concentrate it to increase its potency. He might also expose the bacteria to antibiotics, to make it antibiotic resistant and difficult or impossible to treat. The next and most

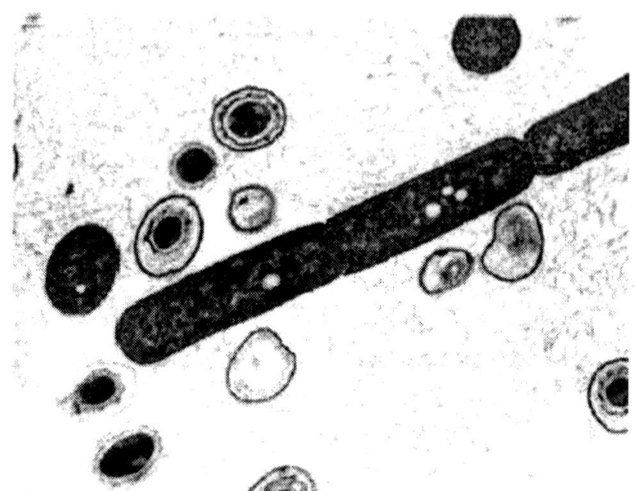

Fig. 16.1. A microscopic view of the anthrax bacteria.

challenging step is to grind it—without killing the bacteria—into a fine powder with particles that are 1 to 5 microns in size.

A micron-sized *anthrax particle* is much smaller than the period at the end of this sentence and invisible to the naked eye. It easily wafts into the air and spreads through building ventilation systems. In this form, it's relatively easy to deliver a dose of 8,000 spores or more, enough to turn a single breath into a death sentence.

Disperse enough anthrax into the air downwind of a major city, and it could infect thousands of people before anyone suspects that anything is wrong. "You can take out 200,000 people in a heartbeat — maybe millions," says C.J. Peters of the Center for Biodefense at the University of Texas Medical Branch at Galveston. "I'm not worried about anthrax in a letter. I'm worried about *weapons of mass destruction.*"

The former Soviet Union turned bioweapons development into a vast state-sponsored industry called Biopreparat, says defector Ken Alibek, who served as Biopreparat's deputy chief until 1992. "We stockpiled hundreds of tons of anthrax and dozens of tons of plague and smallpox near Moscow and other Russian cities for use against the United States and its allies," he recounts in his 1999 book, Biohazard.

Ironically, beginning with Moscow's endorsement of the Biological Weapons Convention in 1972, which outlawed biological weapons, the Soviet Union built "the largest and most advanced biological warfare establishment in the world," with 60,000 employees and 100 facilities in Russia and Kazakhstan.

Iraq, Cuba and India reportedly have biological weapons programs. Before the Gulf War, Iraq legally bought seven to 10 strains of anthrax from a lab supplier, the American Type Culture Collection in Manassas, Va. That prompted authorities to restrict exports of deadly microbes in 1996. Iraqi weapons plants were reportedly destroyed after the Gulf War, but Iraq may still have stockpiles of deadly germs.

Afghanistan also has experience with biological warfare—as a victim, Alibek says. Before the Soviets withdrew from Afghanistan in 1989, Ilyushin-28 warplanes dispersed bacteria that cause glanders, a disease of horses, mules and donkeys. Although not lethal to humans, he says, "it could immobilize an entire division or incapacitate guerrilla forces hiding in rugged terrain otherwise inaccessible to regular army troops—precisely the kind of terrain our soldiers faced in Afghanistan."

The collapse of the Soviet Union brought Biopreparat down with it, and the vast Soviet bioweapons stockpiles have reportedly been destroyed. But Alibek prophetically notes in his book that the threat of biological attack actually increased as the techniques developed in Soviet labs have "spread to rogue regimes and terrorist groups . . . they are cheap, easy to make and easy to use. In the coming years, they will become very much a part of our lives."

Now that Alibek's prophecy has come true, Americans have experienced the power of even a limited biological attack to sow terror nationwide. And the delivery vehicle couldn't be simpler. "You can paint anthrax onto an envelope," says Peters of the Center for Biodefense in Galveston.

The United States manufactured biological weapons at a facility at Fort Detrick in Maryland from 1943 until President Nixon signed an executive order ending the program in 1969. Today, researchers at Fort Detrick have turned to biological defense.

About 1,200 laboratories in the USA study anthrax, authorities say. Much of the anthrax used for legitimate biological research is modified to make it safe for those who work with it. But nobody knows exactly how many such labs there are or how they're using anthrax because no one has ever kept track. "There's no database of who has this stuff, why they have it or how they're using it," Blackwood says, though the Centers for Disease Control and Prevention does register the 5,500 labs in the USA that work with 42 especially deadly microbes.

Anthrax Questions, Uneasy Answers

In the wake of the discovery of the anthrax bacterium in the Florida offices of American Media, Inc., health officials are offering antibiotics to those who worked or spent time in the affected building as a precautionary measure.

But Kevin Keane, spokesman for the federal Department of Health and Human Services, says there is no need for others to take any special preventive actions. "We're not recommending people buy antibiotics or gas masks or anything of that sort. If we have concerns, we will get medication to people who should have it."

Experts on anthrax and other infectious diseases answer some common questions:

Q: Who is at risk?

A: People at greatest risk of dying from anthrax are those who inhale the aerosolized spores. It also can be contracted by eating meat from infected animals or by handling the hides or wool of infected animals, which can allow the spores to enter through cuts or scrapes. Ingested anthrax, which is rare, can be fatal, but the form that occurs through skin contact is usually milder.

Q: How is it spread?

A: Inhalation anthrax—which is almost always fatal if not quickly treated—must be freeze-dried and aerosolized, then inhaled into the lung. If the spores are too large, they will be caught in the nasal passages, where they probab-ly will not multiply. A study in the United Kingdom that looked at workers in a wool mill found that 14% tested positive for anthrax spores in their nasal passages.

Q: Can it be sent through the mail?

A: Yes. Microbiologist Ronald Atlas, co-chair of the American Society for Microbiology's bioterrorism task force and a professor at the University of Louisville, says anthrax spores could survive in powder, which could be put in an envelope and mailed. "It might not be the most efficient way of doing things, but it could be done," he says. "If it was on particles, like a talcum powder, and you opened it and whiffed in some," it could cause disease, he says. But the mixture would have to be inhaled to cause harm, he says. "It would not do it while sitting in the envelope."

Q: How else could it be disseminated?

A: By air. The Johns Hopkins Center for Civilian Biodefense Studies says that, given the right weather and wind conditions, about

110 pounds of anthrax released from an aircraft could spread nearly 121/2 miles downwind. The cloud would be colourless, odorless and invisible. There currently are no warning systems to detect an aerosol cloud of anthrax spores—the attack would most likely not be discovered until patients showed up in hospitals.

Q: Is it contagious?

A: No, anthrax is not passed through the air from person to person or from animal to person.

Q: Has it ever existed naturally in the USA?

A: Yes. In the past six months, outbreaks of anthrax have occurred in deer in Texas; cattle, deer and horses in Minnesota; and bison in Canadian parks. Anthrax spores can remain in soil for decades and can infect grazing animals. "The natural cycle of anthrax in this country is that a deer or cow or sheep gets it, and the animal dies," says C.J. Peters, director of the Center for Biodefense, University of Texas Medical Branch in Galveston. The infected blood of the animal "contaminates the ground, and another cow comes snuffling around, and snuffles up the spores."

Q: Can it be cured?

A: According to the U.S. Army Medical Research Institute of Infectious Diseases, "almost all cases of inhalational anthrax in which treatment was begun after patients were symptomatic have been fatal, regardless of treatment." However, when possible exposure is known or suspected, prompt treatment with antibiotics can be lifesaving.

Q: What antibiotics?

A: Naturally occurring anthrax is sensitive to penicillin and other antibiotics, but because terrorists could create a form that is resistant to antibiotics, the recommended antibiotic is ciprofloxacin.

Q: Does the country have a stockpile of anthrax vaccine?

A: Yes, but only for the military, says former Army Surgeon General Ronald Blanck, president of the University of North Texas Health Sciences Center in Fort Worth. The only U.S. facility where the vaccine is produced, BioPort Corp. in Lansing, Mich., has failed government inspections and has not received clearance from the Food and Drug Administration to release the vaccine it has produced.

Q: How do you test ventilation systems for anthrax?

A: Swabs taken from humans, animals or from surfaces—keyboards, ventilation systems, telephones—can be tested by several methods. They can be placed in petri dishes and the bacteria allowed to grow into identifiable colonies, or pieces of DNA can be cloned through a high-tech technique called polymerase chain reaction. Blanck says the military also has "surveillance devices that can be used in high-threat areas" that can within "a couple of hours" identify biological agents. Samples are added to antibodies that are specific to the organism, showing clearly whether it is present or not.

Building the Ultimate Bioweapon

Stealth viruses triggered from afar like remote-controlled bombs. Designer bugs packed with genes that simultaneously signal millions of human cells to commit suicide. Germs that wipe out the human immune system's ability to combat viruses.

Fanciful as these fearsome innovations may seem, they're edging closer to fact than science fiction. Today, 20 years into the genetic revolution, scientists say that the biotech tools used to make human insulin, interferon and other breakthrough medications could be put to more sinister use.

Military microbiologists equipped with the latest genetic technology, they say, could use it to turn ordinary germs into extra-virulent, drug-resistant superbugs.

Indeed, Australian scientists reported in January that they had created a superbug while trying to make a contraceptive vaccine for rodent control. By inserting a gene for an immune-system chemical into a relatively harmless *mousepox virus*, researchers turned the virus into a monster that kills 100% of its rodent victims by wiping out part of their immune system.

Although mousepox doesn't infect humans, it is a close cousin of smallpox, suggesting that smallpox would be receptive to the same lethal trick.

"Such 'tailoring' of biowarfare agents could make them harder to detect, diagnose and treat. It could, in short, make them more militarily useful and thus increase the temptation to pursue offensive programs," Claire Fraser of the Institute for Genomic Research and Michael Dando of the University of Bradford in the U.K. report in the Oct. 22 issue of Nature Genetics.

Some defense experts reportedly fear that the government may inadvertently increase the risk posed by mutant microbes by funding a major effort to sequence the genomes of more than 100 microbes and stipulating that all findings be posted on the Web. But other biologists argue that the genetic databases will catapult our understanding of biology into new realms.

"In the past, people could only study bacteria that they could single out and grow," says Mary Ann Henkart of the National Science Foundation. "By comparing microbial (*gene*) sequences, you can learn things we never dreamed we would know before we could do these genetic tricks."

Much of the work so far has focused on disease-causing germs and germs that can be used for environmental cleanup. But other researchers are focusing on germs that may shed light on the history of life on Earth, germs relevant to agriculture and germs that live in extreme environments.

Legitimate scientists have tinkered with microbial genes for decades. As early as 1973, scientists spliced a drug-resistance gene from an unrelated microbe into the DNA of the benign intestinal microbe E. coli. Although this pioneering gene-splicing experiment was done by civilians seeking insights into biology, it's exactly the kind of enhancement that might be made by a bioweaponeer.

Bioweapon designers have achieved their own breakthroughs. Although much of their work has been cloaked in secrecy, hints of their accomplishments have surfaced.

Two years ago, a team of leading anthrax researchers led by Paul Jackson of Los Alamos National Laboratory reported that the former Soviet Union had apparently succeeded in combining at least four strains of anthrax into a single bioweapon.

The researchers obtained the bacteria from 11 people who died in a 1979 anthrax outbreak. The outbreak is believed to have resulted from an accidental release of anthrax from a military research facility in Sverdlovsk, though the Soviets insisted for years that the outbreak was triggered by anthrax-contaminated meat. The Jackson team helped dispel the lie, because an outbreak of intestinal anthrax caused by contaminated meat would be caused by one strain of anthrax, not four of them.

The biotechnology revolution has made altering microbes easier by turning gene splicing into an automated, industrial process. Posting the genetic sequences of microbes on the Web will by 2003 provide scientists with an unprecedented resource, the sequences of 250,000 microbial genes.

Comparing genes from other organisms or from humans with those in this library can supply clues to how the genes function and how important they are, pointing the way to new diagnostics, drugs and vaccines.

Scientists have already begun to identify genes in each microbe that are needed for infection and that govern the bug's virulence and resistance to antibiotics. Such information could be used, for example, to splice the genes for anthrax toxin from Bacillus anthracis into less dangerous members of the anthrax family, such as B. cereus, which causes food poisoning.

Such manipulations could create stealth bacteria that are as deadly as anthrax but harder to detect. "The similarity between (bacteria) in the anthracis family suggests you could shuffle their genes back and forth, creating Trojan horse biowarfare agents," Fraser says.

Advocates say easy access to genetic information will benefit scientists working on *biowarfare defense*.

The Defense Advanced Research Projects Agency, or Darpa, spent $167 million on biological defense in the fiscal year that ended last month. Among other things, the agency contracted with civilian laboratories to sequence the genomes of the deadly germs that cause *anthrax*, *Q fever* and *tularemia*. One crucial focus of Darpa research is to develop ways to detect biological agents in time to counter their effects. By layering computer chips with *genetic sequences* from important human, animal and plant germs, scientists are trying to create biowarfare-detection devices.

17

After Effects

In the attempt to identify the lessons learned from a conflict, it must be remembered that every war is unique. The Persian Gulf War had certain unique features, such as six months to deploy and prepare. There was no submarine threat or significant naval surface action. Reinforcements from Germany and the United States did not fear enemy attack en route to Saudi Arabia. Because there was no actual weapons use that stressed the coalition's NBC defense capabilities, it is difficult to identify lessons in that area. Some wonder if the outcome would have been different if Iraq had acquired tactical nuclear weapons earlier, attacked Saudi Arabia in September while only the 82d Airborne Division was in place, possessed a larger arsenal of more sophisticated ballistic missiles, or employed CB weapons in its defense. Not all coalition partners had equal levels of NBC defense preparation. What would have happened if the French or Syrians had refuse to advance against Iraqi forces because of large-area CB agent attacks? The result could have been exposed flanks or holes in the coalition lines, potential breach points for counterattacking Iraqis and potential disaster for American forces.

Saddam Hussein had implied that his forces were prepared to use CB weapons to disrupt and defeat the coalition forces. His army had experience in conducting combat operations in an NBC environment, and his armed forces were experienced in delivering these munitions against Iranian soldiers and cities. By 1990 Iraq had the largest CW production capability in the Third World, with a stockpile of thousands of tons of blister and nerve agents. Iraq had developed and weaponized BW agents, to include anthrax bacteria and botulinum toxin. With ballistic missiles capability, aerial bombs, artillery shells, rockets and spray tanks, this threat challenged the coalition in a very sensitive and vulnerable area. This led to the response by American, European and Israeli politicians that their military response to CB warfare would be "absolutely overwhelming and.... Devastating." While some outside the city of Washington chose to interpret this as a nuclear or possibly chemical weapons response, within the Pentagon this policy was never really defined as a nuclear or massive conventional attack against industrial and military targets. We still do not know if these undefined political overtures were a factor in Saddam Hussein's holding back the use of CB agent munitions.

Congress was not long in seeking answers about NBC defense during the Persian Gulf War. It was impossible to hide the lack of military readiness prior to the initiation of Operation Desert Shield. Based on the GAO's assessment, the US military was not ready for NBC warfare on August 8, 1990. Army spokespersons assured Congress that the troops were well trained and well equipped for CB warfare by February 1991 and that Iraq's offensive NBC capability had been significantly blunted, in both verbal and written testimony. While these statements were true and acknowledged, Congress wanted answers on how the Army had allowed the prior low state of readiness to occur in the first place. In August 1991, as Congress developed the fiscal 1992 budget, the House and Senate appropriations committees (HAC and SAC) raised concerns that the NBC defense program was not adequately funded. The House Armed Services Committee (HASC) raised similar concerns in December 1991. The chairman of the Subcommittee on Readiness, Representative Earl Hutto (D-FL), whose congressional district included Eglin Air Force Base (then the site of the Air Force's advanced development work on NBC defense programs), wrote to Secretary Cheney: While the army is the executive agent for chemical defense, the services are instituting a proliferation of research programs to develop their own equipment because the DoD and the Army have not provided adequate oversight and guidance. The failure of the Army to develop and produce the M-40 mask after twenty years is a symbol of the ineffective chemical defense organization within DoD and the need for radical change to the current structure.

Another obvious issued brought out at the [GAO] hearing was the need for additional training that is more effective and realistic.

The HASC comments observed that the Army had been less than proactive in fielding chemical defense equipment prior to August 1990.

The committee held the opinion that the Marine Corps's Saratoga suit was superior to the Army's BDO (still s hotly contested issue after the war). The members recommended that the Army improve and reinvigorate the management of both equipment and training programs, especially individual protection and medical antidotes. The committee called on the Army to prepare a report on its efforts to improve NBC defense protection and training.

The Senate Armed Services Committee (SASC) concurred, emphasizing the military's immediate need to develop a BW agent detection capability. It also expressed concern about reports that the Army and Navy were not cooperating in this effort and charged the OATSD (HA) to review the situation and take appropriate actions to control this feuding. The SASC also raised how the Army planned for industry production for NBC defense items, as seen with the late shipments of protective clothing and masks. It directed DoD to take necessary steps to ensure the maintenance and stability of the industrial base, and to submit a report on an approach and implementation plan to sustain the industrial base.

The HAC recommended that additional funds be approved for both medical research and development and for the improvement of protective clothing (but not to be spent on the Army's current BDO). Despite the House's addition of $100 million in the previous year's operations and maintenance budget, most BDOs had not arrived until after hostilities were over. Conversely, the House reduced the budget request for smoke and obscurants programs due to program growth and budget execution issues (and perhaps due to ignorance of the success of smoke operations in the Gulf War).

The SAC singled out the M1 CAM, rather than the Army's protective clothing program, for additional funding. Its concerns focused on the possibility that the current protection equipment might be inadequate to meet existing threats worldwide. This concern included DLA's ability to retain the industrial base for protective gloves in the future. The SAC echoed the SASC's desire that the biological detection program be accelerated to field some capability in this area as soon as possible. The committee was particularly worried about the Air Force's NBC defense readiness, as forward air bases were among the most likely targets of large-area coverage weapons. They instructed the Secretary of the Air Force to report on means of improving the capability of tactical contingency forces to carry out their missions on a contaminated battlefield. This report would include ways to use existing DoD facilities and equipment to improve the realism of Air

Force training; determination as to whether or not the Air Force had sufficient manpower and specialists to carry out the NBC defense mission; and the feasibility and desirability of increasing the knowledge of non-NBC defense Air Force members through toxic chemical agent familiarization course (like the Army's CDTF). The Air Force was tasked to consider collocating its Disaster Preparedness School at Fort McClellan, as Lowery AFB was scheduled to be closed. Last, the SAC called for a report on the status of the four services' NBC defense RDA programs.

Official DoD Response

The DoD Final Report to Congress on the Conduct of the Persian Gulf War was release in April 1992. The appendix discussing NBC defense was drafted by the CENTCOM chemical officer, Lieutenant Colonel Silvernail. Accounting for twelve pages of the overall DoD report, Appendix Q (Chemical and Biological Warfare Defense) summarized the highlights and critical issues of DOD's NBC defense preparedness. The appendix acknowledge the initial low readiness of the forces, the extraordinary effort made to correct these weakness, and the initial diplomatic and military measures (Air strikes against the CW/BW plants) to minimize the chance of CB warfare. It noted the tenuousness of the intelligence assessments of the Iraqi BW threat as opposed to the better-established CW threat. The report discussed the Army chemical force structure, assembled from both the active and reserve components, and training measures undertaken by all services during the conflict.

Because Congress and the services pay more attention to the material side of NBC defense than doctrine or organization, Appendix Q emphasized the equipment challenges and successes. The establishment of the JSCC-CDE was seen as a significant part of those successes. The report credited the JSCC-CDE with substantially improving CW/BW readiness of the military. Accomplishments included a rapid increase in defensive readiness, realistic training and good equipment fielding initiatives on the parts of developmental equipment. The report recognized the effort involved in fielding the CAM, XM21 RSCAAL, ANBACIS-II, and XM93 Fox NBCRS vehicles. It asserted while protective masks and clothing may have proved burdensome and initial shortages vexing, soldiers and confidence in their individual protective equipment.

Shortcomings included the availability durability and suitability of protective clothing in the desert. The report acknowledged the shortages of CAMs and their improper use by untrained soldiers, the XM21's false alarm problems and the shortage of Fox vehicles. Collectively protection was clearly inadequate across the board; with the exception of the vehicular CPE gained during the M1A1 tank swapout, there was much room for improvement. Water-based decontamination systems, such as the M12A1s and M17 SANATORS, while adequate for the European theater, were inadequate for desert operations. The report hit on the real logistics nightmare that NBC defense had caused: more than $250 million of worldwide theater reserve chemical defense equipment had been drawn upon to respond to the crisis. The major issues remaining included the need for lightweight protective suits, better integration of collective protection systems, a more adequate biological warfare defense readiness, additional NBCRS vehicles, and a replacement for water-based decontamination systems.

Not identified in the report were some other lessons learned. Protective suits arrived none too soon for the ground war's initiation. The Air Force had canceled its entire collective protection program in the spring of 1990, only to urgently request collective protection systems in September 1990. The Marine Corps's M21 RSCAAL order placed during the conflict arrived well after the conflict. The services' leadership clearly identified the urgent need for these systems during the crisis, but industry could not pivot on a dime for these military-unique applications. This showed the need for careful planning if the services wanted an NBC defense capability in place prior to a conflict.

Chemical Corps Review

Senior chemical officers met at Fort McClellan in June 1991 to analyze their performance in the Gulf War. The official TRADOC summary on NBC defense during Desert Storm stated:

Nuclear, biological, and chemical (NBC) *unit infrastructure is sound*. The rapid fielding of NBC reconnaissance equipment is underway. The Army fielded 49 modified German Fox vehicles during Operation Desert Storm and 75 additional systems are funded in FY93-94. The required NBC fixes are: biological and standoff chemical detection and warning capability; NBC protection clothing to match mission profiles; and lightweight alarm capabilities.

There is a system improvement program that will convert a decontamination company into a reconnaissance company in XVIII ABN Crops in FY93.

If one had to wrap up the Chemical Corps's lessons in one paragraph, that would probably cover the major points. There were, however, other issues to examine, including unit readiness and training, rear area, vulnerability, the effectiveness of active defense against NBC weapon systems, command and control of NBC defense units, logistic support, biological agent sampling and response, smoke operations and the need to invigorate the NBC defense sector of the DoD industrial base.

Unit Readiness and Training

Prior to 1981, Army unit readiness and training in the area of NBC defense was inadequate; no one will debate that. By 1990, the Army had successfully integrate individual survival skills into unit training, such as use of decon kits and protective masks. Its chemical defense doctrine was sound and would work. The weakness was training. The Army had not implemented a training strategy to teach units above the platoon level how to conduct large operations in an NBC-contaminated environment. The lack of realistic training aids and chemical agent simulants for large-area unit training created this low state of readiness. Unit leaders could not train and evaluate their operations with chemical defense equipment that did not indicate if it was functioning correctly during training. It went against the "train as you will fight" mantra of the Army. In the fall of 1990, the solution to this lack of readiness was to rely heavily on the chemical specialist infrastructure that had been built up in the 1980s. Chemical NCOs and officers developed training programs to reawaken rusty individual skills, then developed small-unit operations such as detector placement and crew decontamination drills. Concurrent with these efforts, higher-level staffs included NBC-attack scenarios in their war games. Slowly over the six months of Desert Shied, the US military regained its title as the most highly trained and prepared force in the world. Without a doubt, the integration of chemical soldiers into the combat arms initiated in 1979, form corps down to company level, was the driving force of CENTCOM's defensive readiness.

The majority of the 4,200 chemical soldiers deployed to Southwest Asia had trained in the Chemical Defense Training Facility at Fort McClellan. Many of those chemical soldiers and their leaders stated that their confidence in their equipment and training directly resulted from training in a toxic agent environment. There were scores of non-chemical soldiers in theater who did not trust their masks, protective clothing, or agent detectors to warn and protect them, and they turned to these chemical soldiers for assurance. Chemical soldiers could state confidently that the protective gear, detection and decontamination equipment would work, because they had used the equipment in the presence of actual nerve agents. This was a big plus for the credibility and confidence that commanders had in their chemical soldiers. Major General McCaffrey brought more than 500 of his commanders and their staff to Fort McClellan's CDTF after the war to familiarize them with the toxic agent training; other division commanders did the same.

Reservists had the most difficulty in developing NBC defense skills. NBC defense training in the Reserve Component had been neglected more than in the active duty force. Given the limited time that Reservists actually train as a unit, they generally do not gain expertise in tasks such as setting out agent detectors, running decontamination operations, or operating for long periods of time in protective clothing. Again the chemical specialist infrastructure within the reserve forces was key to training these soldiers prior to the ground offensive. Without this training, the reservists would have been hard pressed to do more than survive in NBC warfare conditions, let alone support the active units in a fast-moving offensive.

Civilian training was a new facet for the *Chemical Corps*. For the first time, it had to equip and train government civilians, industry contractors and media personnel in basic NBC defense and survival skills. This had never been planned for or funded. The resulting demands on equipment and trainers had to be met by chemical officers and NCOs at US deployment centers and in-theater, already tasked to get their combat forces prepared. Again, because of the six-month grace period, it was possible to equip and train the civilians to a level at which they might survive a chemical attack. Asking civilians to operate in a contaminated environment might have been asking too much.

These skills are highly perishable, however. Some *Desert Storm* brigade combat commanders and senior staff members expressed the view after the war that "the threat posed by Iraq was the most formidable and most likely opportunity for weapons of mass destruction to have been used against US forces. Since the use of these weapons did not occur under the most likely set of circumstances, they would never be used and NBC defense training could be significantly reduced or disregarded." Evidence of this exists at today's *Combat Training Centers* (CTCs). At the JRTC, Fort Polk, light infantry leaders tell their troops to keep their masks in their rucksacks to minimize the load. At Fort Irwin's National Training Center, units show up without adequate chemical defense equipment and with soldiers not trained to operate M8A1 chemical alarms. Training in Germany, brigades send their Fox platoons to reconnoiter ahead of the force alone, making them easy kills. Unit and leader success at the CTCs still does not require proper use of decontamination assets. Many combat arms leaders still do not understand how NBC defense operations "fit" into their perspective of conventional warfare.

Rear Area Vulnerabilities

The most difficult are to protect had been the corps, army and theater rear areas, where the majority of the Army force remained vulnerable. It is hard to say anything positive about NBC defense for the rear areas; rather, it was a disaster waiting to happen (but that, fortunately, did not take place). Poor training of reserve support units and government civilians, who made up a large part of rear support, was the first hindrance. In addition, most chemical agent detectors and decontamination devices were up front with combat units due to shortages of these items. Many combat support units had to rely on radio warnings from higher headquarters and M9 paper taped to the tents and vehicles as initial warnings. The sheer number of base clusters (more than one hundred), spread out over literally thousands of square kilometers, made it very difficult to warn everyone of CB agent attacks and predicted contaminated areas. Difficulties in communicating to rear area units meant long delays between Scud attacks and when the individual base clusters were warned.

Most supplies were kept largely in the open, uncovered and vulnerable to persistent CB agents. There was not enough decontamination support to cover all of the division, army and theater support units in the rear area. Accelerated development of protective covers or protective shelters might have done much to reduce that vulnerability. Corps and division commanders remained acutely aware of these problems as they arrived in the theater, and they placed a high priority on the call-up of reserve chemical decontamination companies. Potential CB contamination of rear-area operations was, and remains, a very vulnerable aspect of the Army field organization.

Another difficulty in rear areas was the mixture of Air Force and Army units which had different alerts, warning systems and procedures. Sirens, MOPP levels and MOPP level designations varied, causing confusion where the two services shared the same base. With the movement of the Air Force's Disaster Preparedness School from Lawery AFB, Colorado, to Fort McClellan in 1994, and of the CBR portion of the Navy's Shipborad Survivability School from New Hampshire to Fort McClellan in 1995, efforts to coordinate doctrine and training among the services can finally take place.

One of the most important tools for determining the threat to rear area units (and others in theater) was the ANBACIS-II software. This computerized CB agent contamination-prediction capability allowed commanders at all levels to pinpoint the areas for consideration for contamination hazard surveys and increased protection. This meant fewer soldiers in protective gear and less overall degradation to the force. Reliance on CONUS-based computers and the inability to communicate directly to divisions remain challenges. ANBACIS-II (or similar concepts) without the need of Cray computer support will be further refined to fit into the Army's maneuver control system. Growing emphasis on battlefield digitization calls for just this kind of capability. Far-term efforts point toward a network of CB agent detectors, resulting in near-real time situational awareness of CB agent hazards. Improved prediction of contamination hazards will provide much more useful options for military leaders than merely reacting to contamination predictions after the munitions have landed.

"Active Defense" versus Passive Defense

The air campaign was effective in stopping production of CB agent munitions but failed to destroy delivery systems, munition stockpiles or manufacturing equipment that had been moved. NBC agent delivery systems and newly identified production and storage sites continued to demand the highest priority and attention. Despite this intense effort, Air Force and SOCCOM units failed to stop the mobile Scuds, and the majority of Iraq's air force survived as a threat to CENTCOM forces. Prior to the Gulf War, Air Force planners had never envisioned the difficulties of attacking CB production/storage targets. Concerns that CB agents might escape the destructive power of the munitions was a driving factor behind the extensive ANBACIS-II modeling requirements. The Air Force is currently working on several concepts for munitions that penetrate deep, hardened targets such as storage sites, and neutralize CB agents within them, minimizing the chance of large-area contamination. Offensive munitions do not work, however, unless intelligence finds the targets.

US intelligence agencies failed to identify and track the production and proliferation of CB munitions sites and stockpiles in Iraq. It has become increasingly difficult to track and monitor which nations are developing offensive CB weapons programs. Despite the end of the

Cold War, there are still 100 analysts dedicated to nuclear weapons proliferation to everyone dedicated to CB weapons proliferation. Adding to this misbalance is the near absence of any human intelligence assets in countries that have CB weapons programs.

Legitimate supplies and equipment are commonly used to manufacture CB agents. The advent of a true global economy and the ability to construct front agencies to purchase and move supplies throughout the world market means that nations do not have to buy all their supplies and equipment from one company, or even from one nation. Given this lack of data, intelligence agencies could not significantly identify all CB production and storage sites. Thus, the Air Force could not stop Iraq from using CB agent munitions, as it (and the DoD leadership) claimed air power had at the end of January 1991.

Iraq's Scuds used against Israel and Saudi Arabia could have been armed with chemical warheads. Certainly the capability existed, if not experience, to attack deep targets effectively in CENTCOM's area of operations. Proliferation of ballistic missile technology across the globe continues today. Advances in ballistic missile development, unpiloted and remotely piloted airframes special force's operation and protected underground sites will ensure a constant enemy production capability and threat of CB agent employment. More advanced forms of ballistic missile defense, as well as more effective methods of locating and attacking mobile ballistic launchers, will be necessary to protect the force. The Ballistic Missile Defense office has added the mission of countering ballistic missiles with CB warheads to the future capabilities of a Theater High-Altitude Area Defense.

The Army, as well as the Air Force, attempted to silence the Iraqi CB delivery systems during the battlefield preparation phase of the ground offensive. Each corps drew on additional artillery units above and beyond its normal organizational allotment to counter the Iraqi's long-range artillery and the threat of chemical agent attacks during the breaching operations. In the week prior to the offensive, the corps commanders employed a Soviet-style artillery barrage to knock out systems that might target CENTCOM with CB agent munitions. Without this capability, the ground forces might have been targeted and attacked during the breaching operations by longer-ranged Iraqi artillery firing chemical projectiles. Against an adversary with counterbattery capability, a more mobile enemy force or one with better concealment/deception operations, these massive artillery attacks may not have been feasible.

As later UNSCOM inspection revealed, the majority of CB agent munitions survived the CENTCOM onslaught. Had Saddam seriously wanted to use these corps commanders. Future commanders will not be able to rely on "*active defense*" against CB agent storage sites and delivery systems with 100 percent confidence without strategic and operational intelligence on where those sites are located. Even where this information is available, deep underground facilities exist nuclear attacks, let alone conventional air attacks. What future commanders can count on is increased reliance on chemical defense equipment and more proactive use of chemical defense units.

Command and Control of Chemical Defense Units

The absence of a chemical brigade to coordinate life support and mission assignment for the chemical battalions and non-divisional companies was keenly felt. Often non-divisional chemical companies were directly attached to combat divisions instead of to the chemical battalions supporting that corps. In some cases, a company's three platoons were supporting three different divisions. Division and corps NBCCs had to manage the changing cast of these chemical defense units in addition to attending to their own operations planning, logistics and personnel issues. The non-divisional chemical defense units rotated to new assignments with each new operations order and their rotations were not well managed. Many of the divisions had to coordinate the swaps of chemical defense units between themselves instead of working through a central point.

The chemical defense companies had to search constantly for their logistics and operations support, receiving it from a new source every time they changed organizations, unlike corps-level units that remain a single higher support source while assigned to various divisions. Three chemical battalions operating under the one chemical brigade would have established the command and control relationship and logistics support that these non-divisional battalions and companies required. Artillery and engineer battalions working in support of divisions already use this concept. In addition, a chemical brigade commander (optimally a brigadier general) would have had direct lines of communication to ARCENT, CENTCOM, and the division and corps commander in order to assess their needs better and to communicate the non-divisional chemical defense companies' capabilities. This might have enhanced the flow of intelligence information to chemical officers throughout the force structure; that flow was limited due to the intelligence staffs bypassing the lieutenant colonels in CENTCOM and

ARCENT. Ideally, future commanders will understand that a sound supporting cast is needed in addition to combat power to ensure survivability in early phases of military operations.

However, this is not necessarily the case. The latest attempts to restructure the Army divisions, under Force XXI, has focused on downsizing the manpower from 18,000 to 15,000. One proposal is to remove divisional chemical companies (about 170 personnel) and move to the division's cavalry aviation brigade. The corps chemical brigade would also hold the active and reserve decon companies and the theater Biological Integrated Defense System (BIDS) company, without using chemical battalions for "*middle management*." Whether or not this will reduce a division's ability to train and deploy with its former dedicated chemical companies is not known yet. What is discouraging is the implication that dedicated chemical companies are not vital enough to consider as part of the division main effort. This plan is not set in stone yet, but it does show once again that combat arms leaders are not taking the time to evaluate exactly how NBC defense operations in the future will play out.

NBC Defense Equipment Logistics

Chemical defense equipment (CDE) logistics had been a struggle throughout the conflict. Through the 1980s, the Chemical School had introduced large amounts of new CDE into the Army. However, combat units were not maintaining adequate quantities for contingency operations, nor were they aware what quantities existed within their own units. As a result, when these units arrived in Saudi Arabia, they had to identify their shortfalls and then order the supplies from the United States. ARCENT NBCC had tried to assist by requiring of the two corps a special report to quantify their status, in an attempt to determine the theater CDE shortfalls.

The corps' logistics centers were too busy to implement this process and kept submitting requisitions for more CDE without trying to determine their actual status. This made it next to impossible for ODCSLOG to work up a planning and delivery system to get CDE to the units that needed it most. In addition, there was no policy within FORSCOM for what CDE should accompany deploying individuals, especially those sent through CONUS Processing Centers. These soldiers were told they would receive all their CB defense gear once in theater—which was not true. FORSCOM eventually corrected this problem, but not before thousands of US troops arrived without personal CDE, draining precious theater reserves.

The overall accountability of consumable CDE (protective suits, detectors kits, and decon kits) in theater and throughout the armed forces was poor. Stacks of CDE grew in Dhahran and al-Damman, lost among other supplies. Compounding the problem that chemical officers and NCOs were often held responsible for procuring CDE in peacetime, rather than supply sergeants. During Desert Shield, this arrangement of "*chemical logistics*" in parallel with normal supply continued. Meanwhile, logistics offices were duplicating these efforts in response to their commanders' orders. As an example, one of the chemical soldiers' responsibilities became tracking each individual protective suite, each mask, each agent detector, can of decontaminant, and especially, each piece of new equipment (such as the CAMs and the XM93 NCRS vehicles) as to when it was available and due in. Had logistics experts been procuring and transferring CDE, they might have been able to avoid the shortages encountered and the difficulties of priorizing critical NBC defense supplies. The result was an inordinate drain on worldwide theater reserves, a lack of accountability of stocks and poor delivery results.

With the development of Joint Chemical Defense Equipment Consumption Rates (JCHEMRATES) studies, logistics experts will be able to take back the responsibility. While chemical soldiers will continue to coordinate with their logistics counterparts to maintain a certain asset visibility, logistics experts must take charge and integrate CDE fully with other vital aspects of military logistics. Few other military operations rely so heavy on logistics for success.

Biological Agent Detection and Production

Failure to eliminate the CB warfare threat through active defense emphasized the need for accurate and timely CB agent sampling and response throughout the theater. There has been a long history of inadequate BW defense preparations, even though the US military suspected that biological weapon technology had spread to over a dozen countries, including Iraq. Military and political leadership had always assumed they could treat biological warfare threats like nuclear warfare threats (that is to say, as strategic political consideration), and were not prepared for military operational and tactical realities. The military leadership could also count on its individual protection equipment and decontamination systems, designed primarily for chemical agents, to also counter biological agents.

The lack of a real-time automatic biological detector, lack of a deployment plan, lack of a tested validation process, and the lack of a vaccination policy all handicapped a full BW defense capability. CENTCOM had to react to post-BW attack symptoms rather than relying on a low-level agent detector system that would permit instituting protective measures. Collecting a biological sample from air samplers or tactical units and transporting to JCMEC and forward labs could take form six hours to two days; transportation back to CONUS labs for verification took another day. This did not match the military's "*information age*" concept of operations.

Twelve biological detection teams were active for about two months in Southwest Asia, during which time they collected sixty-three environmental samples and 113 biomedical samples, and used over 2,000 biological SMART tickets for air samples. Less than one percent of these gave positive readings at their sampling points, of which all were confirmed as negatives at the labs. The FMIB identified a number of challenges that it had encountered, in after-action reviews. Primary among these was the need to update the Army's 1980s-era doctrine that relied on post-attack indicators to warn of BW attacks. No military unit in the modern force structure had the responsibility for collecting biomedical and environmental samples.

Chain-of-custody forms used in transporting samples were difficult to employ, and peacetime Air Force and Army safety regulations on transporting hazardous samples had to be ignored in the interests of time. Procedures for collecting and transporting the samples were equally outmoded, failing to include sampling procedures for the Sox vehicles. Containers used to transport the samples back to CONUS laboratories were adequate, mostly because they were commercial products used in similar biomedical operations. However, soldiers using this equipment were unfamiliar with it, not to mention with the collection, packaging, handling and documentation procedures.

The JCMEC itself did not have sufficient communications or transportation assets to cover a three-corps area. It was forced to rely on tactical units for much of the reporting, transportation and handling of samples. During Desert Shield, unit commanders were able to lend helicopters or HMMWVs to transport samples back to JCMEC; during Desert Storm, however, the temp of the battle forced unit commanders to deny such transportation assets to the sampling teams in favor of the more urgent requirements of keeping their combat units supplied and moving. This would have limited quick identification of a BW attack, had it occurred, and could have ultimately cost lives. Another deficiency was the lack of turn-around information from the laboratories in the United States. The Army Tech escort Unit logged sixty-six missions to CONUS laboratories during the conflict, delivering over 240 samples within one-two days of receipt.

The two corps and CENTCOM NBCCs did not receive any immediate feedback from the six or seven sets of chemical samples analyzed at Edgewood or the environmental samples analyzed at Fort Detrick. While this was a result of there being no positive confirmations of CB agents in these samples, the lack of a response unsettled the CENTCOM staff. This made the CENTCOM leadership very reliant on their forward labs for urgent confirmation of any threat. Only sixteen of the 240 samples were analyzed in-theater (they were SMART tickets showing false positives), suggesting that the majority of the samples flown to CONUS were questionable and not based on suspicions of actual CB weapons use but rather for confirmation of negative results.

The lack of biological agent vaccines in an old story by now. While vaccines for both anthrax and botulinum toxin were available to some US and allied forces, the pharmaceutical industry was very reluctant to support the vaccine program. Only two companies of more than ten contacted agreed to produce the vaccines, but not before critical shortages developed that could have doomed CENTCOM. Pharmaceutical companies have stated that the high risk of manufacturing vaccines for biological warfare agents, potential liabilities, high cost, and difficulty obtaining FDA approval made this a no-win situation for them, the result being heavy reliance on government initiatives.

The need to rely on investigational new drugs raised concerns in troops, adding to their fears abut CB warfare. The majority of US soldiers were not vaccinated, due in part to the escalation to a two-corps mission, industrial surge difficulties and lack of a DoD policy for producing and distributing the doses. Division commanders felt that not having enough vaccine was worse for the morale and well-being of their soldiers than having enough vaccine was worse for the morale and well-being of their soldiers than having no vaccines at all.

After the war, General Powell was furious that the lack of a biodefense strategy had nearly "slashed" CENTCOM's Achilles' heel." In a classified memorandum to the Army, he blasted the DoD NBC defense program as inefficient and demanded substantial changes to prevent this error in the future. An interim plan dated March 1992 failed to reach joint consensus; the joint requirements Oversight Council therefore developed a joint Mission Needs Statement for a new biological defense program. A joint body called the Joint Services Committee for Biological Defense, led by ODCSOPS, outlined a DoD Operational Concept for Biological Defense, which grouped needed improvements into detection (point and stand-off), protection, decontamination, and immunization. About a year later, the Office of the Secretary of Defense (OSD) created a special program office, the Joint Program Office for Biological Defense, or JPO-Bio, which would answer directly to OSD rather than to or through the Army. Colonel Gene Fuzy, having led the Army's efforts to develop a biodefense capability, was selected to lead this office, supported by the four services' NBC defense organizations.

Its goals are to develop an interim biological detection point capability by fiscal 1995 and a refined point detection capability by fiscal 2002; develop an interim strategic stand-off biological detection capability by 1997, and field a developed strategic stand-off detection capability by 2004; develop a tactical stand-off biological detection capability by 2005; and develop a biological agent vaccine production plant by 2002. These efforts have thus far been successful. The Army plans to field a biological detection company for Army Corps units by 1997. Each company would feature thirty five Biological Integrated Detection Systems, whose HMMWVs resemble mobile laboratories. A contingency platoon of seven vehicles currently exists, capable of biological agent detection in less than twenty-five minutes. As newer technologies emerge, the BIDS will be upgraded until a real-time capability exists. The Navy has developed several Interim Biological Agent Detectors for the fleet. Future plans focus on developing a modular biological agent detector that meets all services' requirement, networked across the theater to alert all units to potential BW attacks.

The JPO-Bio is working with the service to develop new doctrine for using these detectors, in part through computer, simulations that show potential employment patterns of biological weapons. The Army's manual FM 3-3, Contamination Avoidance, has been radically changed to focus on CB defense and has moved nuclear contamination avoidance to a second manual (FM 3-3-1). It includes a detailed description, based on the Biological Detection Teams' accounts, on how the Army will conduct future biological detection and sampling.

The medical side of JPO-Bio began soliciting industry to bid on the construction of a vaccine production facility and production of vaccines for the four services. To date, no industries have bid or are likely to participate—perhaps because none of the limiting factors of liability, risk and FDA regulations have changed. The technology exists to develop antidotes and pretreatments for just about any CBW agent in quantities necessary to protect the force (at least for those CBW agents that have an available cure). Because there was such a small annual production requirement for these items (Since most of them were stockpiled and not used), there were no industry production lines ready when the military asked for a step-up in production in August 1990. These events may force the Army toward a government-owned, government-operated facility that can run without regard of profit margins and liability suits. This option is being avoided by DoD, given the bend to increase industry participation in the defense sector rather than create more government jobs. Other options continue to be explored, with industry input.

Smoke Generator Operations

There were situations where smoke generator units were allowed to shine, but they were limited in number due to the uncooperative weather and the lack of Iraqi offensive operations. As in the Korean War, many smoke generators units prepared to smoke airfields, logistics areas, and headquarters locations to conceal them from an air threat that never materialized. The KFIA obscuration mission was a definite indication that these missions still have a place on the modern, fast-paced and non-linear battlefield. Also Iraqi smoke operations definitely hindered the Air Force's attempts to knock out Tuwaitha nuclear facility. Deception operations during the movement to tactical staging areas may have fooled the Iraqi military into looking for an offensive up to the middle through Kuwait instead of the actual flanking attack (the Iraqiş have not commented yet).

The 1st CAV DIV successfully used smoke to obscure the several Iraqi units waiting in the Wadi al-Batin. When the raiding party ran into heavy fire, it was able to withdraw under cover of the smoke haze—very helpful, considering that this was a day attack in the (relatively) open desert. The greatest disappointment to the *Chemical Corps* may have occurred when the 1st IN DIV refused the support of two smoke generator companies in its breach operations. First, the use of smoke to obscure river-crossing, obstacle crossings and similar operations is an established and successful operational concept dating back to World War II. Second, two smoke generator companies at one division's beck and call when the normal allocation was one or two platoons represents a staggering amount of resources to discard, presumably after careful consideration of the benefits and risks. In any event, the wind, rain and sandstorm encountered on February 24 would have defeated the whether-dependant smoke operations. Had the weather been better, or had there been some Iraqi response to the offensive, the 1st IN DIV breach may have been very costly in terms of soldiers, resources and the VII Corps schedule.

When the mechanized smoke generator units were tasked to move to the 3rd AR DIV (racing at he head of VII corps), the chemical companies found that the M113A2 chassis could not keep pace with the more modern armored units' M1A1 Abrams tanks and M2/3 Bradley fighting vehicles. Also, the smoke generator units still rely on 55-gallon drums of fog oil, resupply of which is a very inefficient and time-consuming operations. This indicated and need to either modernize the mechanized smoke vehicles to a Bradley chassis and upgrade its supporting logistics or identify a way to project smoke in front of the combat units in the form of projectiles. Since the Artillery Center and School would rather invest in smart projectiles that kill targets, they probably will not be the proponents of an increased capability in smoke projection. The PM Smoke has developed its latest M58 Wolf mechanized smoke system on an M113A3 APC, with a turbo-changed engine for increase mobility.

Smoke funding remains a low priority, even within the *Chemical Corps*. Public Law 103-160 created a special OSD funding line for the highly visible agent detectors protective suits, and non-aqueous decontamination programs. Smoke systems remain an Army-funded budget line, competing against the major defense programs. Many military experts still do not realize the role that smoke operations played in the Gulf War, which impacted negatively on smoke's post-war funding. Yet if one were to ask combat soldiers, they might note that historically smoke generations systems have been the most accepted and successful of the many *Chemical Corps*' programs. Units training at the CTCs always look for and request smoke support. Further input is needed from the combat arms community on priority of effort before unit proficiency and leader experience in training with smoke is lost.

Given the lack of attention that the few successful smoke operations during the Gulf War have received to date, this attention does not seem likely in the near future, despite great potential in reducing enemy observation and target acquisition. With the evolution of smoke technologies that may soon block both infrared and millimeter wave scanners and target acquisition devices, and the increasing lethality of antitank munitions, the combat arms community can hardly afford to ignore the potential benefits. Perhaps with the increased participation of smoke units at the combat training centers and increased war gaming at the Army Battle Labs and Louisiana Maneuvers, this acknowledgment may yet come.

Industrial Base Issues

Industrial base issues are a hot topic for defense firms and Congress these days. Because of the shrinking requirements of a smaller military, DoD must pick and choose what they consider vital resources and which firms should perform those functions in the future. Most of the attention focuses on the "*big boys*": the submarine industrial base, the bomber industrial base, the tank production lines. Up to 1990 there had been little attention to the mostly small firms that supported the production of NBC defense equipment for the military. But as the six months of Desert Shield showed, critically weak areas within the NBC defense sector were (and remain) real war-stoppers.

The NBC defense sector of the DoD industrial base was unprepared to make up the extreme shortages in material for which DoD was asking industry to fill by surge production. The only items that the military had in excess were protective gloves and DS-2 decontaminant; everything else was in short supply and required immediate production to support CENTCOM. Only through a frantic, herculean effort by military and government personnel at depots, logistic centers, R & D centers, production bases and industry offices did the minimal necessary equipment get to Southwest Asia. Even given the full effort of these agencies, the NBC defense equipment necessary to survive and sustain combat operations did not arrive until mid-January.

This is not to say that the air and ground campaigns were delayed or that chemical defense equipment arriving was a precondition to starting operations; these deadlines, however, increased the urgency behind the NBC defense community. Had Saddam Hussein attacked into Saudi Arabia in August or September 1990, and if his army and air force had used CB munitions in the attack our forces could have been frozen in place, these operations significantly degraded because of poor logistics planning. The necessary chemical defense equipment, including protective clothing, masks, decontaminant, agent detectors and medical supplies, was not available when it needed to be. This would have resulted in thousands of American and allied causalities and a great public outcry in the United States, which could have resulted in the withdrawal of US forces from the Gulf. Much of the blame for this lack of readiness goes to the Army for its own reluctance to invest in war reserves of chemical defense equipment. This has resulted in low annual requirements and poor profitability margins, which lead to low bid contracts and less-than-high-quality equipment. There are some poor performers in the NBC defense industrial sector, brought in by the desire to fill contract quotas for small disadvantaged fires or to cater to the low bid, while ignoring high quality standards. These industries will only be weeded out when the overall DoD selection process is improved. Until then, the chemical defense community must work with industry to put plans to place to obtain sufficient quantities of CDE before conflicts erupt. In some cases, these plans for surge productions are being developed.

This issue refers back to the need for careful planning. The overall emphasis in the NBC defense programs remains on research and development, not on their acquisition and sustainment. As a result, the US armed forces have some very fine, sophisticated chemical defense systems—but not in the numbers required to sustain operations. Field commanders and policy makes have no way to measure the benefits of having a certain numbers of detectors, decontamination systems or collective protection shelters over a long conflict. As noted earlier, there are no modeling and simulation efforts that can demonstrate how effectively US forces can defend against CB agent munitions. If there is no definable "*value-added*" in terms of equipment and personnel, there is no push to get these defensive capabilities. As a result, there is little planning with industry on how to best meet the necessary equipment quantities prior to and during a conflict.

CB Defense Research and Development Program

Rather deliberately, there have been no official recriminations within DoD by its leadership against the Army's CB defense program. The Presidential Advisory Committee on Gulf War Illnesses has voiced the opinion, echoed by some veterans' groups and others, that the military has not done well in procuring CB agent detection systems (since there remains the question of whether or not low levels of nerve agents or biological agents were actually in the battlefield environment). Others have bemoaned the heavy protective suits, the older technology used for M17 protective masks, and the lack of alternatives to decontaminants that are highly corrosive and reliant on water. These CB defense programs are well researched and developed, but if one does not realize the limits and benefits of using a system, the user blames the developer for its faults rather than its admittedly untested benefits. Imagine a rookie policeman that had never been shot at complaining that his kevlar vest weighed too much to wear, and one immediately sees the parallel with soldiers complaining about chemical defense equipment. While this book did not allow for a proper discussion on how all these equipment.

Chemical agent detectors such as the M8A1 detector and M256A1 detector kit are designed to give soldiers who are not chemical specialists a device that would maximize time of warning, thus calling for low-level agent detection limits, while begin man portable and rugged. The suite of existing detectors more than adequately meet the soldiers' requirements of low-level agent detection.

The demand for sensitive detector means occasional false alarms (mistaking other vapors such as diesel fuel for nerve agents, or false positives); however, chemical agent detectors do not ignore the presence of chemical agents (not alarming to nerve agents, or false negatives). Combat leaders nerve commented on the false alarm issue, largely because they do not train with detectors and never consider the consequences of false alarms (increased stress, lack of confidence in the equipment, etc.). What they did demand was a "*zero-risk*" approached to CB warfare, which is not duplicated in any other aspect of military R&D; for example, helmets are not required to deflect all bullets nor are armored vehicles required to stop all munitions from penetration, yet paradoxically, chemical agent alarms are required to detect all concentrations of all known agents.

The current suite of detectors already detects low level of chemical agents far before they reach incapacitating or lethal quantities. However, this very feature make the detectors prone to confusing chemicals in the environment with chemical agents. If soldiers demanded zero false alarms instead of zero risk, more reliable detectors would emerge but at the price of higher detection limits and less warning time. To demand both zero risk and zero false alarms in rugged, man-portable packages would result in gold-plated detectors costing may be a hundred thousand dollars each. Given that DoD has not seen fit to order the full necessary quantity of M8A1 alarms in the 1980s, and the future M22 Automatic Chemical Agent Detector/Alarm (ACADA) will not replace the M8A1 alarm on a one-to-one basis (about 40,000 required for the entire force) in the 1990s, what hope is there that DoD would procure these gold-plated ultimate end-state detectors?

There are always compromises made between any current weapons system and its respective gold-plated ultimate objective. In all areas except CBW, DoD determines the cost and benefits of assuming some level of risk in a trade-off between system performance, cost and its effect on military operations. If the Army raised the detection levels slightly to under incapacitating levels and decreased the false alarm rate, the overall cost would not be prohibitive and the operational results would be highly beneficial to the combat arms users. The only way this will happen is if the Army's infantry, armor and artillery leaders (especially the ones that become four star generals and major command leaders) start analyzing the costs and benefits of these options, identify what they really want and what they're willing to compromise on, adequately fund the programs, and work with the Chemical Corps to get these detectors built, Up to now, the chance of that general officer level of commitment does not seem too promising.

Congress Takes Action

When Congress developed the National Defense Authorization Act for fiscal year 1994, it added a requirement to force certain changes in the DoD NBC defense program. This legislation was named Title XVII—Chemical and Biological Weapons Defense, under Public Law 103-160. The House and Senate committees noted some improvements in the overall DoD program since the end of the Gulf War but remained concerned over the need for a sustained effort to strengthen the program. They also recommended DoD assistance in training US and international Chemical Weapons Convention inspectors and monitoring teams. Last, they encouraged the Secretary of Defense to adopt a verification and inspection regime for the 1972 Biological Weapons Convention. The law included five sections which included:

- Section 1701: *Conduct of the chemical and Biological Defense Program.* Improve the joint coordination and oversight of the NBC defense program and ensure a coherent and effective approach to its management. This is to be accomplished though a single office in DoD, a stronger coordinating role by the Army, and a joint coordinated and integrated NBC defense budget for all four services.
- Section 1702: *Consolidation of Chemical and Biological Defense Training Activities.* Moves the Air Force's Disaster Preparedness School would move from Lowery AFB, Colorado, to Anniston, Alabama. This allows the Air Force to use the Chemical Defense Training Facility and increases the likelihood of compatible training of NBC defense specialists.
- Section 1703: *Annual report of Chemical and Biological Warfare Defense* demands an annual report reporting the overall status of the DoD NBC defense program; it includes readiness issues, such

as logistics status of stocks, training and readiness of the armed forces and war game/battle simulations; the status of the DoD NBC defense RDA program, to include future requirements and problem areas; and the military's preparations for the chemical weapons Convention.

- Section 1704: *Sense of Congress Concerning Federal Emergency Planning for Response to Terrorist Threats.* It recommends an increased effort by the Federal Emergency Management Agency to develop a capability to detect, warn and respond to the potential terrorist use of chemical or biological agents, or natural disasters and emergencies involving industrial chemicals or natural or accidental outbreaks of disease.
- Section 1705: *Agreements to Provide Support to Vaccination Programs of Department of Health and Human Services.* This gives the Secretary of Defense and Secretary of Health and Human Services permission to use excess peacetime biological weapons defense capabilities to support domestic vaccination programs. This ability would allow DoD to retain a surge capability to produce vaccines and antidotes for unusual diseases as the armed forces became involved in a future contingency.

So what was the final word on the CB warfare threat? Modern-day chemical defense doctrine was judged to be good, with the exception of some unique areas such as aircraft decontaminations, casualty decontamination and contaminated equipment retrograde procedures. The coalition forces increased their state of CB defense readiness rapidly from very low initially to moderate in six months. The herculean effort moving CB defense equipment, combined with a furious level of training, did improve the overall defense posture to the point that US causalities would have been light instead of the expected thousands. The Fox reconnaissance system, the ANBACIS-II modeling capability, the XM21 RSCAALs and the biodetectors were four vital efforts of the development initiatives that could have been completed in the 1980s with a little more funding and a lot more input form the combat arms community. Chemical agent point detectors may have been too sensitive for tactical operations, judging by the number of false alarms. Collective protection system were inadequate and continue to be critical issue. Individual protection (masks and clothes) were capable of enabling the individual troops to survive, but comfort and performance issues and the procurement shortages kept everyone's nerves on edge. With the exception of decontamination programs, these material fixes are already in the works. We continue to lack are modeling and simulation tools that demonstrate the value of NBC defense equipment in terms of troops and equipment saved.

There is a clear possibility that political sensitive over Gulf War Syndrome could drive CB defense research and development into developing prohibitively expensive detectors and time and resource-consuming decontaminants. With out credible evidence to support the case that CB agents were in any form responsible for these illnesses, it is hoped that our leadership will not suffer any "knee-jerk" reactions to the loud cries of the ignorant. CB defense equipment is meant to minimize the risk to the troops as they accomplish combat missions; if it interferes with their ability to complete the mission, it will not be used and soldiers will die when CB agents are used. Combat leaders need to ask some hard questions and measure the pros and cons prior to reacting to unfounded allegations.

CENTCOM completed its mission without having its CB defense skills fully challenged. Whether that has made it easier to ignore the need to equip and train against the possibility of CB warfare, or whether the military is now on guard, remains to be seen. What is evident is that without a retaliatory capability, US forces must rely on defensive measures and training more than ever before. Failure to develop these defensive measures and training more than ever before. Failure to develop these defensive measures might mean that America's sons and daughters will be killed in future combat operations by an opposing force employing chemical weapons, especially given the US military's past track record. If we lose sight of that important point, within the next twenty years the US military will be defeated in battle or suffer catastrophic consequences as a result of CB weapons use. The last thing our leaders should think is that the Persian Gulf War proved that the US military dos not need to worry about CB warfare anymore.

Agent Orange Revisited

About a year and a half following the end of war, Persian Gulf veterans began coming forward in increasing number with reports of various afflictions. These afflictions were not limited to US active duty soldiers; they appeared in reservists and nationalists Guardsmen, government civilians, and even British and Canadian soldiers. The wide variety of symptoms appearing in individuals scattered across the theater, appeared to have no rhyme or reason. At first the lack of an identified source of the problems from the Gulf War caused Veteran's Administration (VA) hospitals to resist treatment of the unknown afflictions until it was positively disability benefits to veterans with conditions that had not been diagnosed. The main issue was deciphering what illnesses have been caused naturally in the United States, as opposed to illnesses or casualties caused during combat operations in the Gulf, not to mention correctly diagnosing the illnesses.

Cries of betrayal, linking this treatment to that suffered by Agent orange veterans, quickly got action from military and political leaders, whose understood the need to avoid the perception of delaying the treatment of unexplained ailments in groups of returning veterans. Both the House and Senate put forth Persian Gulf Syndrome Compensations bills, but differences over whether or not the VA had the authority to issue the disability benefits created bureaucratic delays in committees trying to resolve differences between the two bills. Medical agencies from all government agencies began researching the possible causes behind the strange symptoms. This search included over thirty government studies during the next year.

It was not until 1994 that medical research began to yield some concrete theories. Gulf War Syndrome (GWS) veterans had brown in number from a few thousand to several tens of thousands but still totaled less than about 10 percent of the deployed forces. The common symptoms identified at the Tucson VA Medical Center included fatigue, skin rash, muscle and joint pain, headaches, memory loss, shortness of breath, sleep disturbance, diarrhea and coughing. These symptoms varied in intensity form soldier to soldier to soldier, and from region to region with no apparent pattern. Common theories exposed by experts included petroleum exposure, stress reactions, depleted uranium, pesticides exposure, smoke form oil fires, indigenous parasites and bacteria, vaccines and nerve agent antidotes, chemical or biological warfare agents, chronic fatigue syndrome and multiple chemical sensitivity. It might be one of these or a combination of factors that had triggered the symptoms. One rumor made out GWS to be a time-bomb virus developed in Baghdad as a revenge-weapon against the coalition forces.

More than 60,000 veterans have signed onto the Persian Gulf Registry. The majority of these have joined the registry because they believe they may be suffering from GWS. The symptoms described on the registry range even more widely than the early reports: abdominal pain, facial pain, chest pain, blood clots, flushing, night sweats, blurry vision, shaking, vomiting, fatigue, swollen lymph nodes, weight loss/ gain, intestinal disorders, sore gums, cough, memory loss, dizziness, inability to concentrate, labored breathing, depression, neurological disorders and leg cramps (among others). In addition, the veterans' families have reported suffering from various symptoms, and some couples have blamed miscarriages and birth defects on GWS. The large range of symptoms, which seem to point to multiple illnesses with overlapping symptoms and causes, are making veterans paranoid about any illness contracted since their return as a possible Gulf War-related disease or agent. The question addressed here is this: are chemical or biological agents, either deliberately used by the Iraqui military or accidentally released by the coalition forces, the sources of the Persian Gulf illnesses? And if so, is the government deliberately concealing this knowledge from suffering veterans?

Without a doubt, the second most popular suspect is exposure to chemical warfare agents (the leading contender being the combined effects of PB tablets and insecticides). The possibility that biological agent exposure might be a cause has been dismissed on the basis of existing extensive research on effect of botulin toxin anthrax, aflatoxin and other biological organisms on the human body. Had soldiers been dismissed on the basis of existing extensive research on effects of botulin toxin, anthrax, aflatoxin and other biological organisms on the human body. Had soldiers been exposed to these agents, medics would have instantly recognized and diagnosed these cases. In any event, extensive and more comprehensive post-conflict diagnosis would have identified such bacteria and viruses in returning soldiers, and to date no such evidence has turned up. Mustard agent, in a similar fashion, has been researched extensively since 1918 in an effort to understand its effects on the human body. As for nerve agent, there are at least three decades of applied research as background reference material as which to identify or discredit nerve agent exposure as a source of GWS. Yet because the Army had ignored NBC defense training, equipment modernization, and leadership development for decades, many veterans continue to see chemical warfare agents as a likely cause of GWS—because of ignorance, not because of facts.

Chemical Agent Exposure Scenarios

There are three general scenarios that serve as basis for the claims of chemical agent exposure. The first possibility is that Iraqi forces might have employed air or ground-delivered CB agents during the air or ground campaigns. Second, bombed Iraqi CB weapon production sites and storage bunkers might have released plumes of agent to drift towards friendly lines. Last, demolition of Iraqi ammunition bunkers, such as those at Khamisiyah, raise the possibility of accidental release as a result of destroying unmarked Iraqi chemical munitions.

Most scholars agree that the Iraqis did not deliberately use CB agents against coalition forces. Evidence gathered to date includes representations of Iraqi military officials upon debriefing, the UN on-site inspections, US intelligence assets, and recent DoD studies. All support a conclusion that there were no international Iraqi chemical weapon attacks, or widespread exposures as a result of any such intentional attacks. Examinations of all the Scud impact areas and the recovered warheads fired at the coalition support this. Numerous division and CENTCOM logs show that all suspected chemical attacks against the coalition turned out to be incorrect reports sent up the chain of command prior to positive confirmation. Fast-moving CENTCOM forces did not find forward-placed chemical munitions at suspected Iraqi locations, while they did capture over 14,000 tons of conventional ammunition. The Iraqi artillery was silenced, the Iraqi air force never returned to the skies, and the few Scud warheads that were CB-capable were kept in reserve.

Even the few *Marine Corps* claims of Iraqi chemical mines, mostly reports of blister agent detections, panned out as false alarms despite positive readings from eager (though inexperienced) Fox operators. The mass casualties that were expected from such attacks, as evidence in the Iran-Iraq War, just were not there. Not one incident could compare to the Tokyo subway incident years later, when Japanese commuters were immediately afflicted by nerve agent vapors. While there were numerous reports of a single chemical agent detections from M8A1 alarms in a single site, confirmed by M256A1 kits and XM93 NBCRS vehicles, indicative of a typical chemical weapons attack.

With the reports of Czech nerve and mustard detection in mid-January 1991, many suspected that low levels of chemical agent released from the bombed CB agent production and storage sites might have affected coalition forces. The Pentagon released its assessment that at last two of the seven Czech and French detections were credible based on ERDEC's analysis of the Czechs' 1970s Soviet-technology chemical agent detectors and interview with the French and Czech militaries. In all seven Cases, the amounts of agent detected were deemed militarily insignificant (much less than 0.4 milligrams-minutes/cubic meter); there were no signs of agent poisoning in any soldiers in that time period; and there was no physical evidence of any-delivered munitions in the area. This led some to believe that the coalition bombing of Iraqi CB production/storage sties could have been the source of the agent.

Yet, of the over thirty suspected CB Agene production and storage areas, only eleven actually stored bulk quantities of chemical agents and munitions (according to Iraqi official claims). Of these eleven, only two Muhammadiyat and Al Muthanna, were seriously damaged by the bombing campaign in February 1991. Approximately 15.2 tons of mustard was damaged at Muhammadiyat, as well as a little less than three metric tons of sarin and cyclosarin mix. At Al Muthanna, stores of approximately 16.8 metric tons of GB/ GF mix were tons of GB/GF mix were apparently damaged. Based on the CIA's worst-case modeling, the farthest chemical agent could travel from these bombings was approximately 300 kilometers; the closest US troops were 400 kilometers away, a difference of 100 kilometers (roughly sixty miles). By these calculations none of the coalition soldiers could have been exposed to the volatile chemical agents released. This was probably why US forces could not confirm the Czech detections at the same sites, nor did any coalition detector alarm between KKMC and the front lines. In addition, no Iraqi, Saudi or Kuwaiti civilians have been reported as chemical agent casualties. The majority of these targets were far from civilian centers.

The Defense Science Board reported released in June 1994 speculated that if chemical agents were released by the bombing campaign, the only possible targets that might have affected coalition forces were the storage bunkers at an Nasiriyah and Tallil. These were the nearest targets, within 150-200 kilometers of friendly forces. To assume that chemical agent exposure would travel such a distance, the bombing would have to release a substantial amount of agent, in excess of sixteen metric tons, beyond the amount consumed in the explosions. The lack of local Arab civilian or animal deaths around those two sites seems to believe that possibility. In any event, DNA modeling of the explosion calculates that a maximum lethal dose would have traveled less than nine kilometers and an incapacitating dose less than ten kilometers. In addition, the rain and wind storms immediately following the An Nasiriyah bombing on January 16 would have dispersed the easily hydrolyzed sarin clouds. To expect that there could be low levels of chemical agent in one spot without high concentrations of chemical agents being detected in another area defies the laws of physics. As a result of these (and other) investigations, the DoD,

DNA, Defense Science Board, Army, CIA, and the Presidential Advisory Committee on Gulf War Illnesses all concur that no US service members were exposed to chemical agents or fallout from bombed chemical weapons production/storage facilities. This all leads to the third possibility—post-conflict demolitions of Iraqi munitions depots.

Depot at Khamisiyah

The Khamisiyah Ammunition Storage Area represents an immense bunker complex near an Nasiriyah spreading out over fifty square kilometers, one of four large bunker areas in southern Iraq storing conventional ammunitions of all types. If featured about 100 ammunition bunkers and several other types of storage buildings. Iraqi personnel moved 2,160 unmarked 122 mm nerve agent rockets form the Al-Muthanna CW production/storage facility to a Khamisiyah bunker just before the start of the air campaign. According to Iraqi officials, the rockets started leaking immediately, motivating them to move 1,100 rockets out of the bunker to a pit area two kilometers away, where they were buried. On February 26, elements of the 24th IN DIV overran Khamisiyah. After the conclusion of the ground war, the 82d ABN DIV occupied the sector. To deny the Iraqis the ability to rearm with the thousands of tons of munitions discovered there, ARCENT undertook immediate demolition activities. On March 2, the 939th Engineer Group tasked the 37th Engineer Battalion with support form one company of the 307th Engineer Battalion and the 60th Ordnance Detachment (Explosive Ordnance Disposal), to destroy the bunkers. Other supporting elements (fire-fighters, technical intelligence teams, civil affairs detachment) were present for a strength of about 430 soldiers.

By accounts taken by the DoD Investigative Team assisting the Presidential Advisory Committee, chemical specialists in the area were told that the ammunition bunkers were assessed not to be holding chemical weapons, as determined by intelligences assets (as noted some Iraqi EPWs had claimed that chemical munitions were marked). While it is unclear if the 82d ABN DIV received world from either 24th IN DIV or XVIII ABN Corps about suspected chemical munitions, Lieutenant Colonek Rick Jackson, the 82d ABN DIV's division chemical officer, took no chances. Fox vehicles and unit reconnaissance teams swept through the area looking for evidence of chemical weapons in the bunkers. They found riot control agents, while phosphorus artillery rounds and empty hollow artillery shells that might have contained TNT, but no sign of chemical munitions. Soldiers did find local civilians and animals living inside the many bunkers; they were evacuated prior to demolition operations.

On March 3, the engineers "prepped" two bunkers with demolitions to test their techniques. During this time, the engineer battalion had M8 alarms operating on their vehicles. The battalion's chemical NCO dressed in MOPP-4 to check personally some bunkers with M256A1 kits. These results were negative. FMIB teams searched for any chemical, laser-guided or optical-guided weapons, and found one rocket of interest. Everything else looked conventional. The engineers blew up the two bunkers without incident. Alpha Company of the 307th ENGBN was destroying munitions at Jalibah airfield thirty kilometers distant that day, also without incident.

On March 4, the engineer teams rigged thirty-eight bunkers, including bunker number 73. While the ammunition was being prepped for demolition, on one saw any markings denoting chemical munitions, nor was there any evidence of chemical agent leaks. In later interviews, Explosives Ordnance Disposal (EOD) personnel stated that they had been aware that they might encounter chemical munitions in any of the demolition missions, and had actively looked for them. The fact that none were detected did not negate the possibility of chemical munitions. Major General James Johnson, commanding general of the 82d ABN DIV, states that his forces had received a chemical downwind-hazard message that forced him to relocate units out of the immediate hazard area prior to the demolition. Most of the engineer task force remained north or northwest of the explosion, while the winds blew toward the east or northeast. The three company commanders in the task force all had had M8A1 detectors mounted on their vehicles, and once outside the three-mile safety zone they had ensured that the detectors were functioning.

Less than an hour after detonating thirty-seven of the thirty-eight bunkers at once, the M8A1 alarm in Bravo Company went off, causing a local scramble to increase MOPP levels. Once their M256A1 kits verified the lack of chemical agents, the unit dropped its MOPP status. Medics reported no casualties or signs of health problems related to chemical agent exposure that day. Because of the falling debris reported, troops moved further away from the bunkers.

On March 5, during heavy trains, a bunker (not bunker 73) which had failed to detonate the previous day was destroyed. Present M8A1 alarms did not alarm, and no further operations were conducted on that day due to poor weather conditions. Because of concern, over a shortage of demolition explosives and the potential for secondary explosions and munition fly-outs, tests were conducted on March 6 to implode four bunkers. No operations were conducted on the following two days. On March 9, the engineers carried out a reconnaissance of the remaining bunkers to be destroyed the following day. The 37th Engineer Battalion operations officer stated that he practically stumbled over stacks of long-crafted munitions in the nearby pit area. The battalion decided to blow these rockets along with the remainder of the bunkers in the area. A 37th Engineer Battalion NCO who set the charges on three stacks of munitions in the pit area recalled that at that time there was not enough explosive material to destroy the munitions completely. Nevertheless, a team set the charges to damages as many as possible.

On March 10, approximately 1600 hours, the 37th ENG BN ignited the fuzes on the explosives, which would detonate the remaining sixty bunkers, most warehouses at Khamisiyah and the munitions stacked in the pit area. The engineer force was about thirty minutes drive form the area, several miles south of Khamisiyah, when the explosion occurred. An EOD NCI from the 60th Ordnance Detachment recalled about six stacks of 122 mm rockets destroyed in the pit,' When he returned a few days after the demolition, pictures taken by this EOD NCO showed many intact rockets. Records from the 60th Ordnance Detachment state that 850 122 mm rockets were destroyed that day. No soldiers reported any ill effects at the time of this demolition or at the time of their return when they assessed the results. EOD operations continued in the area throughout March, destroying munitions at Tallil, the An Nasiryah and other munitions discovered in southern Iraq. When the VII Corps assumed control of the area (as the XVIII ABN Corps departed), the 2d ACR was tasked to recon Khamisiyah's bunkers for CB munitions. On March 23, it reported negative results.

In October, 1991, the UNSCOM inspection teams visited the Khamisiyah area, where they identified three areas holding chemical weapons. At the time, it was not clear whether the chemical weapons identified had been present during the war or whether, as was suspected at other locations, the Iraqis had moved the munitions between February and October 1991. At the pit area, about one kilometer south of the Khamisiyah storage area, UNSCOM found several hundred, mostly intact, 122 mm rockets containing diluted nerve agent (confirmed through sampling and CAMs). In an open area, about five kilometers west of Khamisiyah, inspectors found approximately 6,000 intact 155 mm artillery rounds containing mustard agent (confirmed by CAMs) covered by a canvas tarp. At a third location featuring 100 bunkers, the team noted remnants of 122 mm rockets but not trace of chemical agents, at a single bunker identified as bunker number 73. The Iraqi officials told the UNSCOM team that coalition troops had destroyed bunker 73 earlier that year. These Iraqi statements were viewed at the time with skepticism, because of the extensive and continuous deception by the Iraqis of UNSCOM in its search for nuclear, biological and chemical weapons information.

In March 1992, when the UNSCOM inspectors returned to Khamisiyah, they reported consolidating and destroying more than 450 122 mm nerve agent-filled rockets found in the pit area (that total includes the original 300 that they had found in October 1991). IN addition, they found another 300 intact rockets buried in the pit area; these were sent by UNSCOM to Muthanna's Chemical Destruction Facility. At this time, the focus on investigations was on identifying all the stockpiles of CB agent weapons, not on the possible causes of GWS. As a result, the UNSCOM team and later DIA analysts never considered that agent exposure might have resulted form the destruction of bunker.

In the spring of 1995, along with the formation of the Presidential Advisory Committee on Gulf War Veterans' Illnesses, several agencies were tasked by executive order to cooperate in the search for the possible cause of GWS. The CIA changed of its focus form identifying weapons stockpiles to identifying possible scenarios of weapons releases. The Department of Defense created a telephone hotline for veterans in May 1995 and initiated its Gulf LINK web-page in August 1995. This increased an emphasis on revealing normally sensitive information on topics concerning the coalition's brush with chemical-biological warfare.

In May, 1996, UNSCOM revisited the Khamisiyah site as part of its efforts to verify earlier Iraqi declarations. During this inspection, the UNSCOM teams documented the presence of high-density polyethylene-insert burster tubes, fill plugs, and other characteristics of Iraqi chemical munitions. The rockets had been filled with a combination of the agent sarin and cycloserine, or GB/GF, based on analysis of the rockets' contents UNSCOM had found in 1991 in the pit just outside Khamisiyah storage area. Iraqi officials also claimed that fear of coalition bombing had motivated An Nasiriyah depot personnel to move the intact mustard rounds to the open area five kilometers form the Khamisiyah depot, where the rounds were camouflaged with canvas. This information, combined with a recent intelligence review, led to the Pentagon announcement on June 21, 1996, of possible chemical agent exposure to US troops.

On July 9, 1996, the CIA presented its downwind hazard model to the Presidential Advisory Committee. Modeling of the potential hazard caused by the destruction of bunker 73 indicated that an area around the bunker at least two kilometers in all directions and four kilometers downwind could have been contaminated at or above the level for causing acute symptoms (including runny nose, headache, and miosis). An area up to twenty-five kilometers downwind could have been contaminated at the much lower general population dosage limit. This dosage, identified in Army manuals, is for protection of the general population and is a seventy-two-hour exposure at 0.000003 milligrams per cubic meter, or approximately 0.013 milligram minutes per cubic meter (mg-min/m^3). This dosage is substantially below clinical effects, even threshold clinical effects like runny noses and initial twitches. It is lower than the 0.04 mg-min/m^3 limit recommended for civilian workers over eight hours' exposure time, much lower than the incapacitating dose of 2-3 mg-min/m^3, and significantly lower than the 100-mg/min/m^3 necessary to kill an adult human.

The CIA modelers used a number of assumptions to develop this downwind hazard prediction. As a baseline, they used data from a 1966 incident at Dugway Proving Ground that involved the destruction of a bunker filled with 1,850 GB-filled M55 rockets of characteristics similar to the Iraqi rockets found in bunker 73. The US rockets had had a range of about 15-20 kilometers, and the Iraqi rockets a range of 4–18 kilometers. The CIA assumed that 1,060 rockets had been in the bunker, as was indicated by Iraqi officials. They estimated that the rockets would have been filled with eight kilograms of a 2 : 1 ratio of GB to GF, and assumed it to be 100 percentage pure agent. The CIA model predicted 10 percent of the rockets would be ejected form the bunker, half falling randomly within a 200-meter circle, the other half falling within a two-kilometer circle, based on US military test data. All but 2.5 percent of the agent in the bunker would have been degraded by heat from the explosion and other burning debris, again based on past US tests. The winds were light to the northeast and then to the east, based on modeling and analysis of the videotape of destruction activity at Khamisiyah.

The CIA model, however, did not take into account 37 conventional ordnance bunkers detonating simultaneously with bunker 73. The thermal energy created by explosions and fires in the other bunkers, and by solar heating caused by the increased amounts of smoke, would tend to degrade any surviving chemical agent. The heat would force a column of air, dust and debris near the bunker to an altitude of 800 to 1,200 meters. This rapid vertical spreading would tend to lower ground contamination area and actually shorten the footprint of the model. Scientific evidence and the videotapes show that the agent cloud probably rose to the top of the convective boundary layer, which on that day was between 800 and 1,200 meters. The CIA model had used instead a fifteen-meter height for the explosive plume, because that was the worse-case height for a ground contamination pattern. The model also did not account for atmospheric turbulence that would be associated with a hot desert at midday, which would further decrease the footprint (since in hot sunny weather vapors tend to rise straight up rather than hug the ground).

Later analysis of the Iraqi rockets would show that they held closer to six kilograms of nerve agent rather than eight. The CIA model did not take into account any impurities or degradation of products, although UNSCOM evidence showed that Iraqi manufacturing had had severe quality and purity problems. Nor did the model account for rain effects or ground scavaging (agent penetration into the ground), which would have shortened the downwind hazard further. Last, the model had not yet been scientifically validated prior to its presentation to the President Advisory Committee. These issues did not stop DoD or the Committee from making an estimate of troops exposure possibilities.

Upon receiving this information, the President Advisory Committee deemed it advisable that the Pentagon at least inform everyone that might have been exposed to this general populace dosage—just to be sure. This downwind hazard, as mentioned above, was not a 25-kilometer circle form the depot—it was more of a rounded thin triangle four kilometers wide at its origin and extending outward toward the twenty-five-kilometer point, ending at eight kilometers wide. Early estimates of the number of personnel potentially exposed increased form the initial 430 soldiers (the bunker detail) to include the 770 soldiers form the 82d ABN DIV securing the general area. When the Army reviewed this report, it increased the radius to a twenty-five-kilometer distance around the depot, arbitrarily increasing the number of potentially exposed troops from 1,100 to 5,000 troops. This was done without any justification by data, simply as an additional "*worst-*

case" safeguard. In late October, the Pentagon announced that it had doubled its radius to fifty kilometers to include 15-20,000 troops — again entirely without merit, just to demonstrate that it was "*aggressively reaching out*" to all possible victims. It did not matter if none of the troops actually stayed in the area long enough for what might be termed chronic, long term exposure.

To summarize, the Pentagon reacted to a worst-case, unvalidated scenario that assumed the agent was 100 percent pure agent instead of its actual lower purity; this increased the agent in the rockets by a third; that did not account for atmospherics which would have driven the agent up into the sky rather than toward troops; and that did not account for the added heat from the other exploding bunkers. Based on this faulty scenario, it arrived at the conclusion that troops over two kilometers upwind of the explosion might have at the worst case, been exposed to agent levels deemed unsafe for the general populace—if they stayed in the hazard area for over seventy two hours. Also, despite the lack of any medical evidence that undetectable traces of nerve agent could harm people, despite the most advanced chemical defense equipment in the world and decades of chemical specialist training, the Pentagon accepted a foolish recommendation that there was a possible health risk for over 20,000 soldiers that had been in that area during a three-day period (without knowing if anyone had in fact stayed in the area for three days).

Instead of calming fears as it had intended, the Pentagon increased concerns of veterans and their families and fueled suspicions of a cover-up. The exposed-troops estimate, based on a worst-case model, was dramatically increased in fear of political pressures and the publicity over GWS, increasing the group "*at risk*" from 1,100 troops that didn't even suffer from runny noses to 20,000 that had not been remotely near the site. In an effort to quiet public concerns during an election year over possible nerve agent exposure, the Pentagon ignored its resident experts and made the short-term political effort to gratify the populace and its equally short-fuzed politicians immediately. Instead, it increased fears, raised conspiracy theories, and made its own professionals in the Chemical Corps look foolish, or worse, criminally incompetent.

The media, who up to the summer of 1996 had been skeptical of any claims from the Pentagon regarding CB weapons history in the Gulf War, now enthusiastically accepts the 20,000 number as gospel. Rather than investigating the validity of the CIA model or the Army's reasoning of how it arrived at these numbers, the press sees in this event their having forced DoD to admit failure to disclose this information for years, while others have announced they discovering evidence of the DoD cover-up. Anecdotal stories form sick veterans who did not understand what had affected them, and demands for further investigations into the "*cover-up*" soon took priority over any search for the truth. Trying to cope with the demands for more information, Dr. Bernard Rostker was appointed as the Special Assistant to the Deputy Secretary of Defense for Gulf War Illnesses with a staff of 110 personnel in early November 1995.

"Open Pit" Estimate—More Guesses

Because DoD had acknowledged the results of the CIA model, there was a similar demand that the "*Open pit*" demolition be modeled as well. This time, perhaps because of recognized blunders in handling the depot incident, Dr. Rostker's DoD Gulf War Illness office took a different route. DoD and the CIA planned a series of small-scale demolition tests at Dugway Proving Grounds in May 1997 to replicate the pit explosion, using 122 mm rockets, filled with a chemical simulant called tri-ethyl phosphate, buried in a similarly shaped pit. This simulant chemical has weight and volatility characteristics similar to sarin, but without the lethality. The Gulf War Illness office interviewed the EOD team that had originally set the charges at the Khamisiyah pit to learn how the boxes of rockets had been situated and how it had set the charges. Based upon firsthand descriptions from five soldiers on the EOD team, it estimated the number of rockets in the pit to have been about 1,250, of which less than half had been damaged by the demolition attempts. By placing a series of cards in concentric circles around the pit, the Dugway Proving Ground team was able to blow the boxes in place and record how much simulant escaped the pit, how far it traveled, and how much agent stayed in the soil as opposed to being released. This data was given to computer modelers in the CIA, the Naval Surface Warfare Center, the Defense Special Weapons Agency and the Naval Research Laboratory.

Other information fed the modelers' efforts. Scot and debris patterns around the site allowed the investigators to identify a south-southeast wind pattern (blowing form approximately 335 degrees). Samples taken by the UNSCOM teams demonstrated a 50 percent purity rather than 100 percent, and the rockets now held a correct six kilograms weight of agent. The Dugway data showed that at the most, 18 percent of the agent in the rockets would have been released into the air, with the rest being consumed by the explosion. Of that 18 percent released agent, one percent vaporized into the air, 1 percent released as liquid droplets, 6 percent evaporated form the soil and 10 percent evaporated form the wooden crates. The modelers also identified a major parameter, the "first noticeable health-effect level," which would include symptoms such as pinpointing of the eye pupils (miosis), runny nose, tightness of the chest and eye pain. The approximate levels of these reactions is 2-25 mg-min/m^3. The second parameter was low-level agent presence of between 0.01296 mg-min/m^3 (the general population limit) and one mg-min/m^3.

Based on the cumulative analysis of five different computer models, no troops were exposed to agent levels at or above first noticeable health-effect levels between March 10 and 12, 1991. When the modelers attempted to guess at the downwind hazard form lower levels, they envisioned a plume of agent that extended about five miles south and five miles east of the pit. This may have exposed 19,000 troops, primarily form the 82d ABN DIV, 24th IN DIV, and 101st ABN DIV, to these levels. Based on the surveys returned from 7,415 soldiers in the area (out of 20,000 survey sent out), 99.5 percent of the soldiers had not noticed any physical affects that could be correlated with sarin exposure. Even given this more credible attempt to model these events, these models can not be validated beyond a reasonable doubt; the US government has stopped open air testing of chemical agents, which means these models are based on data that is over twenty-five years old; there were not chemical agent casualties from the war (other than Fisher, whose case was not related to Khamisiyah). Today, depending on the "expert", we hear reports of anywhere from 27,000 to 100,000 troops exposed to low-level nerve agents. Congressional politicians, believing that they are somehow wiser than members of various independent scientific and medical panels, are now calling for the Presidential Advisory Committee to reassess its negative findings on chemical exposure. "It is our belief that more and more scientific evidence suggests that a major cause of ... illness is the synergistic effect of a wide variety of chemicals to which our soldiers were exposed," Rep. Berine Sanders (I-VT) wrote in his letter to the Committee; his letter was quickly signed by eighty-five other House members in June 1997.

If Not Chemical Agents, Then What?

Perhaps the first area to investigate would include occupational hazards that the soldiers may have encountered during the war. For instance, both CARC and DS-2 have hazardous components that might come into contact with the operators in a normal work environment. Some of these could cause health hazards, and these concerns are outlined in appropriate technical manuals, as well as in training courses. Most occupational hazards resulting from using these materials seem to have been avoided. Some unforeseen actions were noted, such as using diesel fuel around encampments as a sand suppressant, burning human waste with fuel oil, fuel leaking into shower water, drying sleeping bags in leaded exhaust fumes, etc. It remains unclear if these activities are connected with GWS, but they were not in a great enough number to account for the GWS complaints.

The most obvious natural cause would be infectious diseases endemic to the desert. The Middle East has a long history of unique diseases, dating back hundreds of years. During the conflict, both AFMIC and the Army Institute of Research, Division of Preventive Medicine, performed work on infectious diseases endemic to the Persian Gulf region and outlined ways in which service personnel should attempt to avoid or minimize their exposure to such diseases as leishmaniasis and malaria. These measures included predeployment information and also treatments, such as using permethrin (a pesticide) on bed netting and the area surrounding beds to repel and flies. Medical labs continue to monitor personnel for these diseases, since variants of leishmaniasis can lie dormant for up to ten years after infection. DoD has since refined guidelines for medical surveillance during deployments.

The Pentagon did not anticipate Saddam's using oil-well fires as a defensive weapon. Accordingly, there was no predeployment information on the effects of exposure to oil-well fires and petrochemicals. DoD did provide guidance after Iraq set fire to over 700 oil wells. Military personnel were advised to avoid the smoke when possible and to practice frequent washing; to use goggles, disposable face masks and scarves; and to alert medical personnel if lung irritation occurred. These oil wells burned for several months. Several organizations sent dozens of doctors, scientists and engineers to research this area, including the Centers for Disease Control (for blood samples) and the Army Environmental Hygiene Agency (for oil in water samples). The blood samples of military personnel in Kuwait showed lower volatile organic compounds than those of oil-well fire-fighters. The water samples showed similarly high concentrations of organic compounds, some of which could have had potential toxic characteristics. A final report was sent to Congress in December 1996.

Some thought that the depleted uranium warheads of the 120 mm armor-piercing projectile might have poisoned soldiers, as this was the first time that the depleted uranium-tipped munitions had actually been used in combat zone. The soldiers most concentrated should have been the tank crews, who regularly carried large loads of the munitions. DoD studies conducted before deployment had shown that the radiation levels were very faint and did not exceed NRC standards. For those feared the uranium would pulverize upon impact on an Iraqi target, thus spreading uranium fragments, the Armed Forces Radiobiology Research Institute released three reports after the war. They concluded that any soldiers who might have been exposed to the depleted uranium radiation were unlikely to have been exposed to hazardous levels of radiation exposure. No soldiers have since exhibited signs of uranium poisoning.

Pesticides used by US forces were accompanied with handling and safety instructions. All products were commercially available and had been tested and approved by the FDA. A less known danger was posed by agricultural pesticides used by Saudi and Iraqi governments and business in and around the area of operations. Because of arid conditions, the amount of arable land is small, mostly surrounding the major river systems; as a result, there is a strong propensity for heavy use of agricultural fertilizers and pesticides in less productive areas. To date, sampling missions have not revealed excessive use of pesticides, although the British government has revealed concerns that this may be a prime cause.

The most popular suspect of GWS are the prophylactics used to counter the effects of chemical and biological agents. The four accused culprits included the pyridostigmine bromide tablets, the botulinum toxoid, the anthrax vaccine and the diazepam autoinjectors. Of the four, only the PB tablets show definite side effects (headaches, nausea, diarrhea, abdominal cramps and other intestinal problems). Many of these had been noted by the soldiers in the field, and perhaps about a third of the force stopped taking the pills, choosing to rely on just the atropine. Still at least two-thirds of the force had taken the PB tablets for about three weeks. There should have been more GWS cases than the 10 percent noted if this was the sole culprit. Several studies within the government and among private organizations continue to study PB effects, yet the Department of defense continues to produce and store it as a nerve agent pretreatment. What might explain the relatively low number of military personnel affected (less than 10 percent) is synergistic effects of hazardous exposure. Combining two or more hazards together, and adding the high stress of combat might result in symptoms that would not appear were an individual exposed to just one factor.

The relatively small number of GWS casualties might also be explained by varying chemical tolerances in each individual exposed. This would certainly answer the question of how so many different symptoms have arisen in this target population. Certainly other multiple-chemical-sensitivity cases match these general symptoms. The question is, what combination of hazards? To date, the focus has shifted to tests in a tenfold increase in the lethality of the insecticide. This has been shown only on cockroaches and has not been confirmed by other sources. Future research is needed on other likely combinations: for instance, petroleum exposure and insecticide, or petroleum exposure and PB tablets.

The Presidential Advisory Committee, in its final report, noted three findings. First, many veterans have illnesses likely to be connected to their service in the Gulf. Second, there did not appear to be conclusive evidence that any one source—pesticides, chemical-biological warfare agents, vaccines, PB tablets, infectious disease, depleted uranium, oil-well fires and smoke or petroleum products—caused the symptoms and illnesses. Third, stress was probably an important contributing factor to the broad range of physical and psychological illnesses being reported. Few veterans wanted to hear that stress, even as a contributing factor, might be partially responsible for their illnesses. Yet a good deal of past medial research on stress-related illnesses does support this view.

Real Medical Evidence

While the public may never be sure about Khamisiyah, it does not appear that these GWS illnesses have any contagious effects on the soldier's wives and children, or upon the ability of a woman to give birth. Major General Ron Blanck, commanding general of the Walter Reed Army Medical Center, testified before the Senate on the medical findings of military research into GWS on September 29, 1994. He reported that prior to the war in 1990 the rate of miscarriages at six Army posts had been 380 miscarriages out of 4,762 pregnancies (7.98 percent). In 1991 at those same posts, the rate was 511 miscarriages out of 6,392 pregnancies (7.99 percent). Compared to an average rate of about 15 percent across the US, the military population fared relatively well. Similar medical evidence shows that the Persian

Gulf veteran is, by most accounts, just as healthy as the average soldier that did not deploy to the Gulf.

One possible explanation is suggested by Dr. Robert Haley of the University of Texas Southwest Medical Center in Dallas. Dr. Haley began his research noting that DoD and the VA had not investigated the string of illnesses as one would an epidemic (that is, by the Centers for Disease Control protocols). The lack of a credible methodology, he felt, could be a reason why there was little progress in narrowing down the causes. He and other researchers initially planned to investigate the stress angle, but a colleague pointed out that the symptoms suffered by GWS veterans closely mirrored brain damage and that most signs had been delayed until months or years after the war. This led to a hypothesis that organophosphate compounds might have had a delayed impact on the human body. While all medical personnel recognize the classic immediate effects of organophosphate poisoning, few physicians were aware of any long-term delayed chronic effects.

There was also reason to suspect that pyridiostigmine bromide might be penetrating the blood-brain barrier, which was previously thought not occur. Studies on hens, exposing them to various combinations of PB and insect repellent, showed that exposure to insect repellent alone would not cause damage. Combining the two however, caused widespread neurological damage to the hens, supporting the idea that PB can penetrate to the brain. Similar animal studies in Britain tend to support the view that combining the two causes severe damage, but no human or lower primate tests have been conducted to verity this supposition.

Dr. Haley decided to focus on one unit, the 24th Naval Reserve Construction Battalion (SeaBees), living primarily in the southern state. These troops had traveled over a good deal of the theater while performing their mission, and accordingly would have had a higher chance of being exposed to any hazards. Two hundred and forty-nine of the 606 veterans volunteered to participate, of which 175 reported serious health problems related to the war. Investigators tested both the sick and healthy veterans' nervous reactions under various physiological, audio vestibular, psychological and blood tests. The team discovered that it could identify three distinct classes among sixty-three of the ill veterans (about 25 percent of the test group). The first group, composed of twelve individual, showed some impaired cognition, having problems with memory, reasoning, insomnia and headaches.

Group two (twenty-one individuals) had more severe problems with thinking, disorientation, vertigo and balance disturbances. These subjects also had the most difficulty keeping a steady job, being twelve times more likely to be unemployed. The last group (thirty individuals) suffered severe joint and muscle pains, muscle fatigue and tingling of the extremities. CAT scans did not show any damage in any of the test volunteers.

When these groups were further screened to identify what they had been exposed to, certain patterns appeared. Group one symptoms were more prone to appear in those that reported wearing flea collars during the war. Group two troops believed they had been exposed to chemical weapons and had used the PB tablets. The risk of joining the last group increased with the frequency and quantity of using the DoD-issued insect repellent containing DEET combined with the sue of PB tablets. In all cases, the illnesses seem to stem from neurological damage caused by chemical exposure. Dr. Haley's explanation is that these veterans may have delayed, chronic neurotoxic syndromes from wartime exposure to combinations of chemicals.

While these studies are remarkable and convincing, there is the possibility that the group two veterans, who feel they were attacked by chemical weapons because they had heard loud bangs and detectors alarming, may have been exposed to a yet unknown hazard. The credibility of these veterans (not their valor) is suspect, since their exposure to chemical weapons cannot be proven or verified by any events during the war. They may have been exposed to nighttime pesticide foggings common during the war or to industrial hazards of Middle Eastern cities. To accept the word of veterans that they were gassed would not be justified without other evidence such as expended Scud CB warheads or bombs found in Saudi Arabia. Even the best modelers supporting DoD cannot confirm that any soldier was exposed to low levels of chemical agents for more than one day. Generally, most medial physicians would categorize chronic exposure cases as exposure to low-level hazard over a long period of time.

It may be years before we discover the real cause of the Gulf War illnesses. There may be good reasons for veterans to distrust at first the government's attempts to find the truth; the media continues to follow the GWS story, eagerly looking for the "*scandals*," the "*hidden files*" that state how the DoD knew the causes all along. I do not think this the case. There are veterans that have suffered and are suffering from an unknown cause or causes, and they should be treated immediately based on the medical evidence of their aliments, regardless of whether they contracted it in the Gulf or in the United States. However, we must also make a case against false legal and slanderous claims by those without scruples or who refuse to acknowledge the evidence.

There are many Vietnam veterans currently in powerful positions in the military and the government, many advocates of the military in the public, and hundreds of thousands of dedicated military personnel in the Army. There are no parallels between the Agent Orange cases of the 1970s and the GWS cases of the 1990s; society has changed, as has the military culture. After some prodding, DoD has responded favorably by opening up the files and treating the soldiers, and is trying to discover the true causes. Perhaps the military system is trying to help its personnel, despite not knowing the causes of these illnesses and without subterfuge.

One thing that I have tried to demonstrate is this: there was no deliberate employment of CB weapons by the Iraqis, and there was no large-scale exposure to chemical-biological agents of the coalition forces. Had the military understood the CBW threat and trusted its equipment, perhaps it could have saved millions of dollars in long, expensive studies and avoided unnecessarily panicking thousands of veterans and their families. At the least, this event should increases the desire of the infantry, armor, artillery and other combat branches to get more involved in developing requirements for future chemical defense equipment. If there are valid concerns about the effectiveness of chemical agent detectors and protective ensembles, the users must get involved, rather than turning their backs as they did in 1973. If military leaders bend to political demands for low-level detectors, they should be aware of the impact on tactical operations (i.e., overly sensitive, very expensive detectors that false-alarm and slow down operational tempo). Education about CB warfare combined with further study and war games are the keys to ensure this situation does not occur again. The last thing we should do is shut down or down-scale the Chemical Corps because the military and public does not trust the experts to protect our armed forces.

18

CONCLUDING REMARKS

On August 2, 1990, as Iraqi tanks crossed the border into Kuwait, US armed forces were not fully prepared to deploy and fight on a CB-contaminated battlefield in the Middle East. Over the last few decades, the Army had focused upon designing equipment for European conflicts. All the latest CB defense equipment had been meant for fighting the Soviets on a European battlefield, and military units in Europe had priority in receiving it. Realistic CB defensive training was the rule (within bounds). Soldiers used chemical protective overgarments (CPOGs) during field exercises. All the tanks had the latest agent filtration systems, and airfields and common posts had collective protection systems ready. The Army and Air Force stockpiled chemical and tactical nuclear weapons in Europe as a theater retaliatory capability (at least until the summer of 1990, when US Army Europe [USAREUR] implemented plans to remove these systems).

Back in the United States, combat divisions training to deploy and fight outside of Europe ignored these preparations, because they did not expect to encounter CB warfare in their theaters of conflict. Because of production delays, many divisions lacked CB defense equipment issued to their higher-priority European counterparts. Unit commanders chose not to purchase chemical protective clothing that probably would not be used, but spent the funds on other training and maintenance priorities. Reserve and Guard units had even less time for training on topics outside of immediate mission areas. This situation made for an unequal level of individual training, unit training and logistics preparations throughout the Army (and other services). Most important, it meant that CENTCOM's forces were not initially prepared for an adversary who used CB agent munitions.

Deployment to Saudi Arabia

General Norman Schwarzkopf first arrived at CENTCOM headquarters in Florida in November 1988, reporting as CINCCENT (Commander-in-Chief, Central Command). One of his challenges was justify the continuation of a command that had no assigned combat units; any forces that were to deploy to the Middle East would be borrowed form CONUS or Europe. Part of this assessment was accomplished through an annual wargame called "*Internal Look*," which tested in the Middle East. Plan 1002, last gamed in 1989, had a scenario assuming that Iran was the main adversary. The Iraq-Iran War had decimated Iran's force but left intact most of Iraq's modern, mechanized units. Syria, the only other major Arab power that might be hostile to the US, focused its military force against Israel, which was not part of CENTCOM's responsibility. General Schwarzkopf decided that 1990 "*Internal Look*" would star the Iraqi forces as the adversary.

Plan 1002-90 would focus on the defense of the Arabian Peninsula from an Iraqui invasion into Saudi Arabia through Kuwait. It assumed twenty-two-divisions opposing force against the VIII Airborne Corps in an established defense-in twenty-one days of warning to mobilize and deploy to Saudi Arabia. Friendly forces included the 82d Airborne Division (ABN DIV), 24th Infantry Division (IN DIV), 101st ABN DIV, a Marine amphibious force, a Navy carrier group, and Air Force tactical fighter wings. The game showed Iraqui armored units, though fiercely attacks by tactical aircraft and helicopters, still able to push nearly 200 kilometers into Saudi Arabia before being stopped around al-Jubayl; XVIII Airborne Corps did hold Dharan, ad-Damman and the Abquaiq oil refineries, at the cost of 50 percent of its fighting force. The exercise stressed the need for tank-killers, such as the tactical aircraft and helicopters, a fast-sea-lift capability, and for quickly developing a strong combat power advantage.

The "*Internal Look*" war game probably did not portray Iraq as using CB agent munitions. Integrating realistic CB agent-cloud behavior, as affected by weather and terrain, into tactical wargaming was too difficult in the 1970s and 1980s. Agencies responsible for developing computer models for CB agent effects did not have the ability to verify or validate their models, given the cessation of open-air testing of CB weapons in 1969. No one had translated the CANE information of effects on troops into war games or quantified how the inclusion or exclusion of chemical defensive equipment would impact casualty results. There was no consideration given to he effects of CB agents on the physiological or psychological state of personnel, or the effects of contaminated equipment on the units' combat readiness or operational tempo. The logistically intensive tasks of resupplying protective clothing, decontaminants, and medical treatments also could not be integrated. Logistic offices had some consumption rates, based on older scenarios and outdated protective clothing, but nothing as well developed as for ammunition, fuel, or other more common general supplies.

In short, since it was too hard to simulate realistic tactical/operational use of CB agent munitions or NBC defense logistics, military gamers chose not to include CB warfare. A certain game might include an intelligence brief that the enemy had the capability to use CB weapons, but that did not mean the enemy would use them. If the enemy did, it was usually seen as the desperate response of a defeated side and a trigger for massive US retaliatory response, often leading to tactical nuclear strikes. In the 1990s, was games still did not feature CB warfare. The same problems remained unsolved. Where models that reflected cloud behavior were used to reflect realistic CB agent movement, war games often stopped as this "*special event*" drained computer power due to its massive memory requirements. Needless to say, CB warfare was rarely welcomed at the war games.

"*Internal Look*" had been an opportunity to examine which chemical defense units might deploy to CENTCOM in support of this scenario. By updating the deployment roster with active and reserve chemical defense units, a plan was made ready for delivering decontamination assets into the theater. The chemical staff infrastructure could also practice requesting and planing retaliatory chemical weapons use. Although the binary chemical weapons program had just been halted in July 1990 after producing a limited quantity of 155 mm binary chemical agent projectiles, there still was a retaliatory capability available in the form of the older, unitary chemical agent weapons. There was also the option of reinitiating the binary weapons program. Given the threat of chemical warfare in the Middle East, the option of relation in kind (in line with national policy) might have to be exercised.

General Schwarzkopf briefed President Bush on Plan 1002-90 at Camp David on August 4, 1990. He described the gamed deployment of the XVIII Airborne Corps. Marine units, and accompanying Air Force and Navy units as the "*Internal Look*" plan had detailed. Schwarzkopf pointed out that the majority of the Iraqui army was not high caliber; the main threat would come from the eight divisions of Republican Guards, the South African 155 mm artillery guns, which outranged the US 155 mm self-propelled howitzers, and chemical weapons delivered by artillery, aircraft or Scud missiles. The Iraqi military's main weaknesses included feeble logistics and strongly centralized command and control. An effective defense would lie in the deployment of over a quarter of a million soldiers, a call-up of reserves, and air superiority which Lieutenant General Chuck Horner had promised could be established in a matter of days. If president Bush wanted Iraq out of Kuwait, it would take an offensive with twice the number of troops, built up over eight to ten months.

When the order to go was issued, the 2d Brigade of the 82d ABN DIV-as Division Ready Brigade 1—began operations to load and depart within thirty-six hours. The 1st Brigade and 3rd Brigade were recalled immediately. Each deployed with a platoon "slice" of the 21st Chemical Company (Smoke/Decon). In seven days, the entire division ready brigade, the division combat aviation brigade, a Multiple Launch Rocket System (MLRS) battery and the 2d platoon, 21st Chemical Company were on the ground in Saudi Arabia. All three airborne brigades were in Southwest Asia by August 24. The 7th Marine Expeditionary Brigade (MEB) at Twenty-nine Palms, California, received the word to deploy on August 8 to fly its troops to the Gulf. They would meet their five Maritime Prepositioning Squadron (MPS) steaming up from Diego Garcia in the Indian Ocean; the MPS vessels held an entire Marine brigade's equipment. The first three met the Marines in al-Dammam on August 14, and rolled out the only heavy tanks (M60A3s) that would be available to CENTCOM until September.

The 24th IN DIV (Mechanized) had started moving even before Major General Barry McCaffrey officially received his marching orders; as commander of the only heavy division of the XVIII ABN Corps, McCaffrey knew the orders were coming, and got his brigades moving toward the Savannah ports. The 197th IN BDE (Mech) (Sep) would join the 24th IN DIV as its roundout unit (a reserve or National Guard unit designated to join an active duty division for wartime deployment) in lieu of the division's National Guard brigade. The 24th IN DIV supplied to the XVIII ABN Corps the heavy punch of M1 tanks, able to counter the Iraqi T-72s. General Schwarzkopf's planners called Fort Hood, Texas, to activate the 6th Combat Aviation Brigade (CAB) with its sixty Apache helicopters. It was expected to deploy to the Gulf within ten days, but it was not ready: the unit was low on spare parts;

all its Hellfire missiles were in storage at Anniston Army Depot, Alabama; its pilots had just come off a training exercise; and it was low on CB defense equipment. CENTCOM turned to the 11th CAB from the 2d Armored Division (AR DIV) (Forward) in Germany to deploy in their place. The 1st Cavalary Division (CAV DIV), the 3rd Armored Cavalary Regiment (ACR), and the Tiger Brigade from the 2d AR DIV at Fort Hood would deploy to offset XVIII ABN Corp's lack of armor. (Initial plans were for the Tiger Brigade to replace the National Guard round out brigade of the 1st CAV DIV). The 101s ABN DIV had units spread out from West Point to Panama and Honduras what altered to the deployment. The 2d Brigade, 101st ABN DIV, began deployment on August 17, but the division would not "close" in Saudi Arabia until October 6.

Schwarzkopf's headquarters moved to Riyadh, Kingdom of Saudi Arabia, on August 24. Already, US intelligence had begun reporting signs of Iraqi chemical warfare preparations. Intelligence sources had reported chemical decontamination equipment near two Iraqi artillery battalions in Kuwait. Admiral Frank Kelso, Chief of Naval Operations, had activated the Navy's hospital ships, the USNS *Comfort* and USNS *Mercy*, to prepare to provide immediate treatment to thousands of expected chemical casualties. General Schwarzkopf's planners issued orders to deploy fourteen fully staffed hospital units to the Gulf. VA hospitals in the United States prepared to receive airlifted chemical casualties. Even at this early stage, the military leadership was deeply concerned over the political and morale-shaking consequences should US forces be exposed to chemical warfare.

Immediate Chemical Defense Support

Lieutenant Colonel Kenneth Silvernail and Major Patrick Fogelson arrived in Dhahran as the CENTCOM NBC Defense Division of J-3 (Operations) on August 9, with the CENTCOM advance party, Silvernail, designated as the Theater Chemical Staff Officer, would receive seven more Army chemical officers by mid-September to form the CENTCOM NBC Center (NBCC). His initial priorities were to develop the chemical unit infrastructure and coordinate the entire coalition's CB defense logistics. CENTCOM would recommend that all soldiers deploy with three unopened sets of protective clothing, a protective mask, three Nerve Agent Antidote Kits (NAAKs) and M258A1 skin decon kits, and a set of replacement mask filters. Army units would discover this goal could not be realistically met, nearly all units lacking adequate quantities of protective clothing and masks.

The Marines, upon inspecting their prepositioned stocks, found their protective suits damaged by heat and petroleum, their protective masks dry-rotted, and mask filters aged past their shelf life. All the Marine Corp's M8 A1 alarms were in an Albany depot supposedly because they had not instituted a radioactive control program (required for the americium isotope inside the detector). The Air Force and Navy were having similar difficulties, findings severe shortages in both protective suits and decontamination supplies. Lieutenant Colonel Silvernail began immediate discussions with the Joint Chiefs of Staff (JCS) and the Army Office of the Deputy Chief of Staff for Operations and Plans (ODCSOPS) over options to increase or accelerate the delivery of any recently fielded or about to be fielded chemical defense equipment to include the M1 CAM, the XM21 RSCAAL, and the XM93 NBCRS. The top priority was increasing the quantities of protective masks, protective clothing, and medical antidotes.

The next CENTCOM responsibility was to coordinate NBC defense operations for all coalition forces. Within the first week after the NBCC's establishment, Lieutenant Colonel Silvernail was tasked to assist the Saudi Arabian Ministry of Defense and Aviation (MODA) to form a Saudi joint-level NBC Staff. He and Captain Paul Schiele conducted a three-day refresher training class (the first of several) for other Saudi NBC School located at King Khalid Military City (KKMC); it was attended by fifty Saudi, Syrian, Egyptian, and Kuwati officers. Saudi Army NBC defense stocks proved to be woefully low—not that three was any shortage of contractors offering to supply the desert nations. The US government was in no shape to assist the Saudi military logistically, barely having enough protective equipment for its own soldiers. The Saudi government did ask CENTCOM's NBCC for support in evaluating the capabilities of the many commercial officers, relying on it to get the best value for the money.

Initially, Headquarters Army Component, Central Command (ARCENT), had a small NBC staff cell, composed of one lieutenant colonel and one master sergeant. The ARCENT NBCC would be augmented with the 63rd Chemical Detachment (JA) from III Corps in September. The JA teams were five-person staff units designed to work one twelve-hour shift, as opposed to the JB teams of ten soldiers. Both augmented division, corps and army headquarters staffs to provide NBC expertise around the clock. Until then, the two soldiers would be sorely stretched to handle the many requests for assistance in chemical defense matters. One of the ARCENT NBCC's first duties was to train the rest of the ARCENT staff on basic NBC defense skills, while assisting XVII ABN Corps in its logistic challenges.

It fell to Colonel Ray Barbeau, the XVIII ABN Corps Chemical Officer, to organize the initial Army chemical defense preparations at corps level and below. Colonel Barbeau, Master Sergeant Zachary, the corps top chemical NCO, and the XVII ABN Corps advance party arrived in Dhahranon August 8. Initial estimates showed a severe shortfall of decontamination assets, especially water-hauling trucks and the battalion-level M17 Lighweight Decontamination System (LDS) "SANATORs." The Army was in the process of accepting an initial delivery of a thousand M17s when troops began deploying to the Gulf in August, but only a few had been issued to his crops. Individual defense equipment (one unopened set of BDOs, a M17A2 protective mask with fresh filters, one M258A1 decon kit, three NAAKs per soldier) was available to support the initial deployment, but it would not support a sustained a chemical warfare environment. The total number of M1 CAMS was only 150 for the entire XVIII ABN Corps. Many units were short their allotment of M81 chemical agent point detector alarms. By the end of August, the Corps NBC Center, manned by the 1st Chemical Detachment (JA), was operational and ready to operate. The 82d Chemical Detachment (JA) would support the corps support command (1st COSCOM) and rear area. The immediate priorities were supporting individual NBC defense training to sharpen forgotten skills, and obtaining additional NBC defense equipment (both consumable protective supplies and hardware).

The troops immediate survival prospects would increase in proportions to how fast they could increase their individual NBC defense expertise, especially Common Task Training and leadership training tasks. All divisions deploying to the Gulf were required to train their soldiers on thirteen NBC defense skills. These skills included the basics of how to put on, take off and maintain the protective mask, how to use the medical auto injectors and how to use of the M258A1 decon kits and M256A1 chemical detection kits. Every soldier used a training set of chemical protective clothing to practice the various MOPP levels, rather than opening their contingency stocks. Most training was conducted in the early morning or evening, allowing soldiers were paying very close attention to CB defense training. Besides enlisted soldiers and NCOs, officers attended the courses, form second lieutenants up through colonels. One chemical officer remarked that the individual CB defense skills were better among the lower-rank soldiers, and an individual's prior knowledge and expertise in this area actually worsened as the rank climbed. This reflected the difference between soldiers who had joined the Army prior to 1980, and those exposed to the "new" Chemical Crops doctrine and training after 1985.

Once individual training had raised the soldier's expertise to an acceptable level, battalions and brigades would move on to practicing unit missions in CB warfare scenarios, using their attached chemical defense units. Each deploying division had its own organic chemical company; the 21st Chemical Company (Smoke/Decon) deployed with the 82d ABN DIV, the 91st Chemical Company (Heavy Division) with the 24th IN DIV, and the 63rd Chemical Company (Smoke/Decon) with the 101st ABN DIV. XVIII ABN Corps had the 101st Chemical Company (Decon) as the crops general support chemical decontamination unit, deploying with 1st COSMOS. These chemical units, in conjunction with the chemical staff soldiers of combat arms companies, battalions and brigades, supplied a large source of trainers for both individual and unit NBC training, both of with would continue through September and October.

Chemical defense units designated to support the XVIII ABN Corps originally included the 415th Chemical Brigade (a reserve headquarters unit without assigned units) and two chemical battalions. The 415th Chemical Brigade was cut in favor of other units, although two chemical battalions did make the deployment schedule. FORSCOM decided to deploy the 2d Chemical Battalion from Fort Hood and 490th Chemical Battalion, a reserve headquarters unit at Anniston, Alabama. The 2d Chemical Battalion, a reserve headquarters unit at Anniston, Alabama. The 2d Chemical Battalion was alerted to deploy on August 10, while the 490th Chemical Battalion would wait for the president's official reserve call-up.

The number-one request for chemical defense unit support in the Gulf was for additional decontamination capability, given the high threat, perceived low training status and the lack of M17 LDSs within XVIII ABN Corps. Colonel Rick Read, chemical division chief in ODCSOPS's space and Special Weapons Directorate, received a number of majors and lieutenant colonels from the US Army Nuclear and Chemical Agency to augment his small staff. They began scouring the Chemical Corps force structure for units eligible to deploy quickly. The first two units tapped included the 59th Chemical Company (Smoke/Decon) from Fort Drum, New York, and the 761st Chemical Company (Smoke/Decon) at Fort Ord, California. Both companies had high readiness levels and were stationed near major airfields; they had the capability of being dual-purpose smoke and decontaminations units. They were to be followed by the 11th Chemical Company and 51st Chemical Company, both theater decontamination units from 2d COSMOS, VII Corps, Germany. Chemical troops in III Corps that would deploy with their divisions included the 68th Chemical Company under the 1st CAV DIV, the 89th Chemical Company (ACR) under the 3rd ACR, and the 44th Chemical Company (Heavy Division), divided between 1st CAV DIV and the Tiger Brigade, 2d AR DIV. The 181st Chemical Company (Decon), a non-divisional chemical unit at Fort Hood, would deploy with the 2d Chemical Battalion at the end of September.

ODCSOPS next turned its attention to the reserves, where nearly 60 percent of the Chemical Corps's strength lay. Under President Bush's initial reserve call-up on August 24, HQ DA alerted a number of decontamination companies, staff detachments and a battalion headquarters unit to report to Fort McClellan. They included the 490th Chemical Battalion, 318th Chemical Company and 907th Chemical Detachment (JB) from Alabama; the 433rd Chemical Detachment (JB) from Georgia; the 327th Chemical Company from Texas; and the 371st Chemical Company from South Carolina. All reserve chemical units stationed east of the Mississippi. River would mobilize at Fort McClellan beginning in early September. As each decontamination company arrived at Fort McClellan, its soldiers refreshed their individual and crew training through the CDTF. The two detachments (907th and 433rd) were scheduled to arrive into theater at the end of September, with the decontamination companies due into Saudi Arabia by October.

The XVII ABN Corps, being primarily light infantry, had one chemical reconnaissance platoon authorized for the entire Corps (within the 24th IN DIV's total would rise to three platoons. These recon platoons were equipped with M113A2 Armored Personnel Carriers (APCs), whose crews were not protected form chemical agent vapors and could not perform reconnaissance on the move. Given the size of the theater and its limited decontamination assets, it was important to have a recon capability to locate and isolate chemical agent contamination quickly. The Fox NBCRSs were officially two years from fielding, and there was little hope that these new vehicles would rush through US production lines. Lieutenant General Frederick Franks, Jr. VII Corps commander in Europe, offered his division' mechanized chemical recon platoons to supplement XVIII ABN Corps's forces.

ODCSOPS, the USAREUR chemical officer, and the Seventh Army chemical officer selected several NBC reconnaissance platoons to deploy immediately.

Assessing the Risk

US Military planners had known of Iraq's successful use of chemical weapons, especially during the 1988 campaigns against Iran. In August 1990, the Defense Intelligence Agency (DIA) and Central Intelligence Agency (CIA) released a number of assessments of Iraq'' capabilities to wage CB warfare against the coalition. (While DIA was aware of the Iraqi nuclear program, there was no suggestion that Iraq had developed any nuclear munitions.)

Analysts identified the major Iraqi chemical warfare agents as mustard gas and the nerve agents tabun (GA), sarin (GB), and GF (cyclosarin, a chemical agent similar to but more persistent than GB). Chemical agents in development included soman (GD), persistent nerve agent VX, and the hallucinogen agent BZ. Iraqi chemical weapon systems included Soviet-purchased 122 mm multiple rocket launchers (with Iraqi rockets sporting larger-than-normal chemical warheads), helicopter-launched 90 mm rockets with chemical warheads (another Iraqi invention), the more conventional 250/500 kilogram aerial chemical bombs, and chemical projectiles for 155 mm artillery guns and 120 mm mortars.

Israeli intelligence also reported the existence of Scud chemical warheads. The weapons of choice would be the 155 mm artillery batteries. DIA pointed out that Iraq had reached the point of self-sufficiency for "*precursor*" agent production, and did not require foreign purchases to develop their agents. Estimates of the chemical stockpile ranged between one and four thousand tons of nerve agents and mustard gas, with a monthly production capability of 150 tons of mustard, five to ten tons of tabun, and twenty tons of sarin. The main complexes of coalition concern were the Muthanna production lines and the three weapon-filling facilities at Habbiniyah.

There were a number of suspected chemical weapons storage bunkers. The two closest to the border were the An Nasiriyah ammunition storage facility and the Ash Shuaybah ammunition storage depot. By the end of August DIA had noticed a flurry of activity as Iraqi forces prepared suspected CW storage bunkers of many of the southern airfields, the nearest one being at Tallil and al-Jahrah. Decontaminations sites were appearing at over half the Iraqi artillery batteries, including those throughout Kuwait. CIA and DIA analysts had not, however, detected any actual movement of chemical munitions to those southern sites.

DIA predicted that Iraq had "*weaponized*" anthrax and botulinum toxin, and was interested in doing the same with clostridium perfringens (which causes gas gangrene), *staphylococcal enterotoxin B* (SEB) and cholera. Candidate biological weapons systems included 250 kilogram aerial bombs, 250/500 kilogram cluster bombs, 90 mm air-to-ground rockets, mortar shells and artillery projectiles, Scud missile warheads, and ground and aerial spray systems (although DIA has not confirmed knowledge of any *weaponization*). Special concern was raised by the reported acquisition of a number of Italian truck-mounted agricultural sprayers, which could be adopted for biological warfare (BW) agent dissemination. Employment of biological agents in Saudi Arabia by Iraqi special forces could not be ruled out, but there was no proof that they had been trained to do so. There were three identical primary nodes of the BW program: the Salman Pak CBW Research, Production and Storage Facility; the Taji suspected BW pilot plant in the northwest suburbs of Baghdad; and the Abu-Ghurayb clostridium vaccine plant a few kilometers west of Baghdad. The Abu-Ghurayb "*infant formula*" plant was suspected of being a backup production plant, given its unusually high security and its state-of-the-art fermenters and driers. The research and development centers at Samarra and Tuwaitha were suspected of supporting the BW program. The offensive BW program was a relatively new aspect of Iraq's CBW program—still growing as its government purchased biological material, fermenters and other equipment form Western nations as late as 1989.

There were a number of suspected BW bunkers with the environmental control characteristics necessary to preserve BW agents. DIA counted as many as thirty-four of them at seventeen different locations, including the ones at Salman Pak. All were located near general munitions storage facilities, and all but one had been built in the late 1970s. As such, they could have had the primary purpose of protecting electronics, fuel-air explosives or "smart" weapons from the heat; then again, they would also be ideal for storing biological or chemical agents. No one had any real evidence to indicate to indicate one way or another.

The official intelligence assessment was that Iraq was "likely to use CW as an integral part of tactical operations to protect key political, military or economic strategic areas." DIA estimated that Iraq was not prepared to launch an immediate offensive into Saudi

Arabia supported by chemical weapons but that Saddam could use such weapons to defend against a coalition attack. The weather and temperature through the fall and winter of 1990 would favor Iraq, since the prevailing winds (blowing east to southeast) and the heat would work against US chemical defense preparations. If the CW production facilities were attacked, Iraq might respond with its chemical munitions capability immediately, in an effort to "use it or lose it" before its poor-quality chemical stocks (estimated 20 to 50 percent purity) lost their potency. Then again, the Iraq is might save the munitions for the expected coalition attack. Potential threats included the use of aircraft and Scuds armed with persistent chemical agents against Saudi airfields and ports, and special forces/ terrorist use of CB agents or other specialized weapons systems in the rear areas.

The coalition was assessed to be at significant risk if Iraq undertook biological warfare. There was no reliable information as to how Iraq might employ its biological weapons, since the Iraqui military had not used them in the war against Iran. No intelligence agency was bold enough to predict or talk about exact details as to the results of an actual biological agent attack against the coalition. The official assessment was that while Iraq had the capability tactically and strategically to deploy BS munitions, they would not be ready to take advantage of any vulnerabilities created by a biological agent attack. The more probable threat was clandestine BW agent use prior to hostilities, as opposed to over BW attacks conducted by planes or Scud missiles.

While DIA, CIA and other agencies felt certain that Iraq would employ CB warfare against CENTCOM, a number of issues remained unresolved. There was no reliable information as to how Iraq might employ its biological weapons, since the Iraqi military had not used them in the war against Iran. No intelligence agency was bold enough to predict or talk about exact details as to the results of an actual biological agent attack against the coalition. The official assessment was that while Iraq had the capability tactically and strategically to deploy BW munitions, they would not be ready to take advantage of any vulnerabilities created by a biological agent attack. The more probable threat was clandestine BW agent use prior to hostilities, as opposed to over BW attacks conducted by planes or Scud missiles.

While DIA, CIA and other agencies felt certain that Iraq would employ CB warfare against CENTCOM, a number of issues remained unresolved. There was no information on Iraqi CB agent munitions markings, or exactly where the stocks were located; no one could guess as to effect such an attack would be, or what steps CENTCOM could employ to combat this possibility. Also, no one knew if there would be any significant CB agent dissemination if a Patriot surface-to-air missiles harmlessly into the jet stream or fall immediately to the group? Chemical warfare experts at DIA and Edgewood had no idea and were unwilling to guess. If Saddam ordered chemical warfare against a CENTCOM force driving into Kuwait, the expected casualties would be high.

As the deployment continued, everyone became convinced that Saddam would use CB agents against he US forces. The US military and political leadership realized how extremely vulnerable its forces were, given the shortage of chemical defense equipment and the poor level of training. There was a fine line being drawn here. The American government had to respond to an Iraqi chemical attack or face possible future. Third World adversaries encouraged by Iraq's success. On the other hand, excessive or massive relation would drive Arab coalition partners from the force. Because of the delay in getting chemical defense units into the Gulf and the acknowledged vulnerability of the soldiers, CENTCOM had to rely on two actions to dissuade Iraqi NBC attacks.

The first action was a massive media focus on CENTCOM's defensive preparedness, beginning with training demonstrations showing soldiers donning their protective masks and getting acclimated to the protective clothing in the desert. News footage showed brand-new Patriot launchers bristled around Riyadh and Dhahran, ready to knock out potential CB agent warhead Scuds. Military spokespersons at the Pentagon, in CNN studio, and the Gulf spoke confidently of their readiness against Iraq's CW capability. Media interest was particularly highlighted by such notable speakers as Colonel (Ret.) Harry Summers and Sam Donaldson describing military NBC defense preparedness. This show of "*expertise*" would, it was hoped, impress Saddam that the use of CB agents would have little or no effect on the military force assembled.

The second action was to retaliate heavily against Iraqi military, industrial and civilian centers in and around Baghdad if any use of chemical agents against US forces was detected. Air force Component, Central Command (CENTAF), developed a plan titled "*Punishment Air Tasking Order*" outlining the massive retaliation options if the Iraqis did use chemical agents. Lieutenant General Chuck Horner laid cut seventeen targets, including the presidential palace, to be hit by allied bombers. His assistant, Brigadier General Buster Glosson, proposed targeting three dams, whose destruction would cause a flood that would destroy much of Baghdad's industrial base. General Schwarzkopf proposed that US politicians should tell Baghdad that if chemical weapons were used, the response would be nuclear—not that it actually would be, he explained, but the forcefulness of the message might strike fear into the Iraqi leadership. Eventually, it was agreed that a combination of political threats and a public show of expertise would be the best option, combined with a broadened conventional air campaign against industrial and military targets if the bluster and showmanship did not work.

Early planning to attack the CBW storage sites brought additional fears. DIA warned that the coalition had to consider a number of probable outcomes, ranging from no release of agent to the liberation of hundreds of kilograms. This could result in significant collateral loss of life unless there was total and complete destruction of all agent at the site. The many factors, including type of agent, wind speed, temperature, inversion conditions, and explosive characteristics, made it too difficult to estimate the results. Ironically, the abandoned US BW program and open-air simulant tests conducted prior to 1969 would offer a basis for further DIA/CIA analysis of these scenarios.

Chemical Corps support Builds

Phones began ringing all over the chemical defense community. Major General Louis Del Rosso, director of the Space and Special Weapons Directorate within ODCSOPS, pushed his Chemical Division into overdrive. Colonel Rick Read's group included Dr. Bob Boyle, a champion of institutional knowledge on BW programs, Lieutenant Colonel Howard Willhoite, a long time sage of chemical defense programs, and Major Ted Newing. Other staff officers form the Assistant Secretary of the Army (RDA) (ASARDA), ODCSLOG, CRDEC, AMC and other agencies began working with ODCSOPS to accelerate chemical defense equipment provisions, set priorities for what was needed, commit resources to make the purchases, and update the Army's policies on chemical defense equipment. Major Newing called Army warehouses to clear out the one thousand M17 SANATORs awaiting for instructions to ship to field units, directing them to XVIII ABN Corps units instead.

Probably the most important chemical defense effort was the Fox program. Lieutenant Colonel Willhoite had won support for the effort to acquire 48 German Fuchs vehicles on a limited procurement urgent acquisition prior to August Because the US Army's Fox NBCRS program was still in research and development, he and Major Newing talked with Brigadier General Joe W. Rigby at ASARDA to negotiate with the German government for the immediate delivery of 30 Fuchs systems, based on the operational analysis and vision of who would be deployed. Unknowing to them at the time, the German government would be deployed. Unknowing to them at the time, the German government would be "*prodded*" by the Bush administration to contribute to the war effort by the US government, and this was one avenue that they were more than willing to assist.

In Germany, shortly after midnight on Sunday August 5, 1990, Major Walt Polley's telephone woke him up. Brigadier General Robert Orton, the Army Chemical School Commandant, was on the other end. He said, "Sorry if I got you out of bed, Walt. You have heard of the invasion of Kuwait by Iraq. Well, the German Army does not know this yet, but the German government is going to give training for the operators at the NBC Defense School (ABC-SeS) in Sonthofen. But also let him know that he can't know' this until the German government tells the German Armed Forces, who will then tell him. The ABC-SeS will train at least four American NBC recon platoons. The first two platoons will arrive in two weeks on 20 August. Can you do it?"

Asked if this was for real, brigadier General Orton assured Major Polley that it was. The German military's NBC reconnaissance course was over three months long, but Orton instructed Polley to shorten the American version to three weeks maximum. He told Polley to notify Oberst Fluegel of his phone call later Sunday and also to work closely with USAREUR for logistics and administrative support. When Major Polley called Oberst fluegel later that day, his son answered the phone; the Commandant was not at home. After apologizing for intruding on the weekend, Polley asked that Oberst Fluegel call him about a matter of extreme urgency whenever he returned, no matter what time it was. Early that evening, Oberst Fluegel called and was told Brigadier General Orton's message. After asking "Is this for real?" he promised the full resources of the ABC-SeS and asked Polley to come in to his office Monday morning to plan the work for this project.

On Monday, *Oberst* Fluegel began quietly to recall selected critical people off their leaves to Sonthofen. *Oberstleutnant* (Lieutenant Colonel) Volker Schmitt (the school S-3 officer, who had overall responsibility for all training courses at the ABC-SeS) and Major Polley pared down the three-month German NBC recon course to a three-week long course, a two-week classroom session and a one-week field session. Once they had identified the critical and essential elements and extracted them from the longer program of instruction, the team began translating the lesson plans into English. Polley contacted Colonel Jan Van Prooyen, the USAREUR chemical officer, to coordinate the transport of NBC recon vehicles form the production lines in Kassel to Ramstein Air Force Base (AFB) and onward to Dharan. Colonel Guenther, head of the Training and Doctrine (TRADOC) Liaison Office at the *Heeresamt* (German General Army Office) was also notified and made aware of the "Germans can't know until officially told through their chain" requirement.

August 8, a holiday marking the Assumption of the Virgin Mary, was spent working on the translations and fitting the selected blocks of instruction into a logical sequence. The *Heeresamt* called *Oberst* Fluegel's home with an urgent message; his wife said he was in the office. Called at the office and asked why he was at work on a holiday, the Commandant said that he had a little work that needed catching up, but that he was planning on returning home soon. Why was the Army Office calling on a holiday? The answer was what Oberst Fluegel had been told on Sunday; he was asked if he thought the German General Army Office should ask the Americans to delay starting their training for one or two weeks past the requested date of August 20. Oberst Fluegel replied that if he could have authority to recall selected personnel from leave and to relax overtime and travel budget restrictions, there would be no problem meeting the start date. He was given those permission.

On August 7, Brigadier General Rigby called the PM NBC Defense Office to inquire how many Foxes they had, where they were, and how soon could they be deployed. The Army had five "*Nunn*" NBC reconnaissance vehicles; two of these were at Fort McClellan for doctrine development, one was at Dugway Proving Ground, one at Aberdeen Proving, and the last was at the General Dynamics Land Systems (GDLS) plant in Sterling Heights, Michigan. On the next day, Colonel Ron Evans, the Project Manager for NBC Defense, was directed to accelerate the plans to field the "*Nunn*" Foxes. His deputy, Lieutenant Colonel Mike D'Andries, as the Product Manager for the NBCRS, suddenly had a change of fortune; after battling a recent loss of project funds, he was struggling to meet demands for as many

Foxes as he could push out the door. The chemical school immediately "Americanized" the two Foxes on site with M60 machine guns, US communications equipment, appropriate US NBC defense equipment and air conditioning, while two crews received ad hoc training at the GDLS facility. Some in the Army Staff questioned the air conditioning, but it was vital to operating the mass spectrometer (the German MM-1) within the vehicle in the desert heat; one hour at 120°F would cause the MM-1 to fail.

There was no time to initiate the GDLS production line, so Lieutenant Colonel Willhoite explored the idea of buying or leasing existing fuchs from the German Army. This had political promise, since the German government could not contribute forces to the Persian gulf because of its constitution but wanted to support the coalition effort publicly. Brigadier General Rigby contacted Thyssen Henchel in Germany about obtaining additional Fuchs to support Operation Desert Shield. He cited to the company president, Mr. Jurgen Massman, the urgent need for a minimum of ten vehicles by mid-August. Since Thyssen-Henschel could not accelerate its production lines that quickly, the Army offered to buy thirty existing German military Fuchs systems. The German Ministry of Defense responded immediately and favorably. The Assistant Secretary of the Army (RDA), on August 11, signed a Justification and Authorization document for the expenditure of $106 million to purchase Fuchs from the German government. Work began at Thyseen-Henschel on August 14 to "Americanize" the thirty German Fuchs. As negotiations continued between the two governments, the German government considered a no-cost loan of the vehicles as part of their nation's support for Operation Desert Shield; on September 4, it offered to lend 30 Fuchs vehicles to the US military.

On August 12, the two "*Nunn*" vehicles at Fort McClellan were shipped to the 24th IN DIV to deploy with the 91st Chemical Company. Captain Vince Hughes and seven NCOs from the Chemical School linked up with the two Foxes at Fort Stewart. Their mission was to deploy with the 24th Infantry Division and to train the 91st Chemical Company's reconnaissance platoon on use and maintenance of the system. The two Foxes made it to the Gulf by August 26, and were immediately pushed out with the end Bn, 4th Regt. Cavalry on reconnaissance mission to protect the 24th IN DIV's deployment. The remaining three "Nunn" vehicles were sent to the GDLS Plant for "Americanization," with the one change, that of adding M240 machine guns for their mounts instead of M60s (which would be the standard for the rest of the Foxes). They would be shipped to Fort Hood after their conversion to deploy with the III Corps forces.

After the other three Foxes had undergone their modifications at the GDLs plant, the Army test community wanted to make sure that they could detect chemical agents in the sand. Some speculated that the liquids agents would soak too deep into the sand for the detectors to sniff out, only to re-emerge as vapor when the heat rose. One official suggested that tons of Saudi Arabian sand be shipped to Michigan on C5As returning to the United States; fortunately, five of the six types of terrain in Saudi Arabia were located naturally at Dugway Proving Ground, from sand dunes to rocky hills, and the special sand transportation was not require. One of the "*Nunn*" Foxes was sent back to Dugway Proving Ground to test this concern. On August 31, Dugway scientists used liquid simulants on the terrain to test the Fox's limits. In all cases, the Fox's MM-1 mass spectrometer was able to identify the agent and its location correctly. Now all the Army had to do was man the vehicle with trained operators.

After evaluating the training capabilities at the Chemical School and Sonthofen and determining the training requirements, Lieutenant Colonel Willhoite and Major Newing outlined a training program. The normal US Army program of instruction, based on a four-week period, was discarded in favor of the fourteen-hour-per-day, seven-day-a week training schedule over three weeks. It was conducted in three phases (one per week): individual training, team training, and for US troops only, mission training. Individual instruction trained the driver and various team members on their specialized skill areas. The team training phase put the four-man crew into the Fuchs simulator, which was a full-scale mock-up in the classroom of the vehicle and its equipment, and also exercised the crew in Fuchs vehicles in short-duration missions within the confines of the post. American crews would work with Chemical School instructors on more detailed reconnaissance missions for the last phase of the training; British and Israeli soldiers, who would later train at Sonthofen, would complete their mission training on their own with their base units. After the training, the crews would marry-up to their refurbished German vehicles, literally rolling off the production lines.

Back at Sonthofen, Major Polley and his German hosts continued to translate and proofread the Fox class instructions. The German practiced their lessons in English, set up the classrooms and stripped several Fuchs vehicles of their equipment. (There was only one- Fuchs simulator available, and only the drivers needed the Fuchs for familiarization). The equipment was moved into classroom bays so students would have hands-on-items for training. They stayed busy with training preparations until August 20, when the first two busloads of American showed up.

Within Seventh Army, the job of getting the chemical reconnaissance platoons to training and then on to Saudi Arabia fell to a working group tagged "*Task Force Fox.*" This task force was formed on August 14 at Montieth Barracks, Furth, Germany, under Lieutenant Colonel W.A. Funderburg, the 1st AR DIV chemical officer, and members of the 69th Chemical Company (Heavy Division). Their mission was to expedite V and VII Corps chemical reconnaissance platoons through their training at Sonthofen, assist in receipt of their Foxes at the Thyssen-Henschel factory at Kassel and deploy them to Southwest Asia from Ramstein AFB. Colonel Barbeau had suggested forming four recon platoons of six vehicles each to equip the 24th IN DIV, 101st ABN DIV, 3rd ACR, and the 2d Chemical BN, allowing for six operational readiness floats. The first two platoons identified for training were the 5th Recon Platoon, 69th Chemical Company (1st AR DIV), and 7th Recon Platoon, 92nd Chemical Company (3rd IN DIV). These fifty-three soldiers arrived at Sonthofen on August 20 to begin their training; they would finish their training by September 7, marry-up with the first ten vehicles coming off the Thyssen-Henschel line, load and deploy to Dharan by September 18.

The second group of soldiers arrived only a week after the first. The 5th Recon Platoon, 22nd Chemical Company (or 5/22 Chem of 3rd AR DIV) and the 5th Recon Platoon, 25th Chemical Company (5/25 Chem, 8th IN DIV) and the stagger their training a week behind the first two platoons. Eight more Foxes would be ready by mid-October and would leave with the third platoon (5/22 Chem) to bring three platoons to full strength of six vehicles each. The 5/25th would then deploy. The first ten Foxes arrived in Saudi Arabia within thirty days of Thyseen-Henschel accepting receipt of American equipment.

About mid-August, General Colin Powell, chairman of the Joint Chiefs of staff, called Major General Gerry Watson, then commander of the Defense Nuclear Agency (DNA) and former commandant of the Chemical School, into his Pentagon office. They discussed Iraq's CB warfare capability during the Iran-Iraq War and the possible threat to the XVII ABN Corps. General Powell had confidence in American soldiers being able to operate in a chemical warfare environment, although it would prove difficult. His greater concerns were Iraq's biological warfare capability and the threat of chemical warheads on Scuds. The biological warfare vulnerability was a real problem, since there were no biological agent sensors in the military, and the Army's vaccine production program had essentially dried up over the last two decades. General Powell asked Major General Watson to get in touch with General Schwarzkopf to talk about the situation. Schwarzkopf shared the same concerns, and asked Watson to develop a capability that would allow CENTCOM to identify a biological weapons attack.

Part of the reason why General Powell had initiated this discussion was that industry lobbyists and contractors were wandering the Pentagon halls hawking various "must have" hardwares. A Californian company, SRI, offered an off-the-shelf black box, a ground-mounted long range stand-off biological detector that used passive infra-red to detect and classify biological agents. These contractors, along with many government officials (including some from Aberdeen Proving Ground), had been on an information campaign to scare Pentagon decision makers with bold threat assessments and unvalidated opinions on Iraqi BW weaponization, warning that something had to be done immediately to avoid catastrophe. This campaign motivated the Army to delicate over $20 million toward a crash biological detector research and development program.

Major General Watson immediately pulled together a DNA team to build a prototype detector that could sense a cloud a biological agents moving toward the force. The team identified as the best approach a flow cytometer operating within an airplane, monitoring the outside environment through airflow samplers mounted on the wings. Similar in concept to the helicopter-mounted "*people-sniffer*" detectors of Vietnam, it would utilize a generic biological organism sampler. It would not positively identify the biological agent, but it would monitor a sharp increase in biological organisms. Samples could then he brought to a forward laboratory for positive identification. By the end of August, the team had begun to build the prototype and developed a test program to run at China Lake, the naval weapons test site. DNA hired a contractor and a plane to begin its tests, which would use biological simulant clouds to assess the effectiveness of the equipment. DNA would also test and evaluate SRI's stand-off system and other commercial options. At the same time, and in response to the same requirement, ODCSOPS directed CRDEC to see what could be resurrected from the old XM2/XM19 Biological Detection and Warming System.

The chemical School had thrown its support behind the Pentagon as well. Brigadier General Orton had established a twenty four-hour operations center at the Chemical School on August 7, with daily war councils in the library's vault. He identified two primary missions for the School. The first was to ensure that all soldiers in the deploying units were trained and prepared to operate in a CB agent-contaminated environment. This would require the School to recommend specific training program for deploying soldiers and their units (especially the chemical reserve units) and to develop special pocket-sized training manuals for soldiers to carry in the desert to refresh them on their defense training. The second mission was to support the necessary training for any special groups of personnel and new equipment. Any new chemical defense equipment, such as the CAMs or XM21s would require special teams to deploy to Saudi Arabia to train the operators. Training support extended to supporting Middle Eastern countries.

On August 7, the Chemical School received a TRADOC tasking to provide an officer to deploy to Saudi Arabia to support the Office of the Program Manager, Saudi Arabian National Guard (OPM-SANG). This office was subordinate to HQ Army Material Command (AMC), with a mission to send technical support and training to the Saudi Arabian National Guard. Major Robert Buchanan arrived in Riyadh on August 17 to head a Mobile Training Team (MTT) that would have the responsibility to outfit and train the Saudi Arabian National Guard in NBC defense equipment. His first responsibility was to train the local government civilians, military service members and their dependents in a four-hour block of individual protection skills. This training was to provide some relief for the psychological stress felt by OPM-SANG, in addition to demonstrating the basic use of protective clothing and masks. A second MTT, led by Captain David Lewis and two NCOs, arrived in the United Arab Emirates in late August to offer a similar program for its military forces. In addition to offering a "*train the trainer*" course, the UAE MTT reviewed the type, quantity, condition, and state of maintenance of the UAE chemical defense equipment, and recommended purchases to address the immediate shortfalls. These MTTs also instructed US citizens living in Saudi Arabia, including the embassy staff, families of the Army Training Mission and employees of Lockheed Corporation, on basic NBC defense skills.

Several other chemical NCOs and officers would arrive by mid-October to augment the MTTs as the first items of a $12.1 million purchase of chemical defense equipment began arriving. This foreign military sale purchase would outfit thirty thousands Saudi military personnel. In addition to training the National Guard troops, the MTTs gradually increased their scope to refresher training for the MODA units. The chemical section developed a "*train the trainer*" program that eventually instructed over sixty thousand Saudi military personnel from October 1990 through March 1991.

Chemical Defense Logistics Issues

Brigadier General Orton tapped Colonel J. Harold Mashburn, who had just arrived at the School during the previous month, and Captain Eric Riecks to augment the Office of the Deputy Chief of Staff for Logistics (ODCSLOG) in the Pentagon. This need had come about since many of the deploying units did not have sufficient NBC defense equipment, could not find their reserve stocks, or had equipment that was damaged beyond immediate repair. While the ODCSOPS chemical section was already assisting ODCSLOG in this area, Orton could see the need for a full-time, dedicated augmentation in ODCSLOG. The two officers began their work on August 10. Three more captains joined them by August 18. Their mission quickly expanded to overseeing the procurement and transportation of all NBC defense equipment for all four services.

This logistics shortage was not unique to the Army. Army division commanders, Air Force unit commanders, Navy fleet commanders and Marine Corps expeditionary force commanders had the responsibility to procure quantities of individual protective clothing, expendable decon kits and detector kits that their forces required to deploy into a potential NBC warfare environment. For decades, these commanders had to decide between spending precious unit operations and maintenance funds on chemical defense equipment that would expire before being used, or purchasing spare parts for weapons systems and vehicles being result the protective clothing shortage grew larger every year. The commanders assumed (wrongly) that if the need was urgent enough, someone in the Pentagon time. Now as their units deployed, all four services screamed for protective suits, which were not available in the numbers required for sustained operations under chemical warfare conditions.

First, ODCSLOG had to determine the availability, serviceability, and quantities of defense equipment, and where exactly it was stored for all four services manually. There was no top-level visibility of chemical defense assets at the units and depots. ODCSLOG accepted the fact that it would have to dip into the wartime and theater reserves worldwide to equip the CENTCOM forces fully. Very quickly the job became a twenty-hour-a-day mission, with two officers chasing down deploying units to ask them what chemical defense equipment they needed, and two others hunting chemical defense equipment all over the world. For instance, it quickly became obvious that the 82d ABN DIV was short significant quantities or protective suits, decontamination supplies and functional protective masks. Through a series of phone calls to Saudi Arabia, the cell gathered the information needed, and at no cost to the deploying units, directed replacement stocks to Fort Bragg from European and US war reserves. This type of detailed unit support kept the team busy throughout the next few months.

The most urgently needed expendable supplies were nerve agent antidote kits and chemical protective suits. The Defense Logistics Agency (DLA) awarded four chemical protective suit contacts in August and September for 1,050,000 suits (estimated contract value, over $83 million). Two companies were already producing suits under contract but would not be able to expand their production lines quickly enough to support the demand. The new deliveries were scheduled for October 1990, but the four new manufacturers did not start delivering the suits units January 1991. They had difficulties adapting to sewing the heavy clothing required. In the past, the Defense Personnel Support Center had awarded contracts to protective suit manufacturers on a lowest-bid-basis. When these small, inexperienced and under financed companies failed to produce, the Army didn't get its suits. This had led to deficit of 43 percent in prepositioned war stocks over the previous five years, with industry agreements to support only 12 to 13 percent of mobilization requirements. Compounding this problem was that the other three services used different protective suits and manufacturers, none of which were prepared to mobilize their production lines in less than three months.

As the buildup in the Gulf continued, forces using the older CPOGs and BDOs had to exchange their uncontaminated suits every fourteen or thirty days, respectively, to retain full protective capability. For a force that was planned to grow to a quarter million by November, this could amount to quite a turnover rate Reserve stocks had to be built up quickly in the event that Iraq attacked into Saudi Arabia. The Army began transferring over 1.1 million BDOs from worldwide theater reserve stocks to the Gulf. ODCSLOG requested chemical protective suits, replacement masks and other chemical defensive equipment from the Army's European and Korean theater reserve stockpiles, and that

US warehouses be stripped. The Air Force quickly stripped US air bases of all older CPOGs and BDOs for shipment.

Filters were another major problem. Soldiers in the theater did not so much as walk to a latrine without a protective mask slung across their waists. Because the Army had anticipated switching to the M40-series masks, filter production for the M17, M24 and M25-series protective masks had ceased. Other NATO countries used the C2 canister, which was incompatible with the current M17A2 and M24/25A1 masks. Soon after the conflict began, the Army contracted with filters (for the M24/25), with initial delivery dates of March and April 1991, respectively. Filter manufacturers, however, required three months to "*ramp up*" their production and overcome startup problems; this set the delivery dates back to June and December 1991. Until those arrived, ODCSLOG would have to continue raiding the global war reserves for their filters. ODCSOPS asked TRADOC and AMCCOM to reexamine the serviceability criteria and change-out doctrine for filters and protective suits to make them more realistic. Because the tendency had been to err on the safe side with respect to suit and filter shelf lives, older but still usable items could presumably be safely issued, saving literally millions of suits and filters and extending the very short supply on hand.

The average temperature for Saudi Arabia in the late summer was consistently 110°F, resulting in a number of equipment problems. The M258A1 skin decontamination kits, filled with alcohol-based liquids, swelled to three to five times their volume, bursting their packets. The BA3517/U batteries for the M8A1 alarms were similarly affected by the heat. Because of low training demands, many the deployment. Some had a performance life of only two hours, while many lasted only thirty-six hours of the expected seventy-two. Low battery levels were soldiers leapt toward their protective clothing and masks. The divisions would were not difficult to produce, no one had anticipated the volume requested, and power cables, so as to run M81A1 alarms off their vehicle batteries.

Many soldiers owing M24 and M25 protective masks reported cracked lenses and peripheral delamination of the facepiece (translation: the one-piece, chemically laminated eye lens popped off). While M17 masks were less vulnerable, many were wearing down and breaking under the heat and the stress of soldiers pulling the fitting-straps tighter. Desert sandstorms could quickly clog the filters, rendering them useless and requiring more frequent changing. When the soldiers began to examine the protective mask technical manuals, they noticed a recommendations to change mask filters every two months in a hot desert climate. The corps NBCC quickly saw a potential shortage in protective mask filters as well as masks and called its AMC logistics representative in Fort Bragg to confirm this estimate. HQ AMCCOM quickly saw the same concern, and adjust the filter change-out rate to once per year.

Then, of course, there were the protective suits themselves. Few soldiers were acclimated to the desert heat in T-shirts, let alone a heavy charcoal-impregnated suit. The butyl rubber gloves and boots caused soldiers' hands and feet soften due to the profuse sweating, making them vulnerable to mechanical injuries and trenchfoot. Sweat also decreased the effectiveness of the overgarments. Hot as they were, however, the suits were the only protection available, and no one would travel far without knowing where his or her chemical suit was. The intense heat limited the soldiers to training in the early morning or late evening hours, while during the day the contigency suits remained close at hand. The leadership had to acknowledge that overreacting to the chemical threat was worse than under reacting. Hard work in the hot BDOs could quickly exhaust the soldiers were able to accomplish the mission, which meant balancing the risk of chemical attack against workload and weather.

At least military personnel were protected; the enormous amount of supplies and numerous maintenance support facilities were unprotected from CB agent contamination, other than in the few warehouses available at the ports and airfields. Covering the supplies with protective sheets would greatly reduce the decontamination required if CB agents were used. The XVIII ABN Corps NBCC requested the Natick labs to accelerate their development of the NBC protective covers then undergoing test and evaluation. The program was not ready for production, but procurement officers could purchase mylar and polyethylene sheets to accomplish the same objective. To augment decontaminant supplies, procurement officers also began local buys of tons of high-test calcium hypochlorite (HTH) bleach. These critical issues drove the crops NBC center to develop a more detailed logistic support request for the NBC defense equipment National Inventory Control Point (NICP) at AMCCOM, Rock Island, Illinois.

Medical Issue Mount

Because of the projected requirement for nerve agent antidote kits, DLA immediately awarded a $2 million emergency contract order for the NAAK autoinjectors to Survival Technologies, Incorporated (STI), a medical supply company based in Maryland. The very fact that there were no fielded biological detectors placed an immediate urgency on vaccines and biological agent antidotes. Since the soldiers would not know when they were being hit with BW agents, they would require medical attention both before (in the form of vaccines) and after (for post-treatment of BW agents) the attack. Vaccines were in critical supply, because of past policy decisions within NATO not to stockpile biological warfare vaccines. As a result, the US Army only made enough vaccines for medical personnel involved with the limited biological defense research effort. Now the military was faced with an adversary that might use BW agents, and there were not enough vaccines. The immediate critical issues were: What BW agents CENTCOM should protect its troops against; how the medical community was to get Food and Drug Administration (FDA) approval to use anthrax vaccine and botulinum toxoid to inoculate the troops; and how enough of the vaccines could be produced prior to an Iraq BW attack.

On August 11, Armed Forces Medical Intelligence Center (AFMIC) analysts briefed Army officials from the Office of the Surgeon General (OTSG) on the Iraqi BW threat; the brief resulted in medical CB defense stockpile assessment and planning. By August 19, the Surgeon General had a good picture of the current status and briefed the four service's logistic chiefs on needs and issues. A Tri Service AD Hoc Medical Working Group met and recommended immediate immunization of the force against anthrax, procurement of more anthrax vaccines and botulinum toxoid and placement of two special analytical laboratories in theater. ON August 23, the Army OTSG discussed with FDA officials the medical emergency needs arising from biological agent threats. The Army Surgeon General recommended to General Carl Vuono (Army Chief of Staff) and Schwarzkopf that the entire force receive anthrax vaccine, and those at the greatest risk receive the botulinum toxoid. Producing more vaccines became a top national priority.

The US military had one source for botulinum toxoid, manufactured at the Michigan Department of Public Health at Lansing Michigan. Two old horses which had slowly built up their resistance to the toxoid, supplied the few thousand doses of vaccine needed annually for academic research and food handling. The Army immediately bought additional horses to build up a stock, although these new horses could not be exposed to the same level as the first two had been and therefore, could not immediately produce as much vaccine. The botulinum vaccine had been given to more than 3000 people at the Army's Medical Research Institute for Infectious Diseases (MRIID) over the past twenty years as a result of potential exposure to the bacterial toxin. The Center for Disease Control in Atlanta had also given the vaccine to thousands of individuals whose work in industry exposed them to this threat. The vaccine protected against five of the seven known botulinum neurotoxins (Type A, B, C, D and E) and was therefore named pentavalent toxoid. Neither agency had reported any serious long-term side effects.

While these vaccines were proven safe for medical researchers, there was no proof that it protected against botulinum toxin used as a biological warfare agent on a real battlefield. This lack of efficacy data was an issue with FDA officials. Under the Food, Drug and Cosmetics Act, all vaccines and products must be proven safe and effective if sold and distributed in the United States or used by US troops. Under this law, unapproved vaccines and treatments could only be used for healthy individuals only under an Investigational New Drug (IND) procedure. Any individual who is given an IND must give informed consent—that is to say, told the potential risks and benefits of the product, orally and in writing, and choose freely whether or not to participate. In addition, the IND procedures call for a controlled environment where safety and effectiveness can be monitored. (Cancer and AIDS research clinics can request such authority to test new experimental drugs on rapidly deteriorating patients). The only problem was that the military could not perform human test trials to determine if the vaccine worked against people exposed to BW agents.

The status of anthrax vaccine was similar. There was not enough vaccine stock immediately available for all of CENTCOM's forces. Other than for the British allies, there was no large-scale production source for anthrax vaccine. In addition, full immunization against anthrax requires a series of three shots two weeks apart followed by boosters at the six, twelve, and eighteen-month marks. This would effectively immunize 85 percent of the force, but the program had to be initiated quickly to build up the inoculations. The FDA decided not to make a fuss about the efficacy of anthrax vaccine. The FDA acknowledged that while the anthrax vaccine had never officially been approved for use as a BW vaccine, it had been used safely on humans in the civilian and military medical field for decades (especially for veterinarians and animal handlers working among sheep and cattle herds). The Army

OTSG had to conduct the necessary safety and efficacy trials for both vaccines while searching for producers, determining a vaccination policy, and delivering the necessary products all prior to any Iraqi BW agent employment.

Getting a license to produce medical chemical and biological defense products was one thing; finding a domestic pharmaceutical company to produce them was another. Despite the United States' premier position as an international leader in health industries, no US firm would take the millions of dollars offered to produce the vaccines and pretreatments. Because the items were still technically (and legally) "experimental," the malpractice insurance required to cover the firms was astronomical, even with government promises of indemnity. Not one trusted that it would be free of lawsuits after the conflict if the vaccines were thought unsafe, whether or not the treatments did their job safely and efficiently. Also, there was little profit in these medical treatments; while other military medical treatments held a dual purpose in public and military health benefits, there was not much call for anthrax and botulinum toxin vaccines outside of the military. Too much risk and too little profit meant no participation from the US pharmaceutical firms.

Overall, the deployment went off as well as could be expected, especially given CENTCOM's initial low readiness status. Because Iraq did not immediately attack US forces entering Saudi Arabia, it appeared that CENTCOM would have a chance to build up its strength. There was a mountain of challenges ahead. There were not enough chemical protective suits, masks or decontamination supplies for more than one large-area chemical warfare attack, let alone stocks for extended operations. The real defense would come from the chemical decontamination units at Fort Hood and other locations in the United States, but they would not arrive until late September at the earliest. The only thing CENTCOM did have was thousands of chemical defense specialists interwoven throughout the force, who would be juggling urgent training, operational and logistics requirements simultaneously. With no modern reconnaissance systems, limited individual defense equipment and a very low level of CB warfare training, combat leaders suddenly realized they had to rely on their chemical soldiers more than ever.

Conclusion

Professor of history Martin Van Creed has written that the rules of war exist to protect the armed forces themselves by defining a common culture code that differentiates an army from a mob. More importantly, he states that these rules carefully define how armies can and cannot be allowed to kill other combatants and noncombatants. These are in effect a societal rule that draws the line between murder and war. Countries that ignore the rules usually provoke punishment, often through annihilation or later war crime trials. These rules of war once covered the use of crossbows, submarine warfare, strategic bombing and mine laying; today of course, they still cover CB warfare.

Over the last century, nations have attempted to restrain the use of CB weapons under these special rules, though more from fear of retaliation than from moral distaste. Because of past association with strategic bombing theories developed between the world wars and after World War II, the advent of nuclear weapons, chemical and biological weapons have been put on the same scale as nuclear devices. Contrary to this view, CB warfare has never resulted in thousands or millions of innocent casualties, the nightmare that has derived the international arms control community to such treaties as the Biological Weapons Convention and chemical Weapons Convention. History has shown that nations continue to develop CB weapons because there are tactical advantages to be gained: when one combines CB weapons use with conventional military tactics against an enemy without a good defense, it dramatically reduces the time needed for victory. IN these days of billion-dollar conflicts, that gets attention. Increasing global proliferation of these weapons drives the need for defensive measures despite these special "rules" of war.

The chemical Corps survived to become part of the Army's twenty-first century military force, not by planned evolution but by world events that constantly demanded that the US military retain an ability to protect itself against CB warfare. In 1972 the Army turned its back on the Chemical Corps because the service's leaders did not see the operational benefits of retaining such combat support. As a result, a decade slipped by without modernizing CB defense equipment; without leaders understanding that CB warfare is a tactical, not strategic consideration; without CB defense specialists staffing combat units and command headquarters; and without the specialized chemical defense companies and biological detection teams supporting combat arms units. While the 1980s featured a great deal of improvement in doctrine development, leadership, education, chemical defense unit build-up and equipment modernization, the GAO report released in May 1991 pointed out the serious deficiencies in the Army prior to Desert Shield. Imagine, if you will the situation in August 1990 if General Creighton Abrams in 1972 had been successful in relegating the Chemical Corps to a special weapons function under the Ordnance Corps. More importantly, will the four services, having looked into the eyes of the dragon, now forget that the threat of CB warfare ever existed during the Gulf War? Or does the US military leader leadership now acknowledge the need for continued reform and further efforts? While the Chemical Corps obviously has room for improvement, its efforts are wasted until the three and four star Army leaders identify these challenges and aggressively support the Chemical Corps in meeting them.

National Policy on NBC Warfare Requires Updating

The US government's policy on NBC warfare has been one of "*no first use*" only since World War II, as the US senate had refused to ratify the Geneva Convention in 1925. Because of the potential threat from Germany and Japan, the US military scrambled for eighteen months to develop a retaliatory capability in the form of mustard and phosgene agent-filed munitions. President Franklin D. Roosevelt publicly stated the government's policy that under no circumstances would the United States resort to using CB weapons unless they were first used by the Axis. If used by Germany, Italy or Japan, the US military would retaliate against munitions centers, seaports and other military objectives.

After World War II, President Roosevelt's policy remained the unwritten rule for most administrations, although the US government had still not ratified the Geneva Convention. President Richard Nixon publicly reaffirmed the policy of no first use of chemical weapons and abandoned the use of biological warfare agents altogether. The Senate's final ratification of the Geneva Convention in 1975 did not change the US policy of retaliation in kind, using the current stockpile of chemical weapons. The re-initiation of the binary chemical weapons program in 1985, meant to replace the aging unitary chemical munitions, forced the Soviets to return to the negotiations table on the subject. In the 1990 Bush-Gorbachev talks, the US government abandoned the future production and storage of chemical weapons, receiving promises from the Soviet Union that it would do likewise.

Now as of April 1997, the broader, multilateral Chemical Weapons Convention treaty has come into play. The CWC treaty outlines a verifiable ban on all production, storage and use of chemical weapons and carries over 180 nations' signatories. This represents a great change from the past policy, of maintaining both a strong defensive posture and a viable retaliatory capability, to one of maintaining only defensive measures. The one policy we knew, which worked for over forty-five years—threatening retaliation by chemical munitions if our forces were attacked with *chemical weapons* - is gone. On the other hand, the CWC treaty affects all countries by, at the least, causing them to go to some effort to shield the size and potential effects of their offensive CB programs. The future threat for US forces will not be continuous hail of chemical rains. Rather, it will be infrequent and inconsistent use of chemical agents to delay and disrupt combat operations, intended to give the opposing force an advantage at key points in the battle.

The US military is at a dangerous transition. It has given up its retaliatory capability and defensive capabilities remain weak, while the CWC treaty's verification measures have not been tested. If our force are attacked with CB weapons, the military leadership will have to choose nuclear or massive conventional retaliation. In a recent war game sponsored by the DoD counter-proliferation office, the players explored a combined CBW scenario in the Persian Gulf: after US carriers were attacked by aircraft armed with biological agent spray tanks, and terrorists attacked Dhahran with anthrax bombs, the United States responded by using nuclear weapons against Baghdad. While this ended the war game, it did not represent a satisfactory or realistic conclusion. This game move did not acknowledge that a US president would have to approve the nuclear attack of a country's capitol, let alone address the implications of attacking an Arab attack against US forces, would the president be prepared for the consequences of a strategic nuclear strike against civilian and industrial targets? Ordering a smaller tactical nuclear strike against military targets is not an option these days; the DoD yielded up their tactical nuclear weapons years ago.

The more realistic option is the massive conventional response, which is also politically and militarily risky. Experience during *World War II*, Korea, Vietnam (and, according to many, the Gulf War) shows that massive conventional bombing produces very little political or military payoff for the effort, while increasing pilot and aircraft exposure to increasingly sophisticated air defenses. In any case, to minimize the threat from CB weapons (e.g., strike production facilities, storage sites, delivery systems), you have to find them first. The intelligence job of finding and identifying these targets has gotten more difficult, not less. An increasingly diverse global economy allows countries to order just about anything they want through dummy companies, academic institutions, and public organization. Taking a page from the superpowers, many countries are investing in deep underground shelters to protect their storage sites and their command, control and communication functions. While the United States can identify most of these facilities, not much short of a nuclear device can get at them.

Military forces cannot predict with 100 percent clairvoyance when or where the CB agent munitions will be used, even with extensive intelligence assets. This meant that US forces would need to retain a strict defensive posture against CB agent use at all times in a theater, increasing logistics demands and decreasing morale. Meanwhile, the enemy needs only a minimal investment in defensive equipment since it controls the time and location of chemical weapons release, thus minimizing effects on its forces. This lopsided arrangement actually increases the possibility that an enemy force would use CB agent munitions, since its chemical weapons will eliminate the US military's high-technology edge. Army studies prove that chemical warfare results in a drop in overall preparedness and effectiveness, anywhere from 25 to 100 percent, depending on the scenario and the troop's level of training. Adversaries using CW munitions will multiply their combat power by degrading the performance of opposing troops that lack defensive equipment or training. Given that current force structure decisions are putting smaller US forces against larger opponents, losing the high-technology advantage will result in being overwhelmed on the battlefield. If we are trying to minimize US casualties, this should not be an acceptable course of action.

Can the US military survive and sustain its forces on the future NBC battlefield through strictly defensive methods? In theory, yes—but it would call for careful planning, expensive stockpiling and extensive training. It requires an aggressive development program that provides state-of-the art defensive equipment. It requires continued reliance on chemical defense units that can decontaminate military equipment and large areas of terrain (such as ports and airfields), while keeping pace with mobile forces. That means maintaining active and reserve units that are ready, well trained and have worked with combat units, integrating CB defense into combat operations. It calls for an increased focus on how combat arms units can minimize the impact of persistent CB agents. By integrating chemical defense training with their mission-oriented combat training, soldiers could learn to fight on contaminated battlefield, making CB warfare irrelevant. This would enable them to retain most of their intended lethality, which today can be seriously degraded, as seen in the CANE tests.

Last and perhaps as important, we need to reexamine our investment in human intelligence sources. The US government needs to remain alert to new and changing dangers such as terrorist use of CB agents and emerging Third World threats. Yet our government has made little attempt to shift its vision in this respect from the *Cold War* to the "*New World Order.*" There are less than fifty CB intelligence analysts in the entire federal government, as compared to nearly ten times that number dedicated to nuclear weapons intelligence. As seen with the intensive research conducted for the Khamisiyah incident, there are few analysts that understand and can validate CB weapons effects. More are needed to track and verity offensive CB weapons programs in countries like Libya, North Korea, Iran and Iraq. Unless this imbalance is corrected, US forces will again have no idea what their opponents have in the way of CB weapons, where the weapons are located, or how to attack them.

The US military must reexamine its policy concerning enemy use of CB weapons, and find a solution that is practical and feasible. Because we are not facing a massive use of CB agents, we can no longer justify a righteous massive retaliation. If massive force is no longer a credible deterrent, US forces in the future will be as fear-stricken as they were when the Scuds filled the skies in January 1991—unless they have full faith in their defensive capabilities.

DoD NBC Defense RDA Program is Still Recovering

Several material areas sorely required attention during the Gulf War. The most evident was the need for improved airlift and sealift capabilities. While C-17 cargo planes, heavy trucks and merchant marine ships will never be as sexy or alluring as F-22 fighter aircraft, Abrams tanks and Seawolf submarines, there certainly was a strong case made when the military had to rely on commercial aircraft and ships older than the generals and admirals in order to get to the theater of operations. Of course, NBC defense equipment was another area of concern. Despite the Gulf War (or because of the lack of CB warfare during this conflict), CB defense equipment continues to struggle on as a small, relatively insignificant portion of the Pentagon's acquisition funds (less than one-fifth of 1 percent).

NBC defense equipment has always been criticized by both the military troops that use the equipment and the chemical specialists that train with it. Protective suits are too hot; protective masks are too restrictive; collective protection shelters are not adequate; decontamination apparatuses use too much water; CB agent detectors false-alarm too often; and medical antidotes can not be trusted. All these complaints came too late for the troops in Operation Desert Storm. These concerns were primarily a result of the combat arms sitting by the sidelines, allowing the Chemical Corps to determine what the combat troops were going to use. The Chemical Corps did deliver detectors that detected chemical agents, protective ensembles that would have saved lives, and decontaminants did work very well. The *BUT* part is that the combat arms units did not understand that getting CB defense equipment that works in only half the equation; there remains such matters as false alarms due to overly-sensitive detectors, hot burdensome suits, corrosive decontaminants. If the combat arms incorporated CB warfare considerations into their war gaming, they might see the benefits and challenges of CB defense equipment, and they might get more involved. This active involvement will become more and more important as the military gives up its chemical munitions and relies solely on defensive equipment.

As a result of Public Law 103-160, there is an increased emphasis on better management of the NBC defense program. With the evolution of the one-star command CRDEC into the two-star command US Army Chemical and Biological Defense Command (CBDCOM) in October 1993, the Army is attempting to put much of its NBC defense program authority under the major subordinate command. The commanding general of CBDCOM also "*wears the hat*" of Deputy Chief of Staff for Chemical Matters, Army Material Command. CBDCOM is charged to mange all NBC defense programs for the Army and to work with the other services to mange better the DoD NBC defense program. CBDCOM will manage chemical stockpile sties, to include Rocky Mountain Arsenal and several programs at Dugway Proving Ground, Pine Bluff Arsenal and other locations. This is not suggest that the Army has gone full circle, back to the single consolidated NBC defense program it had prior to 1962; CBDCOM still has no direct control over medical NBC defense programs or the chemical demilitarization program. But it does have a great deal of authority to request funds conduct studies and procure NBC defense equipment.

Public Law 103-106 also meant reorganization for the entire DoD NBC defense community. The four services have formed a Joint Service Integration Group (JSIG) for joint doctrine and training issues and a Joint Service Material Group (JSMG) for joint material issues, both chaired by the Army, and both including all services as equal partners. The JSIG resides at For McClellan, with the Chemical School's commandant as its chair. Its sister organization, the JSMG, is chaired by the commanding general of CBDCOM At Aberdeen Proving Ground. These groups officially started their functions in January 1995, both overseen by a DoD Joint NBC Defense (Atomic Energy) (Chemical Biological Matters) (or ATSD(AE)(CBM). The joint NBC Defense Board is a high-level, general-officers panel (including civilian acquisition members and officers and to sort our inter services conflicts. The new joint groups may be more effective than their predecessors, primarily since they make recommendations on the annual NBC defense budgets through a joint consolidation Program Operations Memorandum strategy. As the Golden Rule states, those who have the gold make the rules.

The other services still do not trust the Army to control the DoD NBC defense program entirely. The four services still have difficulties agreeing on basic doctrine, or on roles and missions for the future. The other services continue to fight tooth and nail to retain exclusive control over their own destinies in the NBC defense program areas. Each service had its own offices, programs and "*rice bowls*," specifically for NBC defense ever since DoD gave them leeway to initiate their own NBC defense programs in 1960, programs that became further entrenched when the Chemical Corps was down-scaled in 1972. These two joint groups have the budget authority and congressional language to make the tough decisions necessary to reform the DoD NBC defense program, but this does not guarantee any quick or near-term improvements. Existing bureaucracies always fight change, and it will be some time before we see results.

One key to developing better NBC defense equipment may lie in using computer models and simulations to understand CB agent effects on military troops, units and equipment during combat. The Army's "*Battle Lab*" program at six TRADOC schools uses advanced models, simulations and war gaming tools to test new concepts of warfighting and to determine future program requirements. The Dismounted Battle Space Battle Lab at Fort Benning initially had the responsibility for "*weapons of mass destruction*," with NRDEC as its partner, but it focused almost exclusively on individual protection efforts. Other labs, such as the Mounted Battle Space Battle Lab at Fort Knox, the Depth and Simultaneous Attack Battle Lab at Fort Still, and the Early Entry Lethality and Survivability Battle Lab at Fort Monroe, have smaller, but not insignificant, roles for NBC warfare aspects. The Engineer

School and Center initiated its Maneuver Support Battle, Lab, which has taken over the champion role of working "*weapons of mass destruction*" issues, working with the Chemical Corps as it moves to Fort Leonard-Wood. It will be up to these Battle Labs to revisit the issue of NBC warfare on the modern battlefield. To date, there are no proven models of how CB agents affect troops and equipment, and therefore, there is no way to show senior leadership the benefits (or detriments) of fighting with a certain type of CB defense equipment. This is vital to assess the "*value-added*" of these programs. If warfighters, NBC defense subject-matter experts, and industry cannot gain a mutual understanding of NBC warfare, there will be no acceptance or understanding of modern CB defense equipment.

CB Agents and Domestic Terrorism

Terrorist organizations have taken an interest in CB weapons since at least 1972. Prospects for CB terrorism have increased with the international spread of dual-use technologies, increased access to published sources on producing CB agents. US intelligence sources have noted Moslem terrorist organizations conducting chemical defense training at their camps. Simple biological agents such as botulinum toxin can be developed with a moderate amount of education and equipment. They are inexpensive to procure and culture, easy to hide, require far less material than chemical weapons and are very easy to employ in an indiscriminate target-rich area such as a city. Most biological organisms, however, are more difficult to develop, store and disperse safely than chemical agents, lending to a pattern of terrorist groups external to the United States using chemical agents rather than biological agents. This could change, given today's global accessibility of technical and scientific resources.

Chemical and biological agents are inexpensive, easily understood, easily controlled, and easily disperse under a single terrorist's control. As the world's nations have not condemned the use of chemical agent weapon use in Yemen, Afghanistan, Laos, Iraq, etc., terrorists may feel that they can safely use CB agents rather than resort to nuclear devices. Some past examples of CB terrorism include:

1. In 1974, Muharem Kerbegovic was arrested in Los Angles after mailing toxic materials to a Justice of the Supreme Court and threatening to kill the president with nerve gas;
2. In 1980, the Paris police raided a Baader-Meinhof safehouse and discovered a culture of clostridinium botulinum (used to make botulin toxin) in a home laboratory.

3. In 1984, the Rajneesh cult in Oregon was accused of using salmonella to contaminate salad bars in local restaurants in an attempt to influence local electrons;
4. In 1991, German authorities thwarted a neo-Nazi plot to pump hydrogen cyanide into a synagogue.
5. In 1992, the FBI arrested two members of the Patriots Council in Minnesota for possession of less than one gram of ricin, under the Biological Weapons Anti Terrorism Act of 1989; and
6. In 1996, a former Aryan Nation member was arrested for mail-ordering three vials of bubonic plague to his home by giving a false lab code number to the American Type Tissue Collection.

The use of sarin in Tokyo subway system on March 20, 1995, illustrated how easy it is to employ chemical agents in an open society, and how much media attention a small, previously barley noticed group can receive as a result. Between 7:00 and 8:30 in the morning of March 20, several individuals left at least four containers wrapped in newspaper, disguised as lunchboxes, on various trains of three subway lines. Some were placed on hat racks, others on or under the seats. These containers were punctured, allowing its contents to evaporate. Shortly afterward, people riding the three lines bean coughing and complaining of headaches, diminishing vision, and nausea, classical nerve agent poisoning signs. Some collapsed to the floor, and as the trains halted at the next stop passengers rushed out, screaming for help and collapsing on the ground.

By 8:15, police were receiving emergency calls from sixteen subway stations. Tokyo's Metropolitan Police Department dispatched 11,000 police and rescue workers to assist the affected passengers. One assistant station manager, Kazumasa Takahashi, went abroad one train to remove a plastic bag holding a leaking container. He died soon afterward, along with seven others. In all, twelve individuals died, another fifty-four were in critical condition, and more than 5,000 were treated for related symptoms. By 8:45, service on all three subway lines was stopped, with twenty-six stations closed. About three hours after the first attack, the authorities realized they were dealing with a nerve agent. They moved into full response mode, sending police, firefighters and medical response teams into the subways.

The police targeted the Aum Shinrikyo, or Supreme Truth, a Buddhist sect that recruited dissatisfied college-educated citizens, as the probable perpetrators. Several of their members were arrested in Japan, and the police seized bulk precursor chemicals, including phosphorus trichloride, sodium fluoride and isopropyl alcohol. In the sect's building police discovered behind false walls industrial equipment for preparing bulk chemical mixes. As their leader, Shoko Asahara, explained a few days later, these are chemical that can be used for commercial purposes. They also are the prime ingredients for sarin; in fact, the Chemical Weapons Convention specifically names phosphorus trichloride as one of the dual-use chemicals on its "schedule 3" list.

The panic and concern over the next months was largely due to the fact that the Japanese police had been completely unprepared to react to this new form of terrorism. Perhaps more frightening was failure of intelligence agencies or police to predict this attack. There were a number of related cases that stretched back nearly two years, beginning with a case on July 2, 1993, when over 100 residents in Tokyo's Koto district complained of noxious white fumes rising from building owned by the sect. One year later, on June 21, 1994, seven people died and more than 200 were sickened by sarin fumes in the nearby town of Matsumoto. It was later discovered that Aum Shrinkiyo cultists had used a truck-mounted ag-icultural generator to target three judges in an apartment building (they were ruling on a local real estate issue involving cult members). On September 1, more than 230 people in seven town in the state of Nara (in western Japan) suffered from rashes and eye irritation from unknown fumes. On December 1994, material by-products of sarin were discovered in Kamikuishiki; January 4, 1995—the Aum Shrinkiyo filled a complaint accusing a company president of spreading sarin into its facilities in Kamikuishiki; March 5—eleven people were taken to a hospital after nineteen individuals inhaled noxious fumes in a train car in Yokohama (a test case?). On March 15, police discovered three attache cases containing an unknown (but nontoxic) gas. Each case held small motorized fans, a vent and a battery. Despite all this evidence the March 20 episode came as a surprise to the Tokyo emergency responders.

Experts still wonder why more subway riders did not die, considering the high lethality of the nerve agent. One theory rests on these possible speculations. First, the sarin mix was not pure. Later analysis showed that the chemicals were only 30 percent sarin by composition and were therefore not as lethal as they could have been. This design may have been deliberate, contrived to permit the couriers time to flee. Second, the delivery system was crude. Accounts told of the suspected couriers rupturing the one-quart containers immediately before departing the trains, allowing natural seepage to initiate the fumes. Not the most efficient process; a portable fan next to the package would have spread more quickly the fumes throughout the cars. Third sarin is what is known as a *semipersistent* chemical agent—it has about the same consistency as water, taking up to hours to evaporate completely. This would explain why the only individuals who died were the ones traveling in the same cars as the containers like the assistant station manager who picked up the package to remove it from the train. Last, the trains may have had a positive pressure ventilation, using fans to circulate air out of the trains and into the subway tubes. This precaution is a normal engineering method to keep gasses or smells in the subway tubes from intruding into the individual cars; the District of Columbia Metro, for instance, has this feature. In all the Japanese citizens were very fortunate the most survived the physical effects of this deadly agent.

Another subway in Yokohama was attacked a few weeks later on April 19, sending nearly 600 Japanese sent to the hospital for treatment of what was suspected to be exposure to phosgene gas. While this agent is not immediately suspected to be exposure to phosgene gas. While this agent is not immediately lethal, it can kill as the gas hydrolyses within the victim's lungs over a period of one to two days. Many people do not realize that this World War I chemical warfare agent is also a legitimate industrial chemical, used in the textiles and clothing industry as well as plastics manufacturing. As such bulk quantities of the chemical travel across the country every day in tankers on rail cars and trucks; there is no need for illicit manufacture phosgene, it is a very simple chemical compound to synthesize in the laboratory. A third suspected gas attack at a grocery store two days later caused twenty-five people to seek treatment. Because the attack occurred outdoors, the lethal chemical agents may not have their full potency. On May 6, the police defused a binary device that would have again released hydrogen cyanide into a Tokyo subway station.

The Aum Shrinkiyo may have been coming after American citizens as well. A task force composed of representatives of the FBI, Los Angeles police, the Federal Emergency Management Agency (FEMA), Environmental Protection Agency, public Health Service, Centers for Disease Control, and CBDCOM's Technical Escort Unit traveled to Los Angeles airport on April 13 to intercept two Japanese men associated with the cult. These men had in their possession written instructions on how to make sarin and a videotape that indicated an intended attack against Disneyland. Authorities at Disneyland had received a tip that a possible terrorist incident was going to take place over Easter weekend, when their attendance was expected to be higher than average. Although details are still vague, it appears that the terrorist group was planning to release sarin within one of the many theaters of exhibition halls at Disneyland. Because of quick reactions based on the tip, these men were apprehended, and America's version of Tokyo's experience was averted—for now.

Since March 1995, federal agencies have banded together under a program titled "*Domestic Preparedness*," to prevent and respond to acts of CB terrorism conducted within the United States. The FBI leads what is termed "*crisis management*" (what to do prior to a CB terrorist incident), while FEMA leads "*consequence management*" (what happens after the event occurs). Forces were in place at the Atlanta Olympics and the 1996 national political conventions, with a mission to prepare for any sign of CB terrorism. While it was an interim agreement among federal government agencies to cooperate prior to 1996, the Domestic Preparedness program has since been codified by executive order and public law and is under way. This program had just been started when it had its first acid test. Preplanning for large events can be accomplished, but the following case showed the real dangers.

In Washington, DC, on the evening of April 24, 1997, someone left a smelly manila envelope in the mail room of the B'nai Brith offices. Two employees opened the envelope; it contained a petri dish filled with an unknown, red, jelly-like substance and markings that suggested it held anthrax. The police took immediate steps to cordon off square blocks around DuPont Circle, an area that included the Australian Embassy and several traffic commuter routes. Firefighters were called in, as well as the FBI and CBDCOM's Technical Escort Unit. They evacuated the dish, an inside the building, 108 people were quarantined for nearly eight hours as medical technicians at the Bethesda Naval Medical Center analyzed the compound. Meanwhile, the two employee declared they were feeling sick. They along with twelve firefighters' were decontaminated with a chlorine solution.

As things turned out, there was no anthrax in the petri dish. While FBI and city officials praised the firefighters' quick reaction, it was a major overreaction to a minor threat. First, airborne anthrax is the typical biological warfare agent used, due to its much higher lethality than percutaneous anthrax. Since the sample was in a liquid-gelatinous substance, there was no chance of its escaping into the atmosphere. A two hundred-meter safety radius would have been as good as several square blocks; had this actually been anthrax there would have been very little threat to the surrounding area outside the building itself. Second, any biological agent needs time to incubate in a human host prior to causing sings of sickness. Certainly any symptoms felt by the two employees and the firefighters had to be psychosomatic. Exposed personnel could have been treated with vaccines prior to any real dangers to their health. The point here is that, left to their own resources, emergency responders will over-react to CB agents and make the wrong decisions unless they learn more about this area.

The Washington case was a free trial-run for federal counter-terrorism forces and city emergency response forces. It pointed out several challenges: the need for CB defense equipment responders, the need for an expert source of information around the clock and the need to train and educate local emergency responders in how to identify and manage the incident. Trained federal forces will be hard pressed to respond to unplanned emergency events in less than eight to twelve hours. This puts the burden on police, firefighters, emergency medial services, and 911 operators to know how to deal with the threat. It may be that this specialized training and equipment is the best local responders can do is to keep from becoming casualties themselves. If we expect that all the major metropolitan areas require this kind of expertise, a major investment of funds, equipment and time will be required, of which time is probably the most critical.

While the FBI and FEMA have traditionally led counter terrorism and disaster preparedness missions, the expertise on CB agents is in the Department of Defense. This has led to the development of an interagency federal task force and several programs for federal support to metropolitan emergency responders. An ambitious training program has targeted 120 major cities in the US, training their emergency responders to identify and respond correctly to CB agent terrorism. It will take some years, but this interagency task force envisions a certain degree of expertise at the local and state levels that will at least ensure that firefighters, police and emergency medical technicians are not killed rushing into a CB terrorist incident. But it should be understood by all that this will not guarantee against a similar Tokyo subway incident in the US—all it does is minimize the ensuing chaos and the casualties among responding professionals. As in any terrorist bombing incident, few things can minimize the number of civilian casualties other than interdicting the terrorist group itself prior to the event.

There are a number of additional cases, some still classified, where terrorist use of CB agents in the CB agents in the United States has been only narrowly averted. One reason why terrorists have not adopted these weapons more readily in these already unstable times may be the argument of cost versus availability. The 'bang for the buck" comparisons shows that CB agent kill their victims much more cheaply per casualty than bullets or explosive do. Bullets and explosives, on the other hand, are far more available on the open market than CB agent, and they are still effective attention-getters. As long as a terrorist group can achieve its goals with conventional weapons, it will probably do so.

These days, terrorist incidents compete with drive-by shooting, mass suicides, uprising, and international incidents for front-page news. One day soon, exploding a van under the World Trade center resulting in six deaths may not receive much attention. Worse yet, could the next federal building be attacked with CB agents instead of a fertilizer-based explosive? Or will terrorists attack key industrial sites to reproduce the next Bhopal, *Exxon Valdez*, or Chernobyl catastrophe? Is the United States ready to combat domestic terrorism in the form of CB agent attacks? AS one of the most open nations in the world, our society is very vulnerable. One fact remains: in the midst of news stories recounting the falling yen, a major earthquake, and North Korean demands for nuclear reactors, worldwide publicity catapulted the name Aum Shinrikyo, the Supreme Truth, to the homes of billions across the glove within one week. That alone should prompt concerns that others will seek to imitate its efforts.

There is a Future for the Chemical Corps

Future threats are not diminishing in number of volume, despite the successful completion and signing of the Chemical Weapons Convention in 1993. In every corner of the world, particularly in historical and regional conflict areas, proliferation of CB warfare programs continues. Many countries begin with production of industrial chemicals, move into first-generation (*World War I*) chemical agents, rapidly progress into development of second-generation chemical agents (*World War II* and later), and last, biological agent production. While the CWC will continue to put pressure on these countries, the extreme liquidity of the global economy, and the increasing sophistication of other nations' arms programs will make it increasingly difficult for the United States and its allies to control this proliferation. We can be assured that the next major conflict will include the use of CB agent munitions, in an attempt to resolve a conflict before its high price can take its toll and before major powers can be involved.

The US military's future is undergoing its own evolvement, as seen with the Quadrennial Defense Review (QDR) and its successors. With a diminished manpower and budget, a decreasing involvement overseas, and an increasing reluctance on the part of the American public to suffer any casualties in an overseas conflict, the military is searching for a new, defined role. The QDR's language concerning weapons of mass destruction, asymmetric, threats and the threat of ballistic missiles shows that DoD understands the danger exists. Military leaders just have not figured out exactly how they want to combat them. The lack of CB warfare during the Gulf War has caused more questions and theories than would have been the case if the Iraqi military had used these agents. Some emphasis focuses on a "21st Century Land Warrior" program combining protective clothing, mask and integrated CB agent detectors into the troops' combat ensembles. Others insist on more proactive measures, such as Theater High Altitude Air Defense systems and planes with high-powered lasers designed to defeat CB agent warheads on ballistic missiles. The main weakness is a continued search for a technological "fix" for a problem, a search that ignores the need for integrated NBC defense training and trained chemical specialists in future combat forces. The military still needs to test these concepts, using validated computer models that mimic the physical and physiological effects of NBC agents on troops and units, to understand the costs and benefits of these approaches.

Despite their close brush in 1991 with CB warfare, the four services did not immediately acknowledge the need to reform their roles and responsibilities in the DoD NBC defense program. Although the Gulf War division and corps commanders are in high positions throughout the Army today, their near experience with CB weapons use has not trickled down to the new generation of commanders. Despite the worry prior to the conflict over these weapons, some still feel that conventional firepower alone is more than adequate to deal with the threat of CB warfare. This attitude may have explained the many attempts to shut down Fort McClellan since the Gulf War.

In January 1991, the Army leadership recommended shutting down Fort McClellan and moving the Chemical School, claiming that the Army had no special need for toxic agent training such as at the CDTF. Based on the experiences of Gulf War soldiers, the Chemical

School convinced the Base Realignment Committee (BRAC) otherwise. In 1993, the Army proposed moving the Chemical School to Fort Leonard-Wood, Missouri, and keeping the CDTF open; it would fly trainees to Alabama for the specialized training. Again, the Chemical School successfully argued that the CDTF and the School should not be separated, due to the need to integrate up-to-date doctrine, training and equipment into the CDTF. In the 1995 recommendations to the BRAC, the Pentagon recommended the closures of both Fort McClellan and Dugway Proving Ground. The Army's argument to move the Schools (both Military Police and Chemical) was based on a new plan to develop an Army Maneuver Support Command, tieing in the Engineer Center and School with the two other schools to develop an integrated combat support concept. This time, the Army agreed to build a new CDTF at Leonard-Wood in addition to the move. The 1995 BRAC, on a very close (5-4) vote (with two Missouri politicians tipping the results), agreed to this plan.

Chemical officers remain concerned over the potential loss of the Chemical Defense Training Facility. The CDTF will remain active at Fort McClellan until one is constructed at Fort Leonard Wood-at least, as plans now stand. The CDTF has a very successful record of preparing soldiers, both chemical specialists and non-chemical personnel, for the all too real threat of a toxic environment. Tens of thousands of American soldiers have passed through the training, as well as hundreds of British, German, Canadian and other foreign military personnel. This was accomplished while maintaining a perfect record of no training days lost to maintenance or chemical agent accidents. Major General McCaffrey stated: "Then and now, they [soldiers and leaders] wholeheartedly value the opportunity to train with actual agents, real detectors/alarms and real decontaminants. The presence of CDTF-trained soldiers in every company of the Division directly improves our combat readiness. These soldiers have great confidence that their equipment works. Your training program is right on target."

While moving the Chemical School to Fort Leonard-Wood will not stop the Army's NBC defense program, it will disrupt the infrastructure and momentum of CB defense doctrine and training. Also, this plan assumes that there will be no delays in building a new CDTF in Missouri. The last CDTF was a five-year undertaking before the state of Alabama and the EPA approved its operations. Can we assume that Missouri will be more cooperative? If Fort Leonard-Wood cannot build a comparable CDTF by the time of the Chemical School will move at the turn of the century, there will be measurable drop in preparedness.

The attempted closure of Dugway Proving Ground is an even more serious issue. The loss of Dugway Proving Ground would eliminate the one place in the United States where extensive CB agent testing can still be accomplished. Without accurate testing of detection, protection and decontamination equipment with actual CB agents, how will the military be assured of good defensive equipment? As armored vehicles undergo live-fire tests, so must NBC defensive equipment undergo toxic agent tests. The argument for closing Dugway Proving Ground may have centered on the fact that since Congress drastically restricts open-air agent tests, the over 850,00 acres of desert are too expensive to maintain. Since testing with CB agents is all conducted indoors, the argument could be made to relocate the valuable test facilities elsewhere, although the cost would be high. The 1995 BRAC did feel that Dugway Proving Ground's unique

Testing facilities and proving grounds was vital enough to spare, and did not approve its inclusion on the closure list. Some type of ability to perform this testing is necessary. The army has not yet presented an effective argument as to who would assume the responsibility for this testing, and it may not have calculated the total cost of moving the test laboratories to other sites and shutting down the post.

I will not suggest any "*plots*" or "*conspiracies*" to disband the Chemical Corps (although three does seem to be a historical pattern). A cynic would point out that as long as the Infantry Ranger School trained its studies at Dugway Proving Ground, there were few recommendations to close the base (the Rangers left Dugway in 1992). Rather, I will point out that these actions take place without careful thought as to potential consequences. Yes, the Chemical School can still operate at another post. Yes, the testing facilities at Dugway Proving Ground could be replicated elsewhere. But no one has put any thought into minimizing the impact of these moves. Who will maintain the reforms in doctrine and training? Who will continue developing the NBC defense equipment requirements? Who will pick up the mission of testing military equipment to measure its ability to meet the errors of an NBC-contaminated environment? How much time and money will it cost the military to regain these capabilities? As seen with the DoD's attempts to model the Khamisiyah explosion at Dugway, there is still a role for this expertise. It Comes back to the need to maintain that high level of defense in a post-Cold War era, in a political environment that denies to the United States armed forces the use of retaliatory chemical weapons.

The Engineer Corps at Fort Leonard-Wood has a vision of a future combat support relationship. If there is one silver lining in the Chemical Corps move to the future Maneuver Support Command, it is that the Chemical Corps might emulate the successful "*teaming*" that engineers have developed with he combat arms branches. The cooperation seen between the Chemical and Engineer Corps in constructing deliberate decontamination sites in Southwest Asia suggests that there is room for both to grow together within that command. There is little question that the Chemical Corps could learn something from the Engineer Corps' ability to work closely with, and in support of, combat branches. There are two concerns foremost in the minds of chemical officers. History shows the many times that the US Army has attempted to nest the Chemical Corps within another branch (or submerging the potential role of a strong and vital Chemical Corps. The Chemical Corps's mission as a joint service leader, mandated by Congress, as well as its status of an international leader in NBC defense, mandates that it retain its autonomy to a degree. The US military cannot afford the Engineer Corps to assume to a degree. The US military cannot afford the Engineer Corps to assume the Chemical Corps mission within its own. What the Chemical Corps needs is a strong partner, not new management.

The Persian Gulf war should convince most that there is a strong need in this area for a force of full-time professionals. The military was clearly unprepared for CB warfare in 1990, and remains uncomfortable with the concept of CB warfare in 1990, and remains uncomfortable with the concept of CB warfare even today. The Army needs to study the future trends of warfare, analyze potential avenues for future investment and determine how to prepare for conflicts that will include NBC weapons employment. More importantly the Army needs the chemical Corps to develop doctrine and to recommend chemical organizations that fits the future Force XXI concept, and to develop leadership skills to ensure the entire military force has the capability to survive and sustain combat operations in an NBC-contaminated environment. To do this, the Chemical Corps must become a true partner with its sister branches of the Army, as well s its counterparts in the other services. In the past, the *Chemical Corps* has retained a technical specialty; for the future, it must become an integral part of the combat arms teams. The *Chemical Corps* must understand the combat arms' doctrine and leadership demands, and it must communicate its potential to the combat arms into terms their leaders understand in order to achieve these goals.

In closing:

Future US administrations must decide how the Department of Defense should respond to enemy use of CB munitions. The CWC exists, but treaties have never stopped nations from researching and developing more advanced CB agent munitions. Treaties have rarely stopped those same countries from employing CB agent munitions. Faced with the fact that the US military still has problems facing World War I and World War II-vintage chemical munitions, other countries do not have far to go to produce an effective weapons that will disrupt military operations. Arms control experts and politicians who rail against CB warfare research are living in the past. Their transition of the present must come in the realization that while they can strive to limit future warfare, they will never totally eliminate it. Countries find CB agent munitions just too tempting, too easy, to develop, too easy to hide, and too easy to deny having used, to pass up. When the military experts, politicians and arms control experts come to consensus on how best to integrate the trend of chemical warfare into future warfare policy, we can be assured that the United States has a sound national policy and a strong defensive capability in this area. Until then, our forces will remain dangerously vulnerable to CB weapons.

The underlaying reason why politicians, the military, and the public have feared and continue to fear, CB warfare so much is sheer ignorance about its nature. Either they completely underestimate its effects by ignoring the possibility of CB warfare during plans and exercises, or they completely overestimate the CB agents killing ability on the battlefield and in the eight stockpile. *Chemical* and *biological weapons* have never been on the same scale of destruction as nuclear weapons, yet many seem determined to treat them all the same way. At the least, chemical weapons have as much, and as little, potential killing power as any number of conventional bombs, artillery shells, and rockets in use today. Any weapon system is as safe or as deadly as the military force that uses them. As long as the media remains bent on sensationalistic journalism, and as long as novelists such as Tom Clancy and Hollywood screen writers make out CB weapons to be the doomsday devices *du jour*, we may never learn about the true threat of CB warfare to our own forces. Without understanding the tactical nature of these weapon systems, the military and government politicians remain unprepared to plan defensive strategies and will make the wrong decisions. This ignorance will continue until military leaders and politicians make an effort truly to understand the implications of CB warfare in modern combat operations.

We can no longer afford for this divisive battle of arms control experts versus the *Chemical Corps* versus the *combat arms* community. If there is a future vision for the *Chemical Corps*, it is ensure that combat forces can maintain their full mission capability in future wars despite the threat of a CB agent-contaminated battlefield. This call for both highly trained and motivated chemical officers trained and educated military leadership. As General Creighton Abrams once told Colonel Gerald Watson in 1972, it is the infantry and armor combat leaders—not its technical branches—that must decide how to fight and survive on the modern battlefield. The military may not like training for CB warfare, but the Chemical Corp's capabilities and CB defense equipment remain the sole "*insurance policy*" that maintains the United States military's ability to defend itself against the use of CB munitions. Until the *Chemical Corps* specialists are seen as true supporters of the combat soldier, and until the combat arms community comes to grips with the true scope and nature of CB warfare, the potential for future Desert Shield/Storm panics remains.

INDEX